Metaphysics, Method and Politics

British Idealist Studies Series 2: Collingwood

1: James Connelly, *Metaphysics, Method and Politics*
2: Stein Helgeby, *Action as History*
3: Marnie Hughes-Warrington, *'How Good an Historian Shall I Be?'*

Series Editor:
David Boucher, Cardiff University
Editorial Board:
W.H. Dray (Ottowa)
Gary Browning (Oxford Brookes)
Bruce Haddock (Cardiff)
Rex Martin (Kansas)
Guido Vanheeswijck (Antwerp)
Jan van der Dussen (Open University, Netherlands)

Metaphysics, Method and Politics

The Political Philosophy of R.G. Collingwood

James Connelly

ia

IMPRINT ACADEMIC

Copyright © James Connelly, 2003

The moral rights of the authors have been asserted
No part of any contribution may be reproduced in any form
without permission, except for the quotation of brief passages
in criticism and discussion.

Published in the UK by Imprint Academic
PO Box 200, Exeter EX5 5YX, UK

Published in the USA by Imprint Academic
Philosophy Documentation Center
PO Box 7147, Charlottesville, VA 22906-7147, USA

ISBN 0 907845 312

A CIP catalogue record for this book is available
from the British Library
Library of Congress Card Number: 2002102734

www.imprint-academic.com/idealists

Contents

Preface vii
Acknowledgements ix
Introduction. 1
Abbreviations. 4

PART ONE:
Philosophical Method And Metaphysics

Chapter One: The Unity of Collingwood's Philosophy
 1 Introduction 7
 2 The Unity of the Writings: A General Outline 8
 3 Expositors and Critics 17
 4 A Central Thread? 34
 5 Style and Terminology in Collingwood 46
 6 Conclusion 53

Chapter Two: Metaphysics and Method: a Necessary Unity
 1 Introduction. 55
 2 Collingwood and the Characteristics of Philosophy 57
 3 Philosophy and its Method 69
 4 Philosophical Method and the Scale of Forms. 77
 5 *An Essay on Metaphysics* and The Idea of System in
   Metaphysics. 86
 6 Conclusion 95

Chapter Three: Absolute Presuppositions in
Collingwood's Philosophy
 1 Introduction. 97
 2 Beyond Truth and Falsity: Absolute Presuppositions,
   Thought and Change. 97
 3 A Short History of Absolute Presuppositions 115
 4 Philosophical Concepts and Absolute Presuppositions . 141
 5 Conclusion. 156

PART TWO:
The Political Philosophy of Civilization

Chapter Four: Theory, Practice and the Forms of Action
1 Introduction 161
2 Theory and Practice. 162
3 Collingwood's Political Theory and Practice. 177
4 The Forms of Action 189
5 Utility. 191
6 Right 195
7 Duty 199
8 Conclusion. 204

Chapter Five: Political Action
1 Introduction 205
2 The Subject Matter of Political Theory 206
3 Society 210
4 The Body Politic. 216
5 Ruling and Being Ruled 223
6 Punishment 238
7 The Law and Morality 250
8 Conclusion. 261

Chapter Six: Civilization and Barbarism
1 Introduction 263
2 Civilization and Barbarism. 263
3 Civilization as an Ideal 270
4 Conclusion. 284

Chapter Seven: The Dimensions of Civilization
1 Introduction 285
2 Man Goes Mad?. 285
3 Complexity and Intelligence:
  The Role of Critical Thinking 287
4 Continuity: The Place of Order and Tradition 299
5 The Vitality of a Civilization:
  Emotion and the Place of Religion 303
6 Conclusion. 315

Chapter Eight: Conclusion 317

Bibliography 321

Index 331

Preface

This book is an attempt to do two things: the first is to demonstrate that Collingwood's philosophical work as a whole comprises a unity in which, although there was development, there was no 'radical conversion' rendering the later writings philosophically incompatible with the earlier; the second is to display Collingwood's political philosophy as a unified whole. The first task is a necessary prelude to the second, because the second presupposes that writings from different periods of Collingwood's career can be appropriately juxtaposed in the presentation of his political philosophy, a procedure that is open to obvious objection if the presupposition of essential unity is unjustified. The book is accordingly divided into two parts, the first being devoted to an examination of Collingwood's views on philosophical method and metaphysics, and the second to what I have termed 'the political philosophy of civilization'. Although it comprises, I hope, an integrated whole, nonetheless each part can be appreciated separately.

The book as a whole is largely exegetical and constructive in that it draws heavily on Collingwood's writings (both published and previously unpublished) in order to answer certain questions concerning his philosophical development and also to draw together a complete picture of what I believe to be a complete political philosophy of civilization. This is why I have not adopted the approach typified by Peter Johnson's *R.G. Collingwood: An Introduction*. That approach seeks to address Collingwood's arguments individually on their merits, to engage him in a critical conversation in which some arguments might be allowed to stand and others to fall, without reference to the overall issue of the coherence of Collingwood's thought or its development over time. I agree with Johnson that this is an important task because, ultimately, why should anyone care about a thinker's development or the coherence of their thought unless that thought is worth expressing in the first place and has philosophical value for us? However, there is room for both dimensions for, as Collingwood himself remarks in *An Essay on Philosophical Method*, 'the question whether a man's views are true or false does not arise until we have found out what they are'. This book is a contribution to this dimension of study, but I firmly believe that the other dimension is valuable even though I am not practicing it here. Thus a reader would be right to assume that I believe Collingwood's thought of value and hence worth studying, but wrong to assume that I believe that everything he wrote or published was of equal philosophical worth.

For convenience I draw a distinction between published and unpublished material, even though many of Collingwood's manuscripts have now been (and continue to be) published. However, referring to the 'published' and 'unpublished' writings serves as a convenient shorthand to refer, on the one hand, to books and articles published in Collingwood's lifetime (or immediately after his death), and, on the other, to manuscripts which either remain unpublished or were published only in the past few years, typically as addenda to reissued editions of his major works.

Long ago and far away a much earlier version of this book was written as a PhD dissertation. By the 'law of primitive survivals' it undoubtedly still bears marks of this origin, visible to the scholarly eye of readers if not always to my own. But to have cast aside the origin would have meant writing a different book entirely; besides, the original (and its occasional offspring)[1] have established a place of sorts in the world of Collingwood studies, and publication of the book in this form serves to draw together this work in an accessible form.

Collingwood studies have developed apace since I first started reading the unpublished manuscripts in Oxford in 1980. A thriving Collingwood Society which runs popular biennial conferences has been formed, and an annual journal, *Collingwood Studies* (now *Collingwood and British Idealism Studies*) provides an invaluable outlet for much fascinating writing. Many books have been published over the same period of time, including one covering the same territory as this — *The Social and Political Thought of R.G. Collingwood* by David Boucher. There is clearly overlap between the two books; however, their approach and purposes differ; I hope that they complement one another, and that each has something distinctive to offer.

---

[1] Chapters Two and Three were first published in a different form as 'Metaphysics and Method: A Necessary Unity in the Philosophy of R.G. Collingwood', 1990, pp. 33–156.

Acknowledgments

I should like to thank the series editor, David Boucher, for his help and advice on this and other projects over many years. I would also like to thank the inimitable Peter Johnson who has never failed to be a source of conversation, help and information; Josie D'Oro who always asks stimulating questions and Stamatoula Panagakou, for believing so strongly that work of this nature is profoundly worthwhile. Teresa Smith deserves thanks both for giving permission to quote passages from the unpublished manuscripts and for many years of tolerance and forbearance of my questions, comments and activities. Colin Harris and his staff in the John Johnson reading room in the Bodleian Library have been unfailingly helpful and courteous on my many visits there over the past twenty years and can never be praised enough. And, finally, I would like to make special mention of Prof. E.E. Harris, who was kind enough to entertain me at his home in Ambleside and who provides a link with the Oxford of the 1930s.

As always, I am solely to blame for any errors of philosophy, fact or interpretation to be found in the following pages.

In memory of Liam O'Sullivan
who inspired so many of us

Introduction

Any philosophy of civilization or politics must situate its subject matter within the full context of human experience; and similarly, Collingwood's political philosophy of civilization must be situated within his whole philosophy and philosophical approach. This, of course, presupposes that there is an overall philosophical approach and that Collingwood developed a consistent philosophy and consistent method. My claim is, therefore, twofold: first I claim that Collingwood developed a philosophy of politics and civilization, and that this philosophy has its roots in the early just as much as in the later work; and secondly, I claim that Collingwood developed a general philosophy which is for the most part consistent and best regarded as an integrated whole. This second claim, if justified, serves to ground the first claim by eliminating the contention that works from different periods are likely to be mutually inconsistent.

In the nature of things, the second part must come first: the attempt to exhibit the unity of Collingwood's political and social philosophy presupposes the demonstration of the unity of his philosophy as a whole. In drawing upon diverse texts from different periods of Collingwood's career in order to build a picture of his philosophy of civilization and politics, I have first of all to be confident that the procedure is justified. As we shall see in Chapter One, many critics have maintained that Collingwood's work suffered some form of radical break or 'radical conversion'. If this were so then it would clearly be inadmissible to juxtapose texts taken from different periods without first ascertaining either that these texts were unaffected by the 'radical conversion' or that there was no 'radical conversion'. I shall accordingly argue, throughout Part One, that Collingwood's philosophical work is best seen as a developing whole, admitting of differences both of emphasis and content, but not admitting of radical discontinuity. I shall attempt to demonstrate that Collingwood's philosophy is a unity: this demonstration is presupposed in what follows, where I bring together disparate writings on politics and civilization in order to display them as constituting a coherent philosophy.

My presentation of Collingwood's philosophy does not rely solely on published works: a substantial proportion of the material employed comes from unpublished manuscripts. These manuscripts have been used in order to supplement published writings through the use of added detail, and also through the provision of fresh material on all manner of topics either not dealt with in the published works, or at best, dealt with only briefly. Published works are primary in the sense that they, and they alone, were authorised for publication in permanent and accessible form. However, this does not invalidate the use of the manuscripts. Collingwood's intentions in publishing a book are one thing: the difficulties and perplexities which arise in the course of a scholar's efforts to assess these works as a whole are quite another. We are entirely justified in looking at unpublished manuscripts in the hope of answering questions arising from our reading of the published books and articles: and here, while the published works do not cease to be primary, the weight of investigation is necessarily thrown onto the unpublished manuscripts; and if they help us resolve disputes or answer questions which would otherwise be unresolved and unanswered, I hardly think that their importance or value can be denied.

The use of the manuscripts constitutes the core of my presentation. However, the view I take concerning the overall unity of Collingwood's philosophy and philosophical method is not derived solely from the unpublished manuscripts, and could be argued for without recourse to them. But, given that the manuscripts are available in the public domain and increasingly available through re-issue of Collingwood's main works, I thought it important to seize the opportunity presented by these manuscripts to amplify the published writings, to clarify points left unclear or insufficiently developed in them, and to supplement them with fresh material.

In what follows, Chapter One clears the ground, and Chapters Two and Three develop an account of the unity of Collingwood's philosophy, thereby laying the foundations for what follows. In Part Two I begin to construct an account of Collingwood's political philosophy of civilization. Chapter Four addresses Collingwood's understanding of the relation of theory to practice: I correct the slightly misleading account in *An Autobiography* by drawing on manuscript and other sources as well as briefly examining T.H. Green's position. Such a discussion is unavoidable in dealing with any author's social or political thought: in Collingwood's case it is inevitable given the great importance he attaches to the practical relevance of philosophy. I then outline the categories central to Collingwood's moral and political philosophy. The 'forms of action' are characterised and their relation to action as a form of experience indicated.

Chapter Five is concerned with Collingwood's understanding of political action: it includes a discussion of society, community, ruling and being ruled based largely on *The New Leviathan*. It also presents Collingwood's views on punishment, mostly through the use of unpublished manuscripts: and sketches the place of punishment within the overall account of society and community as developed in *The New Leviathan*. Chapter Six addresses the concept of civilization central to *The New Leviathan*: I use that book, along with manuscripts and earlier drafts, in order to draw out the meaning of the concept. In doing so I also bring in Collingwood's interesting discussion of civilization as an ideal which is to be found in an early draft manuscript of *The New Leviathan*.

Chapter Seven, *The Dimensions of Civilization*, takes its title from a phrase Collingwood uses in the 1936 manuscript, 'Man Goes Mad'. The dimensions are emotion, tradition and intelligence and I attempt to indicate how the brief account of these things in 'Man Goes Mad' fits into the much more detailed accounts provided in *The Principles of Art, The Idea of History, An Autobiography* and *The New Leviathan*.

Finally, in Chapter Eight, I summarise and restate the overall thesis of the book.

Abbreviations

Books and Pamphlets

A	*An Autobiography*
EM	*An Essay on Metaphysics*
EPM	*An Essay on Philosophical Method*
FML	*The First Mate's Log*
FR	*Faith and Reason*
IN	*The Idea of Nature*
IH	*The Idea of History*
NL	*The New Leviathan*
OPA	*Outlines of the Philosophy of Art*
PA	*The Principles of Art*
PH	*The Philosophy of History*
RP	*Religion and Philosophy*
SM	*Speculum Mentis*
TLP	*The Three Laws of Politics*
R's P	*Ruskin's Philosophy*

Published Articles

EPS	'Economics as a Philosophical Science'
FN	'Fascism and Nazism'
NAPH	'The Nature and Aims of a Philosophy of History'
OS	'Oswald Spengler and the Theory of Historical Cycles'
Pol A	'Political Action'
PNP	'The Present Need of a Philosophy'
PP	'A Philosophy of Progress'
RFCI	'Reason is Faith Cultivating Itself'

Unpublished Manuscripts

BL	The Breakdown of Liberalism
CRC	Collingwood–Ryle Correspondence
FMC	Function of Metaphysics in Civilization
LMP	Lectures on Moral Philosophy
MGM	Man Goes Mad
NMS	The Nature of Metaphysical Study
NPPS	Notes Towards a Theory of Politics as a Philosophical Science
OCS	Outlines of a Concept of the State
RNP	Rough Notes on Politics
SNEQ	Stray Notes on Ethical Questions
TC	*Truth and Contradiction,* chapter two
WCM	What Civilization Means

Unless otherwise stated, all unpublished manuscripts are to be found in the Bodleian Library, Oxford. Most are available for consultation on microfilm only. For details, consult the catalogue compiled by Ruth Burchnall, available in the John Johnson reading room. For additional detail, see the bibliographies by Taylor and Dreisbach. For details of correspondence, refer to Johnson, *The Correspondence of R.G. Collingwood*.

PART ONE:

Philosophical Method and Metaphysics

Chapter One

The Unity of Collingwood's Philosophy

1: Introduction

The purpose of this chapter is to examine the relationship between Collingwood's writings, to show their points of contact and to display their essential unity. The view I shall be taking is that while Collingwood's thought underwent development and modification, there was no *bouleversement*[1] or 'radical conversion' at any time which might be supposed to have driven a wedge between the earlier and the later works.

The discussion in much of this chapter will be focused on some of Collingwood's expositors and critics: but I shall also address issues concerning his style and terminology in both his published and unpublished writings, thereby shedding light on the relation between early and late works. Chapter Two and Three deal with the philosophical, metaphysical and methodological underpinnings of Collingwood's thought. If Collingwood's thought is to be treated as (in some sense) a systematic whole, for the purpose of examining his political and social philosophy, it must first be shown that it is such a whole.

This chapter is accordingly an exercise in ground clearance: a preliminary account designed to clear up some of the objections to taking Collingwood's thought as a systematic whole. This will make it possible to move on to my own positive restatement of the relationship between the early and the late work, in particular the relation-

---

[1] T .M. Knox's term: see his review of L. Mink, *Mind, History and Dialectic*.

ship between *An Essay on Philosophical Method* and *An Essay on Metaphysics*.

2: The Unity of the Writings: A General Outline

If a writer's work is best understood as an inter-related whole, then the view we take of the whole affects the view we take of the parts. If the unity of the whole can be shown through examination of its principal components, then certain consequences follow. First, that statements and phrases which otherwise seem dark or impenetrable become clear when placed in a wider context which makes their sense manifest; secondly, different works can be used to supplement and correct each other: each book or article or lecture can be appreciated not merely on its own account, but also as a contribution to a wider and more extensive philosophical viewpoint.

For example: if we look at the relation between the two *Essays* — the one on *Method*,[2] the other on *Metaphysics*[3] — and if we adopt the view that they supplement one another, then sense can be made of many other articles, discussions and remarks which might otherwise be overlooked or ignored. For example, it has often been remarked that the early lecture on *Ruskin's Philosophy* reads in same respects like an early formulation of the doctrine of absolute presuppositions[4] but it is less commonly recognised that the same could be said of 'Economics as a Philosophical Science', or parts of 'The Theory of Historical Cycles', or several other reviews or pamphlets. For example, the article on economics states quite firmly that 'what is intended is . . . to throw light on some of the fundamental conceptions which Economists do not so much derive inductively from facts as presuppose in their attitude towards the facts.'[5] And in 'Historical Cycles' we find that 'the philosopher only makes explicit in his own peculiar way an idea which has necessarily been the common heritage of his entire culture' and 'philosophy is only a reasoned statement of ideas common to the culture.'[6]

The reason, I suspect, that the similarity of these passages to the later doctrine of metaphysics as the science of absolute presuppositions has been ignored, is simply that an incompatibility between

[2] *An Essay on Philosophical Method*, (E.P.M.), 1933.
[3] *An Essay on Metaphysics*, (E.M.), 1940.
[4] See, for example, L. Rubinoff in *Collingwood and the Reform of Metaphysics*, pp. 223-232.; Alan Donagan, *The Later Philosophy of R.G. Collingwood*, p. 264.; L. Mink, *Mind, History and Dialectic*, p. 244.
[5] 'Economics as a Philosophical Science', (E.P. S.), 1925, p. 162.
[6] 'Oswald Spengler and the Theory of Historical Cycles', (O.S.), 1927, pp. 313, 315.

Philosophical Method and *Metaphysics* has been assumed; the closeness in the date of these papers to the earlier *Essay* noted; and the conclusion drawn that because the papers are early they must be incompatible with the *Essay on Metaphysics*. If, on the other hand, it can be shown that the supposed incompatibility between the two *Essays* simply does not exist, then a barrier to balanced understanding of these articles is removed.

An even more obvious case of later theories being first developed in earlier works is that of 'Reason is Faith Cultivating Itself'[7] and the pamphlet *Faith and Reason*.[8] Here, again, there is no need to draw these essays into either camp, for there are not two camps but one. The temporal proximity of 'Reason is Faith Cultivating Itself' and *Faith and Reason* to *Philosophical Method* should not divert us from the recognition that these two articles are compatible with both Essays and not with one at the expense of the other.

Finally, in a review of Charles Gore's *The Philosophy of the Good Life* in 1931, we find Collingwood observing that 'the scientists' trust that nature will prove "reasonable" is the presupposition within which all the reasonings of science move, and upon which they all depend ... by faith we grasp *that there is an order* in nature, whereas by reason we discover *what kind of order it is*.'[9] This is manifestly of a piece with the theses of both *Faith and Reason* and *An Essay on Metaphysics*.

In any inquiry into the growth and development of an author's ideas it seems only reasonable to start with his or her own account of the matter. Collingwood wrote his *Autobiography* over the summer of 1938, completing the first draft by 2nd October that year. He received the proofs in February 1939 while on a trip to the East Indies, and he re-wrote the last chapter (Theory and Practice) in March.

During this trip he also wrote the bulk of *An Essay on Metaphysics*. His *Autobiography* was thus written and published before the composition and publication of *The New Leviathan*; written (for the most part) and published before *An Essay on Metaphysics*; and published before although written (for the most part) after *The Idea of Nature* and *The Idea of History*.

Notwithstanding these omissions, I intend to treat Collingwood's account of his intellectual development up to 1938 as largely accu-

---

[7] 'Reason is Faith Cultivating Itself', (R.F.C.I.), pp. 3–14.
[8] *Faith and Reason*, (F.R.), 1928.
[9] Review of C. Gore, *The Philosophy of the Good Life*.

rate, and to use it as a basis for my own account. My reasons for so doing will, I hope, became clear as the argument progresses.[10]

The first thing to note about the *Autobiography* is that there is no mention at any point of a radical change in view on conversion or *bouleversement*. At the very least it would appear that if there was such a shift Collingwood himself was unaware of it. The comments and references in the *Autobiography* to his earlier works make this quite clear. Collingwood states that the logic of question and answer (which was an integral part of the later theory of metaphysics as the science of absolute presuppositions propounded in *An Autobiography* and *An Essay on Metaphysics*) was first developed in an unpublished book written in 1917, *Truth and Contradiction*.[11] This claim can be neither confirmed nor denied in detail as only chapter two of the book is extant; but it can be said that chapter two is both in line with his other early writings and also not incompatible with any later writings.

Religion and Philosophy[12] is mentioned twice; once to be criticised and put firmly in its place as the work of 'a beginner in the art of writing books'[13] and once in order to quote a passage on William James with approval.[14] This passage runs: 'The mind, regarded in this way, ceases to be a mind at all',[15] a judgement with which Collingwood still concurred, and which is explicitly reinforced and developed in detail throughout both the *Autobiography* and *An Essay on Metaphysics*.

Speculum Mentis receives a critical mention as 'incompletely thought out and unskillfully expressed', but the edge of this harsh judgement is blunted by a footnote expressing second thoughts:

> In writing that sentence I have read *Speculum Mentis* for the first time since it was published, and find it much better than I remembered. It is a record, not so very obscure in expression, of a good deal of genuine thinking. If much of it now fails to satisfy me, that is because I have gone on thinking since I wrote it, and therefore much of it needs to be supplemented and qualified. There is not a great deal that needs to be retracted.[16]

---

[10] For the moment I am ignoring the *Autobiography*'s lack of reference to Gentile and Croce: on this, see §5 below.
[11] See *An Autobiography*, (A.), p. 42.
[12] *Religion and Philosophy*, (R.P.), 1916.
[13] A., p. 43.
[14] A., p. 93.
[15] The original passage is on p. 42 of *Religion and Philosophy*.
[16] A, p. 56.

Both *Human Nature and Human History*[17] and *The Principles of Art*[18] receive favourable mentions:[19] the latter reference is of interest as *The Principles of Art* contains a reference to *An Essay on Philosophical Method* concerning the philosophical sense of the term 'difference of degree' where Collingwood states that:

> Here and elsewhere I use this word in the traditional philosophical sense, where differences of degree are understood as involving differences of kind; as in Locke's 'three degrees of Knowledge', where each 'degree' is at once a fuller realization of the essence of knowledge than the one below (more certain, less liable to error) and also a fresh kind of knowledge.[20]

Further, it is structured according to the principles of method developed in *An Essay on Philosophical Method*, and is, in some respects, liable to be misinterpreted if this is not borne in mind by the reader.

Although *An Essay on Metaphysics* (which according to some constituted the definitive statement of Collingwood's later 'historicism') was not published until after the *Autobiography* and receives no mention there, its central doctrines (the logic of question and answer and metaphysics as the science of absolute presuppositions) are there announced briefly but firmly. It must also be remembered that Collingwood began work on *Metaphysics* not only before his *Autobiography* was published, but also before he re-wrote the last chapter and read the proofs. Surely any recognition on Collingwood's part of a fundamental change of philosophical position between his earlier and later writings would have been mentioned here? After all, Collingwood hardly hesitates, both in the *Autobiography* and elsewhere, to acknowledge mistakes and changes of view where he considers it relevant.[21] And is not the absence of such recognition to count for something when one is examining his intellectual development?[22]

---

[17] *Human Nature and Human History*, 1936.
[18] *The Principles of Art*, (P.A.), 1938.
[19] A. pp. 117–8.
[20] P.A., p. 187; cf. E.P.M. pp. 54–5; pp. 69–77.
[21] See for example *Speculum Mentis*, (S.M.), 1924., p. 108, where Collingwood admits a change of view between R.P. and S.M.; P.A., p. 46, where he refers to a mistake in his article 'Plato's Philosophy of Art', 1925) or on p. 228 where he criticizes an argument put forward in his *Outlines of a Philosophy of Art* (O.P.A.), 1925; and p. 56 of A. where he discusses S.M.
[22] Unless, of course, one simply ignores Collingwood's own statement on the grounds either of intellectual dishonesty, or illness, or both. But if we are to assume that a writer is intellectually dishonest, why bother to read any of his books? Do we expect such a man to have anything to say to us? And if illness is the suggested reason, it becomes difficult to comprehend how Collingwood's

In referring to *An Essay on Philosophical Method*, Collingwood wrote that 'I... planned a series, to begin with *An Essay on Philosophical Method*. This I wrote during a long illness in 1932. It is my best book in matter; in style I may call it my only book'.[23] This statement is of considerable importance. It makes it quite plain that *An Essay on Philosophical Method* was to be part of a series: the exact nature of the series was altered after the publication of the *Autobiography*, but the conception of a series remained. In a letter to the Clarendon Press in 1939 Collingwood wrote that *An Essay on Metaphysics* is to be seen as the second volume of *Philosophical Essays* — a companion volume to the earlier *Essay*.[24]

The series was initially conceived as commencing with *An Essay on Philosophical Method*, *The Principles of Art* becoming the second in the series; but by the time of the composition of *An Essay on Metaphysics*, Collingwood's conception of the series had altered considerably. The final series was planned as a tripartite structure with each part comprising two books. Thus in the letter of 3rd June the two *Essays* are brought into line as companion volumes under the general heading *Philosophical Essays*; *The Principles of Art* and the as yet unwritten *Principles of History* were to be companion volumes in the series *Philosophical Principles*; and in a later letter (October 19th) Collingwood wrote that *The Idea of History* and *The Idea of Nature* are to be companion volumes under the general title *Studies in the History of Ideas*.

The half-title of *An Essay on Metaphysics* bears the legend: 'Philosophical Essays: Volume Two', and in the Oxford University Press's dust jacket advertising elsewhere we find the claim that 'this volume continues the series of *Philosophical Essays* begun in *An Essay on Philosophical Method* and is to be regarded as Volume II in that series.' Most commentators have simply ignored this, at least in the sense of refusing to take their status as companion volumes seriously with all that this implies. There are few prepared to give Collingwood the benefit of the doubt and make the effort to treat the two books as companions.

If we are to judge by the retention of their original titles, *The Idea of Nature* and *The Idea of History*[25] were published as companion volumes, but neither is announced. as such, and nowhere is there any indication that together they comprise volumes I and II of *Studies in*

---

later works came to be written at all, leaving aside the question of their undoubted quality.

[23] A., pp. 117–8.
[24] Letter to Clarendon Press, 3/6/39.
[25] *The Idea of History*, (I.H.), 1946.

the History of Ideas. But there is a possible reason for this. Although *The Idea of Nature* is a straightforward study in the history of ideas,[26] *The Idea of History* is not. The latter is really two books bound together within the same covers. Parts I–IV are studies in the history of ideas, a study of the history and development of *The Idea of History*; this part is *The Idea of History* proper. Part V, however, is Collingwood's own philosophy of history, his own metaphysics of historical knowledge. In part it is composed of material from the unfinished *Principles of History* (§3 & 6), in part of 'Metaphysical Epilegomena' delivered as the conclusion to the 1936 lectures on the philosophy of history, and in part of miscellaneous lectures (such as Collingwood's Inaugural and his address to the British Academy).

Thus, 1) *The Idea of History* (as published) contains material from *The Principles of History* and other material of that type, i.e. material dealing not with the history of historical thought, but with the principles of historic thought: the resulting dual character of the book obscures its relation to *The Idea of Nature*. 2) The projected companion volume to *The Principles of Art* was lost for many years and this left that book high and dry and obscured its position in relation to the other late books. 3) The full character of Collingwood's work on *The Principles of History* is misrepresented by the published Epilegomena to *The Idea of History* as Knox saw fit to publish only the part of the manuscripts which Collingwood himself had authorized for publication.[27]

Out of three planned series only one, *Philosophical Essays*, was published more or less as planned — and this series was largely ignored *as a series*. *Studies in the History of Ideas*, which could have been published as planned, was not, and *Philosophical Principles*, which could for the most part have been published as planned, also was not. *The Principles of History* was swallowed up in part by *The Idea of History* and in part by the Clarendon Press for many years, and The *Principles of Art* was left standing as a solitary monument without the support of its companion volumes.

---

[26] In October 1939 Collingwood replaced the sketch of his own Cosmology, which had originally concluded his lectures on 'The Idea of Nature in Modern Science', with the short concluding passage, 'From Nature to History.' This was done, I suggest, not because he was dissatisfied with this concluding passage but because he wished to bring I.N. into line with I.H., which, as he originally planned it, was likewise not intended to contain the concluding 'Metaphysical Epilegomena'.

[27] *The Principles of History* has been discovered and published together with other manuscripts, as *The Principles of History and other writings in philosophy of history*. For an account of the discovery of the manuscripts and their significance see also D. Boucher, 'The Significance of of R.G. Collingwood's *Principles of History*'.

Before progressing further, I should like at this point to anticipate a later discussion by pointing out how much clearer the import and object of Collingwood's later works would have been if they had been published as he planned.

There would have been two volumes of *Philosophical Essays*; the first dealing with philosophical method, and the second with the subject matter of philosophy. These, taken in tandem, would have provided the philosophical underpinning for the historical metaphysics of thought as worked out in the two volumes of *Studies in the History of Ideas*; and would have elucidated both the approach and subject matter of contemporary metaphysics developed in *The Principles of Art* and *The Principles of History*. In other words the tripartite scheme as Collingwood envisaged it would have been mutually supporting: an essay on method, an essay on subject matter; two essays of historical metaphysics displaying an historical scale of forms; and two essays in contemporary metaphysics displaying a conceptual scale of forms. In all these instances reference (whether implicit or explicit) to *An Essay on Philosophical Method* would have made clear the philosophical method of analysis employed throughout Collingwood's works: that is, the method of scale of forms analysis.[28]

T.M. Knox reports Collingwood as having remarked to a friend that 'having propounded a theory of philosophical method, he was now proceeding to apply it to a problem which had never been solved, namely, to the philosophy of nature.'[29] This method was used in both *The Idea of Nature* and *The Idea of History*. The original work on cosmology which is to be found among the unpublished manuscripts and which formed the basis of the original conclusion to the lectures on *The Idea of Nature*, is organised as a scale of forms of the *contemporary* concept of nature and all it implies; the substantial cosmological conclusions to *The Idea of Nature* are organised as a scale of forms.[30] The scale of forms in the book itself is a scale of forms of the *history* of the concept.

As an historical scale of forms, this method of analysis discovers and elucidates the categories used by scientists, the principles which they absolutely presupposed in their work at any given time. It is

---

[28] This also applies to N.L., which, although it has close connections with Collingwood's other writings, was not originally planned as an integral part of a series.
[29] I.N., Prefatory Note. The friend was Knox himself: See T.M. Knox, Review of Mink, *Mind, History and Dialectic*.
[30] This has been published in *The Principles of History*; see also D. Boucher, 'The *Principles of History* and the Cosmology Conclusion to the *Idea of Nature*.'

interesting to note that some philosophers have been misled by the publication date of *The Idea of Nature* into thinking that it was composed after the *Essay on Metaphysics*. They therefore regard it as an application of the doctrine propounded in that book: but, if it was consciously an application of anything, it was an application of the method propounded in *An Essay on Philosophical Method*.[31] Of course, there is no necessity whatever for having to choose between these alternative views (as some would have us do): it is perfectly possible to see *The Idea of Nature* as an application of both the method propounded in *An Essay on Philosophical Method* and of the analysis of metaphysics developed in *An Essay on Metaphysics*. Understood in this way, *The Idea of Nature* tends to confirm the view that the two *Essays* stand together and are mutually supporting.

In *The Principles of Art* Collingwood makes the point that art and craft tend to overlap (an important point often missed by readers of that book) and directs the reader to *An Essay on Philosophical Method*.[32] Later he refers the reader to the philosophical meaning of the phrase 'difference of degree', arguing that it means a difference both of degree and of kind as developed in the *Essay*.[33] The approach to method in the *Essay* is presupposed in the arrangement and approach of *The Principles of Art*, which follows the recommendation that:

> To define a philosophical concept it is necessary, first, to think of that concept as specifying itself in a form so rudimentary that anything less would fail to embody the concept at all. Later phases modify this minimum definition by adding new determinations, each implied in what

---

[31] See for example Donald S. Mackay, 'On Supposing and Presupposing', who writes that '*The Idea of Nature* . . . was intended to be a comprehensive history of the absolute presuppositions of the natural sciences from the early Greek philosophers to Alexander and Whitehead' (p. 10); Stephen Toulmin, who writes of 'the *Metaphysics* and . . . his later *Idea of Nature*', 'Conceptual change and the problem of Relativity', p. 202; A.J. Ayer, who writes that Collingwood's 'view of philosophy as serving only to trace the historical development of the absolute presuppositions of our thought did not convince me, though I now think there is more to it than I then admitted, but I was impressed by the use he made of it in his book *The Idea of Nature*', *Part of my Life*, p. 79; and D.M. Mackinnon who says nothing of chronology, but who sees, correctly, that I.N. and E.M. are companion volumes (the former being an application, arranged according to the principles of scales of forms analysis, of the view of the subject matter of metaphysics propounded in E.M.): 'Collingwood did take *naturphilosophie* seriously . . . no one who has read Collingwood's book (*The Idea of Nature*) or its companion *Essay on Metaphysics* . . . can ever be quite sure that that neglect of *Naturphilosophie* is always a mark of disciplined, intellectual discrimination,' 'Teilhard's Achievement', p. 61.

[32] P.A., p. 22.

[33] P.A., p. 187.

went before, but each introducing into it qualitative changes as well as additions and complications.[34]

This is precisely what Collingwood does in *The Principles of Art* in his inquiry into art and language. He proceeds from the most rudimentary specification to the more advanced and shows how new determinations are generated in each phase. Indeed, as the footnote on page 136 makes clear, Book I is provisional, and it is not until Book III that the full theory of art is given. It is interesting to note that some readers of *The Principles of Art* have been misled, through inattention or through ignorance of Collingwood's method, into taking the provisional statements of Part I for his final utterance; but Collingwood makes it quite plain that his theory of art is not stated until Part III; Part I is provisional ground clearing and Part II is a theory of Imagination which Collingwood regards as a necessary prerequisite for the theory of art proper.[35]

The Principles of History, would have had a similar tripartite structure. At the beginning of the scheme Collingwood wrote that the 'main topics will include, 1) a simple account of the most obvious characteristics of history as a special science, 2) Relations between this and others, 3) Relation of history as thought to practical life. These could be books I, II, III.'[36] Here we have an arrangement in which we start from the basic characteristics of history then place history in relation to other special sciences, noting their points of difference and points of departure, and then, finally, place it in relation to our other activities. And throughout this sequence the concept of history is developed, modified and amended through application, and refined through contrast and opposition with other pursuits and activities.

My suggestion, then, is this: that the two series of *Studies* and *Principles* both represent the concrete application of the view of philoso-

[34] E.P.M., p. 100-1.
[35] One commentator, at least, understood the method employed in P.A.: 'The method of exposition, which is also a method of thought, which Professor Collingwood pursues, may be called a Socratic method. First, without any suggestion of a theory, he tries to disentangle what, as a matter of fact, we all know about art, in the belief that the truth is to be found *in* what we all know about it, through often that truth is not exactly what we at first take it to be. This leaves us with a number of philosophical questions to be investigated, because in stating what we all know about art we make use of words and expressions – sensation, thought, emotion, language – which call for analysis. Lastly, there comes the construction of a Theory of Art, a synthesis of the truths that have emerged and established themselves in the earlier discussions. And it may be said that not the least of the delights of this book is its masterly handling of this method.' Michael Oakeshott, review of *The Principles of Art*.
[36] 'Notes on Historiography', 1938-9, p. 20.

phy developed in the two *Essays*. The two *Essays* taken together form a single approach to philosophical enquiry. This view I hope to sustain in detail in the next chapter; all I would say here is that (broadly) *Philosophical Method* expounds the method, *Metaphysics* the matter.

Here it is apposite to note that in the *Autobiography* Collingwood states quite explicitly that *An Essay on Philosophical Method* is his best book in both style *and matter*: this is hardly the sort of comment one would expect if he had rejected the earlier work. It would be plausible to maintain that a writer might praise the style of earlier work while repudiating its content; it makes no sense at all to suppose that a writer could praise the matter of an earlier work while repudiating its content. I suggest, therefore, that Collingwood's remark is given its full weight. It seems only fair that we presume that a writer of philosophical books knows what he is talking about.

Finally, Collingwood notes that *An Essay on Philosophical Method* was written during a long illness. This is a fact of considerable importance, and we will return to it in considering Knox. What we know from letters is that Collingwood went down with chicken pox in April 1931 and that he was ill with this and complications arising from it for a year. This lengthy illness marked the beginning of the illnesses that were to trouble him for the rest of his life. In the Hilary and Trinity terms of 1932 he had leave of absence from the university. He began writing *An Essay on Philosophical Method* in November 1932 and finished it by June of the following year; it was thus written during and after the protracted period of illness of 1931-2. This fact is of importance solely because, as we shall see, some commentators divide Collingwood's works into pre- and post-illness writings, the pre-illness writings being regarded as superior. Of these pre-illness writings the most notable is taken to be *An Essay on Philosophical Method*. We can now see that this, too, was a post-illness writing.[37]

3: Expositors and Critics

T.M. Knox

Malcolm Knox was a student of Collingwood's at Pembroke College in the early twenties who later became a lifelong friend. He compiled the index to *Speculum Mentis*, and after Collingwood's death was entrusted with the preparation of those manuscripts whose publication Collingwood had authorized.

---

[37] On this see Van der Dussen, *History as a Science*, pp. 3–5.

The Idea of Nature was published in 1945. It needed little editing: Collingwood himself had prepared part of the manuscript, and all that needed doing on the rest was to remove extraneous traces of its original form as lectures. The lectures which formed the basis of *The Idea of Nature* were delivered in Michaelmas Term 1934, Hilary Term 1937 and, in a revised form, Michaelmas Term 1939 under the title *Nature and Mind*, and in Hilary Term 1940 under the title *The Idea of Nature in Modern Science*.[38]

The Idea of History, which was published in 1946, was much more of a problem. The book as published comprises Collingwood's 1936 lectures on the philosophy of history; *Human Nature and Human History* (an address to the British Academy); *The Historical Imagination* (Collingwood's inaugural as Waynflete professor); a review on J. B. Bury; and three sections taken from the unfinished book on *The Principles of History*. Collingwood wrote about a third (90 pages, 40,000 words) of *The Principles of History*; of this Knox used less than half on the grounds that he was 'not satisfied that the quality of all the unpublished material is sufficiently high to warrant publication.'[39] This was despite Collingwood's authorization for publication.

Knox's judgement that these manuscripts were not of a high enough quality for publication had the effect, for many years, of preventing us from judging their quality for ourselves.[40] My concern here is not, however, with Knox's execution of his duties as Collingwood's literary executor, but with his interpretation of Collingwood's thought. This interpretation was presented first and in the greatest detail as the Editor's Preface to *The Idea of History*.

According to Knox Collingwood's writings can be divided into three main groups:

1) *Religion and Philosophy* and *Speculum Mentis*, both of which are early works which Knox maintains that Collingwood came later to regard as juvenilia.

2) *An Essay on Philosophical Method*, *The Idea of Nature* and the bulk of *The Idea of History*. These are the writings of the middle period and, in Knox's estimation, the best. Knox described *An Essay on Philosophical Method* as 'a philosophical classic'.[41]

---

[38] For details see D. Boucher, 'The *Principles of History* and the Cosmology Conclusion to the *Idea of Nature*; Van der Dussen, op. cit., p. 434; T.M. Knox, Prefatory Note to I.N.
[39] T.M. Knox, Preface to I.H., vi.
[40] See Van der Dussen, op. cit., p. 46.
[41] T. M. Knox, review of E.P.M.

3) *An Autobiography, An Essay on Metaphysics* and *The New Leviathan*. These are the later works which are, for Knox, marred by historicism and scepticism. Knox regards *The Principles of Art* as akin in part to the second group, in part to the third.

It is Knox's belief that Collingwood's most important contribution to philosophical thought lies in the works of the middle period. In *Philosophical Method*, he argues, philosophy and history are understood as related but clearly distinct categories, and this he holds is true also of *The Idea of Nature* (excepting the conclusion) and of the bulk of *The Idea of History*.

This happy state of affairs was not to last for long; indeed, the halcyon years lasted only from 1932 until 1936 during which time:

> he had succeeded by 'great toil' in freeing himself from the scepticism of his youth and had forged in The *Essay on Philosophical Method* a weapon which might have enabled him to cut his way through the forest of philosophical problems and erect for himself a habitation which might long have stood serene against the winds of criticism. By 1938 . . . he had relapsed into scepticisms whose falsity he had discerned six years earlier, and, consequentially, had fallen into a dogmatism which in The *Essay on Philosophical Method* he had outsoared; and the result is that enthusiasm for history tended to make him 'turn traitor' to his philosophical vocation.[42]

For Knox Collingwood betrayed philosophy by absorbing it into history, and he finds himself 'compelled to believe that his philosophical standpoint radically changed between 1936 and 1938.'[43] Knox also finds himself having to question the reliability of Collingwood's *Autobiography* both because it fails to record any change in Collingwood's philosophical standpoint, and also because it claims that Collingwood had elaborated his doctrine of absolute presuppositions before he had written *An Essay on Philosophical Method* in 1932, a claim which he finds 'hardly credible'.

On the question of the change in Collingwood's philosophical standpoint Knox draws on the evidence of personal acquaintance. In a review of *Mind, History and Dialectic* by Louis Mink he wrote that 'There was quite a definite change in him shortly after 1936, a change visible not only to me but equally to others who knew him well.'[44] It is impossible to gainsay evidence from personal acquaintanceships, but what exactly does it prove? We may freely accept that there was a marked change in Collingwood's personality, but this goes no way toward answering the strictly philosophical question whether there

---

[42] I.H., xix.
[43] I.H., xi.
[44] p. 150.

was a radical shift in his philosophical standpoint between 1936 and 1938. This question can and should be answered by reference to his writings alone: there is no philosophical reason whatever to suppose that changes in character necessarily mark or imply fundamental changes in philosophical outlook.

By way of explanation for Collingwood's later reversion to the 'scepticism' of his youth Knox invokes the illness which afflicted him in the early thirties. Knox regards all the books written after *An Essay on Philosophical Method* as flawed and marred by the illness which Knox, in his preface to *The Idea of History*, thought occurred *after* the writing of the Essay.

Knox also believes that Collingwood 'suppressed'[45] the original conclusion to *The Idea of Nature*, and replaced it by a conclusion in line with his later 'historicism'. This is doubly false: first there is no evidence that Collingwood 'suppressed' the conclusion. As I have already suggested, the conclusion was most likely changed in order to bring *The Idea of Nature* in line with *The Idea of History* in the series *Studies in the History of Ideas*; to have Collingwood's own cosmology appended to his historical survey of cosmologies would have been an intrusion; and it would also have upset the balance of the series. As we know, the Epilegomena to *The Idea of History* were never originally meant for that volume but for *The Principles of History*; similarly, Collingwood's own cosmology, if it was to be published anywhere, would surely have to be published as *The Principles of Nature*. There is no evidence to suggest that Collingwood planned such a volume, but operating on the assumption that *The Idea of Nature* was intended to parallel *The Idea of History*, that would have been the obvious place for Collingwood's own philosophy of Nature.

Secondly, as more than one commentator pointed out in reviewing the book,[46] the conclusion to *The Idea of Nature* repeats the transition from Science to History which was to be found much earlier in *Speculum Mentis*. Whatever the merits of Collingwood's argument in these two books, the fact remains that on this point Collingwood in 1939 was only reaffirming a conclusion first affirmed fifteen years previously and in a book of which Knox generally approves.

Knox also accuses Collingwood of inconsistency in the later work: he wrote of *An Essay on Metaphysics* that it:

> professes not to expound the author's own metaphysical ideas, but to explain what metaphysics is 'and always has been'. If so, then, on his

---
[45] I.H., x.
[46] C.C.J. Webb, review of *The Idea of Nature*.

own principles, it can hardly be a work of history; and indeed the argument of a crucial chapter 'On Presupposing' is set forth *more mathematico;* even if this were only a matter of form, the argument can still not be made into an historical one so long as we accept what is said about historical evidence and inference in the passage from *The Principles of History* printed below as Part V §3. Philosophy would thus seem to have resisted absorption into history at the very time when its absorption was being proclaimed.[47]

The interesting thing about Knox's remarks is that they make sense only on the prior supposition that the later writings do in fact proclaim the absorption of philosophy by history. If Knox were wrong on this point then the contradiction vanishes: if the later writings are not historicist there is no occasion for surprise when we discover passages incompatible with such historicism; indeed, such passages cease to be witnesses for the prosecution and became witnesses for the defence. Those who maintain a different view can justify their conclusions and use the same evidence Knox uses to convict Collingwood of inconsistency as evidence for consistency.

It might be worth taking a closer look at what Collingwood actually says in the infamous passage from which Knox quotes in his preface to *The Idea of History*. What does Collingwood mean when he writes that 'Philosophy as a separate discipline is liquidated by being converted into history.'[48] Surely the important word here is 'separate'? It is philosophy as a separate discipline which is rejected: what we have then, is an overlap between philosophy and history. The attempt to maintain philosophy and history as separate disciplines is what in *Philosophical Method* is called the 'fallacy of precarious margins'. This consists in assuming that 'the overlap which has already affected a certain area of the class in question can be trusted not to spread, and that beyond its limit there lies a marginal region in which the instances exhibit only one of the specific forms, uncontaminated by the presence of the other.'[49] This fallacy Collingwood avoided by maintaining throughout *Philosophical Method* the cross fertilization of philosophy and history; the question that now arises is whether in his later works Collingwood committed the opposite fallacy of 'identified coincidents.[50] This fallacy consists in the view that because two concepts overlap therefore they are identical. Did Collingwood commit this fallacy? I think not, and I shall quote two passages to demonstrate this. In a letter to Guido de Ruggiero con-

---

[47] I.H., xix.
[48] I.H., x.
[49] E.P.M., p. 48.
[50] E.P.M., p. 49.

cerning *The Principles of Art* Collingwood writes of the science of mind as history — but a special kind of history: 'The absorption is mutual: the product is not philosophy based on history nor history based on philosophy, it is both these things at once,' and later he wrote that: 'the problem of 'the nature of art' should become the problem of the nature of *modern* art; and the solution of this problem is the historical problem (but philosophical as much as historical) of the genesis of modern art.'[51] This is confirmed by a passage in Collingwood's own notice of *The Principles of Art* in which he declares that the book is 'the author's chief work down to the present time . . . Its aim is not simply to add one more to the many extant "theories of art", but to illustrate the author's doctrine concerning the relation between philosophy and history by focusing attention on contemporary art and its problems, and treating these as part of the problem of contemporary civilization.'[52]

These passages demonstrate that for Collingwood philosophy and history were inseparable: philosophy if it was to be concrete had to be historical, and this implied not the absorption of the one into the other, but an overlap between the two. He avoided both the fallacy of precarious margins by denying that they were separate disciplines, and the fallacy of identified coincidents by asserting their difference — i.e. that the area of overlap would consist of both philosophy and history at once. All this is summed up by Collingwood's 'first rule of philosophical method', which is to

> beware of false disjunctions and to assume that the specific classes of a philosophical concept are always liable to overlap, so that two or more specifically differing concepts may be exemplified in the same instance... The traditional way of referring to this principle is to speak of 'distinction without a difference', that is, a distinction in the concepts without a difference in the instances.[53]

As we shall later see this was always Collingwood's philosophical approach: he never denied the autonomy of philosophy, but he did deny that it could exist as a separate subject, and he did deny that it could be studied separately from its historical instantiations. Philosophy, for Collingwood, had to be concrete or it was nothing, and by 'concrete' in the sciences of mind we mean rooted in history.[54]

---

[51] Letter to de Ruggiero, 21st October 1938.
[52] Notice of *The Principles of Art*, p. 314. There is no direct proof that this notice is by Collingwood, but it can be safely attributed on the grounds of style and privileged statement of authorial intention.
[53] E.P.M., p. 50.
[54] This theme is developed and illustrated at greater length in Chapter Two.

I shall now return to the question of Collingwood's illness and examine Knox's use of this in explanation of the faults in the later writings. Knox attaches considerable importance to the influence of illness on the development of Collingwood's views. Before proceeding further it must be said that the use of illness in explanation is a tricky business. First, illness is only ever invoked as explanation when an author's work failed to meet its normal standard: no one ever feels the need to explain away good writing by reference to illness or the author's general state of health — although there were many authors who produced their best work while seriously ill.[55] Secondly, even where illness is called upon in explanation it cannot explain very much. We already know that the piece of writing (or whatever) is flawed before we bring in reference to illness; we also know in what way it is flawed (that is, its philosophical inconsistencies and errors). All that the illness can tell us, then, is that for a work we already know to be flawed there may be an extra-textual reason for its failure. This explanation tells us nothing about the content of the failure, and nor could it — we already know the content prior to looking for extra-textual reasons to explain it. And even if we allow that illness might mar an author's judgement, why should it be supposed that this will result in the expression of a particular doctrine such as historicism?[56]

And here we reach the crux: first, presumably not all supposed failure or error has to be explained this way; and most certainly we cannot always appeal to illness in order to account for an author for which we previously had sympathy producing work with which we disagree. Secondly, if reference to illness is only invoked at that point where an author produces work which is incoherent or not up to his usual standard, then if it can be shown that the work in question is not flawed, not incoherent, and not below the author's customary standard, the author's state of health becomes irrelevant and appeals to it redundant.

If we turn back to Knox we can, I think, show two things: first, that Knox's explanation of what he sees as the unsatisfactory nature of Collingwood's later work is irrelevant as that later work is not in any case discontinuous with the earlier nor is it internally inconsistent in

---

[55] One might mention George Orwell or Elizabeth Barratt Browning.
[56] And even if we do suppose that it issues in a doctrine such as 'historicism', why should this be regretted? Presumably it is only to be regretted if we already have philosophical grounds for objecting to such a doctrine; but those who regard such a view as sound (or at least worthy of serious attention) will find little or nothing to regret in these later views. This is to ignore (for the moment) the question of whether these views in fact amount to a form of 'historicism'.

the way he supposes. Secondly, that Knox's use of the illness by way of explanation fails on its own terms. The first point forms the substance of Chapter Two so I shall not argue it here, but the second point stands in need of elaboration.

Knox had a high regard for *An Essay on Philosophical Method*, which he considered to be both a philosophical classic, and superior to most of Collingwood's other works. *Philosophical Method*, for Knox, represented Collingwood's philosophical work at its best; and it was, he thought, separated from the later work not only through its quality but also through its being on the right side of the dividing line caused by Collingwood's illness. However, it is at this very point that Knox's case breaks down. He believed *Philosophical Method* to be a pre-illness work and hence not marred by the effects of the illness.

On this he is wrong. As Collingwood himself wrote in *An Autobiography* 'this I wrote during a long illness in 1932.'[57] Collingwood was ill from April 1931 for a year; he began to write *Philosophical Method* in November 1932 and completed it in June 1933. Thus the *Essay* was written after a period of serious illness. This fact undermines Knox's position completely. There are two possible ways out for Knox, both of which fail. Either it could be claimed that the later books were affected more seriously by illness than was *Philosophical Method*: this, of course, could not explain why it was relatively unaffected; or it could be maintained that with the progressive seriousness of the illness and the increasing incidence of his strokes, Collingwood's judgement progressively deteriorated. But if this were so we should expect to see a progressive and steady decline in the quality and coherence of Collingwood's later books, but this is not so. Knox explicitly affirms that:

> The *Autobiography* outlines an interesting logic of question and answer which has already begun to be noticed by contemporary logicians. The *specimina philosophandi* in the *Essay on Metaphysics* are brilliant essays in the history of thought. *The New Leviathan* gives some hint of the fruitfulness of applying to ethics the method expounded in 1933, and the value of its sustained defence of our civilized way of life has been recognized even by reviewers not very favourably disposed to Collingwood's other books.[58]

Knox, then, does not regard the later books as uniformly bad, and the book which was *most* affected by Collingwood's strokes — *The New Leviathan* — appears to be a book for which Knox has consider-

---

[57] A, p. 118.
[58] I.H., xxii.

able sympathy.[59] Collingwood himself says in the *Autobiography* that 'I have never known any illness interfere with my power of thinking and writing, or with the quality of what I think and write'.[60] *An Essay on Metaphysics* was written while convalescing from a stroke; *The New Leviathan* amid several debilitating strokes. The question is this: which would we expect to be the more affected by illness and consequent errors of judgement; the writings produced before, or those produced after the serious strokes? The answer can only be those written after, in this case *The New Leviathan* which, whatever its faults, appears free of the historicism and scepticism which Knox claims to find in *Metaphysics*. If Collingwood's judgement was impaired in writing the later books, why is it that the *Autobiography* and *Metaphysics*, which for Knox espouse an objectionable form of historicism, were more seriously affected than *The New Leviathan*, written in the midst of a spate of serious strokes, and which he did not regard as marred by the same flaws? No satisfactory answer is possible given the initial assumption that the illness can somehow be blamed for what Knox finds objectionable in the later writings. At this point it may also be worth noting that of all his books Collingwood considered *The New Leviathan* the only one possibly affected by illness, as he suggested in a letter to the Clarendon Press:

> Part 3 is in manuscript, having been written just before my last stroke. Part 4 which is typed, was written after my stroke and removal to Streatley. If there are any signs of battiness in the whole work, they will occur in Part 4, which should for that reason be looked at with especial care; I find it very difficult to believe that, dictating to a typewriter, I can produce anything but rubbish.[61]

Given the remarks quoted above from the *Autobiography*, this warning should be taken seriously: if there is any place where Collingwood's work was affected by his illness then that place was the last part of *The New Leviathan*.

Knox appeals to the illness only because he is otherwise unable to find reasons for Collingwood's change of viewpoint: here we can agree with him. There are no reasons; but this is not because the shift in viewpoint was somehow irrational and therefore only to be explained by external factors, but because there was no radical change of viewpoint: Knox is attempting, and failing, to explain something that needs no explanation.

---

[59] Knox's Gifford Lectures (published as *Action*) are greatly indebted to the approach and content of NL: see p. 45 and p. 51n.
[60] A, p. 117.
[61] Letter to Clarendon Press, 6 August 1941.

I shall leave Knox here and move onto the work of Alan Donagan who puts forward a similar line to Knox's while revising both his conclusions and his reasoning.

Alan Donagan[62]

Donagan's account of Collingwood's development is in many ways similar to Knox's. Like Knox he believes that the *Autobiography* and *An Essay on Metaphysics* marked a shift to a vicious historicism, but nonetheless there are many points on which they disagree. Donagan agrees with Knox in maintaining that Collingwood underwent a 'radical conversion' at some time between 1936 and 1938, but he disagrees with Knox on two fundamental issues: first, the explanation for this change, and secondly Knox's division of Collingwood's later writings into two groups, the 'non-historicist' and the 'historicist'.[63]

On the first point, Donagan argues that illness may affect a person's judgement in such a way as to cause him to mistake bad reasons for good; but it will not cause him to change his mind for no reason at all. He suggests, therefore, that Knox's account be supplemented by identifying Collingwood's reasons for his change of mind, even if those reasons might appear inadequate to us or, more importantly, would have appeared inadequate to Collingwood himself when in good health.[64]

He then goes on to develop his case by arguing that Collingwood, in writing *The Principles of Art*, came to conclusions concerning the nature of thought incompatible with the position laid down in *Speculum Mentis* and *An Essay on Philosophical Method*.[65] In consequence, he continues, Collingwood could no longer accept the possibility of a non-abstract ontology of the kind put forward in *Philosophical Method*.

Donagan gives other reasons for the change in view, especially the absorption of philosophy by history, reasons which include Collingwood's tendency (noted by Knox)[66] to identify whatever he was doing or studying at the time with philosophy in general; and Collingwood's acceptance of the verification principle as propounded in A. J. Ayer's *Language, Truth and Logic*[67] with the concomitant principle that the propositions of traditional metaphysics are

---

[62] Alan Donagan, *The Later Philosophy of R. G. Collingwood*.
[63] Donagan, op. cit., pp. 12ff.
[64] Donagan, op. cit., p. 12
[65] According to Donagan, the view that thought was necessarily abstract.
[66] I.H., xv.
[67] See Donagan, op. cit., pp. 14–5.

unverifiable. Collingwood then went on to re-interpret these propositions as absolute presuppositions, thus leaving the metaphysician with the historical task of inquiring, not into the truth or falsity of these propositions, but into what they were, who held them and when and why they changed.

On the second point, Donagan rejects Knox's classification of the later books into two groups, the historicist and the non-historicist.[68] In his opinion, the writings after Collingwood began writing *The Idea of Nature* in 1934 contain no major reversal of doctrine, excepting that of the nature of philosophy and its relation to history.[69] Donagan also rejects Knox's division on the grounds that, whatever may be true of the *Autobiography* and the *Essay on Metaphysics*, it is not at all clear that when Collingwood wrote *The New Leviathan* he still subscribed to the view that philosophy could be converted into a purely historical inquiry.[70]

Donagan's alternative interpretation is this: by 1932 Collingwood had planned a series of philosophical books. On the completion of the first book of the series, *Philosophical Method*, he wrote *The Idea of Nature* and the bulk of *The Idea of History*. In 1937 he wrote *The Principles of Art*, the second book of the series. The theory of conceptual thinking developed in that book was incompatible with the conception of philosophy advanced in *An Essay on Philosophical Method*, and Collingwood therefore reconsidered that conception. This he did in the *Autobiography*, the *Essay on Metaphysics* and *The Principles of History*. He then returned to his series, polishing *The Idea of Nature* and writing *The New Leviathan*. *The New Leviathan* showed that the 'historicist' conception of philosophy satisfied him as little as did the 'idealist' conception of *Philosophical Method*.

Donagan concludes that Collingwood's major philosophical work in *The Idea of Nature*, *The Idea of History*, *The Principles of Art* and *The New Leviathan* forms a largely consistent whole which should not be divided into historicist and non-historicist groups.[71] Collingwood put forward two different interpretations of his later philosophy: an idealist one in *Method* and an historicist one in his *Autobiography* and *Metaphysics*. Neither interpretation, Donagan suggests, was adequate to his philosophical achievement.

---

[68] Donagan, op. cit., p. 15
[69] Donagan, loc. cit.
[70] Donagan, op. cit., p. 16.
[71] As Knox did, (I.H., vii); for Knox Collingwood's writings can be divided into three groups, the first being juvenilia, the second non-historicist and the third, historicist, works.

Donagan's interpretation is more subtle than Knox's, but it nevertheless concurs on the major issue: that between 1936 and 1938 Collingwood radically changed his mind on the relation of philosophy to history. Concurrence on this also brings in its train the conclusion that Collingwood's *Autobiography* is 'beyond doubt untrue' in that it (amongst other omissions) fails to record the radical change in his philosophical standpoint.[72]

Clearly, if it can be shown that the two *Essays* are not incompatible; that Collingwood did not undergo a 'radical conversion'; and that the doctrines expressed in *Metaphysics* were no radical new departure but rather the crystallisation of a general view on the nature of metaphysics which had been with him throughout his career (including the years 1932-36 which are supposed to be marked by his commitment to an 'Idealist' view of philosophy)[73] then not only do we have to take the *Autobiography* more seriously as an historical document, but also the whole line of approach characteristic of both Donagan and Knox will have to be abandoned.

Finally, there are one or two further points on which issue might be taken with Donagan's interpretation. Donagan believes that in *The Principles of Art* Collingwood worked out a conception of the nature of thought as abstract which was incompatible with the assumptions of *Speculum Mentis* and the *Essay on Philosophical Method* which are built upon what Donagan calls the 'anti-abstraction principle'.[74] He then suggests that, recognising this incompatibility, Collingwood developed a new theory of philosophy, but that this new theory satisfied him as little as the earlier and that by the time of *The New Leviathan* it too had been superseded.

Donagan's case here rests on the supposition that Collingwood recognised the incompatibility and sought to rectify it: but there is no evidence for this. Even if Donagan's philosophical point is conceded and we accept that the conception of thought as 'essentially analytic and abstract' developed in *The Principles of Art* and *The New Leviathan* is incompatible with *Philosophical Method*'s thesis that there is at least one form of thinking (metaphysics) which is not-abstract;[75] nothing is lost because his interpretation rests upon a view of

---

[72] Donagan, op. cit., p. 1.
[73] Which is what Collingwood claims in a letter to the Clarendon Press (14.11.38): 'I have been for a long time contemplating a short book which should explain to the public what *Metaphysics* is, what it is for, how it works and why the various people who clamour for its abolition ought not to be listened to. I have only lacked the leisure to write it.'
[74] Alan Donagan, 'Collingwood and Philosophical Method', in Krausz, op. cit., p. 13.
[75] Donagan, op. cit., p. 14.

Collingwood's intentions. The question is not whether the two conceptions are incompatible, but whether Collingwood thought them so and acted on that recognition. If he did not, Donagan's case fails because he has failed to supply a plausible motive for Collingwood's 'radical conversion'. And the short answer is that there is no explicit evidence that Collingwood ever saw the supposed incompatibility that Donagan attributes to him and therefore no reason to believe that his supposed change of mind can be explained in this way.

In disagreeing with the interpretation put forward by Knox and Donagan I have freely issued credit notes which I hope to redeem in the next chapter where I present my own interpretation: unless it can be shown that Collingwood's later work marks no radical break with the earlier, then we shall be forced back into a position something like that of Knox or Donagan. Admittedly, the detail of the suggested reasons for the 'radical conversion' would be different, but given the philosophical quality of the proponents of the 'radical conversion' hypothesis, the onus must be on those who deny the charge of historicism and scepticism.

The quantity of commentary and criticism of Collingwood's work has been increasing steadily for the past thirty years. Donagan's book was the first full length book devoted to Collingwood: since then there have been many others.

It is obviously impossible to do more than mention most of these books and articles and essays: I do not aim to provide a tourist's guide to Collingwood interpretation. All I shall do is to briefly examine two books devoted to Collingwood's philosophy, both of which take issue with the 'radical conversion hypothesis' and try to work out and develop a picture of Collingwood's philosophy as a whole. The two books I shall take for this purpose are Louis Mink's *Mind, History and Dialectic* and Lionel Rubinoff's *Collingwood and the Reform of Metaphysics*.

Lionel Rubinoff

Collingwood and the Reform of Metaphysics: A Study in the Philosophy of Mind was published in 1970. Its leading ideas had been developed earlier in review articles, essays and in a commentary to Rubinoff's collection of Collingwood's writings on religion which he brought together in 1968 under the title *Faith and Reason*.[76] The book recast Rubinoff's ideas into a full, detailed and systematic exposition of Collingwood's philosophy. It succeeds in showing the essential

---

[76] L. Rubinoff, (ed.) *Faith and Reason*.

unity of Collingwood's thought, a unity unimpaired by its development. For Rubinoff, Collingwood's thought developed through the elaboration and further exploration of philosophical positions and themes already in principle advanced in the early works, principally *Speculum Mentis*. In criticising Rubinoff's book I am not disputing its general thesis advancing the unity of Collingwood's thought, but rather seeking to draw attention to certain dangers inherent in Rubinoff's particular approach.

If one postulates the existence of a radical conversion in Collingwood's thought, then there is no need to explain apparent contradictions and inconsistencies between books lying on either side of the conversion: one can simply accept their existence, and all one needs to do is to explain why Collingwood moved from one standpoint to the other. This is precisely what Knox and Donagan, in their various ways, seek to do. If, on the other hand, one denies the existence of a radical conversion, this option is closed. In this case it has to be argued, first, that Collingwood actually did or could have held seemingly opposed views at the same time and secondly, that they are not really opposed and thus not in conflict. This line of argument involves the laborious task of resolving prima facie contradictions; of showing the questions they were intended to answer; the level on which they operate, and so on; and all this under the adverse conditions engendered both by the opponents of this view and also by Collingwood's lack of terminological consistency and relative infrequency of cross reference.

Rubinoff sets about the task with spirit and does his job well, but in his zeal perhaps ends up by attempting to prove too much. He has a tendency to ignore Collingwood's development (although he professes to take it seriously) and he tends to view the later works as little more than elaborations in detail of a system already laid down in all essentials by *Speculum Mentis* in 1924.

His central thesis is that the later philosophy is a dialectical outcome of the earlier philosophy; he argues that:

> the history of Collingwood's thought is not characterised by a radical conversion from 'idealism' to 'historicism', but, rather, that the rapprochement which he set out to accomplish in 1916 was actually achieved in *Speculum Mentis* and *An Essay on Philosophical Method* and subsequently applied, in the remainder of his writings, to the interpretation of numerous philosophical problems. My book is an attempt, in other words, at meeting the need of viewing the bulk of Collingwood's

thought as an expression of the programme laid out in *Speculum Mentis*.⁷⁷

The weakness of Rubinoff's approach arises directly out of his taking *Speculum Mentis* as the basic point of reference: the attempt to view the later works as 'the expression of the programme laid out in *Speculum Mentis*' issues in a distortion of Collingwood's philosophical work as a consequence of the skewing arising from the heavy emphasis on this book.

Rubinoff tends to ignore time in Collingwood's thought, that is, to ignore the fact that writing and publishing books over a number of years is an historical process. The point here is that a person's writings are the products of continuous thought, an activity taking place over time and with its own history. No one book exhausts the contents of a writer's mind: each book is a stepping stone. Past thoughts are the stepping stones for present thinking, and present thoughts become the stepping stones for future thinking. The character and direction of future thought cannot be contained within limits set down by present thought, although, no doubt, they are conditioned by it as they are necessarily outgrowths from it.

What Rubinoff sometimes overlooks is the difference between an author developing what was in an earlier work only implicit, and the implicit content itself. The implications of early works are nothing if they are not later taken up and developed. To talk of later works as developing the implications and filling in the detail omitted by an early work is to admit that the early work in question did not contain the doctrine or theory in full. If this is so the later work is no mere sketching in of details but rather the picture itself, and it is only by the use of this picture that the original sketch can be seen for what it was. We often speak of some early essay or chapter of a book as 'anticipating' a later doctrine or theory: it only makes sense to talk in this way if we already know what the later theory is. We view the former in the light of the latter and not vice versa.

Rubinoff's error, then, lies in part with his over emphasis on *Speculum Mentis*, and his insistence that the later works merely flesh out a position already established in principle in that book. Besides ignoring the extent to which a programme is changed and modified in the writing of it,⁷⁸ he ignores or misses an important point about the nature of dialectical implication. Surely it is of the essence of dialectical implication that it looks towards its end, its *telos*? To say that

---

[77] L. Rubinoff, *Collingwood and The Reform of Metaphysics*, p. 24.
[78] As we have already seen, the nature of Collingwood's series underwent several changes.

something contains in principle all later developments is to say that it exists only potentially, not actually.

If we ask for an oak and receive an acorn we naturally feel disappointed: a full understanding must contain reference not merely to the origins of a thing but also to its end. It is therefore a mistake to read the later works in the light only of the earlier (this is to judge the oak by the acorn); it is of equal or perhaps greater importance to read the earlier works in the light of the later, that is, to judge the half-developed by reference to the fully developed. The later writings need criteria for judgement adequate to themselves which are generated within those works and have no prior existence. It is therefore mistaken to judge later works solely by criteria derived from earlier works. My reversal of Rubinoff's approach, I submit, more accurately accords with the idea of a scale of forms, which is the principle of explanation to which Rubinoff himself appeals. If we take Collingwood's writings as constituting a scale of forms then far from judging everything retrospectively in the light of *Speculum Mentis*, we should judge it in the light of its successors. This would more satisfactorily fit in with Collingwood's own judgement 'if much of it now fails to satisfy me, that is because I have gone on thinking since I wrote it, and therefore much of it needs to be supplemented and qualified. There is not a great deal that needs to be retracted.'[79]

Rubinoff sometimes appears to deny that Collingwood went on thinking: this is to do violence both to Collingwood's own statements above, and also to the principles of the scale of forms itself. Surely Collingwood's remarks quoted above also fit his view of the relation between the terms of a scale of forms: 'each term ... has ... a double relation to its neighbours: in comparison with the one below, it is what that professes to be; in comparison with the one above, it professes to be what that is.'[80]

It would seem that if we follow what Collingwood says in his *Autobiography* and *Philosophical Method*, we arrive at a different viewpoint from the one taken by Rubinoff. By way of counterbalance to Rubinoff's maximisation of the importance of *Speculum Mentis* I suggest we accept that (in some sense) Collingwood's works make up a

---

[79] A., p. 56. I largely agree with Passmore's comments both on this passage and Rubinoff's interpretation of Collingwood in general. Passmore makes the point that scholars rarely know exactly what they said in earlier works and that this point is ignored in any picture of a philosopher anxiously attempting to say nothing inconsistent with their earlier writing (J. Passmore, review of Rubinoff, p. 176.).

[80] E.P.M., p. 87.

developing scale of forms, and that the later works often make explicit what in the earlier was implicit. But this suggestion must be carefully balanced by a recommendation to examine the earlier works in the light of the later, given that it is only in the later that promise is translated into performance. Again, we need to stress time. Rubinoff at times writes as if Collingwood's books (post *Speculum Mentis*) could have been written in any order, all being equally the fleshing out of a pre-formed skeleton. But, as Bosanquet reminds us, the skeleton grows with the body and does not come first:[81] the recognition of system is retrospective only and its form grows with its content. It is not possible to lay down the form of a series of works in advance and then expect the content to fall into place; it is not possible to work out the detail and consequences of a pre-existing point of view without modifying, changing and amending that point of view and thereby moving beyond it. Thought necessarily re-shapes its material at each stage of its development and therefore the very attempt to carry out a programme laid down in advance takes us beyond that programme in the act of carrying it out. This renders the original statement of that programme a less than adequate guide to its later fulfillment.

Although I have criticised Rubinoff, I do so precisely because his work is of a high standard. The value of his book (and his articles) as a corrective to Knox and Donagan cannot be overestimated; his stress on the unity of Collingwood's philosophy and his resolute opposition to the 'radical conversion hypothesis' (which very useful term was coined by Rubinoff) has been of great service to all those wishing to come to terms with Collingwood's thought.

Louis Mink

Louis Mink's account of Collingwood's philosophy in *Mind, History and Dialectic* is perhaps the most balanced and perceptive of all: it is because I agree with him the most that I shall say the least about him. Mink is fully aware of the importance of the unpublished manuscripts and especially of the lectures on ethics, both in themselves and also in relation to *The New Leviathan*. At the time he wrote (1969), the unpublished manuscripts were not available for inspection. Nevertheless (of the pre-manuscript accounts) his is the one which needs the least correcting by what they now reveal. As against Rubinoff, Mink lays greater emphasis upon *The New Leviathan* than

---

[81] Bernard Bosanquet, *The Philosophical Theory of The State*, p. 28, footnote, 'It is the old story of forgetting that the skeleton is later than the body, and is deposited and moulded by it.'

upon *Speculum Mentis*: if my objections to Rubinoff are sound, this procedure is fully justified; indeed, it may be this difference of emphasis which accounts for the more balanced and more perceptive account that Mink provides.

Against Knox and Donagan I have argued that the 'radical conversion hypothesis' is false; against Rubinoff I have argued that he succeeds in making everything a little too smoothly fitting and systematic; against Mink I have invoked the unpublished manuscripts which tend to vindicate his line of approach but which he nevertheless could not use in developing his own case.

My own argument draws in large part upon the unpublished manuscripts, and its central claim is that Collingwood's philosophy makes up a coherent whole unmarked by any 'radical conversion'. My next two chapters aim to show how Collingwood's writings can be re-interpreted in such a way as to constitute a coherent philosophy, and in particular I aim to show how the two *Philosophical Essays*, taken together, can be forged into a unified philosophical approach in which both method and subject matter are combined. The succeeding chapters presuppose the earlier chapters and aim to present Collingwood's social and political philosophy in a systematic fashion.

4: A Central Thread?

Throughout this book I shall make extensive use of Collingwood's unpublished manuscripts.[82] The point of so doing is to reinforce the argument for the unity of his philosophical writing by bringing to the foreground recessive features of his philosophy, and by making explicit themes which are otherwise stated only implicitly or in outline.

The question now arising is what sort of unity might we expect to find in the lifetime's work of a philosopher? Here it is perhaps appropriate to take up the metaphor suggested by *Ruskin's Philosophy*:

> when I speak of a man's philosophy, I mean something of this sort. I see a man living a long and busy life; I see him doing a large number of different things, or writing a large number of different books. And I ask myself, do these actions, or these books, hang together? Is there any central thread on which they are all strung? Is there any reason why the man

---

[82] I use the term 'unpublished manuscript' as a term of convenience to refer not only to those manuscripts which still remain unpublished, but also to those which have subsequently been published in the revised editions of Collingwood's books and those reprinted in *Essays on Political Philosophy*.

who wrote this book should have gone on to write that one, or is it pure chance? Is there anything like a constant purpose, or a consistent point or view, running through all the man's work?[83]

My view is that, in the case of Collingwood, there is such a 'central thread': its nature will be discussed below. For the moment I wish only to examine where the evidence for such a thread is to be found. The most important source of evidence is, naturally, Collingwood's published work. Continuity through change and development can be discerned in his published work: it is there for those who care to read him closely and sympathetically; and indeed several commentators have both discerned and described this continuity or 'central thread' with great accuracy. If the thread were not traceable in the lines of the published philosophical writings there would be little point in proving its existence through reference to unpublished manuscripts. The reason for using the unpublished manuscripts in order to highlight the central thread is twofold. First, some of Collingwood's readers have discerned a high degree of continuity and coherence which they have described as accurately as reference to published work alone allows; secondly, this interpretation is contested, and contested by some (for example Knox) who were not only personal friends to Collingwood but who also had access to some (at least) of his manuscripts.[84] These two facts taken together point directly toward the unpublished manuscripts as the possible source of relevant material for resolving the dispute.

The reason is this: on the one hand there are claims to the effect that Collingwood's thought exhibited a high degree of continuity and underwent no radical dislocation; on the other, there are claims that there are radical discontinuities between the earlier and the later work and that there is no possibility of reconciling the two opposed elements in Collingwood's philosophy. In neither case can we assume that the protagonists are limited to knowledge of the published work alone: Knox, the most formidable early proponent of the radical conversion hypothesis, was a personal friend who both read Collingwood's books and heard his lectures; and in his preface to *The Idea of History* he writes of 'others (who) maintain that, while his views developed, the development was gradual and always along the same track.'[85] It is not quite clear to whom Knox is referring, but the point is that there was disagreement about Collingwood's intellectual development even during his lifetime and amongst those who knew him personally.

---

[83] *Ruskin's Philosophy*, (R's. P.), 1922, p. 6.
[84] See T.M. Knox, preface to I.H. and preface to *Action*.
[85] T.M. Knox, preface to I.H., xi.

There are other early commentators who take a middle position on the question. For example, E.W.F. Tomlin who was a pupil of Collingwood's, wrote 'that a change of fundamental importance did occur is undeniable.'[86] But in the same booklet he also writes of *An Essay on Metaphysics* as 'a prolegomenon to *The New Leviathan*' in that its purpose is to define the meaning of civilization understood as a complex of absolute presuppositions;[87] and again, he makes a case for the unity of Collingwood's thought by arguing that Collingwood's principal achievements in speculation were:

> his logic of question and answer, his theory of imagination, his view of metaphysics as the 'science of presuppositions', and his doctrine of history as 'the self-knowledge of mind'. Not merely were these doctrines interrelated, each shed light upon the rest. And they formed in combination an attempt, which the future may show to have been not unsuccessful, to recall philosophy to its traditional responsibilities, as an inquiry into the nature of things, which should at that same time and for that same reason provide guidance in everyday life.[88]

After these early commentators we have the later more systematic presentations by Donagan, Mink and Rubinoff. None of these were pupils of Collingwood's and all relied for their accounts on the published works and such unpublished material as was available to them — which was relatively little.

The arguments over Collingwood's philosophical development have been simmering for fifty years: only now, with the unpublished manuscripts available to public scrutiny, is there a real hope of deepening the inquiry to take full account of all the nooks and crannies of his thought. In principle the question is now capable of resolution with both sides able to appeal to the same publicly available sources for evidence. There is no longer any need for speculative reconstruction of lectures or essays, and no need to rely on ex-pupils' memories of lectures or privileged access to manuscripts, full knowledge of which is denied to others.[89]

It should be stated at the outset that although I have referred to Collingwood's lectures extensively throughout this book, I should not be taken as attempting to provide a full account of their overall contents unless I explicitly declare that to be my intention. For example, much of the evidence for the central thread of Collingwood's thought is to be found in the lectures on moral philosophy he delivered in Oxford from 1921 onwards. I quote from these lectures not so

---

[86] E.W.F. Tomlin, *R.G. Collingwood*, , p. 23.
[87] E.W.F. Tomlin, op. cit., p. 33
[88] E.W.F. Tomlin, op. cit., p. 10.
[89] E.g., T.M. Knox, see preface to I.H., x, xii.

much in order to provide a full and coherent exposition of Collingwood's moral theory, as to provide evidence for the continuity of his thought throughout his intellectual life.

It is my view that these lectures, together with other manuscripts and published books and reviews, show clearly that at no point in Collingwood's thought can a radical break be discerned. These lectures, through their centrality, regularity of delivery, intimate relations with published works and twenty year span of writing and presentation in some way constitute the backbone of Collingwood's thought. Here, if anywhere, evidence for the central thread, constant purpose and consistent point of view, running through all his work is to be found. The lectures will be used as a basic point of reference, a thread of identity making contact at each point with published works and so linking them together in a way in which they do not explicitly link themselves together through cross reference and explicit statement.

Collingwood first lectured on moral philosophy in 1921.[90] These lectures were delivered annually up to and including 1933.[91] They were delivered again in 1940; and his lectures on the 'Theory of Society and Politics', which were a direct continuation of the lectures on ethics, were written for delivery in 1940 and 1941.[92] The 1921 lectures were replaced by an entirely new series written in September 1923 entitled 'Action'. The term 'scale of forms' makes its first appearance in these 1923 lectures, a fact which lends credence to the interpretations of those who argue, with Mink, that 'the scheme of *Speculum Mentis*, regarded now from the standpoint of the *Essay on Philosophical Method*, has the structure of a scale of forms' and that 'the *Essay* ... provides what was missing in *Speculum Mentis*: a theory of philoso-

---

[90] According to A., the date was 1919, but neither in his 'List of Work Done' (1933) nor in the *Oxford Gazette* do lectures on ethics dating back to that time receive a mention.
[91] The lectures were not delivered in 1928 or 1931.
[92] The lectures on politics were a continuation of the lectures on moral philosophy given in Hilary Term 1940 entitled 'Goodness, Rightness, Utility'. According to a prefatory note to these 1940 lectures they were 'written as delivered' and formed a 'continuation of those on Feeling, Appetite, Desire and Will delivered in the previous term'; which were written between December 1939 and February 1940. I can find no other record of Collingwood having delivered lectures on these subjects in the previous term, although he was timetabled to deliver lectures on 'Nature and Mind' and to give 'Informal Instruction' (see Van der Dussen p. 434). These lectures on politics, along with the preceding lectures on 'Feeling, Appetite, Desire and Will' were clearly the prototype of N.L.

phy of which the argument of *Speculum Mentis* can itself be regarded as an example.'[93]

Mink's argument is strengthened by the discovery that the term 'scale of forms' is contemporaneous with *Speculum Mentis*: this gives added plausibility to his claim that *Philosophical Method* presents a logic of dialectical method which is exemplified in the philosophy of *Speculum Mentis* and throughout Collingwood's writings. It also illustrates a point of some importance which is that Collingwood rarely if ever refers to his method in applying it: he proceeds with the job in hand and by so doing exemplifies the method. Typically the method is not explicitly stated in its application, it is carried implicitly and made explicit only in the methodological discussion of *Philosophical Method* itself. This is, of course, in accord with the whole approach of the *Essay*; and the principle that method exists only in its application and not as a ready made formula to be applied *a priori* is formally stated in his 1935 paper on 'Method and Metaphysics'.[94]

In 1926 these lectures were 'much rewritten and expanded from about seventy to one hundred pages ... with some considerable alterations on points of theory.' They were partly re-written in 1927 with a new conclusion replacing the original 1923 conclusion. A new course of lectures was written and delivered in 1929. They were again completely re-written in the summer of 1932, and revised and cut in length in 1933. The methodological introduction to these lectures, which had been growing, cuckoo like, since 1923, was cut out in 1933 'as overloading the course' and took on a life of its own. Suit-

---

[93] *Mind, History and Dialectic*, p. 75. Mink is perfectly correct except in his supposition that the doctrines of E.P.M. arose out of reflection on the structure of S.M. The doctrines of E.P.M. are a logical outcome of reflection upon the philosophy presented in S.M., and not as Mink implies also a temporal outcome. Mink seems to be suggesting that Collingwood first wrote S.M. and only later came to reflect on it and to systematize the principles of philosophical method it exemplified. On the contrary, the central doctrine of E.P.M. (the idea of the 'scale of forms') was already in Collingwood's mind at the time S.M. was published. I do not know why the term 'scale of forms' is absent from S.M. Perhaps Collingwood was reluctant to introduce it before he had fully worked out his principles of method.

[94] 'I do not mean to imply that a philosopher can first of all work out certain rules of method and then go on to apply them as a ready made instrument to fresh problems. It is only by working at problems, of whatever kind, that one can learn to handle them; and when I speak of applying the method to metaphysical problems I would wish you to understand that these and similar problems were always in my mind when I was writing on philosophical method, and indeed long before', 'Method and Metaphysics', 1935, p. l.

ably re-written it was presented as a series of lectures in Trinity term 1933, as 'Philosophy, its Nature and Method'. In June of the same year it was sent to the Oxford University Press and published as *An Essay on Philosophical Method*.

All of Collingwood's lectures existed in intimate relation to his books. His first book, *Religion and Philosophy*, almost certainly contained material taken from his lectures delivered in 1915 on the philosophy of religion. There is considerable overlap between *Speculum Mentis* and the 1923 lectures on moral philosophy: several passages in that book are quite clearly compressed statements of passages which also appear in the lectures.[95] Between 1920 and 1924 Collingwood lectured on the *Introduction to the Theory of Knowledge*. It would be surprising if *Speculum Mentis* and the 1923 paper 'Sensation and Thought' did not contain material from these lectures. In so far as *Speculum Mentis* is an account of the forms of experience and of the problem of knowledge then I think it is reasonable to assume that it contains much that was previously presented in the lectures on the theory of knowledge. In 1924 Collingwood wrote 'Rough notes for a book on the philosophy of Art.' These were rewritten and delivered as lectures in Trinity Term 1925 and published as *Outlines of a Philosophy of Art* in the same year.

An Essay on Philosophical Method began life as a methodological introduction to the lectures on Moral Philosophy; and for the published book betrays this origin in the numerous examples taken from ethics. In 1933, along with the methodological introduction, Collingwood cut out of his lectures on moral philosophy the sections on Matter, Life and Mind. His cosmological speculations, as can be seen from these passages, thus predate the series of notebooks begun after the completion of *Philosophical Method*. In 1934 and 1937 Collingwood lectured on 'Nature and Mind': the origins of these lectures are undoubtedly the passages on 'Matter, Life and Mind' from the lectures on moral philosophy supplemented by the cosmological researches he was pursuing at the time. In 1940 these lectures were revised and presented as 'The Idea of Nature in Modern Science'. They were published posthumously in 1946 as *The Idea of Nature*.

In 1936 Collingwood lectured (as he had done annually since 1926) on the philosophy of history. These 1936 lectures later became parts I-IV of *The Idea of History*. In the summer of 1937 he wrote *The*

---

[95] For example the passages on Convention, pp. 134-8; Utility, pp. 164-176; Duty, pp. 221-231; Absolute Ethics, pp. 304-6.

Principles of Art and lectured on the philosophy of art in both that and the following year during which *The Principles of Art* was published. In Trinity Term 1939 Collingwood lectured on metaphysics. This was from the draft of *An Essay on Metaphysics*, which he had completed in April on board the S.S. Rhesus off Cape St. Vincent.[96]

It is, of course, not uncommon for books to be presented first as lectures, or even lectures first as books, and in this Collingwood is perhaps typical. Books and lectures interpenetrate one another at every point throughout Collingwood's career. Ideas appeared first in one form and then reappeared in another; they underwent development and appeared in print after being matured and polished. Sometimes, most notably with *The New Leviathan*, they underwent a long gestation period and were eventually published long after their initial appearance as lectures. Lectures on moral philosophy from 1921-1940 enables us to see more closely the relations between ideas appearing there side by side but published separately at different times. For example, in my view, the doctrines of both *Philosophical Method* and *Metaphysics* appear side by side in the lectures on moral philosophy, and yet these doctrines are often held to be incompatible. If it is possible to relate these doctrines back to their first appearance in the lectures it may then be possible to re-unite the two works and thus to display them as the two inseparable sides of the same activity of philosophizing. Before going on to make such an attempt, I shall conclude this section by briefly discussing the origin and method of *The New Leviathan*.

In the preface to *The New Leviathan* Collingwood wrote that:

> It was ... in 1919 ... that I began to think out the fundamental ideas of the present book, thereafter revising and elaborating them year after year in experimental forms, accumulating as time went on I will not say how many thousand pages of manuscript on every problem of ethics and politics, and especially on the problems of history which bore on my subject; and imparting my results . . . in lectures to my juniors and in manuscript to such of my colleagues as seemed interested.[97]

The truth of the reference to 'many thousand' pages of manuscript is amply borne out by the quantity of the unpublished manuscripts, which include essays, lectures, papers, notes and, perhaps most important, the lectures on moral philosophy.

Each series of lectures, from 1921 onwards, contained discussions of matters relevant to politics. Sometimes there was less and sometimes more; sometimes there are passages only on law whereas at

---

[96] E.M. Preface.
[97] *The New Leviathan*, (N.L.), 1942, v. (References to N.L. will be to paragraph numbers).

others there were whole sections devoted exclusively to politics and problems of political philosophy.[98] These changes reflect on the one hand Collingwood's concerns and on the other the space available within each course of lectures. Typically, discussions of particular topics outgrew the space available and were either simply cut out, or were cut out in order to take on a new life of their own. We have already seen this process at work with the introduction on philosophical method and the sections on Matter, Life and Mind, both of which had a career subsequent to the lectures both as lectures in their own right and also as books. Precisely the same thing happened to the lectures on politics; the political philosophy to be found in the lectures eventually becoming a series of lectures and later a book — *The New Leviathan*.[99]

The method of exposition employed in the lectures on ethics was the scale of forms. For Collingwood, the central concept of ethics is action: the concepts of ethics were thus to be dealt with by displaying the specifications of the concept of action as a dialectical series or scale of forms, starting with the minimum possible specification of the concept and refining the initial definition until the most adequate possible definition of the concept is reached. The definition of the concept is thus the whole account, the whole scale of forms; each initial definition is a form on the scale; and each definition as modified and amended gives rise to its successor on the scale. The goal is a definition which is the most complete and coherent that we can give. In this scale of forms of action, as Collingwood conceives it, politics is action according to rule, and it occupies a form intermediate between utilitarian or economic action and moral action or action according to duty.

The method employed in *The New Leviathan* is precisely that laid down in the methodological introduction to the lectures on ethics, that displayed in the lectures themselves, and that polished and published as *An Essay on Philosophical Method*. It is related to these lectures both by origin and method. The use of the method is clearly apparent through part one; this should occasion no surprise as this part is quite obviously a straightforward restatement of those parts of the lectures on ethics which were understood as relevant to the inquiry in hand. It is a selection from the totality of the discussion as presented in the lectures and does not pretend to be complete: Collingwood here is following his precept that, 'about each subject

---

[98] See especially the lectures delivered in 1929 and 1940.
[99] The lectures were delivered in 1940 and 1941 and N.L. was published in 1942.

we want to understand only so much as we need in order to understand what is to be said about the next.'[100]

This precept is followed throughout the book: for instance it contains no full or explicit account of punishment. This does not indicate lack of interest in the subject on Collingwood's part as a lengthy discussion of the question is to be found in manuscript entitled 'Stray Notes on Ethical Questions' (1928); there is a substantial discussion in the 1929 lectures on moral philosophy; and shorter but substantial accounts are to be found in the lectures delivered at other times as a part of the sections devoted to law and rules.

The method of scale of forms analysis is employed throughout the book, but not so much where the material dealt with is purely historical and illustrative.[101] For example: Collingwood commences Part Two with a preliminary definition of 'society', its minimum specification: 'All that the word 'society' implies is the fact which I call a *suum cuique*. That is, a one-one relation between sharers or participants and shares... A society is a 'society' constituted by free activity on the part of its members.'[102] The first is a minimum specification of any society, whether of plants or of free men; the second is the minimum specification of society understood as being a society composed of human beings. This minimum specification of the concept is an initial definition of what we understand by the concept; its purpose is to lay down certain minimum necessary features which a society must have. The procedure then is to trace the implications of this provisional definition and to ask, 'What are the necessary consequences entailed by the realization of this concept?'[103] This is precisely what Collingwood is to be found doing in the chapters following. The same method is also apparent in the discussion of civilization, where the chapter 'What "civilization" means: generically', is followed by 'What "civilization" means: specifically'; and this in turn is followed by chapters presenting us with a progressively more complete and adequate specification of the concept of civilization.[104]

---

[100] N.L., 1.16.
[101] e.g., Chapters xiii–xiv.
[102] N.L., 19.64;19.81.
[103] Lectures on Moral Philosophy, 1932, p. 1 and cf E.P.M., pp. 100–1.
[104] It has been noted that the doctrine of the scale of forms underwent some modification in the new leviathan because of Collingwood's introduction of the idea of the law of primitive survivals in which later phases retain an unmodified primitive residue of the earlier phase. See David Boucher , *The Social and Political Thought of R.G. Collingwood*, pp. 95–6, and his introduction to the revised edition of *The New Leviathan*.

I hope that enough has been said to illustrate the extent to which *The New Leviathan* follows the methodological principles expounded in *An Essay on Philosophical Method*. I should like now to turn, briefly, to the other side of *The New Leviathan*: not its method but its subject-matter. It is my contention that *The New Leviathan* exhibits 'in action' the unity of the method and subject matter of philosophy as conceived respectively by the *Philosophical Method* and *Metaphysics*. In *The New Leviathan* he is elucidating the presuppositions of civilization and politics, principally those of twentieth century western civilization, and thus far the inquiry is historical. But, as Kenneth Minogue remarks of Collingwood's predecessor and model, Thomas Hobbes, 'he is not engaged in the practical business of advocacy or justification, but rather in the entirely philosophical activity of exploring the presuppositions of political activity'[105] and thus the inquiry is also philosophical. It is, I believe, true to say with Ficarra, that *The New Leviathan* is 'the most complete realization of his aim to bring about a rapprochement between philosophy and history.'[106] I would only add that the same is true also of *The New Leviathan*'s close relative, *The Principles of Art*: in his preface to that work Collingwood declares that he does not 'think of aesthetic theory as an attempt to investigate and expound eternal verities concerning the nature of an eternal object called Art, but as an attempt to reach, by thinking, the solution of certain problems arising out of the situation in which artists find themselves here and now.'[107]

The principles he is expounding are those of modern art, and the solution of the problem of modern art is the 'historical problem (but philosophical as much as historical) of the genesis of modern art.'[108] For Collingwood at this stage in his career, philosophy and history have to come together through mutual absorption. Neither is reducible to the other: 'The absorption is mutual: the product is not philosophy based on history nor history based on philosophy, it is both of these things at once.'[109]

What form, then, does this rapprochement as represented in *The New Leviathan* take? Collingwood's concern, as always, is to remind us of knowledge we already possess, to enable us to 'know better something which in some sense we know already.'[110] The necessity

---

[105] K.R. Minogue, Introduction to *Hobbes's Leviathan*, xxii.
[106] F.T. Ficarra, *Collingwood's New Leviathan*, p. 12.
[107] P.A., vi.
[108] Letter to de Ruggiero, 12 June 1937.
[109] *Ibid.*
[110] E.P.M., p. 11. Cf. P.A., p. 152; E.M., p. 23; E.P.M., passim; N.L., 1.61–1.88; I.N., pp. 54–60.

for this arises because, at the time of writing, 'it became evident that we did not know what we were fighting for',[111] that 'the whole business was due to the fact that everybody was in a completely muddled condition about the first principles of politics.'[112] Presumably, then, enabling us to 'know better something which in some sense we know already' involves our getting clear about 'the first principles of politics'. Knowledge of first principles is traditionally metaphysical knowledge, knowledge of what Collingwood calls 'absolute presuppositions'. An understanding of the degree of importance Collingwood attached to the relation between metaphysics as he understood it and politics and civilization can be gained from his *Autobiography* and *An Essay on Metaphysics*; but even more illuminating in some respects is the early version of *An Essay on Metaphysics*, entitled 'Function of Metaphysics in Civilization'.[113] This manuscript is the first full and explicit account of the doctrine of metaphysics as the science of absolute presuppositions; and, as in the later *Essay on Metaphysics*, one of Collingwood's central concerns is the relation between metaphysics and civilization.

The remaining manuscript of 'Function of Metaphysics in Civilization' starts abruptly and we find ourselves plunging straight into a discussion of the extent to which those who fought the First World War were unclear what they were fighting about. Following on from a comparison of the metaphysician to the codifier of law,[114] we find the claim that:

> Without this work, done in the studies of lawyers, the problems would indeed have existed, but no one would have known exactly what he was fighting for ... This is what actually happened in the war of 1914-18. [prior to this war] The class of persons on whom by the tradition of centuries the task of bringing to light the hidden presuppositions of everyday thought, whether scientific or historical (I refer of course to the official teachers of philosophy) were treated with a contemptuous neglect ... The result was quite natural. A war of unprecedented violence broke out: and when the belligerents tried to discover what they

---

[111] N.L., iv.
[112] Letter to H.T. Hopkinson, 7th May 1941.
[113] Published in the revised edition of E.M.
[114] Cf. E.M., p. 77. 'A reformed metaphysics will conceive any given constellation of absolute presuppositions as having in its structure not the simplicity and calm that characterize the subject matter of mathematics but the intricacy and restlessness that characterize the subject matter, say, of legal or constitutional history', and E.P.M., p. 198: 'Every particular system is nothing but an interim report on the progress of thought down to the time of making.'

were fighting for, nobody knew. The analytic thinking which ought for half a century or more to have been clarifying the issues had not been done... [and consequently nobody knew what] the fundamental principles at stake were.[115]

What was needed was metaphysics, and it was not forthcoming: the consequences of this lack of or failure in analysis are illustrated in a passage from *An Essay on Metaphysics*: 'The 'pagan' world was failing to keep alive its own fundamental convictions... because owing to faults in metaphysical analysis it had become confused as to what those convictions were. The remedy was a metaphysical remedy. It consisted... in abandoning the faulty analysis and accepting a new and more accurate analysis.'[116]

Such a replacement of a faulty (or perhaps non-existent?) metaphysical analysis by a more accurate analysis is surely precisely the task Collingwood is engaged in throughout *The New Leviathan*: that book is a metaphysics of civilisation, and this metaphysics has a practical purpose: 'what is contained in this book is... the barest minimum which must be known by every member of a 'civilized' country, whatever his profession or occupation, if in the present emergency he is to do his duty as a citizen.'[117]

I hope that the examples cited above are sufficient to indicate, in a preliminary way, the character of *The New Leviathan* as a work of philosophy exhibiting the dual nature of philosophy as the science of presuppositions presented systematically as a scale of forms. The details of this conception of the two *Philosophical Essays* as each dealing with one side of an activity which is necessarily constituted by both sides taken together is presented later: these preliminary remarks serve only to introduce the conception and to draw attention to *The New Leviathan* as a work displaying the concrete unity of the two sides in actual philosophizing.

By way of summary I shall now sketch out the relation of *The New Leviathan* to the lectures on moral philosophy and thereby to other works. The relations I am indicating are temporal and not necessarily conceptual. It would be possible, in principle, for a critic to accept that *The New Leviathan* has its roots in or is directly related to other works and still to deny their compatibility.

The lectures are directly related to *Speculum Mentis* through overlap of material; to the *Essay on Philosophical Method* as its origin; to

---

[115] 'Function of Metaphysics in Civilization', pp. 29–30.
[116] E.M., p. 225.
[117] Unpublished preface to N.L., p. 8.

'Political Action' and 'Economics as a Philosophical Science' as earlier formulations; to *The Idea of Nature* through inheritance of material; and finally to *The New Leviathan* as its original formulation and immediate precursor. In addition, all these books and articles are related to the lectures through their common method.

Thus it is possible to trace direct links, with the lectures as medium, from *The New Leviathan* back to *Speculum Mentis* and the *Essay on Philosophical Method*. This is no mere coincidence: what it suggests is a certain constancy of philosophical attention on Collingwood's part; all these works are the fruits of his philosophizing over a period of some twenty years. They are connected as earlier and later phases in the thought of the same man, and evidence for continuity in the development of that thought is to be found in the lectures. The lectures fill in the gaps between the development of Collingwood's thought and the explicit statements (interim reports) on certain aspects of that thought as issued in book form. What we see is a certain permanence of attention along with a constant restatement of the problems and reformulation of their solutions. The thread of connection is direct, and earlier and later works can be seen as related through common themes dealt with, presented and developed throughout the lectures as delivered over the years. Any attempt to separate Collingwood's work into 'periods' is invalid if what is intended is to show radical breaks or major discontinuities. The lectures on moral philosophy, by displaying the inner connections holding between different phases of Collingwood's thought render such exercises redundant.

The lectures on moral philosophy are, then, perhaps the most important source of evidence for the thesis that Collingwood's thought displays both unity and continuity. Whenever that unity is in doubt appeal will be made to the lectures by way of re-asserting the continuity and unity and so discerning the 'central thread' running throughout his lifetime's work.

5: Style and Terminology in Collingwood

Before proceeding further I shall first make a number of comments on Collingwood's writing style and mode of presentation. Such an examination is necessary because Collingwood's style and manner has very often obscured the degree of interdependence between his books in such a way as to render superficially credible the charge of 'radical conversion' or of maintaining doctrines which he did not hold.

Collingwood rarely pinpointed links or continuities in his philosophical work; the major (partial) exception is *An Autobiography*; but whatever its merits as an account of his philosophical development, it is clearly defective and limited in certain ways. For example, it fails to acknowledge Collingwood's undoubted debt to Italian philosophy, especially to Croce and Gentile. Croce is not mentioned at all in the text, even though Collingwood's first book was a translation of Croce's book on Vico,[118] and he later went on to translate two other books and articles by Croce. It is true that he only acknowledges his debt to Croce in private correspondence, and in a letter to Croce in April 1938 concerning his newly published *The Principles of Art* he explains why Croce's name is 'mentioned ... hardly at all; but that is in accordance with a method of writing which I inherit from a long line of English philosophers, and it will not disguise from you, or from anyone else who knows anything of the subject, the closeness of the relation which connects my thought with your own.'[119] This may all be so, but it hardly explains why Croce's name wasn't mentioned in the *Autobiography*. Elsewhere Collingwood explains that his rule in writing books is 'never to name a man except *honoris causa* ... naming anyone personally known to me is my way of thanking him for what I owe to his friendship, or his teaching, or his example, or all three.'[120]

But this does not fully explain the matter. Surely someone from whom Collingwood was conscious of having learned as much as he did from Croce should have been mentioned by name? And if Collingwood's rule is never to name a man except *honoris causa*, why is the only mention of Croce in *The Principles of Art* a critical one? In a letter to Gilbert Ryle in 1935, he again states that he mentions names only *honoris causa* and that his 'usual practice is to refrain from naming persons who have committed (in my opinion) what I regard as fallacies.'[121] This accounts for the absence of Croce's name from *Philosophical Method*, where (for example) in chapter III §2, 8 he expounds and criticises the main principles of Croce's logic as falla-

---

[118] B. Croce, *The Philosophy of Giambattista Vico*. My criticisms of Collingwood's treatment in A. of his relation to Croce and Gentile should not be taken to imply that Collingwood is mistaken in his account of the history of the content of his thought. Collingwood may have been wrong in failing to mention Croce and Gentile: this does not mean that his assessment of his own intellectual development is false, nor that the rest of his testimony is thereby rendered untrustworthy. See J. Connelly, 'Art thou the Man: Croce, Gentile or de Ruggiero'.
[119] Letter to Croce on 20 April, 1938. The only mention of Croce is in a footnote on p. 46.
[120] Preface to A.
[121] Letter to Gilbert Ryle, (C.R.C.) 9th May 1935, pp. 13–14.

cious,[122] but it does not explain why in the *Autobiography* he denounces the 'realists' by name; least of all can it explain why there is no mention of Croce's name on those occasions where Collingwood obviously agreed with him or was indebted to him. Again, Gentile is criticised but not named in section 9 of chapter III of *Philosophical Method* and he is heavily criticised without being named in the *Autobiography*.[123] But it is clear that Collingwood learnt a lot from Gentile (Croce actually complains that the influence of Gentile vitiates *Speculum Mentis*)[124] and also that he carried on learning from Gentile long after Gentile's conversion to fascism.[125] Gentile joined the Fascist party in 1923 and in his *Autobiography* Collingwood wrote that 'there was once a very able and distinguished philosopher who was converted to fascism. As a philosopher, that was the end of him. No one could embrace a creed so fundamentally muddle-headed and remain capable of clear thinking.'[126]

The natural inference to be drawn from this is that there could be nothing of interest to Collingwood in Gentile's post-fascist writings; that, as far as he was concerned, Gentile, after his conversion to fascism, was no longer to be taken seriously as a philosopher. In this case how do we explain the fact that in a review of a collection of essays in 1937, Collingwood restricts his review so as to 'comment only on a few of the most interesting', and that amongst those he finds worthy of comment is an essay by Gentile entitled 'The Transcending of Time in History'? Of the doctrines propounded in this essay Collingwood remarks that 'This is an important idea, and I believe a true one.'[127] In this case Collingwood is willing to judge Gentile's work in philosophy separately from his politics, and he thinks it good, thereby belying his judgement a year later that no fascist could think straight. If Collingwood learned not only from Gentile's pre-fascist writings but also from late post-fascist writings, why is he so reluctant to say so? H.S. Harris regards Collingwood's silence about Italian influence as deliberate concealment, and goes

---

[122] *Ibid*.
[123] A., p. 158.
[124] B. Croce, 'In Commemoration of an English Friend, a Comparison in Thought and Faith'.
[125] See H.S. Harris, Introduction to G. Gentile, *Genesis and Structure of Society*. Harris detects the influence of Gentile not only in *Speculum Mentis*, but also in *The New Leviathan*, see also H.S. Harris, (ed.), 'G. Gentile, *The Reform of Hegelian Dialectic* (1912)'.
[126] A., p. 158.
[127] Review of *Philosophy and History: Essays presented to Ernst Cassirer*.

on to say that 'we cannot grant, therefore, that his *Autobiography* is, as he pretends, *un livre de bon foi.*'[128]

Another important observation is that the *Autobiography* was written before the completion of *An Essay on Metaphysics*, but published after. Hence, by the time the *Autobiography* was in print Collingwood's statement that 'I did not really feel any great desire to expound the philosophical ideas I have been setting forth in these chapters, whether to my colleagues or to the public',[129] had been superseded by events. Even while working on the proofs of the *Autobiography* he had been writing *An Essay on Metaphysics*, in other words, expounding the very ideas which he had not previously felt any great desire to expound. Again, Collingwood writes of planning a series of books commencing with *An Essay on Philosophical Method* and continuing with *The Principles of Art* as the second in the series.[130] By June 1939, the character of the planned series had been altered considerably: the second volume in the series begun by *Philosophical Method* was to be *Metaphysics*, with *The Principles of Art* having a place as the companion volume to the projected *Principles of History*.

The *Autobiography* was published before *The New Leviathan*, and written after but published before *The Idea of Nature* and *The Idea of History*. Collingwood wrote ten philosophical works all told, including the *Autobiography* itself; of these no fewer than four were published after the *Autobiography* and hence receive no mention there. What this means is that on some of the crucial points in interpreting Collingwood's development we lack his testimony. The reader is thus forced to establish connections and relations between books which are not explicitly made in the works themselves; this quest is also hindered by Collingwood's apparent determination to avoid using the same philosophical vocabulary twice.

This brings us to this issue of terminology, style and the relative lack of cross-reference between books. One defect of the *Autobiography* is its lack of reference to the detailed contents of Collingwood's earlier published works, and this goes together with an almost complete absence of comment on his own terminology. For example, Collingwood writes of *Philosophical Method* as the 'best book in matter; in style, I may call it my only book',[131] but he says nothing of its content, and the concept central to the essay — the scale of forms —

---

[128] H.S. Harris, Introduction to G. Gentile, *Genesis and Structure of Society*, p. 15 and footnote.
[129] A., p. 74.
[130] A., p. 118.
[131] A., p. 118.

does not appear in the *Autobiography*.[132] We are given to understand that he still had a high opinion of *Speculum Mentis*, *Philosophical Method* and *The Principles of Art*, but at no point is there reference to the doctrines expounded in those books, nor is there any explanation as to why their contents were expressed in such widely variant terminology.

I shall try to give an answer to this question of terminology; and in so doing make it clear that the difference in terminology, and the lack of cross reference between, the two *Philosophical Essays*, far from being unusual and therefore standing in need of further explanation, is in fact in line with Collingwood's habitual practice. Nearly every one of Collingwood's books employs a different terminology: the fact that there seems to be no point of terminological contact between *Philosophical Method* and *Metaphysics* should not, therefore, be taken as lending support to the view that they are incompatible.

In dealing with the question of terminology I shall restrict my attention (for the most part) to the following four books: *Speculum Mentis*, *An Essay on Philosophical Method*, *An Essay on Metaphysics* and *The New Leviathan*.

Speculum Mentis is largely written in the language and idiom of traditional idealism: thus it discusses the concepts of dialectic, the concrete universal, absolute mind and absolute ethics, philosophy as absolute knowledge and so on. At the time of writing Collingwood presumably felt happy with this terminology and saw no reason to express himself otherwise, even though he does not employ it in the 1923 paper 'Sensation and Thought' (written and delivered during the period of composition of *Speculum Mentis*) and even despite the fact that he had now coined and utilised[133] the phrase 'scale of forms' which was to play such a large part in the argument and terminology of *Philosophical Method*.

An Essay on Philosophical Method makes explicit the method exemplified throughout *Speculum Mentis*; yet it does not use the term 'dialectic' nor the traditional language of British Idealism that so pervades the earlier book. The two books are without doubt closely related, the later making explicit the method of the earlier and both sharing the same approach to philosophy: it is the terminology alone that differs. *Philosophical Method* is an exposition of dialectical method in new terms: in place of the concrete universal we get the scale of forms; and the method of displaying the articulations of the concrete universal is no longer called dialectic, but is characterised

[132] Except perhaps implicitly on pp. 148–9.
[133] The term makes its first appearance in the 1923 Lectures on Moral Philosophy, §11.

as a form of definition progressing from the minimum specification of the concept through a series of phases differing in degree and kind from their predecessors, each term in the scale summing up the whole scale to that point and both negating and reaffirming the term next below it.[134] Collingwood declares that this method was used by Hegel 'throughout his philosophical works.'[135] There is no doubt, then, that Collingwood's philosophical method is dialectic.

From this it is quite clear that the difference in terminology represents no significant shift or difference in doctrine; but why did Collingwood amend his terminology so drastically? The answer, I suggest, can only be that he thought the employment of the language and idiom of post-Hegelian Idealism would prejudice his chance of a fair hearing for the ideas on method which he regarded as of the first importance for progress in philosophy. Collingwood always objected to labels, and especially resented being labelled himself, especially when the label bestowed was 'idealist' or 'new idealist'.[136] Collingwood, then, eschewed Hegelian terminology for the sake of a fair trial, and presumably also because (as he obviously did not regard this language as indispensable for the exposition of his thought) he felt that he could think out and expound his conception of method better by refusing to rely on ready made terms and phrases and relying instead on a fresh statement in his own words.

Again *An Essay on Metaphysics* uses different terminology, and this also seems to be a consequence of writing for a specific audience. Collingwood knew that he would get no hearing if he wrote in the style and terms of philosophical idealism, or indeed in the terms of *Philosophical Method*:[137] he therefore chose to play the logical positivists on their own pitch and try to beat them at their own game.[138] Collingwood's directing the book at a particular audience had a number of consequences: he had to invent a new terminology;

---

[134] All this seems to be a re-expression, in different language, of Hegel's concepts of determinate negation and sublation (Aufheben).

[135] E.P.M., p. 103.

[136] See, e.g., S.M., p. 13, and the letter to Gilbert Ryle on 9th May 1935: 'why presume me an idealist? I have nowhere in this essay or any other publication or lecture so described myself, and I do not see why you should attach the label to me without giving some reason. I am afraid I resent both the label and the irresponsible manner of attaching it.' See also A., pp. 56-7. Collingwood's claim, however, is at odds with his professed adherence to idealism expressed in S.M., pp. 286-7, 'Croce's Philosophy of History', 1923, and 'Can the New Idealism Dispense with Mysticism', 1923.

[137] For instance, A.J. Ayer in *A History of Modern Philosophy*, p. 193, suggests that E.P.M. belongs rather to the province of *belles lettres* than to philosophy.

[138] For a discussion see J. Connelly, 'Natural Science, History and Christianity: the Origins of Collingwood's Later Metaphysics'.

he had to overstress some aspects of the theory and understress others, thereby leading to a distortion of his thesis as a whole; and the change in language obscures the relation between *Metaphysics* and *Philosophical Method*.[139]

Yet here again, we find covert reference to dialectic, for surely the 'dynamic logic' referred to can be nothing else; and echoes of Hegelian dialectic and the scale of forms are plainly to be heard when Collingwood says that 'strains' in the structure of absolute presuppositions, if too great, lead to a replacement of that structure 'by another which will be a modification of the old with the destructive strain removed.'[140] Collingwood no longer talks of 'philosophical concepts' as he did in earlier, but only of 'absolute presuppositions', and leaves the relations between the two unclear.

Collingwood's final book *The New Leviathan* introduces yet another change in terminology; the scale of forms acts as the backbone of the book, but receives no mention; the doctrine of metaphysics as the science of absolute presuppositions receives no mention; and discussions of matters involving methodological considerations dealt with at length in the *Philosophical Method* are given no cross reference.[141]

It is possible to make some sense of this. The book was intended as Collingwood's contribution to the war effort: as he remarks in 'Fascism and Nazism', 'What our soldiers and sailors and airmen have to fight, our philosophers have to understand',[142] and accordingly we are presented with a restatement of the first principles of politics. *The New Leviathan* was, then, a book for the times, written and published as a book to be taken on its own, with a specific purpose and addressed to a specific audience. If these considerations are granted, then there would have been little point in Collingwood's explicitly relating the doctrines and method of *The New Leviathan* to his other books. Presumably Collingwood reasoned that those interested would take the trouble to look elsewhere if they chose, and draw their own conclusions; while those for whom such things were a matter of indifference would only be repelled by academic cross-reference and irritated by the implicit suggestion that the book could

---

[139] Collingwood deliberately changed his original series so as to make E.M. the companion volume to E.P.M.; but this fact is nowhere mentioned in the preface or text of E.M. itself.
[140] E.M., p. 75; p. 48, footnote.
[141] E.g., N.L., 34.5–34.59 where Collingwood discusses civilization as a scale in which 'Infinity as well as zero can ... be struck out of the scale.' Cf. E.P.M., p. 89.
[142] 'Fascism and Nazism', (F.N.), 1940, p. 176 fn.

not be read alone but carried its companions with it as a snail carries its shell.

I have discussed certain aspects of Collingwood's style which conspire to make interpretation and synthesis more difficult: his changes in terminology, his habit of writing each book according to the principle of what he calls the 'limited objective',[143] and his preference for letting readers work things out for themselves rather than risk boring them.[144] Finally, he tends, at times, to emphasize differences and, at other times, to emphasize similarities: confusion is inevitable if a change in emphasis is automatically interpreted as a significant shift in doctrine. Before attributing a shift in doctrine to an author, the reader must first be sure of the purpose of that part of the text which he uses as evidence: he must first be sure that the view propounded is not merely an avowedly provisional definition subject to later modification and reformulation; he must be sure that the author is not erecting an expository device or hypothesis which he does not hold but finds useful in bringing out a point or tracing connections and implications otherwise hidden from view; and lastly, the reader should be aware of context, and of the possible reasons for the author's choosing on the one hand to bring out the similarities between things and on the other hand to highlight differences.

6: Conclusion

In this chapter I have argued that Collingwood's philosophical writings are best understood as a unified whole. In order to substantiate this claim I have examined some of Collingwood's chief expositors and critics and suggested some criticisms of their work. I then turned to Collingwood's unpublished manuscripts, making the claim that they might help resolve some of the disputes concerning the nature of Collingwood's intellectual development. Turning to particular instances, I argued that Collingwood's lectures on moral philosophy in some sense constitute the 'central thread' at the heart of his thought: and finally I have made some suggestions on the matter of his changing style, terminology and also on the question of the influence of Gentile and Croce.

---

[143] N.L., 31.68.
[144] See the letter to Gilbert Ryle, 9th May 1935, p. 11, 'I know that boring one's reader is the one deadly sin in a writer. I never puzzle him wilfully, and do honestly try to be very plain, but if on a marginal case I find myself asking 'shall I run a slight risk of puzzling him here, or a slight risk of boring him?' I choose the former. And I think my choice justified.' One might remark that as Collingwood's books are never boring (but frequently puzzling) there must have been a considerable number of 'marginal cases'.

Chapter Two is devoted to a more detailed examination of the unity of Collingwood's philosophy; in particular I shall try to establish that his two *Philosophical Essays* are complementary and should be read together as constituting a coherent approach to philosophical problems in which method and matter, form and content, are in necessary unity.

Chapter Two[1]
Metaphysics and Method: A Necessary Unity

1: Introduction

Later, in presenting Collingwood's political philosophy of civilization, I shall be assuming that in so doing I am justified in juxtaposing texts taken from different stages in his academic career and that there is no major obstacle to attempting to cast into systematic form elements which were originally separated both in time and context.

But is this assumption justified? If Collingwood were merely another author of whom it might be said that his thought developed, as is natural over an academic life, then the answer would be a qualified yes: qualified by the need to exercise due caution in weaving together elements belonging to different periods of a developing intellectual life. The problem in Collingwood's case is potentially much more than this. As we have seen, there are many who argue that his thought underwent a 'radical conversion', or *bouleversement* at some time between the appearance of *An Essay on Philosophical Method* and *An Essay on Metaphysics*. If this charge were correct, any procedure based upon the assumption of natural developing unity would be invalid.

---

[1] An earlier version of Chapters Two and Three was first published as 'Metaphysics and Method: A Necessary Unity in the Philosophy of R.G. Collingwood'.

One response might be to argue that my concern is not with metaphysics, logic or epistemology but with political philosophy, and that therefore the issue does not arise. This response would assume that Collingwood's purported 'radical conversion' to historicism left the other parts of his philosophy intact and that therefore it is possible to treat these independently of the debate over the changed nature of his views on the relation between philosophy and history. There are two reasons for rejecting the assumption. First, the issue of historical relativism has direct relevance for politics and political philosophy — what is at stake is precisely the possibility of the existence of political philosophy as a subject independent of political history or sociology. Secondly, it was Collingwood's often repeated claim that philosophical thinking cannot be divided into mutually watertight compartments such that developments in one have no consequences for the others. I agree, and it follows that the possibility of containing the 'radical conversion' in such a way as to prevent pollution of other parts of Collingwood's philosophy cannot arise. For these two reasons it is necessary to preface my presentation of Collingwood's political philosophy with a discussion of the possible existence of a 'radical conversion' in his philosophical thinking; and I shall, in particular, centre the discussion on the relation between *An Essay on Philosophical Method* and *An Essay on Metaphysics*. My conclusion will be that these two essays taken together constitute a necessary unity of philosophical method and subject-matter and that far from being in opposition they are complementary. With this conclusion I am then free to present Collingwood's political philosophy in subsequent chapters, operating on the assumption that there are no insuperable obstacles to treating it as a systematic whole.

In this chapter I focus on Collingwood's views on the nature of philosophy, moving to an investigation of his understanding of the method appropriate to philosophical inquiry. Following a discussion of his conception of the scale of forms I begin to address his understanding of the nature of metaphysics. It is the latter, associated with his later writings, which some critics find to be both in contradiction to his earlier writings and also objectionable in itself as ushering in a vicious form of relativism. The extent to which I accept or deny that charge is postponed to the more detailed discussion found in Chapter Three.

2: Collingwood and the Characteristics of Philosophy[2]

In this section I shall sketch in the general features of Collingwood's conception of philosophy: in subsequent sections I shall attend to more specific concerns.

The following features are characteristic of Collingwood's conception of philosophy: i) It is systematic; ii) It is self-referential; iii) It is criteriological; iv) It is 'thinking about thinking'; v) It elucidates what in some sense we already know; vi) It is categorical thinking concerned with a determinate subject matter; vii) It is an activity, not a result; viii) It conceives its object as activity.

These eight characteristics are interrelated and hence cannot be separated. The above list distinguishes them for the sake of reference and analysis, but should not be taken to imply that they are in any way isolated principles of Collingwood's thought. It will also become clear that the order of exposition is somewhat arbitrary in that from each we find ourselves moving towards every other — it is for that reason alone that it seems reasonable to commence with the proposition that philosophy is systematic.

i. Philosophy is systematic

Collingwood wrote that 'the different parts of philosophy are so related among themselves that none of then can be discussed without raising problems belonging to the rest.'[3] But the systematic character of philosophy should not be mistaken for a misconceived attempt to erect a fixed and final system. Each piece of systematic philosophical thought is a summary of the progress of philosophical thought down to its own time 'and every summary can only be done once, and is therefore final: the problem which it must solve is finally solved'[4], yet 'what is permanent and essential is not this or that system . . . every . . . system is nothing but an interim report . . . but the necessity of thinking systematically.'[5] So we should not strive to erect a perfect system, because 'the truth is not some perfect system of philosophy: it is simply the way in which all systems . . . collapse into nothingness on the discovery that they are only systems.'[6]

Philosophy must present its results in a reasoned and systematic way. This necessity arises both from the fact that the function of philosophy is to explain and render explicit an already systematic body

---

[2] This section owes much to Mink, *Mind, History and Dialectic*, pp. 244-57.
[3] E.P.M., p. 7 (and see R.P., p. 124, I.H., p. 6, P.A., p. 107).
[4] E.P.M., p. 191.
[5] E.P.M., p. 198 (and see E.M., pp. 64-5).
[6] S.M., p. 316.

of thought or experience, and also from the fact that in order to do this, philosophy has to re-present and re-articulate that experience so as to bring out clearly its underlying principles and the relations between them. Again, philosophy can hardly avoid being systematic if its different parts are so related that discussions in each 'part' have consequences for each and every other part. The packaging of philosophical thinking into compartments such as logic, ethics, epistemology and so on is an analytical convenience, and indicates no more than a relative degree of independence. It is possible to discuss logic without raising questions of epistemology: in such a discussion epistemological questions, when they arise, are postponed, 'bracketed off', and left for another time; but this postponement cannot be carried on indefinitely; at some point the implications that logic has for epistemology, and epistemology for ethics, and so on, have to be dealt with. Philosophy, then, must be taken as a systematic whole of which every 'part' shares in the character of the whole: the analytic distinguishing of 'parts' is tolerable only in so far as it is a matter of convenience, and not a matter of policy whereby such distinctions are hardened into separations.

ii. Philosophy is self-referential

If philosophy is 'thinking about thinking' (iv), it must at the same time be an instance of itself; that is, subject and object coincide. This characteristic is not found in, for example, natural science whether the object is not thought (except as an empirically existing aspect of the natural world)[7] but the physical world. As thinking about thinking, philosophy necessarily both asserts the existence and character of its subject matter and exemplifies that character in its own activity. Any account given of the object must, therefore, be at the same time an account of itself, the subject: philosophy is in this sense self-referential.[8]

---

[7] For Collingwood, psychology treats thought not as a criteriological or 'self-criticizing activity', (E.P.M., pp. 107–9), but as a 'self-contained fact' without raising the question whether it is true (R.P., p. 40); it is thus reduced to a mere mental event, on the same level as any other 'event', and hence is understood by the psychologist as essentially external to his own thinking.

[8] E.P.M., p. 129, footnote; S.M., p. 276; E.M., chapters xi–xii; A., pp. 92–5; R.P., pp. 39–42.

iii. Philosophy is criteriological

Philosophy is neither a purely descriptive nor a purely normative science, but inescapably both at once.[9] This is a property not of philosophical propositions as such (that is, propositions taken in isolation) but of philosophical thinking itself. Philosophy is an activity of thought (vii) and should not be identified with the products of thought. Products (or propositions) may be separable into normative and descriptive, but the thought which issues in those conclusions is not only a performance, but also gives itself an account of the success or failure of that performance; and this account, because philosophical thought is self-referential, is inescapably bound up with the performance itself.[10]

Philosophy is the study of thinking, and thinking is always implicitly criteriological, that is, governed by criteria by which the success or failure of each piece of thinking is judged. Philosophy is self-referential; it is an instance of its subject matter and therefore in its own performance exemplifies the principles and criteria of the performance it takes as its starting point, and appeals in judgement to the same criteria. 'In order to study the nature of thinking it is necessary to ascertain both what persons who think are actually doing and also whether what they are doing is a success or a failure':[11] in the case of philosophy the philosopher is also a thinker and is therefore obliged to judge his own performance as a thinker. Philosophy, then, is criteriological in two respects: it judges the success or failure of the performance it philosophizes about and at the same time judges *its own* success or failure as a piece of philosophical thinking, using in the latter instance criteria applying both to itself and to its object.

iv. Philosophy is thinking about thinking

Philosophy is thought of the second degree.[12] It is reflection upon experience which is already rational experience, even if initially unaware of the principles running through it.[13] Thought of the first degree is concerned with an object; thought of the second degree takes thought of the first degree as its object and so is concerned not

[9] See E.P.M., p. 4 and E.M., pp. 107–11.
[10] See S.M., p. 84 and E.M., p. 107. This perhaps explains why philosophy always has as an integral part of itself a philosophy of philosophy: hence the number of books directed to the question 'What is philosophy?' (see E.P.M., p. 2).
[11] P.A., p. 171 footnote.
[12] See I.N., pp. 2–3; N.L., 1.77; 34.51; I.H., pp. 1–2; P.A., p. 167; E.P.M., pp. 172–5; E.M., passim, especially p. 47; A., p. 66; S.M., pp. 85; 256.
[13] See I.H., p. 1.

only with the original object but also with the relation between thought and the object:

> Philosophy is reflective. The philosophizing mind never simply thinks about an object, it always, while thinking about any object, thinks also about its own thought about that object. Philosophy may thus be called thought of the second degree, thought about thought... Philosophy is never concerned with thought by itself; it is always concerned with its relation to its object, and is therefore concerned with the object just as much as with the thought... Philosophy cannot separate the study of knowing from the study of what is known. This impossibility follows directly from the idea of philosophy as thought of the second degree.[14]

Philosophy is, then, thought of the second degree and it studies the thought of the first degree. Thought of the first degree is thought in relation to an object; thought of the second degree is reflection upon this thought, the elucidation and making explicit of the principles presupposed in its operations. Thought of the second degree deals not only with the object of thought of the first degree but also with that thought itself in its relation to its object: it is thus concerned with the question of the necessary conditions for the possibility of a given form of knowledge of the first degree. From this may be derived two aspects of philosophy: the epistemological, 'such as one might group under the question 'how is (for example) historical knowledge possible?', and the metaphysical, 'concerned with the nature of (for example) the historian's subject matter: the elucidation of terms like event, process, progress, civilization, and so forth.'[15] These two aspects are distinguishable but not separable:

> One might put this by saying that the philosopher, in so far as he thinks about the subjective side of history, is an epistemologist, and so far as he thinks about the objective side a metaphysician; but that way of putting it would be dangerous as conveying a suggestion that the epistemological and metaphysical part of his work can be treated separately, and this would be a mistake. Philosophy cannot separate the study of knowing from the study of what is known.[16]

The philosopher, as metaphysician, seeks out and elucidates the principles which run through thought of the first degree and which thereby determine the particular nature of is subject matter; as epistemologist, he or she inquires how those principles operate in mak-

---

[14] I.H., pp. 1–3.
[15] A., p. 77, my parentheses.
[16] I.H., p. 3.

ing the form of experience in question possible and its subject matter knowable.[17]

Philosophy is thinking about thinking, which is to say it makes explicit what was previously implicit in a form of thought or experience. This leads directly to the next characteristic of philosophy, that is, that philosophy elucidates what in some sense we already know: before moving on to examine that characteristic, a further consequence of the conception of philosophy as thought of the second degree is worthy of attention.

If philosophy is not 'one specialized form of experience' but 'merely the self-consciousness of experience in general', as Collingwood maintains in *Speculum Mentis*,[18] then it cannot exist in the absence of experience on which to reflect. Now, we all have experience of some department of thought and action; we all think and act, and these thoughts and actions are constituted and regulated by certain principles. If, as Collingwood maintains, Art, Religion, Science, History and Action are necessary forms of experience then everyone is necessarily familiar with them, but it does not follow that everyone is thereby equally well equipped to philosophize about them: as Hegel notes, 'What is familiar is not known simply because it is familiar.'[19] To philosophize about art we need to have worked hard and long at art itself; looking at pictures is not enough, we must also paint them:

> Everyone enjoys to some extent the beauty of natural objects and works of art, and expresses his enjoyment in acts which are themselves works of art: but this does not entitle him to lay down the law about art. He must first develop and discipline his aesthetic powers by working long and seriously at the technical problems of some medium which should be that of music, painting, or the like, rather than the too familiar and therefore less instructive medium of words. Looking at pictures and listening to music are inadequate for this purpose: the student must learn

---

[17] This Collingwood does through the use of transcendental arguments: his remarks on epistemology directly echo Kant. In A. (p. 77) Collingwood refers (in discussing the philosophy of history) to 'Epistemological problems, such as one might group together under the question 'how is historical knowledge possible?'. Kant writes 'I entitle *transcendental* all knowledge which is occupied not so much with objects as with the mode of our knowledge of objects in so far as this mode of knowledge is to be possible a priori.' (*Critique of Pure Reason*, B.25). Epistemology is, then, for Collingwood, the study of how a form of activity is possible; metaphysics is the study of the principles employed in its operation. For discussion of Collingwood's relation to Kant, see G. D'Oro, 'How Kantian is Collingwood's Metaphysics of Experience?', and *Collingwood and the Metaphysics of Experience*.

[18] S.M., p. 256.

[19] G.W.F. Hegel, Preface to *The Phenomenology of Spirit*, in *Hegel: Reinterpretation, Texts and Commentaries*, p. 406.

to draw and compose. Without this artistic training, the philosophy of art must perish for lack of matter; the philosopher is trying to reflect without having anything to reflect on.[20]

Exactly the same is true of science (and by implication of every other form of experience): 'a man who has never enjoyed a certain type of experience cannot reflect upon it; a philosopher who has never studied and worked at natural science cannot philosophize about it without making a fool of himself.'[21]

We are all familiar with science as a form of experience: we all classify and 'assert the abstract concept', but this does not make us scientists; we are familiar with science but we do not know it.[22] We therefore cannot successfully philosophize about it as we simply do not possess the detailed acquaintance with scientific work which is a necessary precondition for reflecting upon its methods and principles. If philosophy is thinking about thinking it requires thought upon which to reflect: this thought cannot be someone else's, it must be the philosopher's; and it must be derived from first hand experience of the appropriate form of knowledge or activity.

v. Philosophy elucidates what in some sense we already know

For Collingwood, 'philosophy does not, like exact or empirical science, bring us to know things of which we were simply ignorant, but brings us to know in a different way things which we already knew in some way.'[23] It brings to light principles, presuppositions and concepts informing the experience chosen as its subject matter: in making these explicit and in exploring the relations between then we come to know the experience in a different and better way. This principle is ever present in Collingwood's writing, it is found in books, articles, reviews, lectures and essays: the distinction between implicit and explicit knowledge is central to *Speculum Mentis*;[24] *Philosophical Method* is erected on the principle and traces its origin to Socrates; *Metaphysics* presupposes the principle and further clarifies the nature of the principles and presuppositions 'which run through experience and make it a rational whole.'[25]

Prior to reflection, the principles inherent in our thought and action will tend to be implicit rather than explicit; reflection on our

---

[20] *Outlines of a Philosophy of Art*, p. 101.
[21] I.N., p. 3.
[22] S.M., Chapter 5, especially pp. 158–63.
[23] E.P.M., p. 161.
[24] S.M., p. 85n.
[25] E.P.M., p. 174.

experience is philosophy, which 'reveals explicitly the principles which are implicit in what we call everyday experience.'[26] Philosophy, it may justly be said, is the effort to remind us of what we already know perfectly well[27] but 'know' here means not 'fully understood' — but known implicitly as a part of our experience and as the logical foundation of that experience. Accordingly, we may be 'unconscious'[28] of our principles in the sense of being unaware of them; and we might be mistaken as to what they are or what they imply; therefore the job or task of philosophy is not only to bring them to light but also to clear up errors in our conception of what they are.

Collingwood gives a splendid summary of this conception of philosophy at the beginning of his 1929 lectures on moral philosophy, where he suggests that in philosophy,

> the change is from knowing things in a dark or dim or confused way to knowing them in a clear or luminous or distinct way. I do not mean that we come to know them with any greater force or conviction. At the beginning of our philosophical inquiries we may feel as perfectly convinced as it is possible to be, but in general we do not quite know what it is that we are so profoundly convinced of. What we do by these inquiries is to learn our own minds, in the sense of learning what it is that we really think or really want. From this point of view it might be said that philosophical inquiry and argument cannot change people's opinions but can and does change their opinions as to what their opinions really are.[29]

vi. Philosophy is categorical thinking dealing with a determinate subject matter

Philosophy is committed to the belief that its subject matter is something actually existing: philosophy is thus categorical thinking. Its subject matter is thought (philosophy is thinking about thinking) and hence its subject matter is exemplified by the very act of thinking about it: to think about thinking is itself an instance of what is being thought about. Philosophy is reflection upon prior experience or thinking: it is therefore categorical both in the sense that in its own nature it is the same as the experience reflected on (i.e. it is thought)

---

[26] S.M., p. 85, and see I.N., p. 60; O.S., p. 313; E.M., p. 23, 43; E.P.M., passim; N.L., 1.77, 34.15; P.A., vi.
[27] See E.M., p. 23.
[28] See I.N., pp. 1–2.
[29] Lectures on Moral Philosophy, 1929, p. 10. See also I.N., pp. 59–60 and 'Function of Metaphysics in Civilization' where Collingwood describes the Hegelian dialectic as ' . . . not a process by which errors in our presuppositions are corrected. It is a process by which errors *about* these presuppositions are corrected' (p. 41).

but also in the sense that the experience reflected upon is an actually existing experience and the task of philosophy is to render that experience intelligible. Philosophy is constrained, therefore, to treat its subject matter categorically in that it is committed to explaining the actual principles at work in an actual experience of thought rather than hypothetical principles at work in an hypothetical subject matter.

These two aspects of philosophy as categorical thinking — its being an instance of its own subject matter, and taking an actually existing experience as its starting point — cannot be separated. According to Collingwood there can only be a 'philosophy of something' ... when the 'something' in question is 'no mere fragment of the world, but is an aspect of the world as a whole — a universal and necessary characteristic of things.'[30] In other words, for there to be a philosophy of, say, history, 'history must be something more than a trade or an amusement. It must be universal and necessary human interest, the interest in a universal and necessary aspect of the world.'[31] Or, to put it another way, it must be a universal and necessary form of experience.

If there can be a philosophy only of a universal and necessary form of experience, then not only must that experience exist, but it must also exist in the mind of the philosopher. In studying a form of experience the philosopher is studying an actually existing body of thought and experience, historically existing and autonomous,[32] and he is also studying this body of experience as a specification of a form of experience which is universal and as much a part of the philosopher's own thinking as it is of the people whose thought he is studying. Furthermore, it is only because it is universal and necessary that he can reflect upon it; if it were otherwise the possibility of reflection would be a matter of contingency. Collingwood adhered to this general view of philosophy from his first book to his last. Thus he argued in *Religion and Philosophy* that:

> A philosopher has no right to construct the nature of morality out of his inner consciousness, and end in the pious hope that reality may correspond with his 'ideal construction'. His business as a philosopher is to discover what actually are the ideals which govern conduct, and not to speak until he has something to tell us about them ... a hypothetical philosophy is not merely mutilated but destroyed.[33]

---

[30] *The Philosophy of History* (P.H.), p. 2.
[31] P.H., pp. 2–3. This applies, of course, to politics. If it did not, then there would be no possibility of a political philosophy.
[32] E.g., natural science: see I.N., p. 175.
[33] R.P., p. 60.

The full implications of this view are most fully developed in the discussion of the ontological argument in *An Essay on Philosophical Method*. Collingwood argues that the Ontological Proof does prove something, but this something is not whatever God we happen to believe in; rather it proves: 'that essence involves existence, not always, but in one special case, the case of God in the metaphysical sense ... the object of metaphysical thought ... Philosophy stands committed to maintaining that its subject matter is no mere hypothesis, but something actually existing.'[34]

All philosophy is based on experience: it elucidates the principles informing experience and explains it 'by constructing a theory of it, which is nothing but the same experience raised by intenser thought to a higher level of rationality.'[35] Philosophy must, therefore, presuppose the reality of its subject matter: it reaches categorical conclusions about actual experience, not hypothetical conclusions about hypothetical experience. A philosophy not rooted in actual historically lived experience is a philosophy of nothing: this is a point that, on occasions, needs firmly driving home; and Collingwood sought to do just that in the *Essay on Metaphysics*. There, philosophy, in its aspect as metaphysics, is conceived as a historical science, the study of a 'certain class of historical facts, namely absolute presuppositions' and 'it is the attempt to find out what absolute presuppositions have been made by this or that person or group of persons, on this or that occasion or group of occasions, in the course or this or that piece of thinking.'[36] Here, as in *Philosophical Method*, philosophy 'consists of categorical propositions.'[37]

Philosophy is not only categorical thinking, but also thinking about a definite and determinate subject matter: 'there is no science except where two conditions are fulfilled. There must be orderly or systematic thinking, and there must be a definite subject matter to think about.'[38] And a consequence of this is that the philosopher must ask precise questions about precise issues raised by his subject matter: the philosopher can expect only so much precision in his answer as he puts into his question. To ask a general and non-specific question is to get a general and non-specific answer. There is a principle of correlativity between question and answer. 'A highly

[34] E.P.M., p. 127.
[35] E.P.M., p. 173 and see also P.A., p. 167: 'All knowledge is derived from experience; and whatever claims to be knowledge must appeal to experience for its credentials and verification. This is as true of metaphysics ... as it is of railway timetables.'
[36] E.M., pp. 61–2; p. 47
[37] E.P.M., p. 133.
[38] E.M., pp. 13–14.

detailed and particularised proposition must be the answer, not to a vague and generalized question, but to a question as detailed and particularised as itself.'[39] We can only come to an understanding of any philosophical concept through a consideration of its instances; we grasp the essence of a concept through its specification; we cannot simply ask 'What is x?', we have to ask 'How is x specified in this instance and what are its characteristics?' From this proceeds the work of analysis: the definition of a concept taking as a starting point the way such a concept is actually used or specified, examining its most rudimentary and primitive specification, and going on to build up the definition of the concept by drawing out the consequences of the initial definition.[40]

Collingwood's conception of the philosopher's subject matter is well illustrated by an unpublished article, written in 1920, on 'The Philosophy of the Christian Religion'. The occasion of this essay was the appointment of C.C.J. Webb as the first Oriel Professor of the Philosophy of the Christian Religion. Collingwood's concern was to answer those critics who maintained that there could be no such thing as the philosophy of the Christian religion, but only a philosophy of religion in general; and that, in consequence, the new professor was being invited to take up a position as an apologist or advocate of Christianity, in other words to become an ideologist rather than a philosopher. Collingwood rejected this view quite firmly: 'The abstract concept of religion in general — religion with all the characteristics of all the particular religions taken out — is not worth philosophising about.'[41]

> Where the student of the 'philosophy of religion' closes himself in artificial problems, unreal situations and abstract concepts, the student of the 'philosophy of the Christian religion' finds himself face to face with real problems and historical facts and processes. The former has to operate with an abstract idea of God so evasively constructed that it can be taken as equally representative of the God of any religion you like to name: the latter has to study and understand the fully concrete and determinate conception of God held by this or that theologian, and to discover in what way this conception was sound or unsound, fertile or requiring amendment . . . Philosophy is an attempt to discover truth. And there is no truth about the abstract idea of godhead in general, except that such a

---

[39] A., p. 32.
[40] For a full account of the principles of philosophical definition see E.P.M., especially pp. 100–1.
[41] 'The Philosophy of the Christian Religion', p. 10. This was sent to *Theology*, but never published.

thing does not exist and that all questions asked about it are equally meaningless.[42]

Philosophy studies concrete and determinate conceptions; this is another way of saying that philosophy must be rooted in history. This is not to imply that philosophy and history are identified but merely that they overlap: an historically based philosophy rests upon the principle that 'you get nearer to the reality ... by taking it in its historical form rather than abstracting from different parts of the historical form elements which look similar and putting them together.'[43] So understood, philosophy and history can fertilise one another without either being reduced to the other: philosophical truth can only be gleaned from historical reality; in which history is not considered as 'the doubtful story of successive events',[44] it is not a series of externally related events at all, but a sequence of phases each of which turns into its successor through its own immanent rationality.

vii. Philosophy is activity, not result

Philosophy is not a body of propositions or a once and for all system, but a continuous activity of philosophical reflection. No philosophical work is final; each work is an 'interim report'[45] on the progress of thought thereto (progress which can be progress of the philosopher's own thought; the progress of philosophy itself; or the progress of a specialised discipline such as natural science). There is no end to philosophy, no terminus or final resting place: the termination of philosophy could only come about through the death of the activities on which philosophy reflects, that is, through the death of thought itself. The philosopher can never stand at an absolute end; the most he can hope for is a relative end: his 'final' statement can be no more than *Bis hierher ist das Bewusstseyn gekommen*,[46] for by 'reaching this point he already comes in sight of new problems.'[47] Each solution, each question answered, is nothing less than a prelude to a new problem, an invitation to ask a new set of questions.

> Ever since Pythagoras ... invented the word philosophy, in order to express the notion of the philosopher not as one who possesses wisdom

---

[42] *Ibid*, p. 12.
[43] *Ibid.*, p. 11.
[44] Bernard Bosanquet quoted in I.H., p. 143. Compare Collingwood's remarks here with his rejection of a science of pure being in E .M. Chapter 2.
[45] E.P.M., p. 198 and I.N., p. 175.
[46] Hegel, quoted in I.N., p. 174, 'That is as far as consciousness has reached.'
[47] E.P.M., p. 191.

but as one who aspires to it, students of philosophy have recognized that the essence of their business lies not in holding this view or that, but in aiming at some view not yet achieved: in the labour and adventure of thinking, not in the results of it. What a genuine philosopher . . . tries to express when he writes is the experience he enjoys in the course of the adventure, where theories and systems are only incidents in the journey.[48]

This, from *The Principles of Art*, is a continuation of Collingwood's remark in *Method* that 'I know of no philosophy that is not a voyage of exploration whose end, the adequate knowledge of its proper object, remains as yet unreached.'[49] And this conception of philosophy as activity not result is the explanation of Collingwood's enterprise in that essay, where he undertakes to answer the question 'what philosophy is', not through a consideration of its results, ends or objects, but through a consideration of its procedure:

> Philosophy never with any of us reaches its ultimate goal; and with its temporary gains it never rests content . . . it is an activity which goes on in our minds, and we are able to distinguish it from among others, and to recognise it by certain peculiar marks. These marks characterize it as an activity or process; they are, therefore, peculiarities of procedure: and accordingly it is possible to answer the question what philosophy is by giving an account of philosophical method.[50]

viii. Philosophy conceives its object as activity

This principle is a direct consequence of the conception of philosophy as thinking about thinking. Thought is, of its very nature, activity, and hence the philosophical study of thought will study it as activity. Here a philosophical study is opposed to, say, a psychological study which treats thought not as a self critical activity operating according to criteria by which it can judge its own success, but as a mere mental event devoid of reference to its object or to the criteria by which it passes judgement on itself: psychology, in other words, hypostatises activity into substance. A philosophical study must take account of the criteria used in thought's self-criticism, and by studying thought as an activity the philosopher is assimilating it to his own activity in thinking about that thought: he understands it, as it were, from within, his relation to it is an internal one. The psychologist, on the other hand, treats thought essentially from without, as something external to himself; thought is converted into a natural

---

[48] P.A., p. 297.
[49] E.P.M., p. 3.
[50] Loc. cit.

object, a thing, and hence what the psychologist is studying is something of an entirely different character to his thought in studying it.[51]

The principle that philosophy should study its object as activity runs through Collingwood's writing, but it is made especially clear in his work on ethics and politics. What he says of the matter in the essay on 'Political Action' (1928) and 'Economics as a Philosophical Science' (1925) gives a fair representation of his view: in the former he writes 'I propose to take my stand, not on the category of substance and attribute, but on the category of action';[52] in the latter he states that 'the conceptions of value, wealth, and so forth are not ultimate inexplicables; they can be understood, but only by resolving them into the conception of economic action. This resolution is a task for philosophy. Philosophical thought is that which conceives its object as activity; empirical thought is that which conceives its object as substance or thing.'[53]

Thus, for example, philosophical aesthetics deals with aesthetic activity, not with its products: it is for the critic to determine which are good works of art and which are not, and why; the work of aesthetics is the elucidation of the categories of the aesthetic habit of mind. Similarly, it is for the politician or economist to determine into which category various political and economic facts are to be placed; the philosopher's business is to study economics and politics as types of ethical action and to elucidate its distinctive presuppositions or 'fundamental conceptions'.[54]

3: Philosophy and its Method

An Essay on Philosophical Method is precisely that: it is an account of the method and principles employed in philosophical thought, concerned not so much with the subject matter of philosophy as with the way to approach that subject matter. The book is intended to treat only the formal side of philosophy: its purpose is to identify the typical characteristics of philosophical method (as opposed to scientific method)[55] and Collingwood attempts to articulate and defend a method for analysing and elaborating concepts; which method is exhibited in philosophical writing but not always explicitly recog-

---

[51] For the relation between philosophy and psychology, see especially R.P., pp. 39-42; E.M., Chapters IX-XIII, especially pp. 107-8 and p. 115; and A., pp. 92-5.
[52] Pol. A., p. 155.
[53] E.P. S., p. 162.
[54] E.P. S., p. 162.
[55] See Rex Martin, 'Collingwood's *Essay on Philosophical Method*', p. 226.

nised or acknowledged there. His task, as he saw it, was to bring to the attention of philosophers the methodological principles of their discipline, hoping thereby to prepare the way for future progress in philosophy. This is brought out clearly in a letter to the Clarendon Press:

> *Subject.* A systematic treatment of the methods and peculiarities generally of philosophical thought: it is in fact a new *Traité de Méthode*, attempting to disentangle all the relations concerning philosophy (on its *formal* side) and science whether mathematical or empirical. I have been gradually forced to the view that, at present, the progress of philosophy is held up because people will not face these problems of method, and even the best of them are constantly being tripped up by the consequences of this neglect.[56]

An Essay on Philosophical Method is philosophy approached through the peculiarities of its method; *An Essay on Metaphysics*, is philosophy approached through the peculiarities of its subject matter. Just as *Method* says little about the subject matter of philosophy, so *Metaphysics* says little about its method. The former elucidates or develops a method for analyzing and elaborating concepts, specifically philosophical concepts. By a philosophical concept Collingwood means a concept which qualifies reality as a whole, as opposed to a scientific concept which qualifies a limited part of reality.[57] He cites as examples art and ethics (which correspond to what he earlier in *Speculum Mentis* called 'forms of experience' and which in *The Philosophy of History* he declared to be 'universal and necessary characteristics of things)[58] and also various concepts such as unity, reality and goodness, and again, concepts with both a philosophical and non-philosophical phase such as mind and matter: as a philosophical concept matter is the name of reality as a whole, as a non-philosophical concept it is the name of a certain class of things.[59]

Collingwood writes of philosophy as the attempt 'to discern the principles which run through experience and make it a rational whole',[60] but it is not clear that these are equivalent to philosophical concepts in the senses given above, that is, as forms of experience, logical categories and so on. I think it is possible to sort out the relations here and also to show where the 'absolute presuppositions' of

---

[56] Letter to the Clarendon Press, 9th March 1933. This passage forms the basis of the 'blurb' on the dustwrapper of the book.
[57] E.P.M., p. 35.
[58] P.H., p. 2.
[59] E.P.M., p. 34.
[60] E.P.M., p. 174.

the *Essay on Metaphysics* come into the picture.[61] This will be attempted in the sequel.

An *Essay on Metaphysics* tells us a lot about one aspect of the subject matter and activity of the philosopher through the conception of metaphysics as the science of absolute presuppositions: but says little about method. But what it does say is of interest: 'As regards its modus operandi, then, all analysis is metaphysical analysis.'[62] This would seem to identify philosophical and scientific method, but that this is not so is apparent for two reasons: first, philosophy, as metaphysics, is concerned not with the relative presuppositions which constitute the subject matter of ordinary science, but with absolute presuppositions, and this difference in subject matter is reflected in a difference in method.[63] Secondly, metaphysics is not only the science of absolute presuppositions: it also has presuppositions of its own. These presuppositions are, in part, methodological presuppositions: but what sort of presuppositions are these? 'Not only has metaphysics quite definite presuppositions, but everyone knows what some of them are, for as metaphysics is an historical science it shares the presuppositions of all history.'[64]

On the one hand, then, we find that 'all analysis is metaphysical analysis', and on the other hand that 'the problems of metaphysics are historical problems; its methods are historical methods':[65] what are the methodological presuppositions peculiar to philosophy? The answer by implication is that philosophical method can be neither analytic nor historical alone. Metaphysics 'shares the presuppositions of all history', but this is not to say that it is the same as history for in the very same passage we are also informed that the presuppositions of metaphysics are only *in part* those of history: 'not only has metaphysics quite definite presuppositions, but everyone knows what some of them are.'[66] This quite clearly implies that metaphysics also has presuppositions of its own other than those it shares with history. Metaphysics is, therefore, an historical science, but not

---

[61] For discussion see G. D'Oro, *Collingwood's Metaphysics of Experience*, pp. 9–23.
[62] E.M., p. 40.
[63] E.M., p. 45. The difference in method arises because in discovering absolute presuppositions we come to know something better which we already knew in some way; that is, we render explicit the implicitly known furniture of our minds. In making scientific discoveries, on the other hand, we learn something completely new, something of which we were previously wholly ignorant. The characteristic principles of philosophical method are grounded upon this difference in subject matter.
[64] E.M., p. 63, my italics.
[65] E.M., p. 2.
[66] E.M. p. 63, my italics.

merely an historical science: it shares the presuppositions of all history, but these presuppositions are supplemented by the methods and presuppositions of logical analysis.

That this is so can be confirmed by looking at the text of the essay itself. Collingwood asserts that 'the priority affirmed in the word presupposition is a logical priority'.[67] It is not temporal priority, nor is it mere psychological conjunction; hence, metaphysical analysis must be logical analysis. It is not concerned with the temporal order of people's thoughts, nor with the other thoughts they might happen to be thinking at any particular moment; it is concerned solely with the logical priority of their thoughts, 'it deals with things in their logical order, putting what is presupposed before what presupposes it',[68] and this is so irrespective of whether those whose thoughts are studied were aware of what they presupposed.

If we look elsewhere in the book we find examples of metaphysical analysis which cannot possibly be said to be simply historical; for example, the discussion of Causation in Part III C, where history is invoked, and the methods of historical knowledge employed, but the analysis goes beyond any straightforward historical account. The general point is well made by David Rynin:

> Collingwood ... quite explicitly identifies ... metaphysical and logical analysis ... for him ... there seemed to be no inconsistency between describing a study as historical and making essential use in it of the methods of logical analysis ... Metaphysics, the science that concerns itself with the discovery of the absolute presuppositions of systems of thought, examines such systems, using the methods of history, supplemented by those of logical analysis. History tells us what question certain men raised and tried to answer; logical analysis tells us what presupposition they were committed to, having raised those questions.[69]

Metaphysics, then, is neither simply history nor is it simply logical analysis: it is the two fused together to constitute a distinct science which is neither history nor logical analysis alone. It differs from other sciences in its unique subject matter (i.e. absolute presuppositions) and in its method (i.e. philosophical methods).

If we take it that Collingwood understood the method of metaphysics as both historical and logical, then this answers Donagan's objection that if presupposing is not an act of thought, 'but the state

---

[67] E.M., p. 21.
[68] E.M., p. 39.
[69] David Rynin, 'Donagan on Collingwood: Absolute presuppositions, Truth and Metaphysics', p. 330.

of being committed by your questions . . . to accepting something',[70] then it cannot be the object of investigation by a discipline which is concerned solely with acts of thought. In other words, if metaphysics is simply a branch of history, and history deals only with acts of thought (not with what those acts of thought logically imply or presuppose) then metaphysics cannot investigate what Collingwood declares it does investigate. This objection would only be fatal to Collingwood's position if he ruled out everything but historical methods as appropriate to metaphysical investigation; if he did not, but as Rynin suggests, regarded metaphysical method as both historical and logical, then Donagan's objection falls.

Provisionally, then, there is no reason to suppose that either the method or the subject matter of philosophy as discussed in the two *Philosophical Essays* is in any way incompatible one with the other. On the point of method the early draft of the *Essay on Metaphysics* entitled 'Function of Metaphysics in Civilization' is relevant. Collingwood states that:

> The Hegelian dialectic . . . is sometimes represented as if it were a kind of self-corrective or self-critical process by which errors in our fundamental metaphysical presuppositions are eliminated . . . the interpretation is a false one. The self-correction brought about by Hegel's dialectic is not a process by which errors in our presuppositions are corrected. It is a process by which errors *about* these presuppositions are corrected. The metaphysician begins by thinking that what we really presuppose is x; his attempt to isolate x leads him to the discover that if we really presuppose x we presuppose y as well, and so the process goes on. Thus the Hegelian dialectic is in reality Hegel's picture of the method which a metaphysician has to pursue in discovering what in fact the metaphysical presuppositions of our ordinary thinking are. It is not Hegel's picture of a method by which errors in those presuppositions themselves can be removed.[71]

This can be interestingly compared with the statement quoted above where Collingwood says, in 1929, that 'philosophical inquiry and argument cannot change people's opinions, but it can and does change their opinion as to what their opinions really are.'[72] In philosophy we begin with a certain degree of knowledge of our subject matter and come to know it in a new and better way. In *Philosophical Method*, Collingwood puts forward the scale of forms as typical of philosophical method, and develops it in detail as a method for analyzing and elaborating concepts. In that essay he remarks that the method he was outlining had been used by Socrates, Aristotle, Kant

---

[70] Donagan, *The Later Philosophy of R.G. Collingwood*, p. 72.
[71] 'Function of Metaphysics in Civilization', p. 41.
[72] Lectures on Moral Philosophy, 1929, p. 10.

and others, and that 'Hegel . . . used this method throughout his philosophical works.'[73] It is quite clear that this is a reference to the Hegelian dialectic; and indeed, the whole argument of *An Essay on Philosophical Method* might be taken as a restatement of that method in non-Hegelian language in answer to certain critics of Hegel (for example Croce). The method propounded is therefore a dialectical method, and it is precisely the dialectical method of Hegel that Collingwood later, in *Metaphysics*, declared to be the method the metaphysician employs in discovering absolute presuppositions. This identity of method between the two essays goes some way towards establishing their compatibility; but there is still a long way to go; we still have not discovered what precisely that method is nor precisely what the subject matter of philosophy (conceived as metaphysics) is.

My provisional view on the relation between the two *Philosophical Essays* is therefore that *Philosophical Method* is concerned with method, a method which is both historical and logical, in a word, dialectical; and *Metaphysics* is concerned with the subject matter of philosophy, and that what it says about that subject matter is by no means incompatible with what is said in the earlier essay. The two, then, are compatible as regards method; the difference between them lies not in any incompatibility or shift of doctrine, but in their different concerns. *Philosophical Method* presents the presuppositions of philosophical method and says little about the nature of the philosophical subject matter; *Metaphysics* presents an account of the nature and peculiarities of the philosophical subject matter, and says little about the methodological presuppositions of philosophy itself.

If this interpretation is correct, then the two essays stand or fall together. They form two sides of the same concrete activity of philosophy, and neither should be understood as opposed to the other. They are not competing for the same prize, and so there is no need to award the prize of philosophical superiority to either one or the other; to do such a think would be to presuppose precisely what I deny, that is, that they are incompatible and opposed accounts of the same thing. It is worth remarking how little attention has been paid to the titles of these two essays: the commonest reason for setting one essay up against the other is the supposition that they both claim to give an account of philosophy as a whole, and that they give different accounts. I would agree that they give different accounts, and I would point out that mere inspection of their titles would lead one to expect that they would give different accounts. A lot of confusion is

---

[73] E.P.M., p. 103.

cleared up simply by taking the titles of the essays seriously: if we do that we are led to expect that they should be complementary rather than contradictory. If it is objected, for instance, that there is more to philosophy than Collingwood allows in *An Essay on Metaphysics* we can agree, but reply by drawing the critic's attention to first, the passage in the *Autobiography* where, nine pages after declaring metaphysics to be the science of presuppositions, Collingwood goes on to distinguish 'Epistemological problems' from 'Metaphysical problems';[74] and secondly, the fact that *Metaphysics* claims to be 'not so much a book *of* metaphysics as a book *about* metaphysics',[75] just as *Method* is a book about method. We have, then, two books each concerned with a different aspect of philosophical thought; why should anyone suppose them to be about the same thing? What has been said above is, I suggest, more than enough to make us sympathise with W.J. Emblom when, baffled, he remarks, 'Precisely why anyone should infer that in speaking of metaphysics in this latter work Collingwood means philosophy is a mystery.'[76]

An important consideration in all this is surely Collingwood's own view of the matter, and one thing of which we can be absolutely certain is that he himself did not think the two essays in opposition. Now, it is possible of course that he was unaware of the incompatibility of the two essays; but to suggest this is tantamount to suggesting that he no longer knew what he was doing, an interpretation which has already been rejected in Chapter One. But surely it is not plausible to suppose that someone who produced work of the quality of *An Essay on Metaphysics, An Autobiography* and *The New Leviathan* after the serious stroke of February 1938 was incapable of judging his own work. And so far as we can judge his intentions, it is quite plain that not only did he regard the two essays as compatible, but also he wished to bring to the attention of the public their compatibility. This is how he makes his case in a letter to the Clarendon Press of 3rd June 1939: 'It is called *An Essay on Metaphysics,* and is volume II of my Philosophical Essays, that on Method being now regarded as volume I.' This letter explicitly juxtaposing the two essays was written at precisely the same time that Collingwood was supposed to have repudiated the doctrine of the earlier book and undergone a radical conversion to historicism and relativism: at the very least we must accept that Collingwood himself thought he had

---

[74] A., p. 77.
[75] E.M., vii, my italics.
[76] W.J. Emblom, review of A. Donagan, *The Later Philosophy of R.G. Collingwood,* pp. 84–5.

done no such thing.[77] If we take the two *Philosophical Essays* for what I suggest they are — meta-philosophical essays concerning the method and subject of philosophy respectively — then we can see clearly that all of Collingwood's books (post *Religion and Philosophy*) exemplify the unity of form and content as outlined in 'Method and Metaphysics'. *The Idea of Nature* was said by Collingwood himself to be an application of the method expounded in *Philosophical Method*;[78] it is equally obviously a history of the absolute presuppositions of natural science. The first four parts of *The Idea of History* are a history of the idea of history arranged according to the same method; the final part, the metaphysical epilegomena, is (as its title states) a metaphysics of contemporary historical thinking. *Speculum Mentis* is a dialectic of experience arranged as a scale of forms; each form of experience resting upon certain implicit presuppositions which, on being made explicit, effect the transformation into a higher form. *The New Leviathan* arose out of the very lectures in which the concept of the scale of forms took shape and it is thus hardly surprising that it is arranged according to the same principles: it aims to provide a metaphysics of politics and civilization. *The Principles of Art* is a metaphysics of contemporary aesthetic experience, and the degree of its indebtedness to *An Essay on Philosophical Method* becomes apparent if proper attention is paid to Collingwood's procedure in defining art and his references to the *Essay*.[79]

I hope to have shown that the two *Philosophical Essays* represent complementary discussions of related aspects of philosophical thought, and that to take them separately is to mistake the part for the whole, with consequent distortion to our conception of Collingwood's understanding of the whole, the whole here being philosophy as a concrete activity. We now turn to a more detailed examination of Collingwood's conception of philosophical method.

---

[77] F.T. Ficarra's comments are apposite: 'his decision to call *An Essay on Metaphysics* Volume II of his philosophical essays can best be regarded as a deliberate attempt on his part to see that the two essays are viewed together by the public mind and, perhaps to suggest that seeming inconsistencies between the two works are more apparent than real.' F.T. Ficarra, 'Collingwood's *New Leviathan*', p. 13. We might also add that this supposition is given added strength by the series of letters Collingwood wrote to the Clarendon Press in 1939 and also by the fact that Collingwood altered the original title from *An Introduction to Metaphysics* to *An Essay on Metaphysics* in order to bring it into line with *An Essay on Philosophical Method* (letters to Clarendon Press 14/11/38 & 3/6/39).

[78] See T.M. Knox's prefatory note to I.N.

[79] P.A., pp. 22; 187.

4: Philosophical Method and the Scale of Forms

Collingwood's reflections on philosophical method arose directly out of his lectures on moral philosophy, and ultimately out of his lectures on Aristotle's *De Anima* on which he first lectured in 1914.[80] In the first section of this chapter I have described how the method of displaying the determinations of a philosophical concept as a scale of forms was first propounded in the methodological introduction to those lectures; but the question now is, what sort of thing is a 'scale of forms'?

For Collingwood, in philosophy the specific instances of concepts tend to overlap so that two or more concepts may be exemplified in the same instance: 'any distinction in philosophy may be a distinction without a difference, (that is), where two philosophical concepts are distinguished Aristotle's formula may hold good, that the two are the same thing but their being is different.'[81] The subject matter of philosophy, owing to this overlap of classes, does not admit of classification into mutually exclusive species of a common genus of the sort commonly to be found in the natural sciences.

Philosophical concepts are generic; the species of a philosophical genus differ from each other both in degree and in kind[82] and in a philosophical scale of forms 'the variable is identical with the generic essence itself.'[83] Differences of degree between philosophical concepts cannot be measured: this is a consequence of there being, in a philosophical scale, only one set of differences having the peculiar double characteristic of being differences at once in degree and in kind;[84] and the specifications of a philosophical concept make up a scale: 'if in philosophical thought every difference of kind is also a difference of degree, the specifications of a philosophical concept are bound to form a scale; and in this scale their common essence is bound to be realized differentially in degree as well as differentially in kind.'[85]

The terms on a scale of forms are related both by opposition and by distinction. Each term is distinct from its neighbours, but is also opposed to it. This opposition is not, however, absolute: 'if the variable is identical with the generic essence, the zero end forms no part of the scale; for in it the generic essence is altogether absent. The lower end of the scale, therefore, lies not at zero, but at unity, or the

[80] See A., p. 27.
[81] E.P.M., p. 56.
[82] E.P.M., p. 6.
[83] E.P.M., p. 60.
[84] E.P.M., pp. 70–1.
[85] E.P.M., p. 77.

minimum realization of the generic essence.'[86] This seems to imply that all opposition disappears and that we are left only with distincts. But in a philosophical scale of forms there is a fusion of distinction and opposition and therefore the scale does not consist merely of distincts.[87] Opposition within a scale of forms does not imply the real existence of either end of the scale; for example it does not imply the existence of pure wickedness or pure goodness: 'the lowest member of the scale, the minimum realization of the generic essence, is already, so far as it goes, a realization of this essence, and therefore distinct from other realizations; but, as the limiting case, it is an extreme, and therefore an opposite relatively to the rest of the scale.'[88]

Opposition between terms appears at any point in the scale:

> The same relation which subsists between the lowest member of the scale and the next above it reappears between any two adjacent forms. Each is good in itself, but bad in relation to the one above, and hence, wherever we stand on the scale, we are at a minimum point in it; and conversely, however far down we go; there is always the possibility of going lower without reaching absolute zero.[89]

And not only zero, but also infinity, has no place in the scale:

> Each term in the scale ... sums up the whole scale to that point. Wherever we stand in the scale, we stand at a culmination. Infinity as well as zero can thus be struck out of the scale, not because we never reach a real embodiment of the generic concept, but because the specific form at which we stand is the generic concept itself, so far as our thought yet conceives it.[90]

The classes of a philosophical concept overlap so that:

> The higher term possesses not only that kind of (e.g.) goodness which belongs to it in its own right, but also the kind which originally or in itself belonged to its neighbour ... each term, which in itself is simply one specific form of goodness, has also a double relation to its neighbours: in comparison with the one below, it is what that professes to be, in comparison with the one above, it professes to be what it is ... The higher term is a species of the same genus as the lower, but it differs in degree as a more adequate embodiment of the generic essence, as well as in kind as a specifically different embodiment; it follows from this that it must be not only distinct from it, as one specification from another, but opposed to it, as a higher specification to a lower ... as true, it possesses not only its own specific character, but also that which its rival falsely claimed ...

---

[86] E.P.M., p. 81.
[87] E.P.M., pp. 81–6.
[88] E.P.M., p. 82.
[89] E.P.M., p. 84.
[90] E.P.M., p. 89.

The higher term thus negates the lower, and at the same time reaffirms it: negates it as a false embodiment of the generic essence, and reaffirms its content, that specific form of the essence, as part and parcel of itself.[91]

The higher of any two adjacent forms overlaps the lower because it includes the positive content of the lower as a constituent element within itself; but it rejects the negative element in the lower, and this negative element is the denial that the generic essence contains anything more than the lower itself provides. It is this denial that constitutes its falsehood. The lower overlaps the higher in a different sense: it does not include the higher as part of itself; it adopts part of the positive content of the higher while rejecting another part.[92] Taken together, 'the overlap consists in this, that the lower is contained in the higher, the higher transcending the lower and adding to it something new, whereas the lower partially coincides with the higher, but differs from it in rejecting this increment.'[93]

This, in outline, is the scale of forms; and it is a method typical of philosophical writing. In seeking to define a philosophical concept we do not begin with a definition and deduce theorems about the concept from that definition: rather, the whole exposition is the definition, an essay on a philosophical concept 'may properly be described as an extended and reasoned definition.'[94]

'Knowing', in philosophy, is different from 'knowing' in science. In exact science or empirical science we either know something or

---

[91] E.P.M., pp. 86–8.
[92] E.P.M., p. 90.
[93] E.P.M., p. 91. However, it is important to note that some commentators have claimed that in N.L. the doctrine of the scale of forms as originally articulated in E.P.M. is modified. Thus Boucher argues that 'The Law of Primitive Survivals' (9.51), which states that 'when A is modified into B there survives in any example of B, side by side with the function B which is the modified form of A, an element of A in its primitive or unmodified state', means there can be no complete overlap of forms on a scale (*The Social and Political Thought of R.G. Collingwood*, p. 96). There are several possible responses to this claim: it can be accepted, denied or we could adopt a middle position in which we accept it as true of some scales of forms but not of others. For example, it may be characteristic of consciousness or history (where the doctrine of incapsulation can be construed as an expression of the same point in different language, but not in a purely conceptual scale of forms (A., pp. 98–101, 140). This option, of course, wins a reprieve at the expense of conceding the unity and universality of the idea of scale of forms analysis. To deny Boucher's claim one would have to argue that Collingwood's suggestion that the higher of two adjacent forms 'fails to include the lower in its entirety because there is a negative aspect of the lower which is rejected by the higher: the lower, is addition to asserting its own content, denies that the generic essence contains anything more, and this denial constitutes its falsehood' (E.P.M., p. 90), is essentially the same as a primitive survival in which an unmodifed residue is retained in the higher forms of the scale.
[94] E.P.M., p. 96.

we do not: in philosophy there is 'no such thing as a transition from sheer ignorance or sheer knowledge, but only a progress in which we come to know better what in some sense we know already.'[95] Both our knowing and the concept known constitute a scale of forms: both the scale of forms of the concept as we know it, and our knowing of the concept (that is, our philosophical knowledge of the concept in relation to our experience) expresses itself as a scale of forms of the concept. The scale of forms of the concept and the scale of forms of our knowledge of the concept are in the end the same because the knowledge we come to possess is knowledge of ourselves, of our own experience; but now it is knowledge ordered according to its logical priority and progressive adequacy rather than according to psychological contingency. Hence, in philosophizing we can be said to gain knowledge even though the knowledge we gain is knowledge we already implicitly possess. In philosophizing we come to know what we know, and our knowing in relation to our previous knowledge constitutes a scale of forms which coincides with the scale of forms of the concept as we define it in coming to know it. In coming to know the concept better we redefine and rectify our previous definition and so concept and knowledge of the concept grow pari passu: 'in all philosophical study we begin by knowing something about the subject matter, and on that basis go on to learn more; at each step we redefine our concept by way of recording our progress; and the progress can end only when the definition states all that the concept contains.'[96] Philosophical definition starts from already existing knowledge, from the knowledge of the subject matter we already implicitly possess: this follows from the fact that the lowest end of the scale of forms is not zero but unity, and accordingly we begin the process of definition by laying down the minimum that the concept must be — that is, its minimum realization. Thus,

> to define a philosophical concept . . . it is necessary first to think of that concept as specifying itself in a form so rudimentary that anything less would fail to embody the concept at all. This will be the minimum specification of the concept, the lower end of the scale; and the first phase of the definition will consist in stating this. Later phases will modify this minimum definition by adding new determinations, each implied in what went before, but each introducing into it qualitative changes as well as additions and complications. Finally, a phase will be reached in which the definition contains, explicitly stated, all that can be found in

---

[95] E.P.M., p. 106
[96] E.P.M., p. 97.

the concept; the definition is now adequate to the thing defined and the process is as complete as we can make it.[97]

Collingwood assures us that this method of philosophical definition is to be found throughout the history of philosophy, and he cites Plato's definition of the *polis* in the *Republic*. Plato begins with a definition of the 'minimum city' and then develops its implications, adding functions and modifying the original definition, and so on until a fully adequate definition is propounded. Aristotle used the same method in his *Ethics, De Anima* and *Politics*; Kant used it — see for example his threefold definition of the categorical imperative;[98] and Hegel 'used this method throughout his philosophical works.'

We have seen that in defining a philosophical concept its specifications constitute a scale of forms.[99] The scale of forms as it stands at any given moment in our philosophizing represents both the determinations of the concept and also our present knowledge of the concept: our present knowledge of the concept, the concept as now explicitly known, is the scale of forms of the concept so far as our definition extends. But what is the relation between our experience and our philosophical understanding of that experience?

Philosophy is thinking about thinking and therefore is as much about itself as it is about its subject matter; our philosophical utterances must both apply to and be exemplified by that thinking. Philosophy is in the peculiar position of having to justify its own starting point; this follows from the character of philosophy as self-referential. This justification, as a self-imposed task, is only possible if philosophical arguments are reversible: the principles establishing the conclusions and the conclusions reciprocally establishing the principles.[100] This, however, seems to lead straight to a vicious circle: the solution lies in the Socratic principle that philosophical reasoning leads to no conclusions which were not implicitly anticipated by the knowledge we already possessed prior to philosophizing. In philosophy 'known' and 'unknown' overlap and this implies that we may both know and not know the same thing at the same time. This paradox disappears in the light of the idea of a scale of

---

[97] E.P.M., p. 101.
[98] See E.P.M., p. 103.
[99] I have some sympathy for Johnson's view that the scale of forms can sometimes appear to be an imposition on the experience on which we philosophise, determining how it should be understood (P. Johnson, *R.G. Collingwood: An Introduction*, p. 30). However I do not believe this to be a necessary characteristic and I believe that Collingwood is less concerned to impose form than to report his view that philosophical material inherently arranges itself (or is arranged by our thought) in a certain way.
[100] E.P.M., p. 160.

forms of knowledge where coming to know means coming to know in a different and better way.[101] In philosophy the conclusions are anticipated by an experience which possesses them in substance before its reasoning begins:

> The conclusions can be checked by comparing them with the anticipations, and ... by this checking the principles at work in the reasoning can be verified. If this is so, the direction of the argument in respect of principles and conclusions is reversible, each being established by appeal to the other; but this is not a vicious circle, because the word established here means raised to a higher grade of knowledge.[102]

Philosophy is no private spinning of a web of fancy nor reportage of 'news from nowhere'; it does not start from outside experience and then present its conclusions to experience from outside. On the contrary, it is experience itself more thoroughly understood; it is a re-presentation of experience to itself, organised systematically and logically and its purpose is to enable experience to understand itself better.

> If the substance of philosophical knowledge is known to us, however dimly and confusedly, before philosophical reasoning begins, the purpose of that reasoning can only be to present it in a new form; and this will be a reasoned form, that is, the form of a system constructed according to certain principles. The philosopher who unfolds such a system is not spinning a web of ideas from the recesses of his own mind; he is expressing the results of his own experience and that of other people in a reasoned and orderly shape; and at every stage in his argument, instead of asking one question only, as in exact science, namely 'what follows from the premises?' he has to ask another as well: 'does that conclusion agree with what we find in actual experience?' This test is, therefore an essential part of philosophical reasoning, and any argument whose conclusion cannot be subjected to it is philosophically defective.[103]

Philosophy stands, therefore, in a direct and intimate relation to experience because 'there is a continuity between the experience and the theory; the theory is nothing but the experience itself, with its universality further insisted upon, its latent connections and contradictions brought into the light of consciousness.'[104] Experience, then,

---

[101] E.P.M., p. 161.
[102] E.P.M., p. 163.
[103] E.P.M., p. 164. Note how closely this parallels the method which above I found implied within E.M. The method of philosophy is here said to be historical, 'Does that conclusion agree with what we find in actual experience?' and also logical, 'What follows from the premises?' Philosophy is presented neither as the erection of a deductive system nor as simply the recording of what we find in experience: it is both logical and historical, deductive and inductive at once.
[104] E.P.M., pp. 180–1.

Metaphysics and Method: A Necessary Unity

is only relatively and not absolutely, non-philosophical: the conclusions and the experience:

> are names for any two successive stages in the scale of forms of philosophical knowledge. What is called experience may be any stage in this scale; in itself, as all human experience must be, permeated through and through by philosophical elements; but relatively crude and irrational as compared with the next stage above it, in which these philosophical elements are more fully developed.[105]

The theory should not only agree with the experience; it should also explain it: it must:

> perpetuate its substance in a new form, related to the old somewhat as a fact *plus* the reasons for it is related to the bare fact. Consequently, when we ask whether a moral theory tallies with moral experience we are asking whether the theory makes intelligible the moral experience which we actually possess. At every stage in the scale, there is a datum or body of experience, the stage that has actually been reached; and there is a problem, the task of explaining this experience by constructing a theory of it, which is nothing but the same experience raised by intenser thought to a higher level of rationality ... the new and intenser thinking must be thinking of a new kind; new principles are appearing in it, and these give a criterion by which the principles involved in the last step are superseded.[106]

A philosopher is not concerned only to define particular concepts, nor is he or she merely an agent reflecting on his own experience; they occupy a position in a philosophical tradition; and in their philosophizing this tradition is ever present: 'it follows from the peculiar nature of philosophy that each philosopher, if he genuinely does make his own contribution to knowledge, cannot be merely adding another item to an inventory; he must be shaping afresh in his own mind the idea of philosophy as a whole.'[107] Philosophy is a whole whose parts are related as terms in a scale of forms. Each philosophy has reached a relative and not an absolute end; the philosopher is always confronting new problems, problems created in the very solution of the old problems. But the old problems are solved, and real progress is made: 'every summary can only be done once, and is therefore final: the problem which it must solve is finally solved.'[108] Each philosophy is one among many, but as a term in a scale of forms it reinterprets and reaffirms previous philosophies as elements of itself, and in so doing summarises as part of itself the history of phi-

---

[105] E.P.M., p. 172.
[106] E.P.M., pp. 172-3.
[107] E.P.M., p. 184.
[108] E.P.M., p. 191 and c.f. E.M., p. 65.

losophy from which it sprang and thereby elevates itself into a universal as well as a particular philosophy.

Philosophical problems are both permanent and transitory: 'so far as any man is a competent philosopher, his philosophy arises by objective necessity out of his situation in the history of thought and the problem with which he is confronted; but situation and problem are unique, and hence no one philosopher's system can be acceptable to another without some modification.'[109] And this leads to the conclusion that 'the entire history of thought is the history of a single sustained attempt to solve a single permanent problem, each phase advancing the problem by the extent of all the work done on it in the interval, and summing up the fruits of this work in the shape of a unique representation of the problem.'[110]

We have followed through the idea of a scale of forms in sufficient detail for our present purposes; we have become aware of some of the implications and consequences of such an idea of philosophical method, and it should also be now clear that there is in principle no limit to the possible number of scale of forms. There may be a scale of forms of a concept, for example, ethics; of experience, such as we find in *Speculum Mentis*; an historical scale of forms of the development of a form of experience, as is found in *The Idea of Nature* and *The Idea of History*; a scale of forms of experience and philosophy; of concepts and our understanding of those concepts; of mind, as in *The New Leviathan*; of philosophy itself, either historically or of present day philosophy arranged as a scale of forms by subject matter, and so on ad infinitum. In short, wherever and whenever we are dealing with philosophical concepts the scale of forms will make an appearance: and furthermore, according to the principle of overlap of specific classes, these scales of forms will overlap thereby producing on each occasion of overlap a fresh scale of forms.

Granted, then, that there will be at least as many scales of forms as there are philosophical inquiries, there are three particular types of scale that are directly relevant to the present discussion. These are, first, the scale of forms of a philosophical concept — what I shall call the 'analytical scale of forms'; secondly, there is the scale of forms of knowledge or experience, a scale of which philosophical reflection on experience is a part of the scale itself; in this scale experience and the conclusions arising from philosophical reflection on that experience are successive stages in the scale;[111] thirdly, the historical scale of forms of a form of experience (e.g. history) or of philosophy itself.

[109] E.P.M., p. 192.
[110] E.P.M., p. 195.
[111] E.P.M., p. 172.

Among Collingwood's books *The Principles of Art*, *The New Leviathan* and the *Essay on Philosophical Method* display the analytic scale of forms of a single concept or a related set of concepts; *Speculum Mentis* displays a scale of forms of experience; and *The Idea of Nature* and *The Idea of History* (parts I-IV only; part V covers the ground dealt with in the unfinished *Principles of History* which belongs to the same group as *The Principles of Art*) display the historical development of a single philosophical concept, which is at the same time the development of a single form of experience.

True to form, these different scales overlap. For example, in building up an analytical scale of forms in the definition of a single concept, (say in moral philosophy), a philosopher is at the same time reflecting on his or her own moral experience and that experience is a constituent part of a scale of forms of which his or her philosophy is a higher term, a term which in itself constitutes a fully articulated scale of forms of the moral concept. Again, a philosopher, in reflecting upon experience, makes explicit that which was previously implicit and in so doing traverses upwards in the scale of forms of knowledge or experience; this is precisely the phenomenology of the forms of experience as presented in *Speculum Mentis*. But suppose that the philosopher stands, as indeed he or she must, in a philosophical tradition; and further suppose that in reflecting on his or her experience (in this case a datum supplied in part by the history of philosophy itself) and that in propounding this philosophy he has a certain effect on that tradition as a whole, i.e. that philosophy becomes a central and important part of that tradition, a landmark in the philosophical landscape against which lesser philosophers take their bearings: let this be supposed. Here the philosopher's personal scale of forms of knowledge becomes a constituent part of the historical scale of forms of philosophy itself: his or her self-knowledge coincides with an important or fundamental development in the philosophical tradition. Philosophers of this order of magnitude become the 'great' philosophers: these are the philosophers who effected important transitions, who straddled historical phases, ushering in the new by summing up the old. This overlap of scale perhaps goes some way toward explaining why such great attention is paid to the development of the thought of major philosophers: their development matters because of the coincidence of their own pursuit of philosophical knowledge and the development of philosophy itself.

5: *An Essay on Metaphysics* and The Idea of System in Metaphysics

From an examination of philosophical method we now proceed to an examination of philosophy in its metaphysical aspect. In his *Autobiography*, Collingwood begins his account of the nature of metaphysics by stating that:

> Metaphysics ... is no futile attempt at knowing what lies behind the limits of experience, but is primarily at any given time an attempt to discover what the people of that time believe about the world's general nature; such beliefs being the presuppositions of their 'physics', that is, their inquiries into its detail. Secondarily, it is the attempt to discover the corresponding presuppositions of other peoples and other times, and to follow the historical process by which one set of presuppositions has turned into another.[112]

These presuppositions, not being the answers to questions, are neither true nor false; they are thus a peculiar type of presupposition, because 'a presupposition of one question may be the answer to another question. The beliefs which a metaphysician tries to study and codify are presuppositions of the questions asked by natural science, but are not answers to any questions at all. This might be expressed by calling them 'absolute presuppositions.'[113] The *Autobiography* contains the first explicit published account of the concept of metaphysics as the science of absolute presuppositions. This doctrine, along with the associated 'logic of question and answer' was, however, (according to Collingwood's testimony), first expounded in a book written in 1917 called *Truth and Contradiction*. This book was never published, and Collingwood himself destroyed the only copy after writing the *Autobiography*.[114] The logic of question and answer found its way into print in 1924 as Chapter III, §5 of *Speculum Mentis*, 'knowledge as question and answer'. The doctrine of metaphysics as the science of absolute presuppositions did not appear in print under that name until the *Autobiography*, but as I shall argue later, the central ideas constituting that doctrine were already present in Collingwood's writings from 1919 onward.

The doctrine of metaphysics as the science of absolute presuppositions was given its fullest expression in the book written in 1938–9 and published in 1940, *An Essay on Metaphysics*. In this book Collingwood begins by examining Aristotle's *Metaphysics* and extracting from it two different definitions of metaphysics. The first

---
[112] A., pp. 65–6.
[113] A., p. 67.
[114] See A., pp. 47; 74.

is metaphysics as the science of pure being; the second metaphysics as the science dealing with the presuppositions underlying ordinary science[115]. He dismisses the notion of metaphysics as the science of pure being on the grounds that it would have a 'subject matter entirely devoid of peculiarities . . . a subject matter . . . containing nothing to differentiate it from anything else, or from nothing at all.'[116] This elimination leaves metaphysics as the science of presuppositions; and it is this, and its implications, to which Collingwood devotes the rest of the book.

The main statement of the doctrine is to be found in Chapter 2: 'On Presupposing', 'whenever anybody states a thought in words, there are a great many more thoughts in his mind than are expressed in his statement. Among these there are some which stand in peculiar relation to the thought he has stated: they are not merely its context, they are its presuppositions.'[117] This relation is not psychological or temporal: 'The priority affirmed in the word presuppositions is logical priority',[118] and therefore the inquiry into the presuppositions of statements is a logical inquiry.[119]

Collingwood then states his thesis in a series of formal propositions, prefacing them with the remark that 'In expounding these propositions I shall not be trying to convince the reader of anything, but only to remind him of what he already knows perfectly well.'[120]

Prop. 1 Every statement that anybody ever makes is made in answer to a question . . . (and) a question is logically prior to its own answer.

Def. 1 Let that which is stated (i.e. that which can be true or false) be called a proposition, and let stating it be called propounding it.

Prop. 2 Every question involves a presupposition.

Def. 2 To say that a question 'does not arise' is the ordinary English way of saying that it involves a presupposition which is not in fact being made.

Def. 3 The fact that something causes a certain question to arise I call the 'logical efficacy' of that thing.

---

[115] E.M., p. 10. Note that by 'science' Collingwood means 'a body of systematic or orderly thinking about a determinate subject matter.' (E.M., p. 4).
[116] E.M., p. 14. This argument is reminiscent of one Hegel uses, see *The Logic of Hegel*, §86, ff.
[117] E.M., p. 21.
[118] E.M., p. 21.
[119] E.M., p. 30.
[120] E.M., p. 23, c.f. P.A., p. 152. This is, of course, the Socratic principle which runs throughout Collingwood's writing.

Def. 4   To assume is to suppose by an act of free choice.

Collingwood adds here that some suppositions are not deliberately made and hence cannot be said to be assumed: 'all assumptions are suppositions, but all suppositions are not assumptions', E.M., p.27.

Prop. 3   The logical efficacy of a supposition does not depend upon the truth of what is supposed, or even on it being thought true, but only on its being supposed.

Prop. 4   A presupposition is either relative or absolute.

Def. 5   By a relative presupposition I mean one which stands relatively to one question as its presupposition and relatively to another question as its answer.

Relative presuppositions, as answers to questions, can be verified; absolute presuppositions cannot, because:

Def. 6   An absolute presupposition is one which stands, relatively to all questions to which it is related, as a presupposition, never as an answer.

Absolute presuppositions are not verifiable: 'to speak of verifying a presupposition involves supposing that it is a relative presupposition'. The value of absolute presuppositions in science is therefore not their truth, it is their logical efficacy; and logical efficacy does not depend on a supposition being true but only on its being supposed. (see Prop. 3)

Prop. 5   Absolute presuppositions are not propositions.

This is because they are never answers to questions (Def. 6); whereas a proposition (Def. 1) is that which is stated, and whatever is stated (Prop. 1) is stated in answer to a question; 'Absolute presuppositions are never (see Def. 1) propounded. I do not mean that they sometimes go unpropounded ... I mean that they are never propounded at all. To be propounded is not their business; their business is to be presupposed. The scientist's business is not to propound them but only to presuppose them. The metaphysician's business ... is not to propound them but to propound the proposition that this or that one of them is presupposed.'[121]

Ordinarily we tend to be unaware of the presuppositions of our thinking:

> In our less scientific moments, when knowledge appears to us in the guise of mere apprehension ... we are not even aware that whatever we state to ourselves, or others, is stated in answer to a question, still less

---

[121] All definitions and propositions as set out in E.M., pp. 23–33.

that every such question rests on presuppositions, and least of all that among these presuppositions some are absolute presuppositions. In this kind of thinking, absolute presuppositions are certainly at work; but they are doing their work in darkness, the light of consciousness never falling upon them. It is only by analysis that anyone can ever come to *know* either that he is making any absolute presuppositions at all or what absolute presuppositions he is making.[122]

Collingwood does not say that we are *never* aware of pure presuppositions; the point he is making is that awareness of absolute presuppositions is not necessarily an immediate fact of consciousness: the relation between our thinking and its presuppositions is logical, not psychological, and therefore we only come to be aware of our absolute presuppositions by analysis, not by introspection: to know our absolute presuppositions is to be a metaphysician for the day.[123] Metaphysical analysis is both historical and logical: historical in that a given piece of thinking is taken as a historical fact; and logical in that, given this piece of thinking, its absolute presuppositions can be discovered only through analysis of what it logically presupposes. Knowledge of absolute presuppositions is gained through inquiry into the conditions of a particular field of discourse, through analysis of what the thinking under scrutiny is necessarily committed to in being the thinking it is and asking the question that it does. The discovery of the absolute presuppositions of thought is metaphysics: 'Metaphysics is the attempt to find out what absolute presuppositions have been made by this or that person or group of persons, on this or that occasion or group of occasions, in the course of this or that piece of thinking.'[124]

The job of the metaphysician is not only to find out what presuppositions have been made, but also in doing that, to display them systematically in their mutual relations. It is therefore systematic, it must proceed systematically and display its results as a system. As a science it shares the characteristics of all science: 'thinking systematically means disentangling all this mess, and reducing a knot of thoughts in which everything sticks together anyhow to a system or

---

[122] E.M., p. 43; cf. pp. 22; 34; 35–6.
[123] Some have interpreted Collingwood as claiming that we *cannot* become aware of our absolute presuppositions or that, if we did, we could not continue to presuppose them. E.g., Michael Krausz, 'The Logic of Absolute Presuppositions', p. 227–8; R. Harré and M. Krausz, *Varieties of Relativism*, p. 87. This is a mistake arising from misinterpretation of a passage in E.M. (p. 96) in which Collingwood is clearly stating not his own view but that of an hypothetical objector to the practice of metaphysics. For further discussion see J. Connelly, 'A Mistake in the Interpretation of Collingwood.'
[124] E.M., p. 47.

series of thoughts in which thinking the thoughts is at the same time thinking the connexions between them.'[125]

As an historical science metaphysics studies a subject matter which is specified historically, and which is no aggregate of isolated facts but a complex of historical fact: such a complex Collingwood calls a 'constellation',[126] 'there is no such thing as an historical fact which is not at the same time a complex of historical facts.'[127] In studying any absolute presupposition, therefore, we have to study it as a constituent element in a particular constellation of absolute presuppositions.

The question now is what is the nature of a metaphysical system? A metaphysical system is a system in which a given piece of thinking is rendered a coherent whole through the logical analysis of its absolute presuppositions and their relations to other absolute presuppositions, to relative presuppositions, and to the answers predicated upon those presuppositions. Are the constituent elements in such a system related to each other through entailment or strict implication? Is a metaphysical system a deductive system and metaphysics a deductive science? Collingwood's answer to this question is a firm no. He regards absolute presuppositions as logically independent of one another; 'if any of these constituents logically necessitated any other, the first would be a presupposition of the second, and therefore the second would not be an absolute presupposition.'[128] Nonetheless, there is not a simple absence of logical relations between absolute presuppositions: as all alike presuppositions of a coherent piece of thinking 'each must be *consupponible* with all the others; that is, it must be logically possible for a person who supposes any of them to suppose concurrently all the rest.'[129]

A metaphysical system cannot be, then, a deductive system in which the constituent parts are related through strict 'linear' implication; but there is nevertheless a *negative* logical relation between absolute presuppositions; that is, in any piece of systematic thinking its absolute presuppositions must be capable of being supposed concurrently with the rest. The conception of a metaphysical system that Collingwood is attacking here is one in which the deductive systems of mathematics are taken as a model. This he rejects, and must reject, if he is to maintain the view expressed in both *Philosophical Method* and *Metaphysics*, that a philosophical system is not a closed system

[125] E.M., p. 23.
[126] E.M., p. 66.
[127] E.M., p. 66.
[128] E.M., p. 67.
[129] E.M., p. 66.

but an 'interim report'. Only a closed system can be deductively related throughout its parts and any closed system claims to be ahistorical: Collingwood at every point in his career rejected such an ahistorical view of philosophy.

If we look a little closer at the notion of 'consupponibility' we may be able to see more clearly the precise relations between the elements in a metaphysical system as Collingwood conceives them: for, on the one hand a system is not a deductive one, but on the other, it is a system and cannot therefore simply be a random aggregation of elements. In *An Essay on Philosophical Method* Collingwood denies that philosophy is deductive (if that means the deductive reasoning of the exact sciences) or that it is inductive (if that means the inductive reasoning of the empirical sciences). Philosophy is not deductive because philosophy is in the peculiar position of having to justify its own starting point; the arguments of philosophy have a reversible direction 'the principles establishing the conclusions and the conclusions reciprocally establishing the principles'[130] and this is possible as a result of 'the Socratic principle that philosophical reasoning leads to no conclusions which we did not in same sense know already.'[131] In exact science 'the proof is our only source of assurance that the conclusion is true. In philosophy this is not so; we know this normally without any proof at all; and the service which the proof does for us is not to assure us that it is so, but to show us why it is so, and thus enable us to know it better.'[132]

Philosophy differs from inductive sciences in that its data, the initial knowledge, forms the substance of the final knowledge: the initial knowledge is homogeneous with the conclusions. This is not so in the inductive sciences, for there the initial data form no part of the final theory; they are its basis but not its material. In philosophy 'The very same proposition which at first we knew to be true is reaffirmed with proofs in the body of the system',[133] this can never be so for an inductive science. Again, the data of philosophy are never mere facts but universal propositions and this must be so if the conclusions of a philosophical argument are the initial knowledge raised to a higher degree, for the body of any philosophical science consists of universals.

Collingwood sees philosophical method as both inductive and deductive, and he concludes his examination of the ways in which

---

[130] E.P.M., p. 160.
[131] E.P.M., p. 161.
[132] E.P.M., p. 162.
[133] E.P.M., p. 168,

deduction and induction in philosophy differ from deduction and induction in other sciences in this way:

> It is right to describe philosophical thought as deductive, because at every phase in its development it is, ideally at least, a complete system based on principles and connected through its texture by strict logical bonds; but this system is more than a deductive system, because the principles are open to criticism and must be defended by their success in explaining our experience. For this reason, because philosophy is always an attempt to discern the principles which run through experience and make it a rational whole, it is right to call it inductive; but it differs from an inductive science because the experience on which its theories are based is itself an experience of rational living, theorizing, philosophizing. Consequently, because the data from which it begins and which it has to explain are homogeneous with its conclusions, the theories by which it seeks to explain them, the activity of philosophizing is a datum to philosophy, and among its tasks is the task of accounting for itself ... the theory of philosophy is an essential part of philosophy.[134]

All this Collingwood sums up toward the end of *Philosophical Method* in discussing his own procedure throughout:

> The question whether this general view of philosophical thought agrees with experience is a question which I have not postponed until now ... I have been putting it piecemeal at every step in the argument, which has always moved forward in two parallel lines, asking on the one hand 'what follows from our premises?' and on the other 'what do we find in actual experience?' ... I know of no way in which I can travel in the wilds of philosophical thought except by this double method: compass and dead-reckoning, and the finding of my daily position by the stars.[135]

These considerations, I suggest, serve to amend the view of deduction and system provided in *Metaphysics*: and this amendment can best be effected by a further consideration of the notion of 'consupponibility'. Initially I shall be following here the interesting discussion by E.E. Harris in *Nature, Mind and Modern Science*. For Collingwood a constellation of absolute presuppositions cannot be related deductively. Absolute presuppositions cannot be deduced one from another; but they must be 'consupponible'. Consupponibility is a negative logical criterion: to say that a set of absolute presuppositions are consupponible is to say that they can all be supposed concurrently; which is to say not that one can be deducted from another, but that the implications of each presupposition must, at the very least, be compatible with the implications of all the others. The consequence of incompatible implications is the creation of a strain in the constellation, a strain that can only be overcome by the

---
[134] E.P.M., p. 175.
[135] E.P.M., p. 223.

removal of the offending presupposition(s) and the reconstitution of the entire constellation according to a more adequate principle.

Given a particular absolute presupposition, then, we cannot deduce any other; but we can deduce which absolute presuppositions *cannot* be part of the constellation, that is, whose presence would set up a strain in that constellation[136]. Now, this negative logical criterion cannot be negative alone, as Collingwood rightly says in *Method*: 'In philosophy, whatever may be the case elsewhere, it is a rule of sound method that every negation . . . implies an affirmation.'[137] It is these positive implications that I now wish to develop: I shall begin by quoting Harris.

> If absolute presuppositions are to give rise to questions they must have some implications, and if they are to be 'consupponible' the implications of one must, at least in part, be identical with those of another (to say that they must be mutually consistent means no more nor less than this). Consequently, absolute presuppositions must be in some way mutually implicated . . . Once it is realised that to be consupponible is to have compatible implications, it becomes clear that the source of internal strains in any constellation of absolute presuppositions will be some logical incompatibility and we should have to examine the implications of the presuppositions in order to discover this.[138]

All this is well said, but there still remains a degree of ambiguity about the word 'implication'. Collingwood accepts that philosophy is in a sense a deductive science; if we follow Harris's analysis, he is also committed to accepting that absolute presuppositions must have implications; but it is clear that neither Collingwood nor Harris are committed to accepting a deductive system of the sort to be found in exact science or mathematics. The concept of implication being employed here has affinities with so called strict implication in the sense that the bonds of entailment within a metaphysical system are ideally perfectly logical: but such a system is impossible in philosophy for the very good reason that philosophy is as much *inductive* as deductive. Hence, dependent as it necessarily is on experience, no philosophical system can ever be completed; and only a completed, closed, system could ever in principle be a deductive system. What we need to look for is a conception of implication and deduction suitable to express the relations found within the parents of a philosophical system; we need to move away from 'linear inference' and toward a broader conception of deduction and implication.

---

[136] E.M., pp. 48, 74, 76.
[137] E.P.M., p. 106.
[138] E. E. Harris, *Nature, Mind and Modern Science*, p. 34.

Such a conception constitutes, in a sense, the entire argument of *An Essay on Philosophical Method*, but more explicit statements are to be found elsewhere. It is also important to find statements on this matter other than from the essay on Method, as otherwise we run the risk of begging the question in trying to elucidate the relations between *Philosophical Method* and *Metaphysics*.

In his 'Notes on Hegel's Logic' Collingwood argues that:

> Implication is essentially realistic, assuming that the process of thought travels over a previously articulated whole, following out its articulations as they already exist, and leaving them unchanged: dialectic is essentially idealistic, because thought destroys the ladder up which it climbed and therefore there is no world over against thought.[139]

Implication here is seen as something external to the thought which thinks it in the sense that it undergoes no modification in being thought. This form of implication has a place in abstract deductive systems, but in philosophy it has no place: the essence of philosophical thought is its constant revision of its starting point, its procedural self-justification, its pursuit of its own laws, laws which it creates in that pursuit itself. If, in philosophy, we come to know better what we already in some sense knew before, it cannot possibly be the case that we travel along already determined pathways in coming to possess that knowledge. If the lines along which we think have been pre-determined then our knowing will not be a different and better way of knowing what we already know, it will be merely knowing it as opposed to not knowing it.

In a preliminary draft for 'Economics as a Philosophical Science' Collingwood draws precisely the distinction for which I have been looking:

> The concept of utility of the economic good is an a priori ethical category, and ... therefore the science of utility is a branch of philosophical ethics, i.e. an integral part of the philosophy of the spirit. It is misrepresented by being made an empirical science, because its true nature is to be deductive: i.e. not abstractly deductive in the mathematical sense ... but dialectically deductive. We start with the pure concept of utility (economic action in itself) and show how this generates its own determinations.[140]

The crucial distinction is between abstract and dialectical deduction; and using these terms, we can say immediately that the method employed and expounded by Collingwood in *Philosophical Method* and elsewhere is a dialectically deductive one in which a theory is

---

[139] 'Notes on Hegel's Logic', p. 39.
[140] 'Economics as a Philosophical Science — for a section of a comprehensive ethical treatise?', (n.d. c1925), Bodleian Library, Dep. 24/2, p. 1.

presented as a system, a system neither abstractly deductive nor simply inductive, but a dialectical system — a scale of forms.[141] Armed with this distinction and with this concept of system we can now return to *An Essay on Metaphysics* and examine how the conception of system put forward there corresponds to the conception put forward in *Method*.

In his remarks on the nature of a metaphysical system Collingwood concludes that

> It follows that the literary form of a treatise in which a metaphysician sets out to enumerate and discuss the absolute presuppositions of thought in his own time cannot be the form of a continuous argument, leading from point to point by ways of quasi-mathematical demonstrations, as in the *Ethics* of Spinoza. It must be the form of a *catalogue raisonné* as in the fourth book of Aristotle's *Metaphysics*, or in the *Quaestiones* of a medieval metaphysician.[142]

In 'Function of Metaphysics in Civilization' the notion of a *catalogue raisonné* is developed more fully:

> Metaphysics is in the second place a presentation of the principles it discovers, not merely in the form of a catalogue, but in the form of a system. By a catalogue of principles I mean a list of principles stated without any regard for the relations in which they stand to one another. Such a catalogue will be what I call a *catalogue raisonné* if each principle is not merely stated but expanded and commented on in detail, showing how it is used in being applied to this or that kind of case. By a system of principles I mean a treatment in which the relations between these principles form an integral part of the exposition; so that if two principles A and B are inconsistent, an inquiry is constituted into the whole method by which this inconsistency is overcome in the actual application of them.[143]

6: Conclusion

In this chapter I have put forward the claim that a certain conception of philosophy as an activity and as system runs throughout Collingwood's writings; in particular, I have argued that this conception of philosophy unites rather than divides the two *Philosophical Essays*. Thus, in my view, the conception of a scale of forms corresponds to the conception of a *catalogue raisonné*, and hence the method of metaphysics is also the method of philosophy as a whole.

---

[141] See for example Collingwood's remarks on the definition of a philosophical concept, E.P.M., pp. 100–101.
[142] E.M., p. 68.
[143] 'Function of Metaphysics in Civilization', p. 30.

All philosophy partakes of metaphysics,[144] and so all philosophy must partake of metaphysical methods; on the other hand, metaphysics is a part of philosophy and so shares in the methods of philosophy. But there is more to be done if the unity of Collingwood's philosophy is to be demonstrated. Chapter Three addresses this through a consideration of the role of absolute presuppositions in Collingwood's thought.

---

[144] E.P.M., p. 127.

Chapter Three

Absolute Presuppositions in Collingwood's Philosophy

1: Introduction

In this chapter I shall continue addressing the coherence and unity of Collingwood's approach to philosophy, not principally (as in the previous chapter) through consideration of method, but through consideration of Collingwood's understanding of the nature of distinctly philosophical concepts or, in the language of *An Essay on Metaphysics*, the nature and status of absolute presuppositions and their place in thought. This will be done through, first, an inquiry into conceptual change, secondly, the presentation of a history of fundamental presuppositions in Collingwood's thought, and thirdly, a consideration of the relationship between absolute presuppositions and the philosophical concepts identified in the *Essay on Method* and other writings.

2: Beyond Truth and Falsity: Absolute Presuppositions, Thought and Change

In this section I shall make some points concerning the relation between the theory of absolute presuppositions and A. J. Ayer's *Language, Truth and Logic*,[1] on the relation between absolute presuppositions and the thinking which presupposes them; and on the

---

[1] See A. J. Ayer, *Language, Truth and Logic*.

possibility of, and reasons for, changes in constellations of absolute presuppositions.

Ayer divides meaningful propositions into those that are empirically verifiable and those which are analytically true or tautologous: all other propositions, are (for Ayer) 'pseudo-propositions'. The first chapter of the book is entitled 'The Elimination of Metaphysics' and is devoted, as its title clearly states, to the destruction of the possibility of metaphysical knowledge. This book, and in particular this chapter, appears to have been (at least in some degree) the spur to the writing of *An Essay on Metaphysics*.[2]

For Collingwood, Ayer's attack on metaphysics is an attack not on metaphysics, but on pseudo-metaphysics.[3] Collingwood's method in arguing his case against Ayer is not to mount a full-scale onslaught on his position, but to accept his premises while denying that his conclusions follow. In brief, he argues that Ayer fails to eliminate metaphysics for the simple reason that metaphysical propositions are not (as Ayer assumes) propositions, but are, on the contrary, presuppositions and therefore not amenable to the some treatment.

An absolute presupposition stands relatively to all questions to which it is related as a presupposition, never as an answer. For Collingwood, truth and falsity can only be predicated of propositions because they are answers to questions. Absolute presuppositions are not answers to questions and therefore the distinction between truth and falsity does not apply to them. Further, as an absolute presupposition is not the answer to a question it is not, strictly speaking, a proposition at all. In talking of 'truth' and 'falsity', in *An Essay on Metaphysics* Collingwood means by the terms no more than 'what can or cannot be verified', and this is a concession to Ayer's verification principle. He denies the division of all meaningful statements into two exclusive classes of the analytic and the empirically verifiable synthetic by arguing that a third class of meaningful statements, i.e. philosophical statements, exists. His agreement with Ayer is, therefore, only on the surface: he is perfectly willing to let Ayer appropriate the predicates 'truth' and 'falsity' for what can and cannot be empirically verified, and accepts that if this is what truth and falsity mean then absolute presuppositions can be neither true nor false.

---

[2] See E.M. chapter XVI, and A. J. Ayer, *Philosophy in the Twentieth Century*, p. 197. For a discussion of the origins of E.M., see J. Connelly, 'Natural Science, History and Christianity: the Origins of Collingwood's Later Metaphysics', and Rex Martin, Introduction to revised edition of E.M.

[3] E.M., p. 163.

For Ayer metaphysical statements have no truth value because they are not verifiable: for Collingwood metaphysical statements have no truth value because (though meaningful) they are not propositions. My point is that Collingwood goes along, for the sake of argument, with Ayer's reserving of the terms 'truth' and 'falsity' for verifiable statements alone, and that the characterisation of absolute presuppositions as neither true nor false is entirely dependent upon this assumption. If by a 'true statement' we mean one that can be empirically verified, then it is clear that an absolute presupposition cannot be 'true'. However, if the term 'truth' is not restricted solely to what is empirically verifiable then the possibility opens up of a conception of truth not limited to empirical verification, and under which it would make perfect sense to say that absolute presuppositions were true. In formulating his doctrine of metaphysics as the science of absolute presuppositions Collingwood was, I think, anxious to avoid being taken for the very type of metaphysician which the logical positivists denounced. For him to have asserted that 'truth' was not limited to what was empirically verifiable would have amounted to begging the question, that is, presupposing the point at issue by appealing to a conception of truth the very existence and validity of which was precisely what was in doubt. Accordingly he explicitly declines to consider the validity of the verification principle: 'whether [Ayer's] conception of 'verifiability' is sound I shall not consider. I shall assume for the sake of argument that it is; or at any rate that, if not quite immune from criticism as it stands, it is capable of being restated in some such way as to render it so immune.'[4] Collingwood thus accepts the principle of verifiability, and agrees that on its terms metaphysical propositions are neither true nor false; but he denies that they are meaningless: in effect he presents us with a third class of statements which are misconstrued by the positivists as a failed sub-class of empirical statements. He argues that even on the principles of positivism these statements are meaningful, but accepts that according to the conception of truth employed by positivism they can be neither true nor false.

The point is brought out quite clearly in Collingwood's reply to Ryle's article in *Mind*, 'Mr. Collingwood and the Ontological Argument', in which Collingwood is trying to pinpoint the locus of the disagreement between himself and Ryle. What Collingwood says here is important for three reasons: first, it throws light on his conception of metaphysical propositions; secondly it indicates what sort of thing such propositions might be; and thirdly it dates from a

---

[4]   E.M., p. 165.

period when he was supposed to have an entirely different conception of philosophy from that later presented in *An Essay on Metaphysics* and so helps to substantiate the claim that there was no radical break.

> I believe that such propositions as 'God exists', 'Mind exists', matter exists', and their contradictories, do not assert or deny particular matters of fact; nor do I believe that they assert or deny anything which can be adequately described as collections or classes of matters of fact. To assert or deny propositions of this kind, with reasons given for the assertion or denial, seems to me the business of constructive or destructive metaphysics; and what, I suppose, I am objecting to in this sentence of yours is a question begging assumption that Hume was right when he divided all possible subjects of discourse into a) ideas and the relations between them, and b) matters of fact.[5]

In a later letter Collingwood suggests that one of their points of difference 'is connected with your disbelief in synthetic *a priori* propositions, which I do not share; and I think that we are probably agreed that the possibility of metaphysics is bound up with the question whether such propositions are possible.'[6]

The third type of proposition that Collingwood seeks to establish is, then, the synthetic *a priori*; is it justifiable to assume that absolute presuppositions are synthetic *a priori* propositions? We have already given Collingwood's own formal statement of the nature of absolute presuppositions, but in order to establish that they are *a priori* concepts (in some sense) we need to gather together the statements on their nature scattered through *Metaphysics*. 'An absolute presupposition cannot be undermined by the verdict of 'experience', because it is the yard-stick by which 'experience' is judged.'[7] And therefore they are not derived from experience, 'but are catalytic agents which the mind must bring out of its own resources to the manipulation of what is called 'experience' and the conversion of it into science and civilization.'[8] They are what makes argument possible and therefore they are not argued to but from:

> Metaphysics is concerned with absolute presuppositions. We do not acquire absolute presuppositions by arguing; on the contrary, unless we have them already arguing is impossible to us. Nor can we change them by arguing; unless they remained constant all our arguments would fall

---

[5] Collingwood–Ryle Correspondence, (C.R.C.), 9/5/35.
[6] C.R.C., 6/6/35.
[7] E.M., pp. 193–4.
[8] E.M., p. 197.

to pieces. We cannot confirm ourselves in them by 'proving' them; it is proof that depends on them, not they on proof.[9]

Absolute presuppositions, it seems, are in some sense *a priori*: they are not derived from experience, but are brought to bear upon experience in order to render it intelligible. Their validity is not derived from experience: they cannot be proved or verified. The attempt to verify an absolute presupposition is either circular or a category mistake. If we try to verify an absolute presupposition the thought which attempts such verification will either itself presuppose the some presupposition, thus making the presupposition the judge in its own case; or it will not presuppose the presupposition in which case the attempted verification will be irrelevant. It is because absolute presuppositions are logically prior to our thoughts about the world, about reality, our manipulation of experience, that they cannot be proved by being compared with that experience or with reality and found true or false: they are present in all our thought about reality and are not derived from observations about reality. And from this it follows that the idea of checking their correspondence with reality is otiose. Further, they can never be confirmed or made more 'true of reality' through their success in interpreting it. In *Philosophical Method*, discussing the principles presupposed by induction, Collingwood points out that:

> these principles are in no sense confirmed by the successful conduct of the arguments based on them. Unless we assumed them, we could never conduct arguments of this kind at all; but however long and however successfully we go on conducting arguments of this kind, we always know that these assumptions are assumptions and nothing more. What is increased by the success of our inductive inquiries is not the probability of such principles as that the future will resemble the past, but the probability of such hypotheses as that fermentation is due to micro-organisms... The principles on which inductions rests receive in return no support from the inductive process itself.[10]

Absolute presuppositions do not occur in isolation, they occur as elements in a constellation of absolute presuppositions. These constellations are the structural or categorical framework of our thinking (or of the thinking of those whose thought we are studying); but to be the possessor of such a framework is not necessarily to be aware of the framework one possesses. Knowledge of the constellations of absolute presuppositions underlying our thought can come

---

[9] E.M., p. 173.
[10] E.P.M., p. 166. The only important difference between this passage and any to be found in E.M. is that in the later work absolute presuppositions were not held to be assumptions as they are not supposed by an act of free choice.

only from metaphysical analysis. In all our inquiries and practices — in art, religion, ethics, history, science and so on — we proceed by asking questions, performing actions, verifying facts, and the rest; and in so doing we necessarily commit ourselves to certain presuppositions, some of which will be absolute for that particular form of experience. The task of the metaphysician is to examine our statements, questions and actions and ascertain what we are logically committed to in stating, asking and performing them. Now this points to an important fact: our absolute presuppositions are a priori, but they are not temporally prior to our experience. They are logically prior to experience, and such logical priority is perfectly compatible with their arising only in the course of experience. In a commentary on the Preface to the *Critique of Pure Reason* Collingwood makes several pertinent remarks on the nature of the a priori in Kant:

> Kant's view is really that the form itself comes into existence through the act of cognition, and has no separate origin from the matter[11] ... Kant accepts from the rationalists the a priori, but not in the sense of innate ideas ... The Kantian a priori springs out of your mind as it grapples with the problem. It is the activity of thought in the actual work of thinking. The mind is not passive, as the empiricists thought. It does not merely register impressions.[12]

The *a priori* for Collingwood is thus not a psychological a priori but a logical *a priori*: absolute presuppositions are not derived from experience, but it does not follow that they exist somehow temporally prior to the structure of our thought and experience. With respect to experience they are logically prior, but they come into being only as what we are logically committed to in our thought about that experience. This has two consequences: first, that our knowledge of absolute presuppositions is a logical construct derived from an analysis of our thought and action; secondly, that change in absolute presuppositions comes only through the internal working of our thought, through its constant effort to make sense of our experience: change in absolute presuppositions does not come first in time, it comes first only in logic. Rex Martin put this point well:

> Collingwood's notion that an absolute presupposition cannot be separated from the statements that presuppose it leads to the idea that absolute presuppositions are simply a part of scientific practice itself. They are ingredient there as foundation or ground ... absolute presuppositions ... are not propositions; they are objective patterns and structures

---

[11] Commentary on the Preface to Kant's *Critique of Pure Reason*, p. 23.
[12] op. cit. p. 3 (new pagination).

in our ways of knowing. They are neither right nor wrong, true nor false; they just are. We can ... try to formulate and thereby describe them. Indeed, this is the only way we could come to know that they are there at all, or what they are. And such a statement can be ... true or false. These formulations, however, are not simply repertorial in nature; rather, they are logical or dialectical conclusions to complex arguments ... One can become conscious of an absolute presupposition only by formulating it. They must be argued to: one reasons from the explanatory practices and from the knowledge claimed in a given science to the presuppositions that must be involved ... There is no fact, other than the soundness of the arguments involved, that could determine a metaphysical statement to be true or false. In the case of such statements there is no distinction between their truth and their adequate formulation. Absolute presuppositions can be known, but only by reason.[13]

The second consequence of this conception of the nature of absolute presuppositions is that change in them comes through the internal working out of the problems of each individual science or form of experience: change cannot be brought about from without, nor does it arise through the absolute presuppositions changing prior in time to the change in the entire structure of thought. Absolute presuppositions change as the structure of thought changes; it is only in retrospect that we can trace changes in systems of thought to changes in their absolute presuppositions; at the time of the change itself the change in absolute presuppositions is not temporally or psychologically prior but only logically prior. As Martin suggests, 'if our explanatory practices should prove inadequate, in any of a variety of ways, then we change what we do; and it is through such changes that change can occur in the organising conceptions themselves.'[14]

I shall now illustrate this understanding of how absolute presuppositions change using Collingwood's words:

> The essential thing about historical phases is that each of them gives place to another ... because each of them while it lives is working at turning itself into the next ... the metaphysician's business ... when he has identified several different constellations of absolute presuppositions, is not only to study their likenesses and unlikenesses but also to find out on what occasions and by what processes one of them has turned into another ... One phase changes into another because the first phase was in unstable equilibrium and had in itself the seeds of change, and indeed of that change. Its fabric was not at rest; it was always under strain.[15]

---

[13] Rex Martin, 'Collingwood's Doctrine of Absolute Presuppositions and the Possibility of Historical Knowledge', pp. 93–4, and his Introduction to the revised edition of E.M.
[14] Martin, op. cit. p. 93.
[15] EM., pp. 73–4.

The metaphysician has to examine the way in which a given system of thought ' 'takes up' these strains, or prevents them from breaking it in pieces.'[16]

> Where there is no strain there is no history. A civilization does not work out its own details by a kind of static logic in which every detail exemplifies in its own way one and the some formula. It works itself out by a dynamic logic in which different and at first sight incompatible formulae somehow contrive a precarious coexistence; one dominant here, another there; the recessive formula never ceasing to operate, but functioning as a kind of minority report.[17]

The motive power causing change is thus the negativity typical of a dialectical process and therefore the metaphysician 'will expect the various presuppositions he is studying to be consupponible only under pressure, the constellations being subject to certain strains and kept together by dint of a certain compromise or mutual tolerance.'[18] This is, of course, one of the reasons that a metaphysical system cannot be deductive: a deductive system is a strainless structure: for Collingwood the contrary must be true; thought is dialectical and hence change in systems of thought must be dialectical. Change occurs through thought's own dissatisfaction with its own performance: the *nisus* is thought's awareness of its inadequacy, its consciousness of the strains and contradictions to be found in its structure at any one time. To hope for a rigidly deductive metaphysical system is at the some time to will the end of thought; if on the other hand philosophy is a reflection on actual experiences it can no more be a closed deductive system than can the whole of experience.

The most concise of Collingwood's rather irritatingly sketchy discussions of change in absolute presuppositions comes in a footnote:

> People are not ordinarily aware of their absolute presuppositions, and are not, therefore, thus aware of changes in them; such a change, therefore, cannot be a matter of choice. Nor is there anything superficial or frivolous about it. It is the most radical change a man can undergo, and entails the abandonment of all his most firmly established habits and standards for thought and action.
>
> Why ... do such changes happen? Briefly, because the absolute presuppositions of any given society, at any given phase of its history, form a structure which is subject to 'strains' of greater or less intensity, which are 'taken up' in various ways, but never annihilated. If the strains are too great, the structure collapses and is replaced by another, which will be a modification of the old with the destructive strain removed; a modi-

---

[16] E.M., p. 74.
[17] E.M., p. 75.
[18] E.M., p. 76.

fication not consciously devised but created by a process of unconscious thought.[19]

These passages, taken from *An Essay on Metaphysics*, give some indication as to the causes of change: they imply that it arises internally and that it is in some way dialectical; but they do not say how 'strains' are recognised, and the final passage concludes with the remark about 'unconscious thought' which has been the cause of so much misinterpretation. Before proceeding further with the rest of the argument it is therefore necessary to address this issue.

At the outset of *The Idea of Nature* Collingwood writes that scientists, as a result of reflection, discover that they have been working in a methodical way, 'according to principles of which hitherto they have not been conscious.'[20] In *An Essay on Metaphysics* he remarks that 'in our less scientific moments . . . absolute presuppositions are certainly at work; but they are doing their work in darkness, the light of consciousness never falling on them';[21] and later in a footnote he writes of absolute presuppositions changing through a 'process of unconscious thought.'[22]

Some critics, such as Knox and Donagan, have been misled by the use of the term 'unconscious' into supposing that 'presuppositions . . . fall into the sphere of the unconscious'[23] and suggest that changes in absolute presuppositions therefore have to be interpreted 'along the lines of Freudian morbid psychology.'[24]

This is, I suggest, nonsense. First, for Collingwood, presupposing is a *logical* relation: we are unaware of our presuppositions in so far as we do not realise to what our statements logically commit us[25] — the relation between our thought and its presuppositions is logical, not psychological or temporal.[26] To say, then, that we are unaware of our presuppositions is to say no more than we are unaware of the logical foundations of our statements: it is most certainly not to say that presuppositions inhabit a supposedly autonomous 'unconscious'. The point is that our presuppositions have logical connections with our explicit thinking and that they can be logically

---

[19] E.M., p. 48.
[20] I.N., p. 1.
[21] E.M., p. 43.
[22] E.M., p. 48.
[23] T.M. Knox, preface to I.H., xiv.
[24] A. Donagan, *The Later Philosophy of R.G. Collingwood*, p. 271. For an interesting discussion of this issue in a different context, see M. Hinz, *Self-Creation and History*.
[25] E.M., pp. 21–2
[26] I.N., p. 1.

reconstructed through an analysis of that thinking. The need for 'Freudian morbid psychology' simply does not arise.

Secondly, it is quite clear that the term 'unconscious' as used in *Metaphysics* and *The Idea of Nature* means, simply, 'unaware'. Throughout *Philosophical Method* we are assured that philosophy enables us to know better what in a sense we know already: this understanding of philosophy pervades all Collingwood's writing and is the same as the distinction between implicit and explicit knowing. Philosophy makes explicit what in any given form of experience is implicit. The distinction between implicit and the explicit is clarified in *Speculum Mentis*:

> In any given experience there are certain principles, distinctions and so forth of which the person whose experience it is cannot but be aware: these I call explicit features of the experience in question... On the other hand, an observer studying a certain form of experience often finds it impossible to give an account of it without stating certain principles and distinctions which are not actually recognised by the persons whose experience he is studying. Thus an artist constructs his work on principles which are really operative in the construction, but are not explicitly recognized by himself: in art they are implicit, to become explicit only in the criticism of art.[27]

My view that by 'unconscious' Collingwood means 'unaware' is reinforced if we return to *The Idea of Nature* where he states that 'reflection reacts upon the detailed work; for when people become conscious of the principles upon which they have been thinking or acting they become conscious of something which in these thoughts and actions they have been trying, though unconsciously, to do: namely to work out in detail the logical implications of those principles.'[28] There is no 'process of unconscious thought' understood as the actions of an autonomous faculty (the 'unconscious') which works out the logical implications of these principles. Rather, the picture is of conscious thought working out in detail the consequences of principles of which it was unaware but nonetheless logically committed to by its inquiry and the questions asked in the course of its inquiry. Similarly, change in absolute presuppositions is change resulting not from the activities of a supposed 'unconscious' but resulting from the activity of people thinking systematically according to certain presuppositions of which they are ordinarily unaware but to which they are nevertheless logically committed. Change in the structure of the inquiry produces changes in presuppositions which then change 'unconsciously' in the sense

---

[27] S.M., p. 85, fn.
[28] I.N. p. 2.

that those committed to the form of inquiry in question were not consciously aware of changing or seeking to change those presuppositions, but *were* aware of the structure of their thought and its modifications, which modifications logically presuppose different presuppositions and thereby effect a change in those presuppositions.

Thus we are not normally aware of our absolute presuppositions, but we might be, and coming to know what they are does not *ipso facto* mean that we cease to presuppose them (as some commentators have suggested.[29] But change in presuppositions, whether they are explicitly known or not, is not usually brought about directly, but indirectly.

At this point, having considered the blind alley of 'unconscious thought', we can pick up the thread and return to a consideration of why constellations of absolute presuppositions change. As already emphasised, the cause of change in absolute presuppositions is a cause internal to the science or experience concerned: such change may be spurred on by awareness of presuppositions, and so philosophy may have a part to play. But philosophy is no more than reflection on principles, and this is carried on not only by professional philosophers but also by practitioners of the various sciences themselves and, again, the clarification of concepts is carried on in an unselfconscious manner within the sciences themselves simply in the course of their activity.

This is how Collingwood puts the matter in criticizing Hegel, who talks of philosophy as criticism of categories: 'the criticism of (e.g.) chemical categories is carried on not by philosophers but by chemists.'[30] This was written in 1920, and it is clear that he believed here what he believed in *An Essay on Metaphysics*: that metaphysics cannot criticise the presuppositions it discovers, but can only show that they are presupposed. Collingwood emphasises the internality of categorical criticism and change later when commenting on §17, which states that 'the sciences presuppose their object, philosophy proves its'; he argues that this is the 'same old mistake: any given phase of a science takes over its problems as data from the preceding phase, but science *as a whole* posits its own problems in the course of its becoming. The some precisely is true of philosophy.'[31] This parallels the later discussion in *The Idea of Nature* where Collingwood declares that 'natural science, considered as a department or form of human thought, is a going concern, able to raise its own problems

[29] See Chapter Two, fn. 123.
[30] 'Notes on Hegel's Logic', p. 2.
[31] op. cit. p. 4.

and to solve them by its own methods, and to criticize the solutions it has offered by applying its own criteria.'[32]

Collingwood's British Academy lecture of 1936, *Human Nature and Human History*, contains what amounts to a statement of the essential core of the doctrine of absolute presuppositions (although the term does not occur there). This passage is worth quoting at length:

> The positive function of so-called sciences of the human mind has always tended to be mis-conceived. Ideally, they are designed as accounts of one unchanging subject matter, the mind of man as it always has been and always will be . . . They are nothing of the sort, but only inventories of the wealth achieved by the human mind at a certain stage in its history. . . . [e.g.] Kant's *Critique of Pure Reason* analyses the conceptions and principles of Newtonian science, in their relation to the philosophical problems of the day. These limitations are often taken for defects, as if a more powerful thinker . . . would have lifted himself clean out (of his time). So far from being a defect, they are a sign of merit; they are most clearly to be seen in those works whose quality is of the best. The reason is that in those works the authors are doing best the only thing that can be done when an attempt is made to construct a science of the human mind. They are expounding the positions reached by the human mind in its historical development down to their own time.
>
> When they try to justify that position, all they can do is to exhibit it as a logical whole, a coherent whole of ideas. If, realizing that any such justification is circular, they try to make the whole depend on something outside itself, they fail, as indeed they must; for since the historical present includes in itself its own past, the real ground on which the whole rests, namely the past out of which it had grown, is not outside it but is included within it.
>
> If these systems remain valuable to posterity, that is not in spite of their strictly historical character but because of it. To us, the ideas expressed in them are ideas belonging to the past; but it is not a dead past; by understanding it historically we incorporate it into our present thought, and enable ourselves by developing and criticizing it to use that heritage for our own advancement.
>
> But a mere inventory of our intellectual possessions at the present time can never show by what right we enjoy them. To do this there is only one way: by analysing them instead of merely describing them, and showing how they have been built up in the historical development of thought. What Kant, for example, wanted to do when he set out to justify our use of a category like causation, can in a sense be done; but it cannot be done on Kant's method which yields a merely circular argument, proving that such a category can be used, and must be used if we are to have Newtonian science; it can be done by research into the history of scientific thought. All Kant could show was that eighteenth century scientists did think in terms of that category; the question why they so

---

[32] I.N., p. 175.

thought can be answered by investigating the history of the idea of causation. If more than this is required; if a proof is needed that the idea is true, that people are right to think in that way; then a demand is being made which in the nature of things can never be satisfied. How can we ever satisfy ourselves that the principles on which we think are true, except by going on thinking according to those principles, and seeing whether unanswerable criticisms of them emerge as we work? To criticize the conceptions of science is the work of science itself as it proceeds; to demand that such criticism should be anticipated by the theory of knowledge is to demand that such a theory should anticipate the history of thought.[33]

A lengthy quotation, but one rich in implications and which therefore merits scrutiny, not only to enhance our appreciation of Collingwood's understanding of conceptual change and the logical status of basic propositions in systems of thought, but also because the ideas expressed here clearly straddle the disputed transitional years.[34]

Finally, let us consider a passage from Collingwood's notebooks on metaphysics which were started immediately after he completed *Philosophical Method*. The thesis I am presenting is that absolute presuppositions change through the internal criticism, through the dialectic which lies at the heart of any science, inquiry or forms of experience. What I wish to maintain is that, on the one hand, *The Idea of Nature* presents an account of the changing absolute presuppositions of science through its history, and that this links it directly to *Metaphysics* which is an account of the nature of metaphysics and of the nature of absolute presuppositions; and that, on the other hand, *The Idea of Nature* exhibits the history of the absolute presuppositions of science as a scale of forms. *The Idea of Nature* has often been taken as an application of the theory expounded in *Metaphysics*. If 'application' is taken to imply that *Metaphysics* preceded *The Idea of Nature*, this is clearly false. Such a mistake is a consequence of the later publication date of *The Idea of Nature*, which traps the unwary reader into thinking that it was written after rather than before *Metaphysics*. The point is that commentators who made this mistake took it for granted that *The Idea of Nature* was a history of absolute presuppositions and clearly saw no contradiction.

---

[33] I.H., pp. 229–30. See also I.N.: 'All that has been said is a mere interim report on the history of the idea of nature down to the present time. If I knew what further progress would be made in the future, I should already have made that progress' (p. 175).

[34] For further discussion, in the context of a comparison between Collingwood and Bradley's conceptions of metaphysics, see J. Connelly, 'Bradley, Collingwood and the "Other Metaphysics"'.

We know that, on the contrary, not only did *Nature* pre-date *Metaphysics*, but also that it was written as a deliberate attempt to apply the method expounded in *Philosophical Method*.[35] If *The Idea of Nature* is compatible with both Essays then I consider it fair to cite evidence from material written immediately after *Method* in order to throw light on the dialectical principles underlying the change in constellations of absolute presuppositions as conceived in *Metaphysics*.

I draw on notebook A of the 'Notebooks on Metaphysics'. These notebooks were, in part, preparation for the lectures Collingwood later delivered as 'Nature and Mind', and in part preparation for Collingwood's own cosmology. In this passage Collingwood is asking what it is that causes one form in a scale to give way to another which, in the terms of *An Essay on Metaphysics*, is to ask what causes one constellation of absolute presuppositions to give way to another. Collingwood asks:

> Now what about the nisus? i.e. what is the nature of the force which drives us from a lower term to the next higher, or if you like converts that into this? On this subject I have said nothing in the Essay. It is what Spinoza would call an immanent causality: something in the first term which converts it into the second. This causality is of course a teleology ... But of a scale of forms e.g. in ethical theories: does hedonism show dissatisfaction with itself and a desire to became the next thing? Obviously not — it resists every such invitation and seems satisfied with itself. Why does the next thing emerge? a) from fresh moral experience suggesting new aspects of the subject matter: in a word, ab extra, b) by chance, c) through something in the original situation. Of these answers, I submit that we *must* accept (c). The theory is a monad with no windows — nothing can come in ab extra, because the theory itself *determines what is to be regarded as moral experience* (a person with a theory of a certain kind A will not admit that experience of a kind B is moral experience at all). It is not that the theory is dissatisfied with itself, but rather that it is ambivalent: it asserts itself both as A and as B and since these assertions are, apparently at least, inconsistent, it has to ask itself which it really means. On this analogy the nisus should lie in a certain ambivalence of structure in the specific concept itself: it should present conflicting aspects, a bipolar organisation in a state of tension, the tension relieved by passage to the next higher form.
>
> The pattern of a solution therefore should be this: each specific form bifurcates into two aspects. It cannot be a form *of the genus* unless it has both, for either by itself would be a mere abstraction. But the two are in conflict, so related that it cannot be both at once. This conflict can be resolved, but only by breaking down the specific pattern of this form and arriving at a new specific pattern. The force is the conflict itself; persevering in this case means continuing the conflict, and this means *either*

---

[35] T.M. Knox, prefatory note to I.N. and also his review of Mink, *Mind, History and Dialectic*.

going on finding no solution (so called static condition) or finding a solution and breaking through into a new specific form. Why one alternative happens rather than the other is, I think, not for metaphysics to determine.[36]

If we translate this into the language of absolute presuppositions then we arrive at something like the account of change given in the original quotation from *Metaphysics*.[37] The initial structure collapses and is replaced by another; this new structure is a modification of the old with the destructive or negative or contradictory strain removed. A constellation of absolute presuppositions is not an aggregate of particulars: absolute presuppositions are part of the fabric of thought itself and known to the metaphysician only through analysis. Each constellation, then, is an organised whole, the logical foundation of a coherent world of ideas; each constellation has its own structure, its own principle of organisation. If there is a change in our ways of thinking then there is also a change in our absolute presuppositions: but this is not the mere gathering in of a few new absolute presuppositions and the throwing off of a few old ones. The entire fabric of a theory or world of thought is affected by every other part of it: 'A theory ... cannot be dissected into true statements and false statements; every statement it contains has been falsified.'[38] Each element in a constellation is an integral part of a whole which is no mere aggregate of these elements, the presence of each element imparts a 'peculiar quality' to the whole.[39] A change in absolute presuppositions is therefore also a change in the entire structure of the constellation: the old constellation is replaced by a new constellation which not only has a different content as containing new presuppositions and lacking certain old ones, but also has a new form. The new constellation is a new form structured by a new organising principle. The new form differs from the old in degree as a superior representation of the subject matter more adequate to the internal demands of thought; and it differs in kind as a different specification of the concept expressed both through new absolute presuppositions and through a new principle of organisation: the new term in the scale of forms is both a different truth and a better truth.

---

[36] 'Notes Toward a Metaphysic', Notebook, A. pp. 6–8.
[37] E.M., p. 48n.
[38] P.A., p. 107; cf. *Truth and Contradiction*, Chapter Two: 'Thought cannot be patched. A single alteration of detail in a system of thought must be attended by a re-adjustment, indeed a regeneration, of every part of the system.' p. 11.
[39] E.M., p. 76.

We have seen that criticism of absolute presuppositions is an internal process which is generated by the mind's activity in the course of a science or inquiry itself. In this sense we can say that reason is its own criterion, and in this the later Collingwood differs not at all from the earlier, (pace Knox).[40] But the reason involved must always be the internal reasoning of the science or form of experience itself: it can never be the job of the philosopher to come in from the outside and tell the practitioner what to do. Philosophy, in its metaphysical aspect, is nothing more than the elucidation of the principles and presuppositions of any inquiry. It can be done by a practitioner as well as by a philosopher; but in neither case can the metaphysics *in itself* effect any transformation in the inquiry. The transformation arises through the inquiring proceeding now with 'a new firmness and consistency arising out of the scientist's new consciousness of the principles on which he has been working.'[41] Metaphysics cannot criticise absolute presuppositions, it must simply tell us what they are: it cannot change our opinions but 'can and does change (our) opinion as to what (our) opinions really are',[42] and in so doing it enables the practice itself through its clearer understanding of its own nature, to make its own progress in its own way and in its own time. But, in a different sense, metaphysics is critical: not that it can tell us that our absolute presuppositions are false or can in any way directly criticise the ones we do hold; but, if we agree with Collingwood that 'The business of sound theory, in relation to practice, is not to solve practical problems, but to clear them of misunderstandings which make their solution impossible',[43] then we have to accept that metaphysics is critical in the sense that it criticises our conception, our self-understanding, of what we are doing; and its criticism here has consequences for practice. Metaphysics cannot tell us that we are mistaken in presupposing this or that absolute presupposition, but it can tell us that we are mistaken in thinking that we presuppose this or that absolute presupposition.

The question of the relation between theory and practice will be discussed below (pp. 162–77); on the question of the critical element to metaphysics as Collingwood conceives it, E.E. Harris made the general point well:

> What Collingwood calls metaphysical analysis . . . is a method of criticism. It is a process of developing the implications of a proposition and

[40] T.M. Knox, preface to I.H., xviii; and see S.M., p. 45 where Collingwood asserts that criticism must be internal.
[41] I.N., p. 2.
[42] Lectures on Moral Philosophy. 1929, p. 10.
[43] 'Political Action', p. 158.

displaying its connections with others in some systematic body of knowledge the structure of which becomes apparent as we proceed ... But this process cannot go on in vacuo. Only on the basis of a total experience, in the light of which the given propositions from which we begin has meaning and significance, and only by reference to that, can we develop its implications and so discover what it presupposes. And what comes to light as we do so is the systematic structure of that experience itself. Yet, as the system grows, so experience develops and is modified. What was before confused and obscure becomes, by the operation of thought upon it, definite and articulated; ... so that what was before 'known' only vaguely and in 'dim forecast' becomes known precisely and in its explicit relations to the rest of experience.[44]

In a word, self-understanding is dependent upon critical analysis of what we think we know or what we think we presuppose: the more complete our self-knowledge the better we know what we are doing; the better we know what we are doing the easier it is to amend what we are doing if the demands of our science require it.

If for a moment we recall Collingwood's objection to the notion of metaphysics as the science of pure being,[45] we must agree. But what has been rejected is the notion of a study of abstract being: there is nothing in this to disqualify a study of being qua concrete being. Such a concrete being is mind. Rubinoff argues that for Collingwood 'there is only one kind of being which can be made into an object of science, and that is the concrete being of mind.'[46] Now such a science must have a definite subject matter; mind for the psychologist is definite, but it is mind unrelated to its object and studied irrespective of the truth and falsity of its utterances; it is mind studied in the absence of reference to thought as a self-criticizing activity. In other words, psychology studies mind as an object, not as an activity and studies it empirically and not criteriologically: 'The mind, regarded in this external way, really ceases to be a mind at all.'[47] The conception of mind employed by psychology is inadequate.

But. what else might mind be that it may be called 'concrete being'? 'Mind is what it does ... It is nothing except its own activities; but it is all these activities together, not any one separately.'[48] This

---

[44] E. E. Harris, *Nature, Mind and Modern Science*, pp. 36–37.
[45] E.M., p. 14. An objection made on the grounds that a science must be both systematic and about a definite subject matter, and that however systematic a science of pure being might be, its subject matter would be 'entirely devoid of peculiarities; a subject matter, therefore, containing nothing to differentiate it from anything else, or from nothing at all.'
[46] L. Rubinoff, *Collingwood and the Reform of Metaphysics*, p. 162.
[47] R.P., p. 42.
[48] I.H., pp. 226 & 292. Cf. S.M., R.P., N.L., 9.17, O.P.A., pp. 95–6. On the issue of 'mind as pure act' and Collingwood's use of Gentile see H.S. Harris,

conception of mind as 'pure act' runs through Collingwood: and it follows that to study mind is to study its activities; which means that we must study the 'history of mind's activities. We cannot study what mind always and everywhere does, but only what mind has done on certain definite occasions:[49] 'We do not ask what mind is but only what mind does.'[50] What mind does is revealed by its *gesta*,[51] and so the study of mind is a study of 'the wealth achieved by the human mind at a certain stage in its history.'[52] The study of mind is the study of what man has done and thus of what man is.[53] What we study is, then, not being as such; nor is it the 'being' of a mind, for a mind has no 'being' apart from its activity, apart from what it does. We cannot distinguish between what mind is and what it does and study one and not the other: we could not study the 'is', mind's 'being' alone: to attempt such a study would be to try to study a mind which was doing nothing; a mind apart from its thoughts. But if a mind is made of thought[54] there can be no mind apart from thought, which is to say that there could be no mind that was completely at rest.

Mind exists only in its activity, in its movement: it has no being other than what it is doing, and what it is doing is becoming more fully a mind. We might say, therefore, that a mind has no being apart from its becoming; and what follows is that the study of the concrete being of mind is the some as the study of mind in its becoming. Concrete being is becoming: in studying mind we therefore study it historically (as in *The Idea of History* and *The Idea of Nature*), phenomenologically (as in *Speculum Mentis*), as a form of experience (as in *The Principles of Art*), or as consciousness (in *The New Leviathan*).

To resolve philosophy into history, on this view, is not to make philosophy historical — it is to make history philosophical. Philosophy, according to Collingwood's lifelong conception of it, could only become truly philosophical if it became at the some time truly historical. Collingwood summarises his approach in a letter to Ruggiero in 1937:

> A year ago I published a paper on the conception of 'human nature', arguing that what went by that name in the 18th century was really human history, falsely crystallised into a special case of 'nature', and

---

      Introduction to G. Gentile *Genesis and Structure of Society* and his Introduction to 'Gentile 'The Reform of Hegelian Dialectic''. Also Collingwood's brief exposition of Gentile in 'Can the New Idealism Dispense with Mysticism?'
[49] N.L., 9.18.
[50] N.L., 9.16.
[51] N.L., 9.24.
[52] I.H., p. 230.
[53] I.H., p. 10.
[54] N.L., 1.61.

implying that the so-called sciences of mind were faulty in so far as they treat mind as something given, to be analysed like a natural object, instead of something whose only reality is its historical process . . . This thesis involves a programme of recasting the science of mind (including the Crocian science of spirit) into the form of history; not into the form of history *wie sie steht und geht,* but into a form of history, not merely philological but philosophical. The philosophy in it is not, as Croce has said, simply its methodology. The absorption is mutual: the product is not philosophy based on history nor history based on philosophy, it is both these things at once. I think you will understand what I mean, and will very likely say that you have heard it, and thought it, long ago.[55]

For Collingwood, philosophy must be historically rooted; and his name for the aspect of philosophy specifically concerned to study the concrete being of mind is metaphysics. We know, and earlier quotations have shown, that Collingwood's conception of philosophy as necessarily historical can be traced right back to his earliest work: he held this view from the beginning to the end, now emphasising this, now that, but never deviating from his main conviction that philosophy must be 'historical philosophy'. A corollary of this conception is the conception of philosophy in its metaphysical aspect as the science of absolute presuppositions: the question now is, can we trace this view of metaphysics as far back or not? If we can, and if he held that view throughout his life (including throughout the periods when commentators maintain that he held an entirely different view as to the nature of philosophy and metaphysics) then the case for considering that there was no radical 'break' or 'conversion' in Collingwood's thought is strengthened.

3: A Short History of Absolute Presuppositions[56]

We have already seen that *Religion and Philosophy* contains an injunction to the philosopher to study the facts and not to impose theories upon the world: 'his business as a philosopher is to discover what actually are the ideals which govern conduct, and not to speak until

---

[55] Letter to de Ruggiero, June 12th 1937.
[56] In one sense, of course, the history of absolute presuppositions pre-dates Collingwood. For example, the idea of philosophy as the search for fundamental presuppositions can be found in many philosophers. Collingwood's immediate predecessors include J.A. Smith, and F.H. Bradley, who first used the term 'absolute presupposition' in *The Presuppositions of Critical History* (1876), in *Collected Essays*, p. 22. Sir Henry Jones used the terms 'absolute' and 'relative' hypotheses in reference to fundamental presuppositions; for discussion see D. Boucher and A. Vincent, *A Radical Hegelian*. For critical comment on some of the claims made in this section see Rex Martin, introduction to the revised edition of E.M. and Rik Peters, 'Collingwood's Logic of Question and Answer, its Relation to Absolute Presuppositions: Another Brief History'.

he has something to tell us about them.'[57] In his *Autobiography* Collingwood refers to a book he wrote in 1917 entitled *Truth and Contradiction*. This was never published and he declares that he destroyed the manuscript after he wrote his *Autobiography*.[58] However, Chapter Two survived and can be found with the other unpublished manuscripts. This chapter contains a discussion of truth and contradiction which has affinities with the discussion of contradiction in *Ruskin's Philosophy*, the dialectical philosophy of *Speculum Mentis*, the scale of forms analysis of concepts propounded in *Philosophical Method* and the logic of question and answer as presented both in *Speculum Mentis* and in *An Autobiography*. In the latter, Collingwood implies that *Truth and Contradiction* expounded his views on the history of philosophy, the logic of question and answer and the doctrine of metaphysics as the science of absolute presuppositions.[59] However, the surviving chapter of *Truth and Contradiction* does not mention history of philosophy, so the *Autobiography* cannot be confirmed on that point. It does contain a discussion of truth which centres on the notion that 'truth is not a possession but an activity',[60] and this bears a close resemblance to the claims in *An Autobiography* that 'whether a given proposition is true ... depends on what question it was meant to answer',[61] and that truth belongs not to any single proposition, nor to a complex of propositions, but to a 'complex consisting of questions and answers.'[62] Similarly, much of the account of contradiction has affinities with the account given in *An Autobiography*.[63] It also contains a discussion of the relations between theories in which they are conceived as making up a scale very like the scale of forms exhibited in *Speculum Mentis* and expounded in *Philosophical Method*. The significant difference is that Collingwood was dissatisfied with the doctrines of degrees of truth, on the ground that it 'does not succeed adequately in expressing the union of truth and falsehood in every judgement,'[64] but he had not yet at this stage developed the later conception of an overlapping scale whose elements differ not merely in degree but also in kind. On our immediate question — absolute presuppositions — there is silence. From the evidence available all that can be said is that there is nothing which runs counter to the doctrine of metaphysics as the

[57] R.P. p. 60.
[58] A., p. 99n.
[59] A., chapters 5 & 6 and pp. 42 & 74.
[60] T.C., Chapter Two, p. 11.
[61] A., p. 39.
[62] A., p. 37.
[63] R's P. also expresses a similar view to that expressed in T.C.
[64] T.C., Chapter Two, p. 19.

science of absolute presuppositions as I have presented it; but equally there is no direct statement of the doctrine or of anything that could be taken for the doctrine. This does not disprove Collingwood's account of the development of his thought as we simply do not know the content of the missing chapters of *Truth and Contradiction*.

From *Truth and Contradiction* we move to an address presented two years later at the Ruskin centenary conference exhibition at Coniston: *Ruskin's Philosophy*. I have already quoted part of this lecture and I shall take it up again by quoting the succeeding paragraph:

> There are certain principles which the man takes as fundamental and incontrovertible, which he assumes as true in all his thinking and acting. These principles form, as it were, the nucleus of his whole mental life: they are the centre from which all his activities radiate. You may think of them as a kind of ring of solid thought — something infinitely tough and hard and resistant — to which everything the man does is attached. The ring is formed of a number of different ideas or principles, welded together by some force of mutual cohesion ... This central core of convictions ... exists in each one of us, and in that sense every one of us has a philosophy. But for the most part we do not know that we possess it: still less do we know what are the convictions which constitute it. The fact seems to be that a man's deepest convictions are precisely those which he never puts into words. Everything which be says and does is based upon his grasp of these convictions: but just because his grasp of them is so complete, so unquestioning, he never finds it necessary to express them at all. ... (and) we are often quite mistaken as to what these convictions are ... (it is the) attempt to discover what people's philosophy is that marks the philosopher ... only the philosopher makes it his business to probe into the mind and lay bare that recess in which the ultimate beliefs lie hidden.[65]

The close similarity between this and the doctrine put forward in *Metaphysics* is obvious: but there are differences, the most important being that in this address Collingwood treats the fundamental principles as assumptions believed by their holder to be true. However, if we look at this a little more closely the substantive differences evaporate: first, Collingwood's reason for denying that absolute presuppositions were assumptions is that 'to assume is to suppose by an act of free choice.'.[66] Absolute presuppositions are not assumed but presupposed, and presupposition is a logical, not a psychological relation. Exactly the same applies to the 'fundamental principles' of this early address: if they were assumptions they

---
[65] R's P., pp. 6-8.
[66] E.M., p. 27.

would not go unexpressed but would be expressed in the act of assuming them, and if that were so we could not be mistaken as to what these assumptions were. If the 'fundamental principles' of *Ruskin's Philosophy* were ordinary assumptions it would not be possible for Collingwood to go on to say, as he does go on to say, that 'a man's deepest convictions are precisely those which he never puts into words and that we are often quite mistaken as to what these convictions are.'[67] This point is of considerable importance: it appears that before Collingwood explicitly formulated the doctrine of absolute presuppositions he tended to refer to such presuppositions as 'assumptions'. As we shall later see, the context in which the term 'assumption' is used on later (but pre-*Metaphysics*) occasions makes it clear that they are not ordinary assumptions, but assumptions of a special type.

The second difference is that in this address Collingwood refers to these convictions or assumptions as 'true' or 'assumed as true', and at first sight this appears to conflict with the view expressed in *Metaphysics* that absolute presuppositions are neither true nor false. But here again the difference evaporates: these 'central convictions' like absolute presuppositions are never propounded and so the distinction between truth and falsity can hardly apply to them. How can we 'assume as true' something which we never consciously assume in the first place? These central convictions are not derived from experience but are part of our understanding of experience, part of the way in which we approach experience. Collingwood says of one of Ruskin's convictions that 'This principle — the unity and indivisibility of the spirit — Ruskin never questioned and never attempted to prove',[68] and it is easy to see why he did not. In attempting to prove such a proposition we would either presuppose it in our interpretation of things or we would not: either way we are begging the question by presupposing the point at issue. It might be said, 'why should it be presupposed at all prior to proving it?', but this is no way out: assuming for the moment that it would be possible to approach the facts of human history and activity with an 'open mind' (that is without a predisposition to believing in its essential unity or its essential disunity — a possibility which I doubt); then we still could not decide the matter by appealing to the evidence, for it is precisely how that evidence is to be interpreted which is the issue at stake. Given a particular activity or group of activities to study, it would be equally plausible to attend to their diversity, in which case

---

[67] R's.P., pp. 7-8.
[68] R's.P., p. 17.

we go away believing in the *disunity* of the mind; or to attend to their similarity and so go away convinced of the *unity* of the mind. In practice what will happen is that our initial prejudice in favour of one side or the other will be strengthened by our taking evidence favourable to our own viewpoint and ignoring evidence favourable to the opposite viewpoint; or more importantly systematically interpreting evidence according to our initial precepts (which will themselves determine what is to count as evidence) and then using the evidence so interpreted as evidence for those precepts.

The 'central principles' are not judgements; rather they are prerequisites for judgement. They are therefore 'true' in the sense that they really are the principles upon which we think, i.e. in that we do actually presuppose them, but not in any other sense.

The basic point is that absolute presuppositions are not generalisations derived from observation,[69] but are brought to bear upon experience and apply to all possible observations (if they were generalisations they could not be assumed as true or as applying to every possible case) but as Collingwood puts it in *An Essay on Metaphysics*:

> We do not acquire absolute presuppositions by arguing: on the contrary, unless we have them already arguing is impossible to us. How can we change them by arguing; unless they remained constant all our arguments would fall to pieces. We cannot confirm ourselves in them by 'proving' them; it is proof that depends on them, not they on proof... We must accept them and hold firmly to them; we must insist on presupposing them in all our thinking without asking why they should be thus accepted.[70]

Absolute presuppositions are existential commitments arising out of the structure of our thought and action: as logically foundational in that structure they cannot be proved true or false if by that we mean verifying them: our system of thought cannot be checked against reality in order to verify or falsify it; we can no sooner do this than jump out of our own skin in order to take a good look at ourselves.

Ruskin's Philosophy is an interesting and important (though slight) work; and I think that I have showed enough to make it clear that something very like Collingwood's later views on metaphysics is propounded there: about the rest of the text and about its relation to *Truth and Contradiction* I cannot enter into here other than to say that the passages on contradiction and the 'historicist' attitude which

---

[69] See E.M., pp. 149–53.
[70] E.M., p. 173.

Collingwood briefly characterises[71] are very close to what he says about these matters in Chapter Two of *Truth and Contradiction*.[72]

In 'Economics as a Philosophical Science', (published in 1925) Collingwood states that in treating economics philosophically:

> What is intended is ... to throw light on some of the fundamental conceptions which economists do not so much derive inductively from facts as presuppose in their attitude towards the facts conceptions such as wealth, value and the like ... These fundamental or presupposed conceptions of economic science are the subject of this paper. The thesis here advanced is that these conceptions are various aspects of, or various attempts to describe, a certain form of action which ... we shall call economic action.[73]

The similarity between this and the doctrine of metaphysics as the science of absolute presuppositions is obvious and I shall not dwell on it. In 'The Nature and Aims of a Philosophy of History', written in the same year, Collingwood declares that:

> Philosophy of history ... is the study of historical thinking: not only the psychological analysis of its actual procedure, but the analysis of the ideal which it sets before itself ... Historical thought is one among a number of attitudes taken up by the mind towards the objective world ... The philosophy of history must be a critical discussion of this attitude, its presuppositions and its implications: an attempt to discover its place in human history as a whole, its relation to other forms of experience, its origin and validity.[74]

History is to be studied as both an empirical activity and as a form of experience, which means studying it in itself and also in its relations with other forms of experience. The metaphysical aspect is the study of the presuppositions.

In 'Reason is Faith Cultivating Itself' (1927) we find the claim that:

---

[71] R's.P. pp. 9–23.
[72] Rubinoff is right when he says that 'Ruskin's philosophy, ... is probably the closest record we have the of the actual views of *Truth and Contradiction.*' L. Rubinoff, op. cit., p. 230; but I can find no explicit evidence from Chapter Two of *Truth and Contradiction* to substantiate his claim that 'it may be regarded as an early statement of the doctrines of the *Essay on Metaphysics.*' On this we can give no definite answer; Chapter Two itself contains no recognizable statement of the doctrine, but is not incompatible with it; whether such a statement was ever made in another chapter of the book we cannot presently say. For a view which asserts that T.C. does contain such a statement, see Peters, op. cit.
[73] E.P.S., p. 162; (cf. E.P.M., pp. 166–7 on the principles of inductive thinking). What Collingwood says here is substantially the same as his treatment of economic action in N.L., which can best be characterised as a study of the 'presupposed conceptions' of political activity and civilization: it should, in other words, be understood as a metaphysics of politics and civilization.
[74] 'The Nature and Aims of a Philosophy of History', pp. 161–2.

Faith is not irrational, for it is not so much dependent on reason as the ground and source of reason; reason is not the negation of faith, but its development into an articulated system. Every act is fundamentally an act of faith; but it is not a complete act of faith unless it develops into a rational and self-explanatory system of thought... You cannot produce faith by arguing. Faith is presupposed in the argument itself... the function of ratiocination [is] the development of a reasoned statement of what faith finds within itself. [75]

His conclusion is that 'reason is faith cultivating itself',[76] a phrase which could serve as a motto for *An Essay on Metaphysics*. Later the same year Collingwood returned to an examination of the relation between reason and faith in a pamphlet, *Faith and Reason*. Here the account given in the earlier article is continued and developed, through a more detailed picture of the functions, types and content of faith. 'Faith is our attitude toward reality as a whole, reason our attitude towards its details as distinct and separate from each other.'[77] Both reason and faith take three different forms: theoretical, practical and emotional. Faith as theoretical is the knowledge that the universe as a whole is rational; as practical it is the certainty that life is worth living; as emotional it is our feeling towards the world as a whole. Reason as theoretical treats things as objects to be studied and thought about; as practical it is the selection of particular ends to pursue; and as emotional everything excites in us a feeling proper and peculiar to itself.'[78]

> The proper sphere of faith is everything in the collective sense — everything as a whole. The proper sphere of reason is everything in the distributive sense — every separate thing, no matter what. . . . Reason builds upon a foundation of faith, and moves within a system whose general nature must be determined by faith before reason can deal with it in detail.[79]

Faith is the realm of the infinite, the whole; reason is the realm of the finite, the parts of a whole. Faith and reason must lie together or perish: the finite only has meaning as an element in the infinite, and the infinite is nothing but the unity of the finite in its diversity.

> The spirit of faith is shown to be a real spirit by embodying itself in reason, that is, by developing its own assertions, which as undeveloped would be mere abstractions, into a rational system of thought and conduct... Reason, conversely cannot live without faith. The finite is nothing except as part of a whole... Unless there is a whole, a universe, an

---

[75] 'Reason is Faith Cultivating Itself', (R.F.C.I.), p. 118.
[76] R.F.C.I., p. 121.
[77] *Faith and Reason*, (F.R.), p. 140.
[78] F.R. pp. 141–2.
[79] F.R. pp. 143–4.

infinite, there is no science; for there is no certainty beyond the certainty of mere observation and of bare particular fact; whereas science is universal or nothing, and is bankrupt unless it can discover general laws. But this discovery rests on presuppositions concerning the nature of the universe as a whole — laws of thought that are at the same time laws of the real world, not scientifically discovered but embraced by an act of faith, of necessary and rational faith.[80]

The closeness of these views to the central doctrine of *An Essay on Metaphysics* is evident: the absolute presupposition of all science is that the universe as a whole is rational; and the absolute presuppositions of all moral life must be that life is worth living, that the world is open to possibilities and that we are free.[81] The conception of the relation between faith and reason presented in this paper and this pamphlet (and indeed in the other sources which I am presently quoting) is summarised thus in *An Autobiography*: 'metaphysics . . . is primarily at any given time an attempt to discover what the people of that time believe about the world's general nature; such beliefs being the presuppositions of their 'physics', that is, their inquiries into its detail.'[82]

In his review of Spengler's *Decline of the West*, Collingwood again makes some interesting observations on the task of philosophy:

> The philosopher only makes explicit in his own peculiar way an idea which has necessarily been the common heritage of his entire culture . . . All the Greek philosophers, until the decadence, were monotheists; and Spengler knows that philosophy is only a reasoned statement of ideas common to the culture. The monotheism of the philosophers can only indicate a profound strain of monotheism in the whole Graeco-Roman world.[83]

There is, of course, much more to the essay on Spengler than this, but the passages quoted serve, I think, to show the continuity of Collingwood's thought on the nature of philosophy. There is also a highly interesting and suggestive passage in which Collingwood asserts that an 'idea can only live in conflict with its own opposite and unless that opposite is present as an effective force there is no

---

[80] F.R. p. 144.
[81] See E.M. p. 215; I.N. pp. 29–30. This is, of course, a permanent and necessary presupposition (but not the only presupposition) of science, but it is the ground of the other presuppositions, (see below §7). On the presuppositions of moral activity see N.L., chapter XIII; 'The Devil' (on free will); and 'Fascism and Nazism'. For more on the 'emotional charge' attendant on all thought see P.A., chapters VIII and XI.
[82] A., p. 66.
[83] O.S., pp. 313–5.

conflict and no life.'[84] It is Spengler's lack of understanding of this principle that leads him to understand cultures through deduction from one central idea. The passage in its entirety can be read as an amplification of the passage in *An Essay on Metaphysics* which reads: 'where there is no strain there is no history' and proceeds to talk of a 'dynamic logic' lying at the heart of a civilization.[85] This passage runs parallel to the discussion of 'encapsulation' in Chapter XI of the *Autobiography* where Collingwood is trying to account for the revival of Celtic art after the Roman invasion. Another interesting cross reference may be found in the fact that this whole passage is extremely close to the discussion in *Truth and Contradiction* where Collingwood argues that truth 'is an activity partly because every statement must have a contradictory' and that thought is developed only through opposition and hence that without contradiction there could be no thought.[86]

In a review of Charles Gore's *The Philosophy of the Good Life* (1931) Collingwood singled out for attention Gore's treatment of the relation between faith and reason:

> Dr. Gore's view is that they are correlative, so connected that neither can exist without the other. Thus, the Socratic faith in moral values did not rest on argument; but on it, as an ultimate foundation, the fabric of Platonism was built. The scientist's trust that nature will prove 'reasonable' is the presupposition within which the reasonings of science move, and upon which they depend. Anselm's *credo ut intelligam* holds good, therefore, not only in theology but in every department of human thought. All this is profoundly true. But when Dr. Gore says 'it is faith by which we grasp an order in nature', he might have been more explicit, and pointed out that by faith we grasp *that there is an order* in nature, whereas by reason we discover *what kind of order* it is.[87]

This view, expressed before illness and close to the date of composition of *An Essay on Philosophical Method*, goes some way, I suggest, to showing that the conceptions of philosophy propounded in the two *Philosophical Essays* ran concurrently and not consecutively: and that therefore it is a far better procedure to try to reconcile any difficulties that arise between them than to try to separate them and assign them to two different and supposedly unrelated compartments of Collingwood's life and thought.

'The Nature of Metaphysical Study' comprises two lectures given in Balliol College in January 1934 as part of a 'circus' course in meta-

---

[84] *Ibid.*, p. 316.
[85] E.M., p. 75
[86] T.C., pp. 13–14.
[87] Review of C. Gore, *The Philosophy of the Good Life*, pp. 561-2.

physics. Given the date of composition and delivery, these lectures might be expected to be of some interest in ascertaining Collingwood's views on the nature of metaphysics: as we shall see, they show that he understood metaphysics as a study of both the permanent and the transitory; the necessary universal and the historically contingent particular. It is precisely this relation which is of importance in this discussion.

In the first lecture Collingwood begins by describing metaphysics as 'the keep or central stronghold of the castle of philosophy.'[88] He proceeds by conceiving metaphysics as an inquiry in which the empirical or descriptive element is entirely absent: its object, then, is pure; being as such not science or ethics or art of whatever. But, he immediately goes on to say, the notion of pure being is 'a notion which we find it difficult if not impossible to distinguish from nothing.'[89] This leads to the conception that being is not the opposite of nothing but identical with nothing: 'the observation which set us off on this train of inquiry was, that when you *have* grasped the idea of pure being or being in general, you can't distinguish it from nothing.'[90] Being and nothing are the some idea: but we are not denying all distinction between the two concepts, 'only this distinction is one of a peculiar kind: it is a distinction between things which in spite of the distinction are the same.'[91] In finding that pure being is the some as nothing we have found a determination of pure being: pure being sprouts determinations:

> being determines itself as nothing, but this involves finding that it determines itself; that is, discovering that the abstract can, as I say, sprout or grow determinations out of itself, as opposed to receiving them as a gift or burden from somewhere else ... Pure being becomes its own determinations, or *develops* them, for becoming or development is a process of change initiated from within. Pure being is thus not only identical with nothing, it is also identical with becoming'[92] ... The idea of metaphysics in general cannot be grasped in abstraction by a purely formal definition unless we will allow this abstract idea to sprout determinations of its own in the shape of particular metaphysical problems and doctrines.[93]

This dimension of metaphysics is not time-bound or context specific:

> These are not mere instances of metaphysical inquiry ... they are universal and permanent problems and theorems of all metaphysical thought, and you will find that all metaphysicians have at all times and in all

---

[88] 'The Nature of Metaphysical Study', (N.M.S.), pp. 1–2.
[89] N.M.S., p. 4.
[90] N.M.S., p. 7.
[91] N.M.S., p. 7.
[92] N.M.S., p. 11.
[93] N.M.S., p. 13.

places concerned themselves with these ideas, the ideas of being, of nothing, and of becoming, as problems arising necessarily cut of the very nature of metaphysical thought. I cannot explain to you what I think is the general nature of metaphysical study without showing you how that general nature specifies or determines itself into these fundamental problems; and in exhibiting this process I have done all I can towards exhibiting the general character which metaphysical thought has always and everywhere possessed in the past and must always and everywhere possess in the future. But by doing this I have only carried out half of what I conceive my task to be. I have tried to expound the idea of metaphysical inquiry as an inquiry always concerned with the same fundamental problems; being, nothing, becoming, and of course others necessarily arising out of these and their interrelation. Now, this by itself would suggest that the metaphysician always begins again at scratch, having learnt nothing and forgotten nothing since his last incarnation; that the problem is always the same, never advanced or altered in any way by the labour of those who have gone before; that, in a word, there is no such thing as a present situation with which the metaphysician is called upon in a special sense to deal.

This implication would not at all express what I take to be the truth. Every science goes through a process of historical development in which, although the fundamental of general problems remains unaltered, the particular form in which this problem presents itself changes from time to time; and the general problem never arises in its pure or abstract form, but always in the particular or concrete form determined by the present state of knowledge, or, in other words, by the development of thought hereto. This is a universal rule governing all forms of human thought; there can be no reason why metaphysics should be an exception, and indeed the attempt which I have made to formulate the fundamental problems of metaphysics is an attempt which could have been made, in exactly that way, only at the present stage in the history of the world. There is consequently another question to be asked. In this lecture I have tried to answer the question, what is the general nature of metaphysical thought always, everywhere and for everybody? What are the problems with which it is universally concerned? In the next lecture I shall try to answer the question, what are the particular features presented by metaphysical thought today? What are the problems with which metaphysics has especially to concern itself in European countries towards the middle of the twentieth century?[94]

Collingwood begins his second lecture by stating that a period of thought dating from the seventeenth century has closed. Its two principles, which also form the character of modern scientific thought were, first, that nature should be put to the question, through devising experiments and developing theories, and, secondly, that the 'book of nature is written in the language of mathe-

---

[94] N.M.S., pp. 11–4.

matics'; that is, whatever is real in nature is measurable and that this alone demands and admits of scientific treatment.

The first principle depends on the presupposition that 'nature works according to fixed and definite laws, which are exemplified in all that really exists and happens, and that we know in advance of experiment what the general nature of these laws is.'[95] For example, we know independently of experiment that everything in nature has a cause, 'independently and in advance of experiment because unless we did know this, we should not know that experiment could teach us what we wanted to find out.'[96] The second principle presupposes that things in nature are really measurable and that whatever is not measurable is not real:

> This means that things in nature really are extended in space and moving in time, really possess shape and weight and number, but only seem to be, and in reality are not, coloured and scented and sonorous, hot and cold and the like. Whereas Aristotelian and medieval physics had tried in vain to build a successful science of nature on the assumption that all these qualities were equally real, Galileo found it possible to advance and achieve solid results by systematically ignoring secondary qualities as mere appearances, and concentrating on primary qualities as alone real.[97]

Collingwood summarises the argument by emphasising the centrality of these assumptions:

> These two principles are the assumptions on which 17th century science rested, and if that science was to be regarded as real knowledge of the real world these two assumptions must be true. But obviously physical science could not prove their truth; it could only begin to use its own methods when they had been assumed. Their truth was a matter for investigation by metaphysics. Consequently 17th century metaphysics, from Descartes to Locke, took this as one of its main tasks, to prove the truth of these two assumptions. This is a situation so strange to ourselves that I must ask you to reflect on it. No competent judge in the 17th century doubted for a moment that physics and metaphysics were engaged on a co-operative task, playing into each other's hands, each confirming the results achieved by the other. The two fitted each other as a glove fits the hand. The physicist selects certain aspects of nature for study and ignores others; the metaphysician shows that the ones he selects are real, the ones he rejects only apparent. The physicist assumes in advance of any and every experiment that nature must have certain universal characteristics; the metaphysician undertakes to prove that these are the characteristics it must of necessity have. Hence — and this is the key to the intellectual vigour of the 17th century — there is a perfectly harmoni-

---

[95] N.M.S., p. 17.
[96] N.M.S., p. 17.
[97] N.M.S., p. 18.

ous symbiosis of physics and metaphysics; the physicist is assured by the metaphysician that the world really is what in his work he assumes it to be, the metaphysician is assured by the physicist that his a priori theories are vindicated by every appeal to the facts. And neither is subordinated to the other. The metaphysics is not made up to fit the physics, the physics is not deducted from the metaphysics. They develop independently but harmoniously. No wonder that people nowadays who are tired of the squabbles between science and philosophy look back to the 17th century as to a golden age.[98]

Collingwood then observes that, from Berkeley onwards, scientists and philosophers tended to diverge; the philosophers denying that knowledge of anything other than appearance was possible, the science continuing to assume that nature as it knew it was real. It was only in the late nineteenth century that the prevailing phenomenalist philosophy began to be subjected to searching criticism: this was the only alternative to giving up metaphysics and admitting, with the prevailing philosophy, that all knowledge is of phenomena only. This latter line was taken by nineteenth-century scientists: they admitted that all knowledge could only be knowledge of phenomena, but they used the word phenomena without prejudice and assumed all the time that in fact what were called phenomena were realities.[99] Those who chose the former course, that of instituting a searching critique of the prevailing phenomenalism, included amongst their number Ferrier and Grote and Bradley: 'The final outcome and classical expression of this effort is Bradley's *Appearance and Reality*.'[100] Collingwood thought that this book was often grossly misunderstood; and that understood rightly, it is a work of realism, not phenomenalism or subjective idealism: in other words, he claimed Bradley as the 'father of modern realism.'[101]

---

[98] N.M.S., pp. 18-19.
[99] N.M.S., p. 22.
[100] N.M.S., p. 22.
[101] N.M.S., p. 27. On this see also E.M., p. 154; A., p. 16. The analysis of Bradley is developed further in a MS written in December 1933, 'The Metaphysics of F.H. Bradley: An Essay on Appearance and Reality; for discussion see G. Stock, 'Collingwood's Essay on *Appearance and Reality*: some Contemporary Reflections'. Collingwood's assessment of Bradley is, however, qualified. Collingwood is denying that Bradley is a *subjective* idealist: 'In laying down this principle Bradley was founding a new school of metaphysical thought, a school to which almost all philosophers of the English speaking world since 1893 have belonged. The most general name for this school of thought is Realism; but in using that name, with its implied antithesis to Idealism, we must always be careful to think of Idealism as a name not for the objective or absolute idealism of a Plato or a Hegel, but for the subjective or psychological idealism of the nineteenth century.' (p. 27) Collingwood seems to be suggesting that Realism and objective Idealism are not so very far apart: that this was his view is

At this point Collingwood proceeds to an analysis of *Appearance and Reality* and summarises its chief metaphysical doctrines thus: 1) Whatever contradicts itself is not real; 2) Whatever is real is consistent with itself; Collingwood suggests that these doctrines were regarded by Bradley as common place; 3) All appearance qualifies reality, i.e. there is no mere appearance. (This Collingwood regards as 'the crucial and original point in Bradley's doctrine. It marks his revolt against nearly three centuries of phenomenalism, that is, of an attempt to maintain that some appearances at least are mere appearances which in no sense qualify reality.)[102] 4) There are degrees of truth and reality, 'This is the conception ... by which Bradley ... reconciled the denial of mere appearance with the distinction of truth and error.'[103] After further discussing the closeness of Bradley's doctrines to those of the realists and declaring that, in time, the realists might also come to accept the doctrine of the degrees of truth, Collingwood goes on to elucidate the relation between present day metaphysics and present day natural science.

> This, then, is the position in which we stand in metaphysics. After three centuries of attempting in vain to separate appearance from reality, Bradley has shown that the attempt must be given up. Now, the Cartesian metaphysics stood in the closest possible relation ... to the physics of Galileo. How does this new Bradleian metaphysics stand towards the scientific movements of the same age?[104]

Collingwood argues that relativistic physics is realistic in 'that this relativity is relative not to a knowing mind but to a body.' But it is Bradleian in the sense that it is unlike the older physics which distinguished apparent motion from real motion, insists that so-called apparent motions are all real.

> It seems to me that the peculiarity of relativistic physics as distinguished from what is called classical physics lies in its repudiating the distinction between apparent motion and real motion, and this coincides with the peculiarity of Bradleian metaphysics as distinguished from the metaphysics of phenomenalism. Thus, by a simultaneous movement from

---

confirmed by a passage to be found in his 1935 lectures on *Realism and Idealism*. Here Collingwood calls his own position objective idealism and states that it is 'pretty much the same as Whitehead's', and that therefore we might call it realistic as Whitehead does. Collingwood concedes that other realists could disagree with this, but also argues that many realists are subjective idealists or near to it. Collingwood's view is , 'I, like Whitehead, think that the object of perception really is what we perceive it to be only as what Whitehead calls an element in an actual situation that includes as other constituent elements not only the context but also the perceiver.' (p. 54).

[102] N.M.S., p. 26.
[103] N.M.S., p. 26.
[104] N.M.S., p. 28.

both sides, and without any collusion or mutual interference, the breach between physics and metaphysics which dates from Berkeley has been in principle bridged, and there is strong hope, unless I am deceived, that we may be entering on a new era of peace and co-operation between these two branches of human thought, perhaps no less fruitful than the 17th century.[105]

At this point Collingwood turns his attention to the science of mind:

1893, which saw the publication of *Appearance and Reality* saw also the publication of a paper describing how traumatic hysteria — that is, hysteria due to a mental shock in the past — could be cured by bringing up in the patient's mind a clear memory, with all its appropriate emotional accompaniments, of the original shock. That paper, by a young neurologist called Freud, was the death warrant of the old psychology, and the first successful attempt to show how the abnormal psychology of insanity, where what we think is mere appearance, could be linked up with the normal psychology of processes in which what we think is reality. The constant effort of Freud and his school, in spite of many aberrations, has been to break down the division between normal and abnormal psychology, or rather to reinterpret that division in terms of a scale of degrees of self-consciousness. The normal or healthy mind is a mind relatively high on that scale; the abnormal or morbid is one relatively unable to achieve consciousness of itself; and the process of becoming sane or healthy in mind is a process of coming to know oneself. Obeying Spinoza's precept to form a clear and healthy idea of one's own passions, and trusting Spinoza's promise that when we have done this *passio* as such will disappear and be replaced by *actio*.

This is a psychology which fits the metaphysics of Bradley . . . as a hand fits a glove. If the real is the self consistent, it follows that conflict in the mind is an appearance, to be removed by clearer self-knowledge; if all appearances qualify reality, these conflicts, however morbid, are not mere disease but realities at a low level of self-consciousness; if there are degrees of reality, they are progressively resolved as the mind becomes more truly a mind, more aware of itself.

Here again, then, there is a kind of pre-established harmony between the new metaphysics and the new psychology — and these facts, I suggest, give an orientation and an impulse to the work of the modern metaphysician. His special task, I conceive, is this: to begin from Bradley, with the principle that all appearances belong to or qualify reality, and with that principle in mind to approach the physics of Einstein and the psychology of Freud in the same spirit of free co-operation in which Descartes approached the physics of Galileo, or Locke that of Newton: to think out such ideas as consciousness and unconsciousness, sublimation and repression, four-dimensional space-time and a finite universe, with a clear understanding that these ideas cannot be mere fictions of the human mind, having no basis in reality, for that would make them mere appearances, and there are no mere appearances. It is for the metaphysician of today to work out a general conception of reality into which these

---

[105] N.M.S., p. 29.

findings of modern science will dovetail naturally: to the mutual comfort and confirmation of metaphysics and science. This is an opportunity granted to metaphysics 300 years ago, when the foundations of modern science and modern psychology were being laid; now for the first time it is offered again, at an intellectual crisis in which are being laid the foundations of a new age . . . (this) is how we ought to conceive the special nature and function of metaphysical inquiry at the present time.[106]

I have quoted at length from these two lectures because I consider them to be of some importance in tracing the development of Collingwood's thought. The similarities to the later doctrine of *An Essay on Metaphysics* are obvious; certain differences are also apparent. I shall now deal with these differences and see whether or not, after examination, the substance of the difference cannot be overcome.

One difference might be that in these two lectures Collingwood regards science and metaphysics as simultaneously arriving at the same conceptions and so fitting each other as a 'hand fits a glove'; the task of the metaphysician being to analyse and elaborate these conceptions, the task of the scientist to operate in accordance with them. In *An Essay on Metaphysics* he often writes as if the science came first in time, and metaphysics arrived afterwards: however, as can be seen from taking a close look at what he writes in that essay, this is not his true view. 'The priority affirmed in the word presupposition', he affirms, 'is logical priority.'[107] In other words, the presuppositions of science, which are the object of investigation for metaphysics, are *prior* to the practice of science, where by 'prior' is meant not temporally but logically prior. However, reflection upon what these presuppositions are and what they mean and imply is temporally posterior to the science. This would seem to indicate that the science must come first and the metaphysics second, but here again we must be careful. First, to talk as if metaphysics has nothing to do until science has been operating with the new conceptions for some time is to ignore the historical side of the question. Prior to any given conception being employed in science or analysed by metaphysics, both science and metaphysics have already been in existence, each with its own inherent problems and methods and each with problems and methods derived from the other. Science and metaphysics constantly cross-fertilise one the other, and so it is a matter for little surprise that conceptions and doctrines should arise simultaneously in both as a result of the internal necessity generated by the progress of each discipline: and this brings us to the second

[106] N.M.S., pp. 29–31.
[107] E.M., p. 21.

point. Even if we accept that, in some sense, the particular inquiry comes first in time and reflection upon that inquiry second, it is still a mistake to suppose that there are periods of inquiry lasting a number of years followed by periods of reflection lasting for a similar time. Collingwood discusses this very point in *The Idea of Nature*, and what he says there is directly relevant to what he says in the above two lectures.

> Such a contrast between 'periods' of non-philosophical thinking and subsequent 'periods' of philosophizing is perhaps what Hegel meant to assert in his famous lament, at the end of the preface to the *Philosophie des Rechts*: 'When philosophy paints its grey in grey, a form of life has aged; and grey in grey does not enable us to make it young again, but only to know it. The owl of Minerva begins to fly only at the coming of dusk.' If that was what Hegel meant, he made a mistake . . . in fact, the detailed work seldom goes on for any length of time without reflection intervening. And this reflection reacts upon the detailed work; . . . What I have just said may be put by saying that natural science must come first in order that philosophy may have something to reflect on; but that the two things are so closely related that natural science cannot go on for long without philosophy beginning; and that philosophy reacts on the science out of which it has grown by giving it in future a new firmness and consistency arising out of the scientist's new consciousness of the principles on which he has been working.[108]

This is very much to the point. Nowhere in the above lectures does Collingwood say or imply that philosophy, specifically Bradley's philosophy, arose in a vacuum. On the contrary, it arose out of reflection on the prevailing phenomenalism, that is out of reflection on philosophy's own problems; and also out of reflection on the science and intellectual life of its time. The four principles which Collingwood abstracts from Bradley were not simply Bradley's inventions nor were they simply derived from the science of the time: they were both at once, arising out of the progress of philosophy, the progress of science and their mutual relations. Further, as was only to be expected, neither the principles nor the science continue in their work without each reacting upon the other. The principles propounded by Bradley further both our understanding of science, and science's understanding of itself; and the work of science continually provides a spur to reflection and subsequent modification of the principles which were first clearly enunciated (but not necessarily originated) by philosophical thought.[109]

---

[108] I.N., pp. 1-2.
[109] Although Collingwood does not mention the point, his own E.P.M. is both a continuation and a refinement of Bradley's work. His doctrine of a scale of forms differing in both degree and kind arose out of a dissatisfaction with a scale

The second difference between these lectures and *An Essay on Metaphysics* is that in the lectures Collingwood refers to the principles underlying seventeenth century science as *assumptions*. These two principles or assumptions are discussed in the later *Essay* as the 'absolute presuppositions' of seventeenth century science.[110] In that later work Collingwood says that 'To assume is to suppose by an act of free choice';[111] in this sense, the two principles of seventeenth century science are not assumptions. They were logically presupposed in the workings of natural science since Galileo, not assumptions made consciously and temporally prior to that science. In writing that 'the book of nature is written in the language of mathematics' Galileo was declaring that the presupposition that what is real in nature is measurable must be made; he was not asking that it be assumed as true: 'he was making a fighting speech'[112] on the side of scientific progress. He was rejecting an Aristotelian science of quality in favour of a 'Platonic' science of quantity, and he was doing this not by saying 'assume this' but by declaring that his way of doing science was the only way in which, at the time, progress in science was assured; that this science absolutely presupposed that mathematics was applicable to everything in nature, and that therefore the progress of science depended on this presupposition being made.

The third difference between the lectures and *Metaphysics* concerns the 'truth' of the assumptions employed in 17th century science. Now, if I am correct in denying that they are assumptions, then, as absolute presuppositions, they can be neither true nor false. In discussing *Ruskin's Philosophy* above, I addressed this question, and concluded that in *Metaphysics*, Collingwood meant by true and false what can or cannot be verified. In this sense of 'true and 'false' the two principles *cannot* be verified: they are presupposed prior to observation and hence no observation could serve to verify them. They are not generalisations derived from observations, but absolute presuppositions constitutive of the world of nature as we observe it. If we find nature to be amenable to mathematical treatment that can only be because we presuppose it at the outset of our inquiry: there could be no possible sense in which we could empirically prove, (and prove for every possible case) that the world of nature was essentially an applied mathematics and hence that math-

---

which (like Bradley's) differs only in degree. On this see also T.C., which shows Collingwood attempting to come to terms with Bradley's doctrine of degrees of truth and reality while not accepting it in its entirety.
[110] E.M., p. 250 and Part IIIA.
[111] E.M., p. 27.
[112] E.M., p. 250.

ematics was applicable to everything in it. To prove such a proposition we should have to examine each realm of nature (prior to our scientific examination) to see whether or not it was measurable. In so doing we would either presuppose that it could be measured, thereby rendering our measuring superfluous because adding nothing to our already existing certainty that nature could be measured. Alternatively, we might not presuppose that it could be measured, and thus either defer our scientific inquiry until it had been proved that every possible aspect or realm of nature, past, present and future, could be understood as an applied mathematics (which is logically impossible), or we might take the view that the only way to see whether something is measurable is to try to measure it, in which case we would in effect do all our measurements twice — leading to the conclusion that it would be more economical to have presupposed that mathematics was applicable to everything in nature from the outset. This would of course lead us back to the original presupposition.

The same sort of argument applies to the four principles which Bradley enunciates. None could be said to be derived from experience, if this means that they have been observed or verified. They are not derived from experience because they are our means of interpreting what we find in experience. We hold these presuppositions not because they have been proved or empirically verified (which they could never be as they are what makes such verification or proof possible) but because the necessity of our thought leads us to think in these terms.

For example, how can we possibly know, empirically, that all appearances qualify reality? To answer this question empirically, we are, as it were, on the wrong side of appearance; our experience is of appearance, but we believe it to be not experience of mere appearance, but experience of reality appearing. Yet at no point can we apprehend reality apart from its appearance to us; for us reality is as it appears to be for us, not as it is in itself. We cannot, therefore, look at the matter from the standpoint of reality and empirically verify that appearances do indeed qualify reality; rather, we are led to assert that all appearance qualifies reality and that hence there is no mere appearance because the inner necessity of our thought leads us to that position. In this sense, therefore, these principles are not verifiable and cannot be regarded as true or false in the sense in which those terms apply to propositions which are the answers to questions (i.e. to relative presuppositions). We are justified, I therefore maintain, in describing these metaphysical principles of Bradley's as absolute presuppositions.[113]

Yet it is not false to maintain that the job of the metaphysician is to prove the truth of these presuppositions; all that has to be established is that by their 'truth' Collingwood does not mean their truth as propositions about empirical matters of fact. Collingwood himself tells us what is meant by asserting the truth of a metaphysical proposition: 'it seems to me that what we mean in calling a metaphysical proposition true is that we do actually presuppose it in our thinking':[114] asserting the truth of an absolute presupposition is the some as asserting that we do actually presuppose it. But this is not the end of the matter. If Collingwood uses the terms 'true' and 'false' in relation to absolute presuppositions merely in the sense of 'what can or cannot be empirically verified' this leaves open the possibility that there may be another (stronger) sense in which it would be correct to say that absolute presuppositions were true or false. [115]

An absolute presupposition is absolute for the science or inquiry in which it is made: logically absolute and therefore not in need of empirical verification. Absolute presuppositions are not propositions as they are not answers to questions and the metaphysician's business is not to propound them but to propound the proposition that this or that one of them is presupposed.[116] But there is still an answer to be made to those who ask why we do presuppose this or that presupposition and this answer is provided by investigation into the history of thought: 'a mere inventory of our intellectual possessions at the present time can never show by what right we enjoy them. To do this there is only one way: by analysing them instead of merely describing them, and showing how they have been built up in the historical development of thought.'[117] Our intellectual possessions (that is, our absolute presuppositions) are not derived from experience but are 'catalytic agents which the mind must bring out

---

[113] See E.M., where Collingwood deals with Ayer's treatment of Bradley: 'In his chapter on "The Elimination of Metaphysics" he gives further examples: Bradley's sentence 'the Absolute enters into, but is itself incapable of evolution and progress which he evidently takes to be the statement not of an absolute presupposition made on occasions of a certain kind but of a would-be proposition about an empirical matter of fact which is not even in principle verifiable and therefore has no literal significance . . . ' E.M., p. 164.
[114] 'Function of Metaphysics in Civilization', p. 45 (cf. E.M. & A. pp. 66–7).
[115] On this see J. Connelly, 'Bradley, Collingwood and the 'Other Metaphysics''.
[116] E.M., p. 33.
[117] I.H., p. 230. Cf. S.M., p. 309, 'The life of the spirit cannot be described except by repeating it: an account of it would just be itself.'

of its own resources to the manipulation of . . . experience and the conversion of it into science and civilization . . . If they were once lost, they could never be recovered expect by repeating the same kind of process by which they were originally created.'[118]

Absolute presuppositions can, therefore, be justified by investigation into the history of thought: we can answer the question why people think in terms of a particular presupposition or category by investigating the history of their thought and the history of that category and show how they came to think in that way. This is indeed one of the functions of the metaphysician.[119] Now it is at this point that we can begin to bring in mention of the metaphysician justifying absolute presuppositions or proving them true. If we accept that absolute presuppositions are 'catalytical agents which the mind brings out of its own resources' then it follows that the history of the absolute presuppositions of a civilization or science is a history of the mind(s) (i.e. thought) of that science or civilization. The essence of mind is thought, that is, rationality: thus if we are investigating the history of mind we are investigating the history of rationality. In investigating mind historically it is a fair assumption to make that change in its categories and principles arises not through contingency or accident but out of the internal requirements of that thought itself. Collingwood at the end of *An Essay on Philosophical Method* suggests that just as the assumption that nature is rational is not only legitimate but obligatory for the scientist, so the assumption that the history of thought has been on the whole rational and a record of achievement and progress is both legitimate and obligatory for the philosopher.[120]

This, I think, provides the answer. By studying the history of thought the metaphysician is at the same time tracing the development of different modes of thought, of different presuppositions, categories and principles which thought has developed out of its own resources: the metaphysician is still not free to say that we ought not to think in a certain way, i.e. that a particular absolute presupposition is empirically false. The most he can do is to justify our present thought and its presuppositions by exhibiting it as the outcome of a sequence of rational thought; and also pinpoint tensions and strains in the fabric of our thought. In so far as this results in conceptual change this change comes about not through an absolute presupposition (or group of presuppositions) having been proved false, but through their having become unnecessary or leading to

[118] E.M., p. 197.
[119] A., p. 66 & E.M., pp. 73–4.
[120] E.P.M., pp. 225–6.

false conclusions. Thus they would not be rejected as false but because they were no longer a necessary part of our thought.

David Rynin makes several acute observations on this point:

> We may reject a 'whole system' in favour of another 'simpler' one when each is able to account for the facts, or when one, but not the other is incompatible with experience, i.e. with the outcome of crucial tests, or rather entails them; but it is not the case, necessarily, that when one whole complex is rejected its absolute presuppositions are rejected with it, although they may be; nor is it the case that if the absolute presuppositions are rejected, they necessarily are rejected as false. All that logic requires is that we reject the system as a whole when we can derive false statements from it, i.e. that we acknowledge that not all the premises (assumptions) can be true. Which is the culprit neither logic nor methodology can of themselves tell us, and a fortiori they cannot tell us that all the absolute presuppositions are false, or that any are for that matter. Methodology does tell us to reject the less simple of competing systems otherwise equally reconcilable with the facts. But this does not rest on the assumption that some of the absolute presuppositions of the more complex systems are false, but only on the assumption that the simpler system is more useful or efficient.[121]

Conceptual change takes place, then, not through the rejection of absolute presuppositions as 'false' or 'untrue', but through the relative explanatory power of competing conceptual systems. And the question of 'progress' in thought depends not on the superior 'truth' of a constellation of absolute presuppositions, but on their capacity to explain. Philosophical progress is a scale of forms in which we consider there to have been progress when (as Collingwood put it in his 1936 lectures on the philosophy of history) 'thought in its first phase, after solving the initial problems of that phase, is then, through solving these, brought up against others which defeat it; and if the second solves these further problems without losing its hold on the solution of the first, so that there is gain without any corresponding loss ... there is progress.'[122]

In so far as the metaphysician is engaged, in the present day, with present day principles and categories of thought, his work of elucidation, definition and clarification will be a part of the rational process he is reflecting on itself, and hence his activities will be critical in that through his work the principles on which we think will be more fully understood and our thinking clearer and better. Rational change comes about through rational understanding of the principles lying at the heart of our thought: the better our grasp of those principles the more powerful our thought and therefore the greater

[121] Rynin, op. cit. pp. 321-2.
[122] I.H., p. 324.

the pressure to modify that thought when it is felt to be inadequate. And ultimately we have to ask the question 'how can we ever satisfy ourselves that the principles on which we think are true, except by going on thinking according to those principles and seeing whether unanswerable criticisms of them emerge as we work?'[123]

The metaphysician cannot anticipate the history of thought, but can only approach it internally. His work is a contribution to the internal development of thought, and progress in thought is solely due to the internal demands and requirements of thought itself, of which the logical analysis of the metaphysician acts as the grit in the oyster. Dorothy Emmet makes the point well by suggesting that Collingwood could be described as a 'radical idealist' for whom all that we are left with is the developing system of thought itself. In this system, she suggests, we cannot ask whether ideas expressed in this system are 'true of reality', because:

> There is no relation between the system of thought and a reality outside it. Our criterion of objectivity must be found within the system itself; and the criterion is not that of truth and falsehood ... but of whether certain assumptions are necessarily made at certain stages in order to make possible the development of the dialectical process of the system of thought itself ... The criterion which disciplines the process is internal to the process itself ... 'truth' here must mean that answer to a question which the evidence at our disposal obliges us to give. The strength of this coherence theory is ... that it recognises that in thought we cannot get outside the boundaries of experience, and compare ideas with things in themselves, or 'real' physical objects in themselves. We can only be aware of anything in so far as we know it through the interpretive forms of our experience.[124]

This, it seems to me, expresses precisely what Collingwood was driving at. Systems of thought change according to their own internal dynamic and according to their own internal criterion: by exhibiting the history of a constellation of absolute presuppositions the metaphysician is also justifying them and in a sense proving them true. The metaphysician cannot say that an absolute presupposition is true or false in itself; but even though limited to propounding the proposition that this or that absolute presupposition was or is held by this or that group of people, the very recognition that a particular absolute presupposition is being made is a recognition of its 'truth':

---

[123] I.H., p. .230.
[124] D.M. Emmet, *The Nature of Metaphysical Thinking*, pp. 75–7.

if it is being made then it is being made (or has been made) as a consequence of the inner necessity of the developing system of thought.[125]

Perhaps we can ask a further question: how absolute are absolute presuppositions? Clearly for each science or form of inquiry at any given time absolute presuppositions are logically absolute; but might it not be that from the point of view of philosophy they lose their absoluteness? What I do not mean is that the metaphysician is in a position to ask of an absolute presupposition (as Donagan suggests they can do)[126] whether it is true or false. This would be to convert it into a relative presupposition, that is, into a proposition which is the answer to a question. I do not mean this, because I wish to retain the understanding of absolute presuppositions as absolute: that is, not as answers to questions but as logically prior to all questions. By suggesting that an absolute presupposition can, when viewed philosophically, lose its absoluteness, I do not wish to deny that within the system of thought in which it functions it remains absolute. To suggest that absolute presuppositions could be converted into relative presuppositions simply by asking of them whether or not they are true or false is to deny that absolute presuppositions exist. The point I am making is this: given the existence of absolute presuppositions (and all that connotes); is it not the case that the metaphysician in delineating a constellation of absolute presupposition, in presenting it as a *catalogue raisonné* (or a scale of forms) in which the conceptual connections are clearly defined, and in placing that constellation within an historically developing scale of forms of constellations of absolute presuppositions; is it not the case that he is displaying what we might call the 'relative absoluteness' of absolute presuppositions? Each absolute presupposition is absolute relative to its position in the developing system of thought of which it is an integral and necessary part; but equally, as a constituent in the developing system of thought it is only relatively absolute. It is absolute at any given moment, but (seen from the point of view of the whole historical sequence) its absoluteness is relative to the internal demands of that whole sequence. Thus each absolute presupposition is relative in respect of the whole, and it is the whole itself which is truly absolute.

Metaphysics, as an historical science, cannot view the developing system of thought (e.g. science or history) from any absolute standpoint for the simple reason that the system is still developing: the

---

[125] See E.M., p. 28, where Collingwood claims that the logical efficacy of a supposition does not depend on its being supposed to be true. The 'truth' of an absolute presupposition in such a system is its logical efficacy.
[126] Donagan, op. cit., p. 76.

most the metaphysician can say on issuing his interim report is, 'so far has consciousness reached'; but even though he reaches only a provisional, a relative and not an absolute end, he is nonetheless viewing the historical sequence as a whole so far as it has come, and in so viewing it he can discern the relativity of presuppositions which when first trade, were absolute. All this is implicit in Collingwood's injunction to the metaphysician 'to follow the historical process by which one set of presuppositions has turned into another.'[127] It is also exhibited in the history of systems of absolute presuppositions provided in *The Idea of Nature* and *The Idea of History*.

Errol Harris summarises the argument:

> The metaphysician ... discovers the absolute presuppositions of science ... by reflection upon the nature of the experience which the science investigates. The form of his argument ... is 'If our experience is to be such as it is and if such-and-such propositions are to be made in science, then such-and-such presuppositions ... are necessarily implied'. But the principles he discloses, though *a priori* for the scientist (absolutely presupposed by him), are so only because of the admitted nature of experience. Experience, as we have it, is prior to the absolute presuppositions and is presupposed in them. If our experience were other than it is, the a priori elements in science would be different. Accordingly, the presuppositions which are absolute for science are for philosophy relative to experience. They are the defining characteristics of experience.[128]

From the point of view of experience as a whole, then, we may say that absolute presuppositions are relative; or, as Harris expresses it, 'the presuppositions which are absolute for science prove to be relative when viewed philosophically. Using Kantian ... language we may say that they are empirically absolute but transcendentally relative.'[129] Harris goes on to assert that absolute presuppositions, viewed philosophically, are no more than the basal hypotheses of the sciences, and that therefore it is perfectly in order for the philoso-

---

[127] E.M., p. 73. This is not the same claim as that made in E.M. (pp. 97–8) where Collingwood discusses the possibility of an absolute presupposition being converted into a relative presupposition. This might occur, but I am attempting to establish a conception of all absolute presuppositions as (viewed historically and philosophically) 'relatively absolute'. It is not that they lose their status as absolute within the system of thought of which they are constitutive; but that each particular system of thought, seen in the light of the whole historically developing system of thought, is only a part of the whole, i.e. is relative and not absolute: or, to put it another way, each particular system is a term in an historically developing scale of forms and therefore the absolute presuppositions of each particular system are absolute only relatively to each system, and are only relatively absolute in relation to the scale of forms as a whole.

[128] E.E. Harris, *Nature, Mind and Modern Science*, pp. 37–8.

[129] Harris, op. cit., p. 36.

pher to criticise and cancel them. This, of course, is denied in *An Essay on Metaphysics*, and rightly.[130] Here Harris's view damages Collingwood's account by detracting from the self-supportive character of the sciences; for, as Collingwood repeatedly asserts, 'to criticise the conceptions of science is the work of science itself as it proceeds; to demand that such criticism should be anticipated by the theory of knowledge is to demand that such a theory should anticipate the history of thought.'[131]

The sense in which we are justified in saying that absolute presuppositions are 'empirically absolute and transcendentally relative' is not the sense in which philosophy, qua philosophy, is entitled to dictate the conceptions and presuppositions of the sciences. It is simply the recognition that, viewed from a standpoint encompassing the entire developing system of experience and thought (of a science), the presuppositions which were absolute in their particular context appear as only relatively absolute when set against the whole sequence of which they were a necessary, but now superseded, part. Against this general background presuppositions which were once absolute become relative to the whole: not just that they are superseded, but also that, in a sense, from this viewpoint, even their original incarnation as absolute presuppositions loses its character as absolute in the light of their later supersession. Explicitly absolute presuppositions are absolute; implicitly, as an integral element in an evolving system of thought they are only relatively absolute.

At this point I shall not pursue further the other obvious difference between the lectures on metaphysics and the *Essay on Metaphysics*, the notion of metaphysics as the science of pure being: this will be dealt with below. Neither shall I dwell on the 'Function of Meta-

---

[130] Harris, op. cit., p. 36, and see E.M., Chapter XV. Collingwood is right to deny that it is the business of the metaphysician to 'cancel' or 'remove' absolute presuppositions. He did, however, make a mistake in identifying 'presuppositions' and 'hypotheses'. From this it follows that he interpreted Plato as enjoining the philosopher to 'remove' or 'cancel' absolute presuppositions. If, on the other hand, we take 'hypotheses' to be not absolute presuppositions, but rather hypotheses as to the content of our absolute presuppositions, then E.M. fits into place with E.P.M. and also agrees with itself. Earlier we saw Collingwood presenting Hegel's dialectic as a method by which the philosopher corrects errors *about* our presuppositions, not errors *in* our presuppositions. The metaphysician starts with certain hypotheses as to the absolute presuppositions in his field of study and as the inquiry progresses some hypotheses are confirmed and others not. If one of the hypotheses is incorrect then it is 'cancelled' or 'removed' and another is advanced in its place. This account of the nature of hypotheses in metaphysics also accords with Collingwood's statements in E.P.M., see chapter VIII, 'Deduction and Induction'.

[131] I.H., p. 230.

physics in Civilization' as the main points of immediate interest have already been considered. It neither throws little new light on the development of Collingwood's thought nor adds significantly to the account of the science of absolute presuppositions presented in *An Autobiography* and *An Essay on Metaphysics*. There is, however, one obvious difference: at no point does its argument invoke or rely on the logic of question and answer.[132]

Now that this short history of the development of the conception of metaphysics as the science of absolute presuppositions has been completed, we can move on to a fuller discussion of the types of philosophical concept and the question of the permanence of absolute presuppositions and the permanence of philosophical problems.

4: Philosophical Concepts and Absolute Presuppositions

What sort of concepts are typical of philosophy? We have already seen that philosophy as metaphysics studies absolute presuppositions; that the specific classes of a philosophical genus do not exclude one another but overlap one another; and that philosophy studies the principles running through experience: but we have not yet answered the question of the relation between these things, nor do we yet know what a 'philosophical concept' is. Certain concepts, Collingwood reminds us, have long been known as exceptions to the rules of classification. The Aristotelian categories, e.g. goodness, are predicable under all the categories;[133] the *unum, verum, bonum* are predicable of anything whatever; the concepts of identity and difference are predicable of anything including each other; being and nothing were claimed by Hegel to be indistinguishable from one another, and so on.[134] Concepts of this type were called by the scholastics 'transcendental concepts'.

In his 1929 lectures on moral philosophy Collingwood wrote that:

> Philosophy deals with conceptions of a peculiar kind, namely those which in traditional philosophical language are called transcendentals. A 'universal' conception (in traditional philosophical language) . . . is one which holds good of a number of particulars, each of which is an instance of it . . . Now a 'transcendental' is a conception of which everything is an instance. *Quodlibet ens*, we are told, *est unum, verum, bonum*. In other words, Unity, Reality and Goodness are said by this ancient

---

[132] For a discussion of 'Function of Metaphysics in Civilization' in this context, see Rex Martin, Introduction to the revised edition of E.M.
[133] E.P.M., p. 32.
[134] Mink, *Mind, History and Dialectic*, p. 69.

maxim to be transcendentals. Whenever we can say 'everything that exists is X' then, whatever term that can be put in the place of X, that term is a transcendental.[135]

He then goes on to point out that everything is an instance of every transcendental, and that there is therefore no point in trying to show the meaning of a transcendental conception by producing instances of it. We have no way of knowing which transcendental conception a particular object is meant to be an instance of: each will be an instance of all transcendental conceptions: for example, a book is a unity, a reality, a plurality and so on.[136]

There are some concepts which have a dual significance; they are used in different ways and undergo a regular and uniform change in meaning when they pass from one meaning to another. These concepts may be said to have two phases, a non-philosophical and a philosophical phase.[137] The two phases are closely related, but nonetheless there is a definite distinction: a non-philosophical (or empirical) concept applies only to a certain class of things, whereas a philosophical concept applies to every possible instance, that is, to reality as a whole:

> When a concept has a dual significance, philosophical and non-philosophical, in its non-philosophical phase it qualifies a limited part of reality, whereas in its philosophical it leaks or escapes out of these limits and invades the neighbouring regions, tending at last to colour our thought of reality as a whole. As a non-philosophical concept it observes the rules of classification, its instances forming a class separate from other classes; as a philosophical concept it breaks these rules, and the class of its instances overlaps those of its co-ordinate species.[138]

An interesting illustration of the nature of concepts with dual significance is given by Collingwood in his 1930 pamphlet, *The Philosophy of History*: 'if anyone says that matter and motion are the only things that exist, he is talking not physics but philosophy. The biologist studies organisms; but Professor Whitehead, when he says that the world is an organism . . . is being a philosopher, not a biologist.'[139]

We have now established that philosophy studies a particular type of concept: philosophical or transcendental concepts; but what we do not yet know are the variety of different types of philosophical concepts. In *The Philosophy of History*, Collingwood maintains that

---

[135] Lectures on Moral Philosophy, 1929, p. 2.
[136] *Ibid.*
[137] E.P.M., pp. 33–4; also E.P.S., pp. 162–3 where Collingwood distinguishes empirical and philosophical concepts.
[138] E.P.M., p. 35.
[139] P.H., p. 1.

the philosopher studies those attributes of things which they share with all other things whatever; in doing this the philosopher might use, say, an egg, as an instance of unity and existence and so forth, but a stone or an ink pot would do equally well. There is no philosophy of eggs or ink pots or stones: 'Philosophy studies the universal and necessary characteristics of things: science their particular and contingent characteristics.'[140]

Thus, if there is to be a philosophy of history, history must, like the logical categories, be a universal and necessary characteristic of things:

> When we speak of the philosophy of art, the philosophy of religion, the philosophy of history, and so forth, either we are abusing language and confusing our minds, or else we are suggesting that art or religion or history is somehow a universal and necessary characteristic of things, not merely a particular and contingent characteristic of a certain group of things . . . If the philosophy of art is the study of certain things called works of art, and of the minds of certain people called artists, then it studies only a selected part of the world, not the world as a whole; it is science, not philosophy; and its methods ought to conform to the model of scientific (in this case psychological) research, not that of philosophical thinking. If it is to be a branch of philosophy, it must be able to show that, in the sense in which it uses the word art, every work is a work of art, locomotives and business letters no less that statues and sonnets; it must even show that natural objects are *objets d'art*, and that every man is an artist. 'The philosophy of something' is a legitimate phrase only when the 'something' in question is no mere fragment of the world, but is an aspect of the world as a whole — a universal and necessary characteristic of things.[141]

What this implies is that in addition to the logical categories or transcendentals studied by philosophy, there is another type of transcendental concept which is also studied by philosophy. This type of concept is what Collingwood calls in *Speculum Mentis* 'a form of experience': each concept of this kind is a universal and necessary category or habit of mind or as Collingwood describes them in the 'Die' manuscript 'a universal or necessary form of human activity.'[142]

Some philosophical concepts are logical categories which operate as logical presuppositions of all experience and thought; other philosophical concepts are forms of experience.

---

[140] *Ibid.*
[141] P.H., p. 2. There might have been less confusion and fewer misunderstandings of P.A. had this been borne in mind by its readers.
[142] 'Outlines of a Philosophy of History', 1928 , p. 1, written in le Martouret, Die, France.

The subject matter of philosophical study is, then, twofold: first a study of the logical categories of thought; this is precisely the role Collingwood reserves for metaphysics in the first lecture on 'The Nature of Metaphysical Study' quoted above. The study of such categories, their interrelationships and their transformations must always be at the heart of philosophy qua metaphysics. There is no evidence that I can find to substantiate the claim that Collingwood ever denied the existence of such categories: therefore I would maintain against Knox[143] that Collingwood at no point ceased to believe in 'the possibility of metaphysics as a separate study, distinct altogether from history, a study of 'the One, the True, and the Good.' These categories, as transcendental concepts, must be and must always remain the object of study by metaphysics. However, as is clear from the lectures on 'The Nature of Metaphysical Study', metaphysics will always be more than this. These categories are a necessary prerequisite for all thought and are predicable of all reality; but metaphysics has a history of its own and, therefore, the precise way in which we approach these questions (being, nothing, becoming; *unum, verum, bonum*, etc.) will alter over time and with the philosophical context in which these predicates are employed. The character of the objects of which they are predicated will likewise alter. Further, as Collingwood insists, metaphysics not only has its own history, but also studies a subject matter with a history of its own, and the example he gives in the lectures is that of the relation between metaphysics and physics — an historical relation in which metaphysics deals not only with the timeless and necessary attributes of any possible science, but also with the time-bound particular presuppositions and methodological problems of each. This brings us to our second point: the subject matter of philosophy is not restricted to the timeless categories alone; it also comprises particular inquiries, sciences, activities, and so forth. What it studies are not only the categories of all possible experience, but also the historically existing character of particular aspects of experience. It therefore studies for example the history of science and the history of historical studies[144] and it studies art, religion, ethics, politics and history as contemporary activities.[145] In each of these activities we are presented not with a single unchanging subject matter, but with a subject matter which undergoes change and development; and philosophy studies each subject matter not as a timeless entity but in

---

[143] Preface to I.H., x–xi.
[144] As in I.N. and I.H.
[145] As in P.A., R.P., the Lectures on Moral Philosophy, N.L., the Epilegomena to I.H, and S.M.

its change and development; and furthermore, it does this because it sees this as the only possible entry point into the subject matter as a whole. Such a subject matter is conceived by philosophy as articulated into a series of specifications; historically specified as the history of the subject matter or analytically specified as the specifications of the concept at any one particular moment.

This is all very well but, as Collingwood would remind us, there can be no philosophy of anything which is not a universal and necessary characteristic of things: if we are to study, philosophically, a subject matter that is from first to last in a condition of change and development, we can only do so on the assurance that the subject matter is also from first to last in some way the some subject matter, and that this subject matter is no empirical concept but a philosophical concept, a universal and necessary characteristic of mind. In other words, if we are to study the history of science, we need to have an assurance that what we are studying is not only a particular discipline but also a form of experience: if history were not a form of experience but only what historians do it could not be studied philosophically.

What, then, is the relation between a particular discipline such as science, and the form of experience, the philosophical concept, of science? How is it possible to study the latter through the former, and what relation do successive phases of scientific thinking bear to one another? Lastly, if metaphysics is the science of absolute presuppositions, how does it escape being a merely historical science and become a philosophical science? Which is to say, what is the principle of continuity by which we can characterise successive constellations of absolute presuppositions as somehow belonging to one and the same universal and necessary characteristic of mind?

To answer these questions we will have to turn back to Collingwood's manuscripts. In the manuscript of 1927 entitled 'The Idea of a Philosophy of Something, and in particular, a Philosophy of History',[146] Collingwood is concerned, as the title suggests, with what it means to be a philosophy of anything, with what sort of things can be the objects of philosophy, and with the question of the relation of, e.g. history, as a form of experience to the way professional historians proceed. Philosophy deals with the universal and necessary: 'a philosophical concept is universal in the sense that it

---

[146] Reprinted in the revised edition of I.H. My exposition of this manuscript draws upon Van der Dussen in *History as a Science*, pp. 133–7.

arises necessarily whenever anybody thinks about a subject . . . the concepts which comprise the body of philosophy are transcendentals.'[147]

Now, as we have already seen, there are two types of transcendentals, the logical categories and those with which Collingwood is concerned here: that is, categories of mind. Collingwood mentions art, action, science and history as transcendental concepts, and accordingly, the philosophy of history is 'The exposition of the transcendental concept of history, the study of history as a universal and necessary form of mental activity.'[148] Besides this transcendental concept of history there is also an empirical concept of history: the actual practice of historians. The some holds for art and science and the rest. However, the empirical concept also has its transcendentals:

> every work of (e.g.) art (that is, every operation of the mind qua work of art) must display a number of different characteristics which are the transcendentals or categories of art . . . Thus the relation between the particular work of art and art in general is parallel to that between a particular philosophy such as the philosophy of history and philosophy in general.[149]

A concept, such as history, can be both a philosophical and a non-philosophical concept: it has two phases, each phase being related systematically to the other. Each can be the object of philosophical study, the one as itself a transcendental concept, the other as characterised by transcendental concepts. And *these* transcendentals are, I suggest, absolute presuppositions.

> History . . . as an empirical concept, means the investigation of certain arbitrarily defined problems known as historical problems . . . If on the other hand history means the acquisition or possession of historical knowledge, and not merely the retelling of certain parts of it to others, it must be a transcendental conception. For the object of this knowledge is not the history of England or the history of this or that particular empirical thing, but history as such, whatever history there is, everything historically knowable; and this is a perfectly universal conception. Moreover it is a necessary conception, in the sense that it is implied as a condition in all mental activity . . . Thus history is a transcendental conception, like art and science, when regarded as a pure form of activity; though it becomes, like them, an empirical conception when it is arbitrarily restricted to certain specialised embodiments of that form. If anyone says 'that isn't history, because there isn't a book about it in the historical section of the library, or because a professor of history would

---

[147] 'The Idea of a Philosophy of Something . . . ' xviii–xix.
[148] op. cit. xxv.
[149] op. cit. xxii–xxiii.

not bother to lecture about it, or because it never occurred to the people concerned to call it history', he is using a perfectly legitimate criterion to exclude it from history in the empirical sense, but he is not even attempting to deny that it is history in the transcendental sense: that is to say, that it contains those characteristics which, in a more conspicuous degree or form, confer the name of history upon the things generally so designated. For the empirical concept is nothing but the prima facie application of the transcendental concept.[150]

In philosophy of history we are, then, doing two things: first we are studying the transcendentals of the empirical concept of history — the absolute presuppositions of historical thinking at any given time; secondly, we are studying the historical consciousness itself, history as a form of experience. We approach the latter through the former, and must do so as a form of experience has no objective existence apart from its specialised embodiments; and in studying history (or any other form of experience) we must also relate it to the other forms of experience and trace the connections between them. In studying (say) history qua a form of experience we are studying the permanent (the transcendental conception of history itself); in studying history qua historical practice, we are studying the transitory (the historically conditioned and changing principles of historical practice at a given time). And the philosophy of history therefore means

> bringing to light the principles used in historical thinking, and criticising them; its function is to criticise and regulate these principles, with the subject of making history truer and historically better. It thus arises by an absolute necessity out of the practice of historical thinking, and the historian can evade the necessity of engaging in the philosophy of history only so long as he can evade entangling himself in the problems of methodology; that is, the problems of how he ought to handle historical materials and what kind of result he ought to aim at attaining . . . the philosophy of history, so understood, is the methodology of history. Arising spontaneously in an unsystematic form out of actual historical work, it cannot ever be expressed in the form of a completed doctrine; it must consist of topics raised and discussed in the shape given them by the peculiar circumstances in which they arise; and the natural method of treating it is by isolated and self-contained discussions.[151]

Philosophy of history so understood is the philosophical analysis of the presuppositions of the practice of history.

Collingwood then goes on to draw a distinction between what he calls 'ought questions' (for example, whether the historian ought to pass moral judgements on his characters?) which are generally ques-

---

[150] op. cit. xxiii–xxv.
[151] op. cit. xii–xiii.

tions over which the historian has a free choice in the presentation and interpretation of his materials, and 'can' questions (for example, whether the historian determine why things happened, or only what it was that happened). Questions of this latter sort are not matters of choice for the historian but conceptual limits defining the scope and limits of his historical reconstructions. 'Ought' and 'can' questions are interrelated, and they all 'revolve around one central question, the question of the fundamental nature, meaning, purpose and value of history: the question: what is history?'[152] The question, what is history is, specifically, 'Is it a genuine form of knowledge, or is it an illusion? Can it really make good its claims to be a mental discipline and an approach to reality, or is it a confused mass of heterogeneous and half-developed tendencies of thought? If it is a genuine form of knowledge, what place has it in knowledge as a whole, and how is it related to other forms?'[153] The question, 'what is history?' is important for Collingwood because in his opinion a properly thought out concept of history is an indispensable condition for the solution of the various methodological questions arising out of historical practice itself.

Finally, on the relation between a transcendental concept and its specific embodiment:

> There are thus three aspects of the philosophy of history. First, as a complex of particular methodological problems, growing immediately out of historical thinking. Secondly, as the attempt to answer the question, what is history? Thirdly, as identical with philosophy in general. Now clearly, these three aspects are in no sense three distinct departments of the subject. They are bound up together in such a way that neither can exist without the others. The first is the *matter* of *the* philosophy of history; the second and third together make up its *form*. The matter is a mere plurality of particular philosophical problems, in themselves chaotic, shapeless, capable of enumeration to infinity; the form is a unity which brings unity into this matter by relating its parts to one another in the light of a whole which is the form itself.

Only by coming to know what history is can we hope to solve the methodological questions arising from its practice; but it must be remembered that there is no history apart from the practice of history: 'it is only in this concrete experience of historical work and its difficulties that I can be said to know what history is at all. Take away the matter, and the form becomes an empty and worthless formula.

---

[152] op. cit. xiv.
[153] op. cit. xiv–xv.

The form makes the matter intelligible, the matter makes the form actual.'[154] The relationship between a transcendental concept interpreted as a form of experience, and an empirical concept, is this: the empirical concept is the prima facie application of the transcendental concept, its specialised and historically situated embodiment. Each empirical concept has its own transcendental concepts, that is, each empirical concept shares in the character of the transcendental concept or form of experience itself, and derives its status as an object worthy of philosophical attention from that association. If we ask, how is it possible for the principles underlying each empirical concept to be transcendental? the answer is this: each philosophical concept articulates itself into a scale of forms in which its specific classes overlap. Each specification of the philosophical genus is a specification of the philosophical concept itself, and therefore shares its characteristics. In the language of the 1929 lectures on ethics:

> This kind of articulation, in which a concept is divided into two opposite determinations which coexist in every instance, is called *dialectic* and it is the characteristic structure of the conceptions proper to philosophy . . . The articulations of this, or dialectical type are called, to distinguish them from species, moments . . . The idea expressed in calling these things moments was that they coexisted in their instances, instead of excluding one another . . . the moments into which a transcendental conception is articulated are thus all present in every instance of the concept.[155]

The opposites are not both present positively; one is present positively and the other is present negatively: 'the concepts of philosophy are invariably analyseable into opposites of which they are the synthesis . . . action is a transcendental and therefore its moments are also transcendentals'[156] The answer to the question is therefore that the transcendental concepts found in the empirical concepts are moments or specifications of the fundamental transcendental concept or form of experience.

We can only study a form of experience through the mediation of its empirical specification, either historically or contemporaneously. The permanence of a form of experience is guaranteed by its character as a universal and necessary form of human activity; but at any given moment that universal and necessary activity will express itself in a quite individual way, according to concepts which constitute its character at that moment and which give way to different

---

[154] op. cit. xv–xvi.
[155] Lectures on Moral Philosophy, 1929, pp. 16–19.
[156] op. cit. p. 35.

conceptions in the course of its becoming or development.[157] The structure of the whole will be that of a scale of forms: this may be an analytic scale of forms exhibiting the articulation of a philosophical concept at a particular time; or an experimental scale of forms exhibiting the relations between a form of experience and other forms of experience on a scale of forms of experience itself; or an historical scale of forms exhibiting the concept, as empirically specified, in the course of its development over time.

The question now remaining is that of the place of absolute presuppositions in such a scheme. We have already examined a particular type of transcendental (or type of absolute presupposition), that is, the logical categories such as being, nothing and becoming, which are necessary conditions for all discourse and experience. These categories are not subject to change (other than in their interpretation); but neither are they constitutive of forms of experience; they are, so to speak, free floating with respect to forms of experience. If forms of experience are universal and necessary and therefore permanent, this implies that some at least of the absolute presuppositions constitutive of such forms are equally permanent and necessary. Are there absolute presuppositions which are both constitutive of particular forms of experience and also necessary and permanent? On a superficial reading of *An Essay on Metaphysics*, the reader may come away with the impression that all absolute presuppositions are always in a continuous process of change. This impression is, I am sure, false. In the essay Collingwood clearly suggests that some presuppositions may be made *semper, ubique, ab omnibus*.[158] This is promising, but not sufficient; the way it is put implies that some presuppositions may be universal and permanent but that then again they may not. In other words, that whether they are held *semper, ubique, ab omnibus* is a purely contingent matter confirmable only historically. What I am looking for is something stronger than this, that is, an admission that certain absolute presuppositions are universal and necessary.

Collingwoodian arguments are typically transcendental arguments of the type: 'given this form of experience, what are the conditions which make it possible?' In *An Autobiography* Collingwood referred to questions of this type as epistemological, 'such as one might group together under the question 'how is historical knowl-

---

[157] See, e.g., O.P.A., p. 95: 'Because the process of the spirit is a conscious process . . . it does not merely travel through a fixed cycle of changes but finds every passage past a given point altered in significance by the consciousness of what has gone before it' and see S.M., pp. 57; 317.
[158] E.M., p. 47.

edge possible?"[159] By the use of such arguments we can justify the absolute presuppositions which constitute this form of experience; but if the argument is used on a form of knowledge which was not permanent and necessary, then our transcendental deduction would only prove that (given that form of knowledge as presently constituted) these conditions and presuppositions are necessarily present. This is no more than providing the necessity of the presuppositions relative to that form of knowledge: if the form of knowledge alters or ceases to be, the presuppositions go with it. In other words, such a deduction is circular, proving only that if we are to have the knowledge that we do in fact have, then we must make the presuppositions that we do in fact find ourselves making.[160]

This, however, is not the whole story: if there are forms of experience which are universal and necessary then there will also be absolute presuppositions that are universal and necessary. Historically speaking, the development of a form of experience will appear as a sequence of changing absolute presuppositions each of which makes it what it is at any given time, and so far, the picture presented above is correct. But it is not the whole of the truth: we can only intelligibly talk of change where we can also talk of something which changes; as G.R.G. Mure put it, 'wherever there is change, a single subject enters whole into every phase of the change, and yet in every change suffers a gain or loss of completeness,'[161] which is to say, with Kant, that only the permanent can change. If the history of (say) science, were nothing more than a history of changing constellations of absolute presuppositions then such a history would not be possible. It would not be possible even if, as they would, the constellations of absolute presuppositions overlapped. Such overlapping could not provide the continuity needed: we can only talk of a scale of forms of a concept where that concept enters whole into every phase: with a contingently overlapping series of presuppositions there could be no possible guarantee that the overlapping forms constituted a scale of forms of the same concept. But Collingwood found no difficulty in writing of the history of science, or of the history of other concepts: and this could only be because he believed that there was something permanent and universal underlying the changing specifications constituted by changing constellations of absolute presuppositions.

A transcendental concept or form of experience is universal and necessary, and as such must be constituted by certain absolute presuppositions which, as its outward expression, are also universal

[159] A., p. 77.
[160] Cf. I.H., p. 230.
[161] G.R.G. Mure, 'Change: Part II', §37.

and necessary. If we can find evidence of absolute presuppositions which Collingwood himself explicitly admits are universal and necessary then this will be an indication that the form of experience which they characterise is also. Or, again, if we can find presuppositions which are not declared in themselves to be universal and necessary, but which are constitutive of a particular form of experience, and if that form of experience is a universal and necessary one, then we can deduce that the presuppositions (as the necessary conditions of the latter) are equally universal and necessary. The procedure is that suggested by A. J. Watt: 'if one could show of a certain node of thought and discourse, both that any rational person would need to engage in it, and that it required a certain presupposition, the argument would constitute a form of justification of that presupposition.'[162] I think this can be done, and I shall demonstrate it, briefly, in the case of history and in the case of science.

In discussing the historical imagination Collingwood suggests a possible candidate in the form of a criterion which 'is the idea of history itself: the idea of an imaginary picture of the past. That idea is, in Cartesian language, innate; in Kantian language, a priori. It is not a chance product of psychological causes; it is an idea which every man possesses as part of the furniture of his mind, and discovers himself to possess in so far as he becomes conscious of what it is to have a mind.'[163] Here we have an absolute presupposition which is universal and necessary, and which is 'the idea of history itself'; in other words: no historical imagination, no history. If this presupposition is (as Collingwood declares it to be) a necessary possession of every mind, then this points to the conclusion that history itself is equally a universal and necessary activity of the mind. This is, of course, precisely what we find him claiming elsewhere.[164] The historical imagination, I conclude, is a permanent and necessary presupposition; it is permanent and necessary in direct consequence of its being a defining characteristic, the fundamental expression of the transcendental concept of history itself. The history of the idea of history is only possible because there is an idea of history; without the concept of history itself being present from first until last, the history of the changing conceptions of that idea could never be written, for it would be not one history, but many histories, an infinite number of possible histories each with nothing more than a certain chance resemblance in common. In so far as the idea of history constitutes a

---

[162] A.J. Watt, 'Transcendental Arguments and Moral Principles', p. 41.
[163] I.H. p. 248
[164] See, for example, *The Philosophy of History*, 1930.

scale of forms, it can constitute it only as a scale of forms of the philosophical concept of history.

The case of science is perhaps even more interesting. In *An Essay on Metaphysics*, Collingwood corrects Aristotle's account of the absolute presuppositions of his time.[165] He does this not on the ground that he had failed to notice an absolute presupposition which simply happened to be there, but on the ground that he failed to notice an absolute presupposition which logically *must* have been there. The passage runs:

> Aristotle thought, and he was not the only Greek philosopher to think it, that by merely using our senses we learn that a natural world exists. He did not realize that the use of our senses can never inform us that what we perceive by using them is a world of things that happen of themselves and are not subject to control by our own art or anyone else's. I have already pointed out that the existence of such a world is a presupposition, the first and fundamental presupposition, *on which alone any science of nature can arise*. When Aristotle described it as a fact discovered by the use of the senses, therefore, he was falling into a metaphysical error. For his own science of nature, no less than for any other, the thing was in fact an absolute presupposition. This metaphysical error was corrected by Christianity.[166]

And, we may add, it was corrected by Christianity not in the sense that it was later presupposed whereas formerly it was not; on the contrary, they corrected the error because they saw that for the Greeks to have had a science of nature in the first place it *must always have been presupposed*. What we have in this passage is an epistemological argument to the effect that 'the use of our senses can never inform us that what we perceive by using them is a world of things that happen of themselves', along with a metaphysical argument to the effect that therefore we can only know of such a world by absolutely presupposing it, and that if there is to be a science at all then this must be absolutely presupposed.

---

[165] E.M., p. 215.

[166] E.M., p. 215, my italics. By the phrase 'metaphysical error' here Collingwood means something much stronger than mere failure to report the presence of an absolute presupposition. He means not only that this absolute presupposition was a necessary one for any science of nature, but also that Aristotle's 'metaphysical error' consisted in his belief that the use of his senses could inform him that what we perceive is a world of things which happen of themselves. Collingwood is thus maintaining both that the absolute presupposition is universal and necessary (and that therefore a failure to report its presence must always and everywhere by a metaphysical error); and also that some propositions cannot, by their very nature, be derived from experience, and that this is one of those propositions. Collingwood is not therefore for all his professions, what W.H. Walsh calls a 'metaphysical neutralist'. W.H. Walsh, 'Collingwood and Metaphysical Neutralism'.

Now, this absolute presupposition therefore differs from the other absolute presuppositions which Collingwood discusses in the Essay in being a necessary presupposition for the existence of science itself, (rather than a merely contingent or transient presupposition made by natural science at a particular stage in its history).[167] However, this presupposition may be necessary for the existence of any natural science, but it is only if natural science itself is a universal and necessary form of experience that this presupposition itself becomes universal and necessary, made *semper, ubique, ab omnibus*. We are given no direct assurance in *An Essay on Metaphysics* that science is such a thing; on the other hand there is, as far as I can see, no objection to supposing that Collingwood still regarded science as a universal and necessary category of mind when he wrote the *Essay*. Such a view of natural science is apparent in the concluding remarks to *The Idea of Nature*, which were written at about the some time as *Metaphysics*; and, of course, it is a point constantly being made in the earlier works from which we have quoted.

At the time of writing *The Idea of Nature*, there can be no doubt that Collingwood understood natural science to be a universal and necessary feature of experience; and in this work we find precisely the some account given of the necessary presuppositions of natural science. The three presuppositions of Ionian science, according to Collingwood, were: '1) That there are 'natural things' . . . 2) That 'natural' things constitute a single 'world of nature' . . . These two points are indispensable presuppositions of any science of nature . . . 3) That what is common to all 'natural' things is their being made of a single 'substance' or material. This was the special or peculiar presupposition of Ionian physics; and the school of Miletus may be regarded as a group of thinkers who made it their special business to take this as their 'working hypothesis' and see what could be made of it: asking in particular the question 'that being so, what can we say about this single substance?' They did not consciously treat it as a 'working hypothesis': it cannot be doubted that they accepted it as an absolute and unquestioned presupposition of all their thinking; but the historian of thought, looking back on their achievement, cannot fail to see

---

[167] E.g. concepts such as 'every event has a cause' or that natural science is essentially an applied mathematics, of which Collingwood writes (E.M., p. 254) that it is by 'no means an indispensable presupposition for any science of nature' — a statement which clearly implies that there are presuppositions which are indispensable.

that what they really did was to test this idea of a single universal substance and to find it wanting.'[168]

These two indispensable presuppositions constitute the 'Idea of Nature'; the particular character of 'the Idea of Nature at any moment is constituted by the 'special or peculiar presuppositions' held at the time. This is precisely what I was looking for, and it is important that the evidence was drawn both from *The Idea of Nature*, which was written before Collingwood's supposed conversion to historicism, and also from *An Essay on Metaphysics*, written after that supposed conversion. I hope that the interpretation of Collingwood's theory of absolute presuppositions presented in this chapter makes clear what Collingwood means when he says that:

> In part, the problems of philosophy are unchanging; in part they vary from age to age, according to the special characteristics of human life and thought at the time; and in the best philosophies of every age these two parts are so interwoven that the present problems appear *sub specie saeculi*, and the special problems of the age *sub specie aeternitatis*.[169]

In the foregoing I hope to have established that, in principle each form of experience is constituted by certain indispensable presuppositions; that as the form of experience is a universal and necessary category of mind so too are those presuppositions; these presuppositions remain constant throughout the history of that form of experience in its empirical application and specification although what is understood by them will change with each phase of the development of the concept; that the character of each phase of a form of experience is constituted by the variable or 'peculiar' presuppositions; and that the matter of philosophy is given by the absolute presuppositions of the empirical application of the form of experience it studies and the form is constituted by the form of experience itself. The form of experience is the whole which 'brings unity to this matter by relating its parts to one another in the light of a whole which is the form itself . . . The form makes the matter intelligible, the matter makes the form actual.'[170]

What remains permanent is the philosophical concept itself, that is, the form of experience; what changes are the specifications of that concept, each phase being a specification of that concept constituted by a constellation of absolute presuppositions. Each phase overlaps its neighbour, and the guarantee of continuity is the permanent and

---

[168] I.N., p. 30. Nathan Rotenstreich overlooked the fact that his comments concerning permanent presuppositions in I.N. apply equally well to E.M. ('Metaphysics and Historicism', p. 198).
[169] I.H., p. 231–2.
[170] 'Idea of a Philosophy of Something . . . ', xv–xvi.

continuing presence of the presuppositions which constitute the form of experience itself, and in this way we are able to maintain both the permanence of philosophical problems and also their historical relativity:

> The entire history of thought is the history of a single sustained attempt to solve a single permanent problem, each phase advancing the problem by the extent of all the work done on it in the interval, and summing up the points of this work in the shape of a unique presentation of the problem. In a history of this kind all the philosophies of the past are telescoped into the present and constitute a scale of forms, never beginning and never ending, which are different both in degree and in kind, distinct from each other and opposed to each other.[171]

5: Conclusion

There are, of course, many questions which I have to leave unanswered: to answer them all would mean far exceeding the limitations of this book. All that I hope to have achieved in this chapter is some indication of the extent to which Collingwood's philosophy has to be taken whole if it is to be thoroughly understood; and the recognition that taking it in parts and setting each part against each other is to do a disservice to Collingwood's philosophical achievement.

I will conclude this chapter by quoting a passage from the 1921 lectures on ethics, which, in my view, and read in the light of all that has been said above, make clear Collingwood's understanding of the nature of philosophical problems and the extent to which they are permanent or not. This passage should be understood as representing and summarising all those other passages in his other books in which Collingwood discusses the existence of permanent problems in philosophy. All these discussions have been in their various ways, misunderstood through one sided interpretation (made inevitable by a failure to recognise that where Collingwood deals with only a part of a problem, he is not thereby suggesting that what he is dealing with constitutes the whole of the problem). It was always Collingwood's way to stress one thing at one time and another at another time. Such a habit implies not a change of view, but merely a change of aspect: what I now hope to be able to do is show how all these aspects are aspects of the some thing and hence not opposed to one another but complementary as presenting different sides of the same truth.

---

[171] E.P.M., p. 195.

The task of a history of ethics would be (did such a history exist, for I am not acquainted with one) to show how one single problem (what is action?) was restated from age to age in different terms, now in terms of criterion, now in terms of faculty and so on, and to trace the dialectical development of these subordinate ethical concepts as transformations of the single concept of action.[172]

---

[172] Lectures on Moral Philosophy, 1921, pp. 5-6. Cf. A., p. 62: 'The history of political theory ... (is) the history of a problem more or less constantly changing, whose solution was changing with it.' This passage, seen in the light of the above quoted passage, becomes more obviously compatible with the passage quoted from E.P.M. on the preceding page. The difference lies in emphasis, not substance: after all, Collingwood does not hesitate to assume that both Plato and Hobbes are propounding political theories. The concept of politics is identical in its difference: as Collingwood writes on the some page, 'Plato's Republic and Hobbes's Leviathan are about two things which are in one way the some thing and in another way different. That is not in dispute. What is in dispute is the kind of sameness and the kind of difference.'

PART TWO

The Political Philosophy of Civilization

Chapter Four
Theory, Practice and the Forms of Action

1: Introduction

Part One has argued that we are justified in taking Collingwood's philosophy as a coherent whole which developed over time but underwent no radical or fundamental change requiring that we regard it as cleaved into two mutually incompatible philosophical positions. Taking this as my premise, I am able to proceed to draw together Collingwood's political philosophy of civilization.

Any philosophy of politics must situate politics in relation both to political practice and to the other forms of practical action. The first question is, then, 'What is the relation of political theory to political practice', and this is a sub-species of the more general problem of the relation of theory to practice in general. The second question is, 'How is this activity — politics — related to other practical activities such as economic or moral action, and what are its defining characteristics?' This chapter will accordingly be devoted to an examination of Collingwood's answers to these questions which were central to his whole approach to philosophy — so much so that Johnson refers to the nature of the unity of thought and action as his 'big worry'.[1] It is the centrality of this concern for Collingwood (typified by the opening pages of *Speculum Mentis* and the final chapter of *An Autobiography*) which also explains the digression in the section on Collingwood's own political theory and practice.

---

[1] P. Johnson, *R.G. Collingwood: An Introduction*, p. 147.

2: Theory and Practice

Sooner or later in the exposition of an author's moral or political theory the question of their conception of the relation between theory and practice will arise. I shall now try to give some sort of an account of Collingwood's understanding of the relation between theory and practice.

Speculum Mentis opens with the resounding declaration that 'all thought exists for the sake of action. We try to understand ourselves and our world only in order that we may learn how to live.'[2] In *The New Leviathan* Collingwood likewise insists that thought is primarily practical, and that practice is prior to theory, both in logic and in fact. However, although we may agree with what Collingwood says here, the question of the precise relation between the two things remains to be explained. To answer this involves looking not at the texts where Collingwood simply asserts that there is a relation between theory and practice,[3] but at the texts where he details more precisely what he takes the specific character of that relation to be. I shall take as my starting point Collingwood's remarks about T.H. Green in his *Autobiography*, look at what Green said about the matter, and then examine Collingwood's more considered position.

In talking of Green, Collingwood is seeking to draw a contrast between a philosophy which saw itself as relevant to action and a later (realistic) philosophy which denied that philosophy was relevant to action.

> The school of Green sent out into public life a stream of ex-pupils who carried with them the conviction that philosophy, and particularly the philosophy they had learnt at Oxford, was an important thing, and that their vocation was to put it into practice . . . the philosophy of Green's school might be found, from about 1880 to 1910, penetrating and fertilizing every part of the national life.[4]

As opposed to the realists, 'the school of Green had taught that philosophy was not a preserve for professional philosophers, but everyone's business.'[5] The realists — Cook Wilson, Prichard, Joseph, Carritt — taught that as nothing is affected by being known, moral theory could make no difference to moral action. For Collingwood the consequences of this point of view were disastrous:

> The pupils, whether or not they expected a philosophy that should give them, as that of Green's school had given their fathers, ideals to live for

---

[2] S.M., p. 15.
[3] See for example, A, Chapter XII: 'Theory and Practice'.
[4] A., p. 17.
[5] A., p. 50.

and principles to live by, did not get it; and were told that no philosopher (except of course a bogus philosopher) would even try to give it. The inference which any pupil could draw for himself was that for guidance in the problems of life, since one must not seek it from thinkers or from thinking, from ideals or from principles, one must look to people who were not thinkers (but fools), to processes that were not thinking (but passion), to aims that were not ideals (but caprices), and to rules that were not principles (but rules of expediency).[6]

The result of this was twofold. Because it taught that thought was pointless it was, first, the best possible training for producing a generation of potential dupes for every political, moral, commercial or religious con man; secondly, it could only convince those pupils that 'philosophy was a silly and trifling game,[7] a futile parlour amusement. In Collingwood's view the realists not only deliberately expunged any notion that moral philosophy might be relevant to life: they rejoiced in it and were proud of their handiwork; at last they had

> eradicated from the philosophical schools that confusion of philosophy with pulpit oratory which was involved in the bad old theory that moral philosophy is taught with a view to making the pupils better men. They were proud to have excogitated a philosophy so pure from the sordid taint of utility that they could lay their hands on their hearts and say it was no use at all; a philosophy so scientific that no one whose life was not a life of pure research could appreciate it, and so abstruse that only a whole-time student, and a very clever man at that, could understand it.[8]

In these famous passages Collingwood is using Green as a stick with which to beat the realists. His main contention is that Green taught moral philosophy as a thing of practical value, in which the philosopher could give 'ideals to live for and principles to live by'; and that the realists taught that moral philosophy could have no possible effect on practice (that there was a complete divorce between theory and practice) and, further, that anyone who thought otherwise was intellectually deficient or evilly motivated.[9] Whether or not Collingwood was right in his characterisation of the Realists' standpoint or in his view of the consequences of their teaching does not matter here (although his reasons for disagreement with the Realists on the nature of the relation between knowing and what is known and its effects in moral philosophy are important and will be returned to). What does matter is what Collingwood says of Green: he seems to be saying that Green was a sort of philosophical moral-

---

[6] A., p. 48.
[7] A., p. 50.
[8] A., p. 51.
[9] A., pp. 50-1.

ist, a philosophical conjuror who produced moral prescriptions out of his philosopher's hat. However, Green was certainly nothing of the sort, and as we shall see, neither was Collingwood.[10] His main objection to the Realist position was that they thought moral theory could make no difference to moral practice; he thought that it did, and also that Green thought that it did. When he invokes Green here he is not so much exploring the precise nature of the relation between theory and practice as enlisting Green on his side in common opposition to the Realists. What Green actually said I shall now briefly go into.

Green thinks that moral theory is of value to moral practice, but that it can be so only negatively and that it presupposes a pre-existing disposition to morality.

> Any value which a true moral theory may have for the direction of conduct depends on its being applied and interpreted by a mind which the ideal, as a practical principle, already actuates. And it will be as well at once to admit that the value must in any case be rather negative than positive; rather in the way of deliverance from the moral anarchy which an apparent conflict between duties equally imperative may bring about, or of providing a safeguard against the pretext which in a speculative age some inadequate and misapplied theory may afford to our selfishness, than in the way of pointing out duties previously ignored.[11]

Again, theory can be of value in preparing our moral character for the crises and emergencies that will at times befall us: not that at the moment of acting we would reflect on moral theory; but rather that dispassionate theorising about morality, the analysis of the meaning of moral terms, can do a good deal towards preparing us for such emergencies by making us sensitive to the leading issues involved and enabling us to discern the elements despite merely personal considerations.[12] At the moment of acting we act as it were intuitively and not by 'going over the theory of virtue in one's mind: but such an intuitive judgement in fact 'represents long courses of habit and imagination founded upon ideas.'[13] In other words, our 'intuitive' action or moral judgement flows not through some faculty of intuition but from our whole moral character, and what that charac-

---

[10] That this is so can be independently confirmed by the testimony of his ex-pupils. For example, Shiela Grant Duff: 'I thought that moral philosophy would teach me how to live and political philosophy would teach me how states should be governed, but this, I found, was not the case and it was from R. G. Collingwood that I learnt my mistake.' *The Parting of Ways*, p. 46.
[11] T.H. Green, *Prolegomena to Ethics*, §311.
[12] See *Prolegomena to Ethics*, §317 and W. D. Lamont, *Introduction to Green's Moral Philosophy*, pp. 153–4.
[13] *Prolegomena to Ethics*, §320.

ter is depends both on what we have made of ourselves and on the quality of our thought about moral issues and our reflection about the origin and validity of moral ideas.

Green concludes his remarks on the practical value of moral theory by making the point that moral theory has beneficial effects on moral practice not by seeking to moralise, but simply by being good moral theory.

> It may thus fall to the moral philosopher, under certain conditions of society and of intellectual movement, to render an important practical service. But he will render it simply by fulfilling with the utmost possible completeness his proper work of analysis. As a *moral* philosopher he analyses human conduct; the motives which it expresses, the spiritual endowments implied with it, the history of thought, habits and institutions through which it has come to be what it is. He does not understand his business as a philosopher, if he claims to do more than this. He will not take it for a reproach to be reminded that no philosopher can supply a 'moral dynamic'. The pretension to do so he would regard as a great impertinence. He finds moral dynamic enough in the actual spiritual nature of man, when that nature is regarded, as it is his business to regard it, not merely in its hitherto performance, but in its intrinsic possibilities. If he cannot help wishing for more, that is an incident of the very aspiration after perfection of conduct which constitutes the dynamic. His immediate business as a philosopher is not to strengthen or heighten this aspiration, much less to bring it in to existence, but to understand it. As a man and a citizen, indeed, it is his function to serve as its organ; to give effect to it in his own conduct, to assist in communicating it to others. And since in being a philosopher he does not cease to be a man and a citizen, he will rejoice that the analysis, which alone forms his employment as a philosopher, should incidentally serve a purpose subordinate to the 'moral dynamic' — that it should help to remove any obstacle to the effort of the human soul after a perfect life.[14]

Green's views are conveniently summarised by Lamont: 'philosophy doesn't make good men bad; perhaps it does not make bad men good; but it helps all men to see more clearly the implications of the practical ideals actuating them, and therefore helps to make good men better.'[15] From this, it would seem, given what Green says about the relation between theory and practice, that if Collingwood

---

[14] *Prolegomena to Ethics*, §327. Green's position is close to Bradley's: 'There cannot be a moral philosophy which will tell us what in particular we are to do, and also it is not the business of philosophy to do so. All philosophy has to do is 'to understand what is' and moral philosophy has to understand morals which exist, not to make them or to give directions for making them, political philosophy has not to play tricks with the State, but to understand it; and ethics has not to make the world moral, but reduce to theory the morality current in the world. If we want it to do any more, so much the worse for us.' *Ethical Studies*, p. 193.
[15] W.D. Lamont, op. cit., p. 161.

expects Green to give 'ideals to live for and principles to live by' he is going to be disappointed. But Green's position is, in fact, very similar to Collingwood's when he descends from generality into the detail of the relation between theory and practice. What he opposed was a view which regarded theory as utterly irrelevant to practice; and what, positively, he was suggesting was not that the philosopher qua philosopher constructed moral ideals and principles out of nothing and passed them on to his pupils, but that moral philosophy, reflection on our moral ideals and practices, does make a difference to our practice and that the philosopher should therefore not act and talk as though it does not. If the utterances of the moral philosopher clear up our ideas about morality, and if in the light of those clarified ideas we act differently or better, then in a sense the philosopher is giving us ideals and is giving us principles: but he is not doing this by spinning them out of nothing; he is doing it by making us more clearly aware of the moral ideals and principles that we do hold and which actually guide our conduct. I shall now substantiate this by looking more closely at what Collingwood himself has to say.

In 'The Present Need of a Philosophy', Collingwood puts forward the view that philosophy can neither descend 'like a *deus ex machina* upon the stage of practical life and, out of its superior insight into the nature of things dictate the correct solution for this or that problem,' nor can it be a merely analytical and theoretical thing 'that is no more able to influence the processes which it describes than astronomy can influence the movement, of the stars.'[16] For him the truth lay between these two extremes. The philosopher is neither a pilot, nor is he a mere spectator: what present day philosophers should provide is a:

> philosophy showing that the human will is of a piece with nature in being genuinely creative, a *vera causa*, though singular in being consciously creative; that social and political institutions are creations of the human will, conserved by the same power which created them, and essentially plastic to its hand; and that therefore whatever evils they contain are in principle remediable. In short, the help which philosophy might give to our 'dissatisfied, anxious, apprehensive generation' would lie in a reasoned statement of the principle that there can be no evils in any human institution which human will cannot cure.[17]

However valuable the reasoned statement of this principle might be, and however important the philosopher's task in consequence, the question of how exactly such a principle is related to practice and how precisely it affects practice has still been left unanswered.

---

[16] P.N.P., pp. 262–3.
[17] P.N.P., pp. 264–5. There is a clear echo of Vico's *Scienza Nuova* in this passage.

To find the answer we shall do well to begin with Collingwood's remark in 'Political Action': 'The business of sound theory, in relation to practice, is not to solve practical problems, but to clear them of misunderstandings which make their solution impossible.'[18] Here we have an attitude similar to that of Green's — that theory is negative with respect to practice in that it cannot enjoin particular actions. But theory is not indifferent to practice. Sound theory does not solve practical problems but it can help to make them soluble: how does it do this?

In 1939 Collingwood added the following comment to the original text of his lectures on moral philosophy as first delivered in 1933:

> At the end of the last lecture I was pointing out that when we begin to think of ourselves as performing certain activities which hitherto we have been in the habit of performing thoughtlessly, or without self-consciousness, the effect of this change is normally a disturbance or disorganisation of such activities. There is no activity of our minds, I said, of which our own thought is content to be a mere spectator; it will have its fingers in the pie, often to the pie's destruction — you must please pardon me for insisting upon this. I do so because it is a very obvious and familiar truth which when I was an undergraduate the leading teachers of philosophy in Oxford were in a conspiracy to deny. There was in those days a thing called Realism in Oxford, whose main article of faith was that 'knowing makes no difference to its object' . In support of this dogma it used to be asserted that astronomers, by coming to know how stars move, do not make them move differently. This may (for all I know) be true, though I should be sorry if I were asked to prove it; but where knowledge takes the form of self-knowledge it is flagrantly and indubitably false.[19]

In opposition to the Realist view that 'knowing makes no difference to what is known'[20] Collingwood was at pains to assert that it most certainly did; and that this was especially important when we were dealing with the sciences of mind in which what is known is no external object but the knowing mind itself.[21] Now, for Collingwood all philosophy is self-knowledge and therefore any philosophical

---

[18] 'Political Action', (Pol.A.), p. 158.
[19] Lectures on Moral Philosophy, 1933. p. 33. Collingwood then goes on to point out that 'the skill which vanishes can be built up again and raised to a higher power by the same thought which disturbed it.'
[20] The form of wording in A, p. 44.
[21] This echoes strongly the doctrine of S.M. In A. he writes that he had recently re-read S.M. for the first time since it was published (p. 56n). That is, he had re-read S.M. shortly before writing the additional note to the 1933 lectures on moral philosophy and it is interesting to note how this addition is so powerfully reminiscent of S.M. The addition also serves as a valuable supplement to the famous passage on p. 44 of A. in which Collingwood presents his refutation of the Realists' doctrine that knowing makes no difference to what is known.

theory about our knowledge does not leave that knowledge unaltered: as he says in a passage already quoted, philosophy cannot change our opinions but it 'can and does change (our) opinions as to what (our) opinions really are.'[22] The question now is, how does the self knowledge brought on by philosophizing make a difference to what we do? If we now know what our opinions really are, how does that affect our practice? Collingwood gives the answer to this in the *Autobiography*: it ought to be familiar to every human being that:

> In his capacity as a moral, political, or economic agent he lives not in a world of 'thoughts'; that if you change the moral, political and economic 'theories' generally accepted by the society in which he lives, you change the character of his world; and that if you change his own 'theories' you change his relation to that world; so that in either case you change the ways in which he acts.[23]

One of the consequences which Collingwood lays at the door of the Realists in their espousal of the principle that knowing makes no difference to what is known is that it represented an attack on moral philosophy: 'moral philosophy, from the days of Socrates down to our own lifetime, had been regarded as an attempt to think out more clearly the issues involved in conduct, for the sake of acting better.'[24] The new moral philosophy proposed by Prichard would study the workings of the moral consciousness 'as if they were the movements of the planets' and would make no attempt to interfere with or affect that moral consciousness; this approach was seconded by Russell, who proposed, on similar grounds, the exclusion of ethics from the body of philosophy. Collingwood then drew out and elaborated the difference in attitude which the Realist philosophy induced in the teaching of the subject, as against the attitude towards teaching evinced by the school of Green.

> The 'realist' philosophers who adopted this new programme were all, or nearly all, teachers of young men and young women. Their pupils, with habits and characters yet unformed, stood on the threshold of life; many of them on the threshold of public life. Half a century earlier, young people in that position had been told that by thinking about what they are doing, or were about to do, they would became likely on the whole to do it better; and that some understanding of the nature of moral or political action, some attempt to formulate ideals and principles, was an indispensable condition of engaging creditably in these activities themselves. And their teachers, when introducing them to the study of moral and political theory, would say to them, whether in words or not — the most important things that one says are often not said in words — 'Take this

---

[22] Lectures on Moral Philosophy, 1929, p. 10.
[23] A., p. 147.
[24] A., p. 47.

subject seriously, because whether you understand it or not will make a difference to your whole lives'. The realist, on the contrary, said to his pupils, 'If it interests you to study this, do so; but don't think it will be of any use to you. Remember the great principle of realism, that nothing is affected by being known. That is as true of human action as of anything else. Moral philosophy is only the theory of moral action: it can't therefore make any difference to the practice of moral action. People can act just as morally without it as with it. I stand here as a moral philosopher; I will try to tell you what acting morally is, but don't expect me to tell you how to do it.'[25]

What sort of differences does knowing make to what is known, when the knowing is moral philosophy, and the known is the moral self? In *An Essay on Metaphysics* Collingwood writes that 'if a mind is something which has opinions as to what it is trying to do, its possession of these opinions will in certain ways complicate its behaviour.'[26] And presumably if our opinions or our 'opinions about our opinions' alter, our behaviour alters also. Collingwood develops this point in *Speculum Mentis*: 'Of everything that a mind in the full sense does, it gives itself an account as it does it; and this account is inseparably bound up with the doing of the thing.'[27] Later he suggests that 'those who give a false account to themselves of their own experience, so deform that experience that it loses its highest qualities and actually becomes something not altogether unlike what they falsely think it.'[28] This is because:

> The mind, having formed a false conception of itself, tries to live up to that conception. But the falseness of the conception just means that it cannot be 'lived up to'. There is therefore a permanent discord between what the mind thinks it is and what, on the strength of that conception, it does . . . The result is an open inconsistency between theory and practice.[29]

This makes Collingwood's views on the relation between theory and practice fairly clear. Practice is not something other than theory: on the contrary it is through and through theoretical; it operates according to principles and presuppositions (even if 'unconsciously') and reflection upon these principles and presuppositions inevitably intrudes, at some point, upon the practice itself. For example, difficulties arising in a scientific theory may need, for their solution, deep reflection upon the first principles of that science and may even, in the end, necessitate or demand a revision in those first prin-

[25] A., pp. 47–8.
[26] E.M., p. 107.
[27] S.M., p. 84.
[28] S.M., p. 295.
[29] S.M., p. 250.

ciples. Clear and accurate thinking then becomes a prerequisite for future progress; without a clear understanding of our principles and presuppositions we cannot hope to perform well as scientists nor to engineer the conceptual revision which will make progress possible. If we give the full version of the passage quoted above we can see that this is what Collingwood means:

> Of everything that a mind in the full sense does, it gives itself an account as it does it; and this account is inseparably bound up with the doing of the thing. Thus every activity is also a theory of itself and, by implication, of activity in general; but not necessarily a true theory. For instance, every scientist has some way of telling himself what he is doing, some logical theory as to the nature of science; but this logical theory may be and often is a quite unsound one. Nor can its defects fail to influence the immediate scientific practice of the man who holds it; bad fashions in logic have always had detrimental effects on actual science.[30]

A similar account holds good for moral action. If my beliefs about the nature of the world, of my place within it, about my capacities and inclinations and powers, are false then my actions will be rendered false also. My actions will not 'fit' the world in which I move and they will not 'fit' because the flaws in my thinking lead directly to flaws in my action. If I examine my beliefs — both my beliefs about how the world is and my beliefs about what my own fundamental beliefs or presuppositions are — I can come to correct the mistaken account of my own experience which has been the cause of my practical error. When I understand what I really want, what I really believe, what I can really do; when I make an effort to resolve the contradictory opinions or impulses; when I do all this I will be better equipped to face the world and better able to resolve the practical difficulties that arise in the course of my dealings with the world.

My theory, even if by 'my theory' I mean a set of practical rules, cannot tell me what exactly to do — no theory contains within itself the rules for its own application — but my possession of it, my understanding of the nature of moral action and its component parts, prepares me for what lies ahead. As Knox rightly remarks: 'for a philosopher the interesting question is: what is duty? And this is the important question for the layman too, because unless he has some sort of answer to give he will be unable to answer the further question: what is my duty here and now?'[31]

The grasping of fundamental principles and distinctions equips the agent for the facing of moral dilemmas and moral difficulties: when these arise he or she can act the better because they know what

---
[30] S.M., pp. 84–5; see also I.N., pp. 1–3.
[31] T.M. Knox, *Action*, p. 176.

is at stake and are aware of the leading issues involved. Although at the time of acting my deliberating may be far removed from dispassionate theoretical analysis, the very fact that I have done such theoretical analysis in the past serves as a preparation for the deliberation necessary to resolve the practical problems.

The intervention of theory into practice at moments of crisis or breakdown in practice is an important part of the relation between the two: but it is not the only one. Perhaps equally important is the way in which moral theory, though enabling us to more fully understand moral practice, reconciles us to various aspects of that practice that at first appear unreasonable or irrational, but which, once understood, can be seen as rational and necessary for an ordered and happy way of life. One example might be the need to form habits: that is, for us to create our moral character in such a fashion that we habitually act well. Life would be intolerably difficult, if not impossible, if we eschewed the cultivation of habits and settled dispositions, and sought a mode of conduct that would subject our every single act to scrutiny and deliberation. Of course, habits may be bad habits or they may become bad through force of circumstance (such as when we find ourselves in a situation in which our habitual response is inadequate or is simply irrelevant or would actually be immoral). In such circumstances moral deliberation is necessary if we are to do what is required of us; reliance on habit[32] or on ready made rules of behaviour will not suffice. In these circumstances we proceed 'directly from our knowledge of the situation to an action appropriate to that situation, without passing through the stage of formulating a rule appropriate to the situation.'[33]

We can grant that habitual following of rules is not the only kind of moral action without in any way detracting from its value; and its value lies precisely in that for the most part this is how we do behave. In so far as moral theory can indicate to us that this is so, and that therefore the cultivation of settled habits of behaviour and the formulation of general rules of conduct is a valuable and necessary part of moral life, then that moral theory will enable us, through understanding the inherent rationality of these things, to act better. Moral action according to rule also has an objective side, namely Law, and this we will come to later; but there is also a type of action according to rule which is not morally indifferent (for no action can be altogether morally indifferent) but which for the most part stands out-

---

[32] When we speak of 'habits' in the moral sense we mean the habitual following of certain rules: the content of our habits is given by the particular rules we typically follow.
[33] A., p. 103.

side questions of moral worth. Such action we call caprice or in the case of collective caprice, convention. Many of our habits and the habits of our society or community are of this sort: we habitually eat at certain times and in certain attire; we play certain sorts of games; and we act towards others in certain sorts of ways. It would not be immoral to act otherwise than we do, but in a sense it would be wrong: these conventions and the habits associated with them are a rational part of our moral life fulfilling a similar function to that which acting according to moral rules fulfills on a higher level. They make our lives possible; they leave relatively unimportant matters to be dealt with in the course of our habitual routine, thereby freeing our mental and moral capacities from the drudgery of constantly having to choose how and when to do these things.

I bring in the question of the value of convention for this reason: the pointing out of the place of convention in our lives is an important thing and one which moral theory is well suited to do. Further, those who learn moral theory and learn it thoroughly will be able to appreciate the value of convention and understand its character and peculiar rationality; this understanding may be of inestimable value in their lives and thus be an example of the relation between moral theory and moral practice. Moral theory here does not do anything or tell us to do anything: it merely points out the value of something we habitually do and shows that it has a place in our lives even if that place is often misunderstood.

That recognition of the facts of convention can make an impact on a person's life I shall now illustrate through reference to the testimony of a distinguished ex-pupil of Collingwood's — Sir Tom Hopkinson. Tom Hopkinson went up to Pembroke College in 1923 and was a pupil of Collingwood's from 1925–27, reading Greats. Both he and Collingwood knew that he was no academic, but this did nothing to mar their friendship nor did it diminish the value of what Hopkinson learnt from Collingwood — especially from Collingwood's lectures on moral philosophy.[34] The lectures that Hopkinson heard were the course first delivered in 1923 entitled *Action*: these lectures stirred his mind and he later recalled the effect they had with gratitude. Hopkinson is an important witness not only because his testimony illustrates the way in which theory can affect practice, but also because he was himself an essentially practical man. I shall first quote part of the relevant passage from the lectures and then Hopkinson's comments.

---

[34] See H.T. Hopkinson, *Of This Our Time: A Journalist's Story 1905–50*, p. 301 and H.T. Hopkinson 'Robin Collingwood'.

> It is usual to abuse convention and regard it as an altogether bad thing, one which ought to be resisted and one which if it is allowed to affect us will destroy our freedom and make us slaves and moral cowards. This is true in the same sense in which it is true that play is a childish and infra-moral thing. But in any other sense it is wholly false. Like play, convention is an early stage in the development of the moral consciousness but a necessary stage, and one which cannot be passed over; and, also like play, it is a relaxation of the pressure of the full blown moral life which in its right place is a necessary and beneficial rest. A man who earnestly debated with himself whether he ought to dress for dinner when he knew other people were doing so would be a fool: and a man who kicks at such conventions as fashion in clothes, the social habits of his own and other countries, having bridesmaids and a cake when he marries his wife and black clothes and a hearse when he buries her, is equally a fool. The fashion is not an irrational or degrading thing, any more than cricket is an irrational or degrading thing: it is a corporate game whose rules if carefully examined may be seen to be full of an unconscious reason and whose pursuit, if done in the right spirit, gives life a beauty and a cheerfulness which those who defy convention would crush out of existence. Because these people are virtuous, stern moralists and unbending puritans, are there to be no more cakes and ale, no more ball dresses and uniforms and bank holidays and days of national sorrow and joy? The value of convention is not explicitly a moral or even a utilitarian value: it is a value of a lower type than these and must not be substituted for them or set above them; but it is a real value of its own, and conforming to conventions simply because they are conventions gives every rational being a peculiar and not at all despicable pleasure though convention as a complete guide to life is dead, convention still, has its place as a subordinate principle, regulating matters which we regard as unimportant, and the source of a quite particular form of enjoyment or pleasure — the pleasure of good fellowship, of joining in the activity of others not because these activities are inherently useful or admirable but just because they are activities in which we are allowed to join.[35]

It must be this passage which Hopkinson remembered so clearly many years after:

> Lastly, I had lost that precious possession — from which we all cry to be delivered yet which few of us can contrive to live without — a routine. Any established way of life will became at times tedious and constraining, but it frees one from the burden of deciding, 'what shall I do now?' Twenty years and more before this time, at one of his crowded lectures in an Oxford hall, I had heard Robin Collingwood speak in praise of convention: 'It may be a nuisance,' he said, 'to have meals at fixed times, but what a much worse imposition it would be to have to keep thinking throughout the day, 'Do I want to have something to eat?' 'And from there he had gone on to an examination of convention and routine, and

---

[35] 'Action': Lectures on moral philosophy, 1923, pp. 60–1. cf. the sections on convention in S.M. (written the same year): pp. 234–8; 280; 226–7.

their value not only in the external arrangements of life, but in the complex pattern of our human relationships.[36]

When we turn from the relation between the theory and practice of the individual to the relation between the theory and practice of a civilization or society, we find exactly the same thing reproduced at a different level. In the original (later superseded) preface to *The New Leviathan*, Collingwood states that 'What is contained in books I-IV of this volume is . . . the barest minimum which must be known by every member of a 'civilized' country, whatever his profession or occupation, if in the present emergency he is to do his duty as a citizen.'[37] As Collingwood made clear in a letter to his friend Crawford, 'everybody concerned (with the outbreak of war) was in a completely muddled condition about the first principles of politics.'[38] Operating on the principle that 'What our soldiers and sailors and airmen have to fight, our philosophers have to understand',[39] Collingwood seeks to gear philosophy to political considerations. Philosophy, thus conceived, has the duty of informing a civilization what its fundamental convictions really are, whether it wants to listen or not: the discharge of this duty has a practical intention and practical consequences — the 'function of metaphysics in civilization' is the analysis of its thought and practice in order to elucidate its guiding principles, presuppositions and beliefs; the importance of this Collingwood remarks on in 'Fascism and Nazism'.

> The vital warmth at the heart of a civilization is what we call a religion. Religion is the passion which inspires a society to persevere in a certain way of life and to obey the rules which define it. Without a conviction that this way of life is a thing of absolute value, and that its rules must be obeyed at all costs, the rules become dead letters and the way of life a thing of the past. The civilization dies because the people to whom it belonged have lost faith in it. They have lost heart to keep it going. They no longer feel it as a thing of absolute value. They no longer have a reli-

---

[36] H.T. Hopkinson, op. cit., p. 301.
[37] Unpublished Preface to N.L., p. 8. The practical intention of N.L. is made even more evident if we reflect that it was originally intended to be not in four, but five parts. The fifth part was intended to deal with 'how a society which considers itself civilized should behave in the face of this revolt' against civilization, 'it is the last of these five questions that constitutes the real subject of the book' p. 6. It would seem that Collingwood was prevented by illness from producing quite the work he originally intended.
[38] Letter to O.G.S. Crawford on 14 April 1941.
[39] 'Fascism and Nazism', p. 176n.

gious sense of its rules as things which must at all costs be obeyed. Obedience degenerates into habit and by degree the habit withers away.[40]

In addition, it may be that we do not know what our fundamental convictions are, in which case our practice will degenerate to such a point that our civilization fails. For example, we fight wars over we know not what, for we know not what. The result of such a war could not be victory for either side because there is no clear sense in which we know what has been won or 'what new course of conduct it enabled them to pursue.'[41] In other words, we might fail because our civilization was: 'failing to keep alive its own fundamental convictions . . . because owing to faults in metaphysical analysis it had become confused as to what those convictions were. The remedy was a metaphysical remedy. It consisted . . . in abandoning the faulty analysis and accepting a more accurate analysis.'[42]

The relation of theory to practice, as I find it in Collingwood's writings, is essentially negative in that theory can enjoin no particular actions or dictate particular policies; but it is positive in that is makes a difference to practice, and in so far as good theory is an inseparable adjunct to good practice. The moral world is a world not of objects but of thoughts, and therefore our knowledge of that world is also knowledge of ourselves: in giving an account of our thoughts and principles moral theory is providing the means of gaining self-knowledge. False understanding of our own principles, opinions, capabilities and inclinations distorts our practice: the only remedy for such distortion is a revision of our 'opinions as to what our opinions really are'. Such a revision is the result of theoretical reflection, and therefore in tracing the consequences of this reflection on individual and collective conduct we can trace the indirect (that is, non-prescriptive) though nonetheless real, effect of theory on practice.

I shall conclude this section by quoting at length the passage with which Collingwood concluded his 1933 lectures on moral philosophy. This passage is the only text we possess whereby we can see exactly what Collingwood means by giving his pupils 'ideals to live for and principles to live by'; it is interesting that his advice is entirely general, non-partisan, and recommends no particular actions other than what really amounts to an injunction to think carefully and think for yourself. These lectures, he says, were not

---

[40] F.N., p. 168.
[41] 'Function of Metaphysics in Civilization', p. 29.
[42] E.M., p. 225.

chiefly meant simply to prepare students for their examinations, but to:

> direct your thoughts towards the fundamental problems that are concerned with the life of action. The life of action is a life we all have to lead; there is no escaping it, whether by retiring from the world into a contemplative life or by living in the world under the command and leadership of others to whom we entrust our souls; and the problems that it presents are not academic problems, arising only when we begin to think about it but non-existent in the living of it. Had that been so, moral philosophy would have been no fit study for men whose interest lies in action itself; but as it is, we cannot act without thinking what we are doing and why we do it, and clearness of thought about these matters is a condition of acting wisely and firmly.

Collingwood continues by remarking that everything he has said is meant to have some application in practice and to contribute towards the task of deciding how to live. He then remarks that:

> Everywhere you will hear people saying that they want a leader. Demand creates supply, and leaders are forthcoming. But before you swear allegiance to any of them, I would ask you to remember this. If you find a leader worth following, you must offer him followers worth leading. You can only do this if you are so far independent of any leader as to live in a way that deserves the name of living before you find him. How are you to do this in the chaos and darkness of the world into which you have been born?

He then offers three general rules for life:

> The first and greatest rule of life, as it seems to me, is the old rule, know yourself. You must take pains, when you want something, to find out what it is that you really want. If you do not, you will find later that you have been pursuing things under the mistaken belief that you want them, and making it impossible to gain the things you really want. You must take pains, when you are doing something, to find out what it is that you are really doing. When you choose a course of action, you must take pains to find out what are the real reasons for your choice. This sounds simple, but there are a 1000 impediments in the way: fear and shame of your real desires and real motives, fear that we shall have to forego something we greatly desire when we found out that there is something else we desire more, every kind of hypocrisy and cowardice, which make self-knowledge the hardest thing to compass. But in so far as we achieve it, we are lifted above dependence on things outside ourselves, whether ready made institutions or ready made leaders, and we are certain of happiness, so far as happiness is a thing that man can find.
>
> The second rule is, respect yourself. Resist the temptation to belittle human nature by writing it down to the lowest level. Think that every

desire, every impulse, every feeling which you find in yourself, and therefore in other people, has a right to be there, and demands not to be repressed or hidden away from sight, but to be fitted somehow into the map of life. There are higher and lower elements in our nature, but the lower elements are not purposeless, and cannot be killed without fatal damage to the whole, nor ignored without fatal ignorance of the whole. Respect not only your reason but your passions; not only your conscious mind but your unconscious mind; not only your mind but your body.

The third rule is, orientate yourself. In all activity there is process or development, movement from one element to another: see that the arrow which in your mind's eye is drawn on the diagram of your activities points in the right way. For example: passions like fear and anger represent activity breaking down and disintegrating into emotions: therefore point your arrow away from anger and fear, and never do anything because you are angry or afraid. Again, love begins as a mere animal appetite, but points from the first towards an effort to realize a perfect human nature, and in the last resort points to the love of God. Never, unless you wish to paralyse your will and frustrate your deeper desires, invert the order of things and treat love as a mere animal appetite to which these other things have been attached as a kind of fig-leaf to conceal the crudities of sex from prudish eyes.

With these rules in mind, I would say to you, when you look for shelter behind institutions or leaders, don't look for help to things outside you. Look inside yourselves. Learn not to be frightened of what you may find there. Learn to look deeper and deeper, solving the perplexities you find at one level by penetrating to the one below. In a world where institutions have broken down and leaders have failed, this resource is still open to you; it is the resource men have always had in such times, and it has always been enough. If you can look deeply enough into yourselves, you will find, what you will never find elsewhere, the means of building a new world for your more fortunate children to inhabit.[43]

A stirring peroration — but even at this point relatively abstract and analytical; it amounts to a reminder of the value of self-knowledge and self-understanding — in other words of exactly what he takes philosophy to be.

3: Collingwood's Political Theory and Practice

In *An Autobiography* Collingwood wrote that he was working at a *rapprochement* between theory and practice. I examined his understanding of the relation between theory and practice. This question is, however, distinct from the question of the relation between Collingwood's *own* theory and his *own* practice. We know that he maintained that there was a clear relation between the two things, abstractly considered; but is such a relation discernible in his own

[43] Lectures on Moral Philosophy, 1933, pp. 127–30.

thought and actions? And if it is, what precisely were the political views he held?

In what follows I shall present Collingwood's political views and I shall also argue that his political views did not undergo a sudden shift from right to left in the late nineteen thirties. Before proceeding I shall briefly say a little more about the *rapprochement* between theory and practice. In *An Autobiography* Collingwood writes that he held three different attitudes towards the division between the contemplative life and the practical life.

> There was a first R.G.C. who knew in his philosophy that the division was false, and that 'theory' and 'practice', being mutually dependent, must both alike suffer frustration if segregated into the specialized functions of different classes. There was a second R.G.C. who in the habits of his daily life behaved as if it had been sound; living as a professional thinker whose college gate symbolised his aloofness from the affairs of practical life. My philosophy and my habits were thus in conflict; I lived as if I disbelieved by own philosophy, and philosophized as if I had not been the professional thinker that in fact I was . . . But underneath this conflict there was a third R.G.C., for when the gown of the professional thinker was a disguise alternately comical and disgusting in its inappropriateness. This third R.G.C. was a man of action, or rather he was something in which the difference between thinker and man of action disappeared.[44]

Collingwood then goes on to draw a distinction between a 'gloves-on philosophy', such as that purveyed by the 'realists' and a 'gloves-off philosophy', such as Marx's.

> The first and third R.G.C.s agreed in wanting a gloves-off philosophy. They did not want a philosophy that should be a scientific toy guaranteed to amuse professional thinkers safe behind their college gates. They wanted a philosophy that should be a weapon. So far, I was with Marx. Perhaps all that stood in the way of a closer agreement was the second R.G.C., the academic or professional thinker.[45]

The second R.G.C., he explained, had had his tranquility disturbed and comments that he is not writing an account of recent political events but is rather engaged in: 'writing a description of the way in which those events impinged upon myself and broke up my pose of a detached professional thinker.'[46]

Collingwood thought of himself as re-establishing the unity between the first and third R.G.C.s: he seems to be implying that he was no longer a detached professional thinker, but a man whose thoughts and actions were now one. The major change in his politi-

---
[44] A., pp. 150–1.
[45] A., p. 153.
[46] A., p. 167.

cal attitude, it seems to me, was not so much a change in his support for particular policies or parties, as a change towards a lived embodiment of his principle that 'all thought exists for the sake of action', following a change in his attitude towards the British Government. He no longer accepted its own self-estimate and was no longer inclined to believe in its honesty or political integrity. I shall adduce evidence to support the first part of this claim in the sequel; the immediate question is, what does this 'lived embodiment' comprise?

Collingwood had an acute sense of the possible value of his practical services: he saw quite clearly that his contribution to action was best made through taking seriously his work as a philosopher and producing work which was not only philosophically sound but also practically useful. Everything after *An Autobiography* was written with an expressly practical purpose. *An Essay on Metaphysics*, 'Fascism and Nazism', *The Three Laws of Politics* and *The New Leviathan* were all written for a practical purpose; and in each of them he was clear to to what his job, as a philosopher, was. The philosopher's task was to 'cackle' because: 'what our soldiers, sailors and airmen have to fight, our philosophers have to understand'[47] and his practical response to the perils around was to sacrifice the completion of *The Principles of History* in order to write *The New Leviathan*.

According to T.M. Knox and R.B. McCallum, both of whom knew him well, Collingwood was politically Conservative for must of his life, but turned sharply to the left in the late nineteen thirties. Thus Knox wrote that 'in politics, and in college business, he was on the conservative side for most of his life, but his views turned sharply to the left when the attitude of the British Government to the European Dictatorships seemed to him to be too supine.'[48] This general statement I take as a starting point: in what follows I shall try to fill it out in detail, and also query the extent of this leftward turn in the light of the continuity I find in Collingwood's expressed political attitude.

During the First World War Collingwood moved to London to work with a section of the Admiralty Intelligence Division. Although he regarded the war as 'an unprecedented disgrace to the human intellect'[49] he clearly had no objection to his war work, nor any inclination towards pacifism or conscientious objection.[50] His

---

[47] F.N., p. 176.
[48] T.M. Knox, 'R.G. Collingwood'; see also R.B. McCallum, 'Robin George Collingwood'.
[49] A., p. 89.
[50] Pacifism is rejected in 'War in its Relation to Christian Ethics', and conscientious objection in S.M., p. 315 and N.L., 29.9–29.98.

attitude towards the peace settlement which followed the war is clear and sharp:

> A war of unprecedented ferocity closed in a peace-settlement of unprecedented folly, in which statemanship, even purely selfish statemanship, was overwhelmed by the meanest and must idiotic passions. We had been warned some time ago, by Norman Angell, that in modern war there would be no victors in the sense that no party could be enriched by it; but we now learned that in another sense too there ware no victors: no party whose morale rose superior to it; no group of statesmen who, by the end of it, had not become a mob of imbeciles, capable only of throwing away all the opportunities their soldiers had won them.[51]

What precisely was wrong with the peace treaty? In a word, the absence of principle: 'the peace treaty which ought to have laid down the principles governing the policy of the party that dictated it, and to have worked out their practical consequences, laid down no principles whatsoever, and is of importance in history only as a declaration of intellectual bankruptcy.'[52] After the War Collingwood supported the League of Nations.[53]

Collingwood always opposed both class war and socialism. In *Speculum Mentis* he rejected socialism, which he labelled 'the substitution of economics for justice' and 'the declaration of a class war which is the explicit negation of the state.'[54] But equally, he argues against 'commercialism, or the overthrow of law by profit and the replacement of statesmen by business men.'[55] Again he rejected both 'militarism or the seizure of the state by that science of war which the state has devised to serve its own ends',[56] and conscientious objection.[57] This characteristic rejection of both opposites will surface again later. Collingwood refuses to allow their self-substantiality; to embrace either is to embrace a false abstraction. Each, understood in context, requires the other. Militarism is right in so far as it recognizes the need for a state to defend itself, but wrong in so far as it implies that this is the end of the state; conscientious objection is right in so far as it recognizes the sphere of private conscience, wrong in so far as it fails to recognize the necessity and rationality of law.

Of course, part of Collingwood's reasoning about practical politics is rooted in his view that historical understanding undermines

---

[51] A., pp. 89–90.
[52] F.M.C., pp. 30–1.
[53] 'The Spiritual Basis of Reconstruction', 1919, pp. 14–15.
[54] S.M., pp. 227–8.
[55] S.M., p. 229.
[56] S.M., p. 229.
[57] S.M., p. 305.

certain universalist political claims. For example, he wrote to his fellow archaeologist, F.G. Simpson, that 'political doctrines may work in Russia or Germany, and may fail to work in England owing to the Roman element which we still inherit, and that — here I would strongly oppose certain 19th century notions, including some of Marx's — there can be no such thing as an international culture, proletarian or any other, that ignores differences of historical background.'[58] Similar arguments are also expressed in his discussion of political progress in 'Political Action', where he also denied 'the commonplace of socialism, that government by a certain class is *eo ipso* government in the interests of that class. What is really wrong about government by a class . . . is not that it governs in a political interest, but that it governs with a partial conception of the interest of the whole.'[59]

Collingwood certainly, it would appear, objected to socialism; but did this make him a political conservative? Again, it would appear not: he was clearly not opposed to reform as such (although, as we have seen, he objected to mischaracterisations of the notion of reform). For example, he regarded the passing of domestic service a good thing[60] and in *An Autobiography* he wrote that 'the social legislation of . . . Asquith's first ministry, was such as I could not but approve' but he disliked the manner in which this legislation was advertised — promising voters 'ninepence for fourpence' was the negation' of his political principles. [61]

In his 1929 lectures on the philosophy of history, and later in *The New Leviathan*, Collingwood repeated the view that certain political doctrines were not self-sufficient as they abstracted from an historically concrete whole. Thus he remarked of Marx that:

> 'his antithesis between a present age of capitalism and a future age of socialism is vitiated by the fact that capitalism and socialism are co-existent tendencies in the economic organisation of one single age. If capitalism should disappear, socialism could not survive it, for socialism is essentially an opposition to capitalism; what would survive would be a quite new type of economic organisation.[62]

In *The New Leviathan* Collingwood treated the relationship between aristocracy and democracy and argued that properly understood, they are not hostile to each other, but 'mutually complementary. Each of them gives a partial answer to the question: 'How

---

[58] Letter to F.G. Simpson, 17/6/25.
[59] Pol. A., p. 165.
[60] Pol. A., p. 169.
[61] A., p. 156.
[62] Lecures on the Philosophy of History, 1929, p. 20.

shall we make the ruling class as strong as possible?'[63] Adherents of democracy urge wider participation; adherents of aristocracy urge restricted participation. The practical solution to the problem lies in the dialectical interplay between these two tendencies.

By 1936, Collingwood had become disillusioned with the League of Nations: in August of that year he wrote 'Man Goes Mad' of which Part One, 'The Marks of Madness', is devoted to a warning against 'the resolution of the state into a fighting machine', that is, against the militarism which he had also rejected in *Speculum Mentis*. He argued that the League of Nations cannot do away with war as it either perpetuated it through actions taken in order to suppress it, or rested content with disapproval, in which case it is ignored.

Collingwood hated militarism, but he argued that certain wars had to be fought, and certain threats resisted. With the rise of aggressive German Nazism and British appeasement to it, he began to argue strongly in favour of British re-armament. On the eve of the Oxford by-election of 1938, Collingwood sent A.D. Lindsay, the anti-appeasement candidate, a letter of support:

> My dear Lindsay — I am leaving for the East tomorrow but I cannot go without sending you my deepest good wishes for your success in your candidature. I do not think that the country has ever in all its history passed through a graver crisis than that in which it is now involved. I am appalled by the apathy with which our situation is regarded by a great many of us, and by the success which the Government has had in keeping the country as a whole from knowing the truth. Your candidature shows that the spirit of English democracy is not extinct. I hope that it still survives among those who have to vote next week.[64]

Nor is this all: Knox records that 'in 1938 he felt so strongly about the policy of appeasement that he went to the headquarters of the Labour Party and begged its leaders to oppose that policy with all their strength.'[65]

In *An Autobiography* Collingwood wrote that 'my attitude towards politics had always been what in England is called democratic and on the Continent liberal.'[66] What this meant was amplified in the preface to his translation of Guido de Ruggiero's *The History of European Liberalism* where he expresses the essence of liberalism thus:

> Liberalism... begins with the realisation that men, do what we will, are free; that a man's acts are his own, spring from his own personality, and cannot be coerced. But this freedom is not possessed at birth; it is

---

[63] N.L., 26.12–13.
[64] Letter to A.D.Lindsay, 20/10/38.
[65] T.M. Knox, review of W.M. Johnston, *The Formative Years of R.G. Collingwood*.
[66] A., p. 153.

acquired by degrees as a man enters into the self-conscious possession of his personality through a life of discipline and moral progress. The aim of liberalism is to assist the individual to discipline himself and achieve his own moral progress; renouncing the two opposite errors of forcing upon him a development for which he is inwardly unprepared, and leaving him alone, depriving him of that aid to progress which a political system, wisely designed and wisely administered can give.

These principles lead in practice to a policy that may be called, in the sense above defined, Liberal; a policy which regards the State, not as the vehicle of a superhuman wisdom or a superhuman power, but as the organ by which a people expresses whatever of political ability it can find and breed and train within itself. This is not democracy, or the rule of the mere majority; nor is it authoritarianism, or the irresponsible rule of those who, for whatever reason, hold power at a given instant. It is something between the two. Democratic in its respect for human liberty, it is authoritarian in the importance it attaches to the necessity for skillful and practised government. But it is no mere compromise; it has its own principles; and not only are these superior in practice to the abstractions of democracy and authoritarianism, but, when properly understood, they reveal themselves as more logical.[67]

This conception of liberalism lies at the heart of *The New Leviathan*: indeed, that work reads as an extended definition and analysis of this conception. In particular, we may focus on Collingwood's understanding of the relation between democracy and authoritarianism. It is plain that the treatment of the dialectic between democracy and aristocracy in *The New Leviathan* is an application of the same principle. Similarly, Collingwood understands the relations between political parties as essentially dialectical: 'to hasten the percolation of liberty throughout every part of the body politic was the avowed aim of the Liberal party; to retard it was the avowed aim of the Conservative party.'[68] In his view (a view which might appear ideologically naïve and certainly not one typically associated with an adherent of the left) the two parties were in fundamental agreement: both wanted the process of percolation to go on, but both

[67] G. de Ruggiero, *The History of European Liberalism*, vii–viii.
[68] N.L. 27.79. Collingwood defines the term 'dialectic' by its opposition to the term 'eristical'. 'What Plato calls an eristic discussion is one in which each party tries to prove that he was right and the other wrong. In a dialectical discussion you aim at showing that your own view is one with which your opponent really agrees, even if at one time he denied it; or conversely that it was yourself and not your opponent who began by denying a view with which you really agree. The essence of dialectical discussion is to discuss in the hope of finding that both parties to the discussion are right and that this discovery puts an end to the debate.' N.L. 26.58–60.

knew that there was an optimum rate for change that had to be determined according to circumstances. The Liberal party represented the engine on the vehicle of progress, the Conservative party the brake. However, at this point Collingwood argues that the eclipse of the Liberal party in the twentieth century was a result of its failure to grasp its dialectical relations with the Conservative party.

> The Conservative who described his party as a brake on the vehicle of progress understood that the vehicle must be propelled. Did any Liberal understand that it must have a brake? ... I think not ... They pictured themselves as dragging the vehicle of progress against the dead weight of human stupidity; and ... they believed Conservatives to be a part of that dead weight. Conservatives understood that there must be a party of progress. Liberals never understood that there must be a party of reaction ... That was why the Liberal party disappeared. It was not because the Labour party arose and by degrees took its place as the party of progress; if the Liberal party had known its business it would have absorbed the Labour party instead of being replaced by it. It was because the Liberals did not understand the dialectic of English politics.[69]

It would appear that Collingwood regretted the passing of the Liberal Party; and bearing in mind his dislike of class-war, he probably did not welcome the rise of the Labour Party. Furthermore, if the Liberal Party failed to understand the dialectic of English politics, it is certain that the Labour Party understood it less. In so far as the Labour Party denied the dialectic of politics, so far, I suggest, would Collingwood object to its rise.

Both in NL and in the earlier 'Man Goes Mad', Collingwood is concerned to establish the dialectical relation between the political parties as against the relations holding under non or anti-democratic regimes.

> From the point of view of one who does not understand that political life is dialectical, it is easy to bring two opposite criticisms against the two party system ... First, that the two parties are rivals, wasting in friction energy that would be more usefully spent in getting ahead with the work. But the two parties were not rivals. They were agreed in fundamentals. They were united, and consciously united, in work which everyone in those days considered important: controlling the rate at which freedom percolated through the body politic. What the partisan of tyranny objects to is that freedom should percolate at all; he wants the body politic to be saturated with servility.
>
> Secondly, that the parties were not rivals; that they merely posed as rivals, wasting energy in a pretence at rivalry. They were combining, says one, to exploit the proletariat. They were united, says another (or perhaps the same), to bolster up a cretinous parliamentary system; when a party with the courage of its convictions would have defined its policy

[69] N.L., 27.93–7.

and carried it out through thick and thin. But the two parties, though agreed on fundamentals, differed in function, one was charged by common consent, with seeing that the process (of the percolation of freedom) did not fall below the optimum velocity; the other that it did not exceed it.[70]

A similar view of the two directions of attack upon the 'liberal' or democratic system had been earlier expressed in *An Autobiography*:

> After the war the democratic system was threatened by two powerful rivals — there were two elements in that system, one of which was inherited by each rival. On a Lockian basis of private property the democratic tradition had erected a system of representative institutions designed to promote the good of the nation as a whole ... the Socialists ... agreed with the democratic tradition in aiming at social and economic betterment for the entire people, but proposed to achieve this aim through the public ownership of 'means of production'. Then came Fascism in Italy and National Socialism in Germany, which agreed with the democratic tradition in making private property their first principle: but in order to preserve it they abandoned, not only the political institutions of democratic government, but also the aim of social and economic betterment on which those institutions had been directed.[71]

Collingwood rejects both socialism and fascism; indeed, he thought fascism could best be understood as 'capitalist Socialism: a system in which the machinery of socialism had been turned upside down in order to connect it up with a different prime mover, namely, the desire of Capitalists to remain Capitalists.'[72] Both, in addition, were based on the idea of class (whatever their claims) and as we have seen, Collingwood had a hatred of the doctrine of class-warfare. The democratic tradition, if uncorrupted, could, he maintained, stand against these trends. But it had been corrupted — by Lloyd George, by Chamberlain, by the *Daily Mail* — and no longer preserved its old strength. Before this point he had believed that parliamentary democracy 'was still working well enough to perform its proper function of an antiseptic against class war', and he had consequently rejected socialism; he had also rejected fascism as an 'incoherent caricature of Socialism's worst features' [73]

All this had a common ancestry in the discussion of 'Modern Politics' which comprises Section II of 'Man Goes Mad'. He began by stating that 'there has been a collapse of liberalism in the modern world'. The essence of liberalism is:

---

[70] N.L., 27.85–9.
[71] A., pp. 156–7.
[72] A., p. 158.
[73] A., p. 159.

the idea of a community as governing itself by fostering the free expression of all political opinions that take shape within it, and finding some means of reducing this multiplicity of opinions to a unity . . . The one essential of Liberalism is the dialectical solution of all political problems: that is, their solution through the statement of opposing views and their free discussion until, beneath this opposition, their supporters have discovered some common ground on which to act.[74]

Liberalism rests on the theory that political activity and political education are inseparable; that politics is not a matter of expertise in which some can govern free from criticism, nor the views of others be dismissed as valueless to the community. It holds that politics is a normal form of human activity and should be shared as widely as possible; and that:

political activity circulates through the community, and governments gain strength from enlightened and cooperative criticism on the part of their subjects. The more political thought and experience, the better the government is likely to be. The aim of a liberal system is political education as well as the solving of the political problems of the community. Political education occurs in the school of political experience, not as a separate activity.[75]

Liberalism is not, however, a finished product but rather 'has been, not so much something done, as something in the doing'[76] nor can it flourish in all conditions. It does not flourish in war or emergency; nor where the people are 'internally rotten with crime and violence.'[77]

In Collingwood's view there were two directions of attack on liberalism. The first is from the right. This suggested that liberalism replaced action by talk, that it lacked efficacy; and that the apparatus of political dialectic should be replaced by government by experts. The claim was that we are in an emergency, and that therefore liberalism will not work. In effect, the fascist was claiming that there is a permanent state of emergency: where a militaristic country is concerned, this is true. If war is the sole end of the state then liberalism was rejected simply because it is political: 'The first French Republic fought for liberty and the rights of man; these gangster governments suppress liberty and deny the rights of man, in order that they may fight.'[78]

The second attack came from the left which argued that liberalism was a charade which failed to live up to its own principles, and that

[74] M.G.M., p. 16.
[75] M.G.M., p. 17.
[76] M.G.M., p. 18.
[77] M.G.M., p. 19.
[78] M.G.M., p. 20.

its rhetoric masked the reality of exploitation. The remedy it proposed was class war. The socialist programme was, in a sense, liberal in that it sought the fulfilment of certain liberal principles, unlike the right which did not. But it was liberal only in principle and not in method. Class war is war and is therefore opposed to liberal method. If it is objected that class war is not in the future, but has been already going on for a long tine, then the objection can be seen to rest on a confusion: 'it is based on a confusion between the general idea of conflict or struggle, and the special form of struggle which is properly called war. Healthy political life is conflict, but it is political only so long as it is dialectical.'[79]

War, on the other hand, is non-dialectical: 'a class conflict within the limits of a liberal political system is dialectical: one carried on in the shape of a class war is non-dialectical.'[80] For Collingwood, Marxist socialism was composed of relics from the past. It derived the idea of a wise ruler imposing his will on the people for their own good from the age of enlightened despotism; it derived the idea of a dualism between revolution and crisis as against the end of conflict (i.e. the idea of a millennium) from eighteenth century utopianism; and it derived the idea of war as the consummation of political activity from the romanticism of Hegel. All three ideas, Collingwood contended, were obsolete and, further, they had been refuted by the very liberalism which they sought to destroy: 'in all of these ways, Socialism is, in spite of its affiliation with Hegel's dialectic, radically undialectical. Liberalism is the true heir of the dialectical method.'[81]

So far we have seen that Collingwood adhered to liberal or democratic principles; that he supported the League of Nations up to 1936; that he disliked fascism and socialism; that he opposed pacifism and appeasement and militarism; that he rejected proposals for eugenics (and indeed any other intervention of a like kind); and that he thought the British empire a good thing. His changes of mind, such as they were, concerned matters such as the value of the League of Nations (which he rejects in both 'Man Goes Mad' and *The New Leviathan*, the stability of liberal democracy as a result of political corruption (which is not so much a rejection of liberal democracy as a complaint about those who were working it), and the political honesty of the British 'National' Government after 1935. He regarded the National Government as corrupt and dishonest. He deplored its attitude toward the Spanish Civil War, and its appeasement in the face of Hitler revolted him.

[79] M.G.M., pp. 22-4.
[80] M.G.M., p. 23. See also N.L., 10.96-30.99.
[81] M.G.M., p. 25.

Collingwood may have moved to the left somewhat in his later years — if all of the above adds up to a movement towards the left; I tend to agree with David Boucher when he remarks that 'the suggestion that Collingwood moved radically to the Left in his *Autobiography* is largely illusory. Collingwood did not abandon the principles of liberalism; he believed that everyone else had.'[82] Clearer still is the fact that (despite rumours) Collingwood did not become a Marxist. The extent to which some people (for example, Joseph Needham) had a desire to read Marxism into his work is quite extraordinary.[83] Needham was convinced that Collingwood had become a Marxist and he wrote not only to *The New Statesman*, but also to Collingwood himself on the occasion of the publication of *An Autobiography* to tell him so. In that letter he claimed that the *Autobiography* contained clear evidence of Marxism, and wrote that: 'the only criticism which occurs to me is that Marxism is brought in somewhat abruptly on page 152. For those who have any eyes to see, many earlier remarks lead up to it, e.g. pages 50, 61, 95 & 148, but just a single sentence or paragraph would have supplied the connection.' All of this reads as so much wishful thinking on Needham's part. The passages he alludes to merely state that there is and should be a connection between theory and practice, and there is nothing particularly 'marxist' about any of them. Moreover, the passage on page 152 makes it clear that Collingwood was 'never at all convinced either by Marx's metaphysics or by his economics': Collingwood is praising Marx for being 'a fighter, and a grand one' and for seeking to solve practical problems and to make the world better. This hardly adds up to a conversion.

Both *An Autobiography* and *The New Leviathan* contain ample evidence that Collingwood did not accept either Marx or socialism. Toulmin reports that before Collingwood died, 'dark rumours had begun to circulate that he had been converted to Marxism, perhaps even to Communism'.[84] Rumour is powerful, but frequently false:

---

[82] D. Boucher, *The Social and Political Thought of R.G. Collingwood*, p. 153.
[83] Needham wrote to Collingwood on 14th January 1940 and also made the same claim in a letter to *The New Statesman*, pp. 174–5, as did R.H.S. Crossman in 'When Lightning Struck the Ivory Tower', pp. 222–3. H.J. Laski in his review of *The New Leviathan*, *New Statesman*, pp. 97–8, argues that 'whereas the *Autobiography* suggested that Professor Collingwood was, if not on the road to Moscow, at any rate prepared to consider a ticket for that journey, this volume seems to prove the basis for a sophisticated 'Vansittartism' which is asserted rather than proved'. A. Quinton writes of Collingwood's 'sudden, late acquisition of enthusiasm for Marx', *Thoughts and Thinkers*, London: Duckworth, 1982, p. 36.
[84] S. Toulmin, 'Conceptual Change and the Problem of Relativism', p. 219.

the evidence of his writings suggests otherwise. I do not doubt that, as Knox and McCallum maintain, Collingwood's politics swung away from a general conservatism and towards the left; but I do question the interpretation. It seems to me that the difference between the earlier and the later Collingwood in respect of practical politics lies not in any change of political principles, but rather in a growing unwillingness to accept at face value the statements of the British government, together with a greater insistence on promoting a relation between theory and practice.

Collingwood adhered to the same basic political principles throughout his life: in later life, however, he reacted to the dishonesty of the government and the failure of the League of Nations with strident denunciation and increasing awareness of the failure of politicians. It is perfectly possible that he did this without any fundamental alteration in his political attitude: the evidence I have presented is insufficient to establish any firm conclusion either way; I hope only to have succeeded in throwing some light on the question of Collingwood's personal political convictions.

4: The Forms of Action

From this consideration of Collingwood's understanding of the relation between theory and practice, we now pass to an examination of his conception of action as a transcendental specification of this concept and then to the specifications of this concept — the forms of action.

Action is a transcendental concept, a universal and necessary form of experience. A transcendental or philosophical concept is a generic concept whose specifications are articulated as a scale of overlapping forms. Each moment of a transcendental concept is itself a transcendental, that is, a universal applicable to reality as a whole rather than a concept qualifying a limited part of reality. Action, as a genus, is specified in a number of ways[85] but here we are concerned only with the forms of practical reason: utility, right and duty. Collingwood argues that the distinction between these three forms of action is not accidental or arbitrary: 'It is a philosophical distinction; one which is made not because we choose to make it, but because we cannot think about the subject at all without making it.'[86]

Economics as a philosophical science studies actions in so far as they are utilitarian, that is, means to ends; Politics as a philosophical science studies actions in so far as they are regularian or action

[85] See N.L. and the contents to the lectures on moral philosophy as given above.
[86] E.P.S., p. 166.

according to rule; Ethics as a philosophical science studies action itself, that is, the genus action (of which utility and right are specifications) and in particular its highest embodiment — 'moral' action or duty.

Collingwood summarises his general approach in *An Autobiography*:

> My notion was that one and the same action, which as action pure and simple was a 'moral' action, was also a 'political' action as action relative to a rule, and at the same tine an 'economic' action as means to an end. The problems of moral theory, in the broader sense of the word moral, could thus be divided into (a) problems of moral theory in the narrower sense, that is problems concerned with action as such; (b) problems of political theory, that is, problems concerned with action as the making, obeying or breaking of rules; and (c) problems of economic theory, or problems concerned with action as the procuring or non-procuring of ends beyond itself. There were, I held, no merely moral actions, no merely political actions, and no merely economic actions. Every action was moral, political and economic. But although actions were not to be divided into three separate classes — the moral, the political and the economic — these three characteristics, their morality, their politicality and the economicity, must be distinguished and not confused as they are, for example, by utilitarianism which offers an account of economicity when professing to offer one of morality.[87]

The concept 'action' is articulated into its specific classes which overlap one another, thus for example, 'all moral action has within it a subordinate element of economic action'. Each class or phase of the concept is constituted and defined by its own particular fundamental conceptions (or absolute presuppositions): the specific characteristics of each type of action is given by the presuppositions which together constitute a form of action through their characterisation with action under certain categories. For example, in studying economics philosophically, Collingwood writes, 'what is intended is to throw light on some fundamental conceptions which economists do not so much derive inductively from facts as presuppose in their attitude towards the facts.' These conceptions include 'value', 'wealth', and 'exchange', and his thesis is that 'these conceptions are various aspects of, or various attempts to describe, a certain form of action which, for the sake of a provisional name, we shall call economic action.'[88] The fundamental conceptions enumerated above together constitute a constellation of absolute presuppositions, which constellation, as a specific case of action, is definitive of economic action or utility.

---

[87] A., pp. 148–9.
[88] E.P.S., p. 165

As an account of economic action these presuppositions serve admirably (which statement is strictly speaking tautologous as they are constitutive of that form of action) but as an account of action as a whole they are inadequate. They retain their value in describing economic action, and in being a subordinate element of the other species of moral action; but as an element in political, or in dutiful action, they are modified by their context. The difference is one of degree in so far as political and 'moral' action are progressively more adequate accounts of action per so; and one of kind in so far as each phase of the genus 'action' is a specific and unique characterisation of that genus.

We shall now look a little more closely at the form of practical reason. I shall follow, in the main, the account given in *The New Leviathan*: 'On any one occasion when a modern European answers the question: "why did you do that?" he will answer: 1) "Because it is useful." 2) "Because it is right." 3) "Because it is my duty."'[89]

5: Utility[90]

To call a thing useful is to call it useful for something: the question then arises, 'useful for what?' A thing is useful for a purpose; thereby my act, x, is a means to an end beyond itself, y. In this complex y is the end and x the means; but what is the essential characteristic of this sort of relation? Positively, to say that I choose x as a means to y is to explain why I choose x, but it is only a partial explanation. The relation between means and ends is not necessarily a time relation: it may be, and often is, the case that means and ends are simultaneous: 'what is essential in the relation between means and ends . . . is that there should be a logical interrelation such that each plan, the means plan and the end plan alike, is checked and corrected by reference to the other.'[91]

In planning the end, y, we must also plan the means, x: the choice of y necessitates the choice of x; but this necessitation works the other way round also. Carrying out the deed x is also to begin carrying out the deed y. The means have no meaning apart from the end to which they are the means, and further, the ends and means are mutually necessitated because the distinction between 'means' and 'end' is a distinction within a course of action, not between one course of action and another. For example, if I get rid of weeds by

---

[89] N.L., 14.65–14.68.
[90] This account of the forms of practical reason owes something to A.J.M. Milne, 'Collingwood's Ethics and Political Theory'.
[91] N.L. 15.46.

pulling them up, there is only one operation, the pulling itself. The end is to get rid of the weeds and the means is the pulling them up, but the distinction between end and means is not a distinction between two different operations or deeds (it cannot be): it is an analytic distinction between two aspects of the one operation, the pulling up of the weeds. If the relation between means and ends were a time relation such that one always preceded the other, then it would be plausible to maintain that there were two deeds and not one. Plausible, but not true: first, as we have seen, the relation is not necessarily a time relation and therefore we cannot build our account upon the presupposition that it is; secondly, where the relation appears to be a time relation the appearance is deceptive. Where the end is temporally as well as logically distinct from the means, we are tempted to say that there are two deeds, not one. In a sense this is true in that there may be two distinct physical acts, but it is not true in the sense here being discussed. Our immediate act, the means, is not good in itself but is good only as a means to an end. Whatever goodness it possesses, then, it possesses by virtue of its relation to that end. If the end were to disappear or if the end were never achieved in experience, the goodness of the means would disappear with it. In either eventually we are left with an irrational action: a means which is a means to nothing; the grin of a Cheshire cat has more reality and value. The goodness of the end, if it is really to make the means good also, must be a goodness confined not to the end alone (as opposed to the means), but the goodness of a whole of which means and end are constituent elements. However, it is precisely the inability of utility qua utility to conceive this or take account of it which marks its breakdown. I shall illustrate this point by reference to the 1923 Lectures on Moral Philosophy.

> If I am doing A for the sake of B, what am I doing? Not A, because I am not willing A as such at all. Not B, because B as such is not in my power. I am not willing either A or B as such; I am willing a whole of which A and B are parts. And yet I am not willing A as a true part of the whole AB, because the value of the whole AB is, in my opinion, altogether situated in B; and hence arises the paradox that, of the whole AB, the only part possessing value is B; but the only part I am doing is A. Thus utility leads to the situation of 'jam tomorrow, never jam today', what we are actually doing is always for the sake of something which is never realised in the past, but always hoped for in the future.[92]

Utility begins to break down because it implicitly recognises the goodness of the means as a reflection of the goodness of the end, without recognising or accepting that the end can never be the

[92] 'Action': Lectures on Moral Philosophy, 1923, p. 49.

source of the goodness of the means unless both means and end are conceived as belonging to a whole in which goodness belongs not to a part but to each part only as a constituent element of the whole. This denial constitutes its falsity.

On its positive side utility is identical with rightness and duty: 'The implication of x by y in planning, and the converse implication of y by x in execution, is the general characteristic of practical reason as such, and is found in every form of practical reason.'[93] What distinguishes utility from right and duty, as we have seen, is its insistence on the separation of the means and the end, with the means sharing in the goodness of the end only in so far as it is a means to it. The attempt to limit rational action to this marks its breakdown: if goodness belongs to an end conceived not as an integral part of the same whole and sharing the goodness of that whole, but to an end conceived as separate from the means, the end will never be reached and hence the means will never actually become good. This is one of the negative characteristics of utility: 'it is because utility stops short where it does, explains only so much and no more, that utility is only utility and not rightness or duty. Its differential is the peculiar limit of its rationality.'[94]

There are two further negative characteristics. Utilitarian action involves a decision about both the ends plan and the means plan; but both are indeterminate. For utility, the specific detail of the means and of the ends is a matter of indifference. The means plan must be specific enough to ensure the desired outcome, and the ends plan must specify the aimed for state of affairs in sufficient detail for it to be envisaged and brought about; but in both cases means and ends can be realized in several ways and so far as utility goes it does not matter which way. Utilitarian action deals with individuals, but 'each is an indefinite individual, required to satisfy certain specifications, but free to vary so long as those specifications are satisfied.'[95] In other words, utilitarian action makes plans that cannot be carried out solely on its own terms because the plan cannot specify the details of the situation in sufficient detail. There are elements in the execution of the plan that must be settled in the performance itself, and of these elements utility, qua utility, takes no account. The details which are unspecified by the plan are free to vary and are undetermined by the utilitarian action itself: they are decided capriciously as the action is effected. It is this element of caprice that renders utility imperfectly rational.

[93]   N.L., 15.51.
[94]   N.L., 15.52.
[95]   N.L., 15.72.

There is a second way in which utilitarian action is capricious: it cannot decide what state of affairs is to be its end; for utility there is no reason for choosing one end rather than another. If an action is good as a means to an end then that is what its goodness is, and the nature of the end is irrelevant. This point is not developed in *The New Leviathan* itself; although it is implicit there. Utilitarian action presupposes criteria by which we can judge what is of value, and what we should choose as our ends. Utility itself can only supply the criterion 'that what is of value is that which is useful': this, even if we provisionally accept it, remains inadequate. The capricious element still remains: there are many things that are useful, hut equally, they may well be useful to quite different ends, by what criterion do we choose one of these things as our end? At this point we can take the argument a stage further in displaying the inadequacy of utility as a complete account of practical reason. If we consider that utility gives us no reason for choosing one end rather than another, and that utility by separating ends and means, postpones its consummation, we begin to move beyond utility towards a different conception in which the end is not utilitarian and the means is an element of the end. The means becomes a part of the end and the end is contained in the means; while the end is chosen not capriciously but rationally, not for its utility but for its intrinsic value. Such a development of the argument shows the necessary progress of utility to other types of action: the tendency to halt the necessary progress is the tendency to replace utility as an element in the moral life with utility as the whole of moral life; that is, the tendency to replace utility by utilitarianism.

The point is beautifully summarised in a highly interesting passage of Collingwood's diary of a voyage, around the Greek islands, *The First Mate's Log*. In this passage he is reflecting on the possibility of justifying, as part of the community, the monks in the monastery at Santorin. On what grounds would outsiders who do not accept the people of Santorin's own account justify the presence of the monastery?

> What would the right grounds be? Social utility, you say. Nothing in the activity of one man or class or men is good unless it is useful, for its utility is what constitutes its goodness. I reply that this cannot be true, because it is self-contradictory. An action is useful because it leads to some other action. If this second action is desired only for its utility, that is as much as to say it is desired only because it will lead to a third action. Sooner or later, this series must end; an action must be reached which is desired not only for its utility but for its own sake: not only because it is expected to lead to something else, but because in itself it is regarded as good. If utility is the only goodness, if nothing is good except in so far as

it is useful, there is no utility and therefore no goodness: just as, if no commodities had any value except an exchange value, none would have even exchange value, because no exchange would be worth making. To judge all human action by the standard of utility is like establishing a paper currency in which notes can be exchanged only for other notes, never for gold and never for food or drink, tobacco or railways tickets or the services of professional men. To have a currency of that kind is to be bankrupt; and the same name applies to having only a utility test for the value of human activities. Sooner or later the judgement that something is good because it is useful rests on the judgement that something is good in itself, irrespective of whether or not it is also useful. This shilling is some good to me because it is useful to me and not for any other reason; and it is useful to me because by exchanging it I can get things that are good in themselves, things I desire for their own sakes: a fire when I am cold, a meal when I am hungry, or a lift in a bus when I am tired. Nothing is disqualified for being useful by being good in itself; a lift, which is good in itself as constituting a rest for weary legs, may also be useful as bringing a man nearer to his destination; but it is only because some things are good in themselves that anything can be useful. The utilitarian trick of judging the worth of all human activities by assessing their utility is therefore logically nonsensical, and hence unworthy of anyone who claims to be an educated and enlightened person; and it is morally disastrous, because it is the first step on the road to moral bankruptcy brought about by some process in the moral life analogous to inflation in economic life. Inflation pushed to extremity means that real commodities, the things we really want to buy, cannot be bought; all we can handle is stuff that is called money; but nobody wants money, people want the things that money can buy, and if money cannot buy things it forfeits the very name of money. So the moral bankruptcy of which I speak is the experience of finding that life is not worth living, because everything one does is done in the hopes of purchasing by its means a satisfaction which never comes. The way to avoid this moral bankruptcy is to stop judging the value of actions in terms of utility, and to judge them in terms of intrinsic worth.[96]

From here we can move on to another form of practical reason and see whether it fares any better.[97]

6: Right

In regularian action or action according to rule, we choose to do something because that something is right, that is, because it conforms with the rule. A rule is a kind of purpose:

---

[96] *The First Mate's Log*, (F.M.L.), pp. 150–1.
[97] The account of utility in F.M.L. proceeds straight from utility to the concept of intrinsic worth, but I shall follow the order of exposition in N.L. and discuss Right next.

> It is a *generalized purpose*: not the purpose to do one thing on one occasion ... but a purpose to do things of a certain kind on all occasions of a certain kind. This is a *regularian principle* or *rule*. To act on a regularian principle is to decide upon a general way of behaving, defined as involving some act of a specific kind and when some occasion of a specified kind arises.[98]

Regularian action is political action and 'the capacity for "political action", understood as the regulation of life according to definite rules is universal in man.'[99]

The rule is only a part of regularian action: there is also the decision to obey or disobey that rule. Again rules have to be made before they can be obeyed or broken. The making of rules is often, but not necessarily, a social thing; we may and often do make rules for ourselves alone. The simplest case of regularian action is the case of someone making rules for himself: this must be understood before we can understand the more complex case of someone making rules for someone else to obey.

For Collingwood, regularian action is capricious, but not to the same degree as utilitarian action:

> A utilitarian action never fully explains why just this action and no other is done. The same is true of regularian grounds, though in a different way. This is because the regularian ground is a generalization, expressly admitting of alternative realizations ... A rule only specifies *some* act of a certain kind. The application of it to a given occasion bids me to perform one, and only one, of the acts which would conform to its specification. The acts which so conform may be many or few; which they are, depends not on the rule but on the circumstances; if they are many, I have got to choose between them, but the rule cannot tell me how. From the regularian point of view my choice between the alternatives is a matter of caprice. Regularian explanations, like utilitarian explanations, are at best partial explanations. *They never explain why a man does this* act; they only explain why he does *an act of this kind*, one of the alternative actions specified by the rule.[100]

Regularian action is a valuable and necessary part of all action. Just as convention and habit have their value as a part of our lives, so regularian action has a definite place as a part of our moral lives, albeit on a higher level of rationality. The element of caprice which flaws regularian action is its indeterminateness. It is flawed, as utilitarian action was found to be flawed (although not to the same extent): the flaw arises from the fact that no rule can carry within itself ready criteria for governing its own application. The criteria,

---

[98] N.L., 16.31–16.32.
[99] 'Notice of Political Action', p. 355.
[100] N.L., 16.6–16.63.

from the point of view of regularian action, are external or capricious: as we shall see later, from the point of view of moral action *as such*, the criteria are rational and the element of caprice disappears.

Regularian action fails through its inherent element of caprice, but there are other reasons why regularian action is not self-sufficient. Regularian or political action has its own conceptions and particular values: 'orderliness, regularity, submission to a rule which applies equally to all persons,'[101] 'the political good is order as such.'[102]

This is clear, but why are these things desired? Within regularian or political action this question does not arise, order is simply presupposed as the very condition of political action. Again, we may ask, how should we institute order? What rules shall we make? In regularian action there are two decisions which have to be made: a) what rules to obey, that is, what rules we ought to make and b) the decision to obey them in relevant circumstances, which includes the decision how to obey them. These questions cannot be answered from within regularian action itself. We might look to utilitarian explanations, but these would fail: for example, the habit of queuing cannot be given an adequate utilitarian explanation: 'it does not save time; it is definitely opposed to the interests of the strongest and most active individuals; and it demands an extraordinary degree of discipline when you are at the end of the queue and the train is about to start.'[103] Its value is not utilitarian but political, its goodness the goodness of orderly conduct, observance of rule. Neither can we give a regularian explanation. To say that, as a rule, it is better to act according to rule is to beg the question. Order, and the particular rules and laws which are its expression, cannot be explained by reference to anything outside themselves, they can only be explained as being of intrinsic value. Order is good in itself, and good rules and laws are good in themselves: they are good in so far as they really are rules and laws: 'the goodness of a law consists in its being really a law — that is, a principle really worked out in thought so as to apply to a particular region of practice, really laid down as binding within that region, and really obeyed or observed within the limits of its application.'[104]

Law, then, is good in itself; but the recognition of what is good in itself is not accountable for in the terms of regularian action. Regularian action (like utilitarian action) serves in its own particular way as an end. For utility the end is served by something understood

[101] Pol. A., p. 162.
[102] Pol. A., p. 166.
[103] Pol. A., p. 162.
[104] Pol. A., pp. 160-1.

as separate, that is, by the means: for right the end and the means are conceived not as separate but as conjoined — a rule 'stands upon its own legs, justifies itself. It is immediate.'[105] This may be so, but if we remember the two kinds of decisions involved in regularian action (decisions about what rules to obey and decisions to obey them), we may add that there are occasions on which right gives way to the demands of a higher form of action.

To recognise something as right is to recognise it as being in accordance with a rule; that is, we recognise the thing not in its individuality but merely as an instance of a type. This recognition is a necessary part of regularian action and therefore a necessary part of all action: but it is not able to account for two things that need explanation. First, we need to be able to explain why we come to make this rule rather than that, and this presupposes that we can recognise intrinsic value. Secondly, we need to be able to explain why, on certain occasions we a) obey a rule in this or that unique way (that is, we have to be able to explain why we do what we do with respect to those features of the action which the rule itself leaves open); and b) we need to be able to explain why we at times break rules or; c) why we (on occasion) leave rules to one side as inadequate and; d) we need to be able to explain what we do on those occasions where you find yourself in a situation which you do not recognise as belonging to any of your known types.

The making of rules, the implementation of rules, the breaking of rules, the leaving aside of the rules, the acting in unfamiliar situations for which we can find no rules; these all demand a feature of consciousness which the regularian consciousness alone cannot provide. Rules can do everything except implement themselves, and the implementation of a rule requires an act of judgement that cannot itself be referred to a rule without the risk of infinite regress. We can only explain how these things are possible if we go on to discuss a type of action in which we act according to our recognition of things as good in themselves (that is, not good relative to an end or to a rule) and in which we act not according to certain features which we abstract from a situation, but according to the unique qualities of the situation itself. Just as utilitarian action presupposes things which are intrinsically good, so regularian action presupposes a kind of action 'which is not determined according to rule, and where the process is directly from knowledge of the situation to an action appropriate to that situation, without passing through the stage of

---

[105] Pol. A., p. 164.

formulating a rule appropriate to the situation.'[106] It is to this sort of action that we now turn.

7: Duty

Utilitarian and regularian action are not self-sufficient because they a) lack determinacy, i.e., they leave certain aspects of the action which they seek to explain open, and these aspects, from their point of view, can be fulfilled only capriciously; b) neither can account for itself: utility presupposes an end which is good in itself; and right presupposes a form of consciousness which is capable of formulating rules and a form of action which can proceed without reference to rules.

In acting according to rules we are moving among certain standard types of situations: we recognise the situation and apply the rule which we normally apply in such a situation. The question now is, how did the rule arise in the first place?

> You may know this rule, but how do you know it? Either because of your own experience or someone else's. In either case a certain body of experience has been accumulated before the rule could be known to anyone... (the existence of a rule presupposes experience of acting in situations where there was no rule) ... There must, therefore, be a kind of action which is not determined according to rule, and where the process is directly from knowledge of the situation to an action appropriate to that situation, without passing through the stage of formulating a rule appropriate to the situation. And it must be very common, for a vast deal of it must go to the formulation of even the most trivial rule of conduct.[107]

Such a kind of action is ubiquitous not only as a result of our having to act in situations for which we have no rule, but also as a result of the fact that every piece of utilitarian or regularian action is not determinate and so requires supplementation by action proceeding directly from a judgement of the particular requirements of the situation in all its individuality. The inadequacy of utility and of right lies in the fact that neither can explain why we do *this* act; each can only explain why we do an act of this *type*: but no situation is merely a type of situation, and hence no act can be merely a particular type of act either.

Every act, therefore, demands something over and above its features as a utilitarian or regularian action, and this we might call improvisation. Improvisation is an element in all actions: but there are occasions when it determines the whole of an action.

> The first kind of occasion on which it is necessary to act without rules is when you find yourself in a situation that you do not recognise as

[106] A., p. 103.
[107] A., p. 103.

belonging to any of your known types. No rule can tell you how to act. But you cannot refrain from acting. No one is ever free to act or not to act, at his own discretion . . . You must do something. Here you are, up against this situation; you must improvise as best you can a method of handling it. The second kind of occasion on which you must act without rules is when you can refer the situation to a known type, but are not content to do so. You know a rule for dealing with situations of this kind, but you are not content with applying it, because you know that action according to rules always involves a certain misfit between yourself and your situation. If you act according to rules, you are not dealing with the situation in which you stand, you are only dealing with a certain type of situation under which you class it. The type is, admittedly, a useful handle with which to grasp the situation; but all the same it comes between you and the situation it enables you to grasp. Often enough, that does not matter; but sometimes it matters very much.[108]

As we have seen, all actions are in some degree improvised, even where we are content to act according to a rule. Improvisation represents a stage higher than the stage of rule following. In order to improvise, that is, in order to act in a manner fully adequate to the unique exigencies of the situation, what is needed is practical insight; without such insight our actions will fail. Whence comes this insight? It cannot come from rules for it is what enables us to apply the rules: it comes instead from historical understanding: 'What history can bring to moral and political life is a trained eye for the situation in which one has to act.'[109] Ready made rules are not sufficient in themselves; we must also develop a kind of insight which can tell us what rules to apply, not in a situation of a specific type, but in the situation in which we find ourselves.[110]

Improvisation in the light of insight supplied from historical knowledge is a more adequate and less partial explanation of action; but so far it tells us only how it is possible to go beyond utility and right; we still need to know in what way we must go beyond these other forms of action. Improvisation as an account of duty is necessary but not sufficient. We have discovered how it is possible to fill in the gaps in our actions, but we still need to know why we come to make particular rules and why we choose to do this particular act in these particular circumstances. We are still looking for the differentia of duty.

The first step in moving beyond regularian action is the recognition that rules exist only in being consciously obeyed.[111] In this sense, obeying a rule is the same as making a rule. It is this fact which

[108] A., pp. 103-4.
[109] A., p. 100.
[110] A., p. 101.
[111] 'Utility, Right and Duty', p. 13.

regularian action as such does not recognise: in merely following a rule we assume that the rule arrives ready made, whereas the truth of the matter is that 'all genuine rules are constantly being reshaped in their application; it is only in the application of it that a rule has any genuine existence. This so called application, which is also the recreation or re-affirming, of a rule, is nothing but the element of universality that is present in all volitions.'[112] An action, therefore, cannot be merely regularian, even though every action is in some degree regularian; every act in accordance with a rule is not only an instance of the rule but also a creation of the rule. The concept of action according to rule therefore presupposes a type of action which creates the rules it obeys: action of this sort, which rejects the letter of ready made rules in pursuit of their spirit is autonomous action or action pure and simple. It contains its explanation within itself: it not only follows rules but chooses which rules to follow; in this we begin to glimpse the concept of duty.

A consequence of this is the possibility of a 'one-off' rule.[113] We normally think of rules as general, applying to a number of cases; but this is to misunderstand the nature of a rule and to confuse generality with universality.

> The universality of a rule does not depend on its applying *de facto* to a number of instances. It depends on our being able to distinguish relevant from irrelevant features of the one instance that we are considering ... this universality of the decision cannot therefore be an inductive universality for it is not arrived at ... by considering an actual plurality of cases in which similar decisions have been actually made; it is an a priori universality, that is, we know in advance of their actually occurring that it would apply to all other cases of the kind if any others arose ... Thus a rule may be a universal, though it not only does apply but can only apply to one unique instance only.[114]

We have now reached a point where we can see how rules are generated, and also how, through the overlap of concepts, all action (including duty) can be understood as action relative to a rule; but so far we have concentrated on this side of the question alone. The existence and the consciousness of action 'pure and simple' makes possible the existence of the other forms of action; however what we are now interested in is not the extent to which this form of action makes possible the other forms of action, nor in the characteristics it has in common with those forms of action, but the characteristics specific to it as *dutiful* action.

---

[112] Lectures on Moral Philosophy, 1933, p. 93.
[113] 'Utility, Right and Duty', p. 13.
[114] Lectures on Moral Philosophy, 1933, pp. 94–5.

> An act done for duty's sake is an act whose value lies in itself, not in anything beyond itself; it is an act conceived not as a means but as an end in itself . . . I do it simply because it is my duty, not because I hope to get anything by it . . . the completeness and self-containedness of a dutiful action are due to its inclusion of everything else in itself.[115]

Duty is good in itself, and it is this that is the ultimate ground for the other forms of action. As we have seen all action presupposes an end that is good in itself: the recognition of such an end is a prerequisite of duty, and acting in accordance with such an end is duty itself.

I shall conclude this section by returning to *The New Leviathan*. Duty arises through consciousness of obligation or debt: such obligation is logically although not necessarily temporally prior to the discharging of the obligation in the dutiful action. Consciousness of obligation is called conscience, and it is one of the defining characteristics of duty that its goodness depends not only on the external aspect of the act (for instance regularian action where the motive of the person in obeying a rule is irrelevant to its goodness), but crucially on the intention with which I do the act, 'as Kant has shown, my will is the source of the goodness of a dutiful act; its goodness is merely a name for the fact that I dutifully chose to do it.'[116] Collingwood states this again, quite clearly, in 'Political Action': 'Nothing has moral worth, I submit, except the will of a moral agent. If that is so, the moral good and moral activity, are not related as end to means: they are identical.' To do good and to be good are the same.[117] The morally good action is a dutiful action.

When we do our duty we do not do it for anything: we do it *because* it is our duty.[118] Duty has two special characteristics: 1) determinacy and 2) possibility:[119]

> Duty admits of no alternatives. Whatever is my duty is an *individuum omnimodo determinatum*. There is only one of it; it is not one of a set of alternatives; there is nothing that will do as well. In the first place it is my duty and nobody else's . . . Secondly, any duty is a duty to do 'this' act and only 'this', not 'an act of this kind. . . Hence dutiful action, among these three kinds of rational action, is the only one that is completely rational in principle; the only one whose explanations really explain; the only one whose answer to the question; 'why did I do that action?' (namely, 'because it was my duty') answers precisely that question and not one more or less like it.[120]

---

[115] 'Action': Lectures on Moral Philosophy, 1923, pp. 83–4.
[116] *Ibid.*, p. 84.
[117] Pol. A., p. 159.
[118] N.L., 17.4.
[119] N.L., 17.5.
[120] N.L., 17.51–17.55.

The doing of our duty is not the *idea* of our duty: the idea of duty is an abstraction: the business of conscience is to tell us that we are under an obligation; what conscience cannot do is to tell us what the obligation is.[121] The answer to that question can only be arrived at through thinking through what the situation requires: it demands a combination of logical thought and historical insight, and the conclusion we arrive at is that this act and no other is our duty. There cannot be conflicting duties for there is only one duty; when we talk of conflicting duties we are really talking about conflicting claimants for the title of duty. The idea of duty is abstract and thus indeterminate — but it is the idea of duty which activates our conscience. What our actual duty is is not an abstraction. Duty in general is a specification like utility or right and is realized in different ways; 'but my present duty is not . . . 'My present duty' . . . is a phrase which at any given time applies to only one thing or person . . . and many different acts have been at different times my present duty.'[122] In other words, the idea of duty is abstract and general, while any particular duty is concrete and particular and admits of no other alternative. It is this which differentiates duty from right and from utility each of which admits of alternatives in its application.

The remaining characteristic of duty is possibility. 'Whatever a man is under obligation to do is an act which that man is here and now able to do.'[123] Kant was right to say that ought implies can, he was wrong for embedding it in a regularian theory of duty. We cannot be obliged to act in accordance with conflicting rules; again, as 'no rule can enable me to decide between the alternatives of which it bids me do one',[124] how do we then choose? We cannot have more than one duty and yet here we are enjoined either to follow conflicting or contradictory rules or to choose from a set of alternatives between which we cannot choose. To say in cases like these, Collingwood maintains, that ought implies can, is nonsense.

Towards the end of the chapter on duty Collingwood provides us with an admirably concise summary:

> When a man says that such and such an act is his duty, or that it is not, or wonders if it is, what does he mean by the phrase: 'his duty'? A man's duty on a given occasion is the act which for him is both possible and necessary: the act which at that moment character and circumstance

---

[121] N.L., 17.56–17.58.
[122] N.L., 17.83.
[123] N.L., 17.6.
[124] N.L., p. 123, fn.

combine to make it inevitable, if he has a free will, that he should freely will to do.[125]

And in his 1932 lectures, he clarifies the analytic distinction between right and duty:

> Doing our duty, therefore, involves two things. First, it means putting our will into a certain state; secondly, it means acting in certain ways, doing certain things, as a result of having our will so disposed. The first of these is the only thing to which the name duty or obligation strictly applies: the second is properly not what it is our duty to do, but what it is right to do.

He then concludes that 'the action as a whole may be called either doing our duty or doing the right thing, but what makes it right is the action performed, whereas what makes it duty is the fact of victory in the moral struggle.'[126]

8: Conclusion

This chapter has addressed the relationship between theory and practice, both in general terms and also in relation to Collingwood's own personal politics. This latter consideration was necessary principally because some commentators have sought to draw general conclusions about Collingwood's philosophical work and development from their perception of his personal politics. My purpose was to show the irrelevance of this approach. I have also introduced and examined the forms of action as developed by Collingwood in his lectures on moral philosophy and in *The New Leviathan*. From this we now proceed to a specific consideration of one of these forms of action: the regularian side of action or political action.

---

[125] N.L., 17.8
[126] Lectures on Moral Philosophy, 1932, p. 92.

Chapter Five
Political Action

1: Introduction

In a review of *The New Leviathan* H.J. Laski remarked that 'Professor Collingwood has made his book extraordinarily difficult for the reader to understand by the method it follows. It reads rather like a forcible arrangement of a great pile of notes than a clear and coherent account of its subject.'[1] In making this claim Laski was nearer the mark than he knew. *The New Leviathan* is essentially an arrangement of passages originating from the lectures on moral philosophy, from essays and articles on moral and political theory, and passages written expressly for the book. In each case the relevant passages were revised and modified, but their origin was undoubtedly the 'I will not say how many thousand pages of manuscript on every problem of ethics and politics', which Collingwood refers to in the Preface.[2] The reason for the book taking this form, it seems to me, is twofold: first, Collingwood was fully aware, after a number of debilitating strokes, that he was dying and so had little time left to devote to the task.[3] Accordingly, he adopted the system of numbered paragraphs as the most efficient way of reducing the sheer volume of material to some sort of order. Secondly, his writing was impaired as a result of the strokes, and he was thus compelled to use the typewriter, with which he found great difficulty. The use of numbered paragraphs lends itself to the task of overcoming physical disabilities which prevented handwriting and presumably induced fatigue; this along with the ease of reference it makes possible, permits the writing of a book where the production of a continuous narrative would be too

---

[1] H.J. Laski, review of N.L., p. 97.
[2] Preface to N.L., v.
[3] Collingwood suffered strokes, of varying degrees of severity, in January–February 1938, March 1938, Summer 1940 and January 1941. This last stroke left him paralysed and speechless.

great a mental and physical strain. This is, of course, conjecture; but not I think far from the truth: Collingwood had, after all, written all his previous books and lectures in a longhand narrative in the form of a continuous argument: in order to account for the radically different style of *The New Leviathan* some such explanation seems to be required.[4]

The New Leviathan is both dense and diffuse; it contains both complex sustained arguments and single, seemingly trivial, throwaway remarks. It is certainly hard to understand. Accordingly, while giving an account of the concept of society developed in that book I shall supplement what I find there with material from unpublished manuscripts. Again, *The New Leviathan* is in several ways incomplete; incomplete not in the sense that it attempted completeness and failed, but incomplete in the sense that it deliberately omitted discussion of anything not directly relevant to its main thesis. Thus it contains no discussion of punishment, or of the relation between law and morality: it intimates the place within the general scheme these things occupy, but of a systematic account we find nothing. An account of Collingwood's political philosophy which aims to be even minimally complete must, I submit, include reference to these matters, and I have therefore gone to the unpublished manuscripts to make good the deficiency.[5]

2: The Subject Matter of Political Theory

For Collingwood, politics as a philosophical science deals not with 'the state', but with political action. If politics is to be a philosophical science it must be shown that political action is an autonomous category of ethics.[6] Philosophical concepts are transcendentals: 'Political action, being identical with action in general so far as this organises itself, is a transcendental';[7] there can therefore be a philosophical theory of politics conceived in terms of action, but not of politics conceived as substance.

[4] For circumstantial evidence see the letter to W. Von Leyden written on 31st May 1941: 'There is much that I should like to talk to you about, but I cannot write except in a scrawl barely legible to myself and not at all to anyone else; and this machine, which I am trying to use instead of a pen, is a tedious thing and difficult to keep under control', 'Philosophy of Mind: An Appraisal of Collingwood's Theories of Consciousness, Language, and Imagination', p. 20. See also D. Boucher, *The Social and Political Thought of R.G. Collingwood*, chapter three.

[5] For an extended discussion of *The New Leviathan*, including Collingwood's relationship with Hobbes, see D. Boucher, op. cit, chapters two and three.

[6] 'Notes Towards a Theory of Politics as a Philosophical Science', (N.P.P.S.), p. 1.

[7] Lectures on Moral Philosophy, 1929, p. 108.

Now, the state is typically conceived as a substance with attributes: so understood there cannot be a philosophical theory of the state; 'in reflecting on politics, the conception of political life must be treated not as substance but as subject.'[8] To conceive the state as substance is to conceive it empirically, as an existing empirical fact; a fact with attributes, a thing with predicates. The problem arising from such a conception is this:

> If you think of politics as a thing, the state, or a number of things, the various different states, having this and that attribute, then the mere 'thingness' of the state, as so conceived, implies a rigidity of conception, an intransigence of behaviour, which gives rise to a simple destructive dilemma. If the state gives way to the trade unions, or signs the covenant of the League of Nations, *either* it is surrendering its sovereignty and therefore ceasing to be a state, or it is merely showing that it never possessed such a thing as sovereignty, and therefore ceasing to *pretend* to be a state. In either case the state is a discredited superstition.[9]

Politics can, then, in Collingwood's view be studied philosophically only by resolving it into the study of political action understood as an autonomous category of ethics, (and so a universal and necessary feature of all human activity). Given this view it is quite clear that political philosophy cannot concern itself solely with the study of the 'state': if political action is universal it cannot be constrained by the limits of an actual state; and the theory of politics cannot be so constrained either. Political theory must study politics wherever and whenever it occurs, that is, whenever there is action of any kind; its task is to grasp 'the conception of rule and all that it implies'[10] — for example, command, authority, ruler, rules and so on, and to exhibit these as elements of all rational action. Just as politics is found elsewhere than in the 'state', so the 'state' contains elements that are other than political. As an historical fact the 'state' shares the characteristics of all facts: it may be primarily political, but 'like all empirical facts it must exhibit the transcendental characteristics of all reality'[11] and therefore will have diverging functions and responsibilities. It will exist as an aggregate of functions bequeathed to it historically or functions left over by other bodies: it will thus have economic and religious and scientific and other functions belonging to it *de facto*. The point is this: as historically existing, the 'state' will inherit functions not of themselves inherently politi-

---

[8] 'Rough Notes on Politics', (R.N.P.), p. 1.
[9] 'Political Action', p. 156.
[10] Lectures on Moral Philosophy, 1933, p. 99. (Hereafter these lectures together, with those from other years, will be cited as L.M.P. along with the date).
[11] L.M.P., 1929., p. 107.

cal; as empirical, it will be necessarily involved with non-political activities. How should it deal with this state of affairs? 'Its success in dealing with these questions depends on the firmness with which it grasps its own essentially political character, and realises that it can and must deal with them only so far as that character at once compels and enables it to do so.'[12] Collingwood's view on the question of the legitimate extent of state interference appears to be that the state can intervene only a) for political reasons, b) where such intervention is necessary as a consequence of the political failure or inability of the activity with which it interferes, c) where such interference is seen as the job of the state.[13]

So far I have written only of the 'state', by which has been meant the state as an empirical fact; I have shown that, for Collingwood, there can be no philosophical theory of the state so conceived, and that the philosophical theory of politics deals not with 'states' but with political action. However, there is a perfectly genuine sense in which it is permissible to talk of a philosophical theory of the state, and this is where we mean by 'state' not a thing or substance, but an activity. So understood the state is 'the collective name for a certain complex of political actions.'[14] the theory of the state becomes a study of the political aspect of life, and especially a study of this aspect as an organised whole by which the life of a community is regulated. In order to illustrate Collingwood's view of the nature and scope of political theory I shall quote from the lectures on moral philosophy delivered in 1933. This passage also has the merit of throwing light on Collingwood's understanding of the relation between history and philosophy, especially on the remarks in the *Autobiography* concerning the theory of the state.[15]

> Politics as a science has an empirical part and a philosophical part. There are certain institutions, or organised complexes of human activity, which exist for the purpose of making and administering universal rules: these are generally called states, and on its empirical side politics may be described as the theory of the state. But the making and carrying out of rules is by no means an exclusive function of the state, nor yet its only function.
> Conformity to rule is a characteristic of all action whatever; there is no institution, whether state, church, school, club, or family, which does not make rules and impose them on its members, and there is no individual human agent who does not make rules and impose them on himself; and on the other hand the state, as a concrete historical institution, can-

---

[12] L.M.P., 1929, p. 107.
[13] See notes on R.M. MacIver, 1927.
[14] Pol. A., p. 157.
[15] A., pp. 61–3.

not confine itself to the making and administering of rules or laws, it must to some extent interest itself in economic and moral questions as well as political questions in the strict sense of the word. Consequently there cannot be a philosophical theory of the state, there can only be a descriptive, empirical, or historical account of it; the philosophical theory of politics can only be a theory of the political element which, though people are perhaps readier to discern its presence in the state than elsewhere, is not confined to it but is coextensive with human life.

There is, therefore, a certain equivocation attaching to all the concepts of political science, according as they are understood empirically or philosophically. Empirically considered, the state is merely a certain type of historical phenomenon.

It is a type of organisation which has never confined itself to the strictly political function of making and enforcing rules, nor has it ever tried to monopolise that function as it exists in the life of its citizens. It is therefore idle to attempt a deduction of the proper functions of the state from the principles of philosophical politics. In order to understand the state we must appeal not to philosophy but to history.[16]

The state as we know it is an entirely modern thing, profoundly different in its essential character from, for example, the ancient Greek polis, which from our point of view was at least as much a church as a state, being based on a common religion and regarding the maintenance of this religion as its *raison d'être* nor is it to be expected that the state as we know it will survive indefinitely into the future. But philosophically the state is a mere name for the political function in human life; and in that sense it is an eternal necessity, for this function must be carried out in the consciousness that it is a function distinct from others. The same analysis will apply to the other concepts of politics.[17]

In the passage from *An Autobiography* Collingwood stresses the historically bound nature of the state and insists on a recognition of the difference between the state as Plato and Hobbes conceived it, both in its empirical and in its ideal nature. This accords with the passage from the 1933 Lectures on Moral Philosophy.

If by 'state', however, we understand neither an empirically existing thing with certain historically contingent powers and limitations, nor a theory of such a thing which conceives it as a substance with attributes, but instead 'a complex of political actions', then there can be a philosophical theory of politics. Such a theory would have a history on both its theoretical and empirical side. Theoretically it would be a study of the political element in all action:[18] such a study must originate as the study of actual historical conduct. Empirically it would be a study of actual states and therefore historical, but philosophical in that it would conceive of the state as a cer-

---

[16] This paragraph was inserted later, probably in 1939–40.
[17] L.M.P., 1933, pp. 99–100.
[18] A., pp. 148–9.

tain type of activity. This activity would be political activity understood as a universal and necessary feature of human life and it would be studied in its historically determinate manifestations as the activity of a society organising itself politically. So far, then, as political science is a theory of political action it is a philosophical science, and the sameness of its object is the sameness of a universal (not an abstract, but a concrete or philosophical universal — in other words, a scale of forms); so far as it is a theory of the state, the sameness of its object is the sameness of an historical process. In practice these two elements are so interwoven that the permanent problems (what is political action?) appear *sub specie saeculi*, and the special problems of the age (the nature of the state) *sub specie aeternitatis*.

3: Society

A society is not a class: the members of a class are related by resemblance; the members of a society are related as parts of a whole. There is such a thing as the class of members of a society: in this case belonging to a society is a point of resemblance among its members, and thus the members of a society can be said, by virtue of this resemblance, to constitute a class. This is the only sense in which the members of a society are the members of a class: Collingwood's aim here is to show that a society cannot be reduced to a class of its own members.[19]

Collingwood draws a distinction between a 'society' and a society. What they have in common is that in each there is a one to one relation between its members; each member has a share in something divided among them. This one to one relation between sharers or between participants and sharers, Collingwood calls the *suum cuique*[20] of that society. All societies have a *suum cuique*, and so far all are the same, but a 'society' may be any such whole with parts related by participation: it may be a society of plants, or of sub atomic particles:[21] Collingwood does not object to this usage, but he is concerned to remind us that there are societies that are more than this. In order to do this he draws on the concept of *societas*. So conceived a societas is a relation between *personae* (that is free men)[22] arising through contract, that contract being the joint activity of free agents.[23] It is the conscious and free foundation of certain types of

---

[19] N.L., 19.37–43.
[20] N.L., 19.64.
[21] N.L., 19.59–61.
[22] Originally Roman citizens who were capable of suing and being sued.
[23] N.L., 19.57.

'society' that provides our criterion for distinguishing 'society' and society; society is the narrower and historically prior concept:

> The difference between a 'society' and a society is this: each of them has a *suum cuique* in each of them the members have a share in something that is divided among them; but in a society proper the establishment and maintenance of the *suum cuique* is effected by *their joint activity as free agents*. A society is a 'society' constituted by free activity on the part of its members.[24]

A society, then, is a whole composed of free agents whose will alone maintains the *suum cuique*, which is to say, whose will alone maintains the society itself. The *suum cuique* of a society (as opposed to a 'society') is a conscious arrangement:

> There is no living together unless something is shared; not as a family likeness may be shared, but as a family umbrella or a family hut may be shared; that is, by an arrangement binding upon all the members of the family as to the conditions under which it is at each one's disposal; the sum total of such arrangements forming what I call *suum cuique* of the community.[25]

A society is not a mere aggregate of its members (it is not a class), but neither is it anything over and above the organised activities of those members.[26] To say that it is more than the sum of its parts is true; but if this is understood to mean that it is the sum of its parts plus something else (another particular) then it is false. What the parts of the whole have in common is their sharing or participating in the character of the whole; and what makes the whole a whole is the character of the parts as sharing certain things. What they share are not similarities, or personal attributes, but the property of being in a certain active and conscious relation with other parts: that is they share an organising principle: what makes the whole more than the sum of its parts is that organising principle which enables the parts to share a common life.

The distinction between a 'society' and a society is a distinction between a non-human and a human state of affairs. As we are concerned solely with human states of affairs the distinction is no longer necessary; but an analogous distinction is necessary, and this is the distinction between a society and a community. A community is a

---

[24] N.L., 19.8–81.
[25] *The Three Laws of Politics*, (T.L.P.), p. 4.
[26] Pol. A., pp. 168–9. 'We speak of a society, but the society is not anything except the people in it. Its actions are their actions', and N.L., 21.27: 'If a society consists in the practical social consciousness of its members it follows that a society is nothing over and above its members. It has no will but the will of its members; no activity but the activity of its members; no responsibility but the responsibility of its members.'

state of affairs in which something is shared by a number of human beings — this state of affairs is the *suum cuique* of the community.[27] A society is a type of community, and it stands in relation to a community as a society stands to a 'society': that is, it is the narrower concept. What the members of a society share is not possessions or even the *suum cuique* alone, but something more: a social consciousness or will: 'A society is constituted by the social will of the partners, an act of free will whereby the person who thereby becomes a partner decides to take upon himself a share in a joint enterprise... A society consists of people who are free and know themselves to be free.'[28]

Social consciousness necessarily involves the consciousness of freedom and the recognition of freedom in others. A society must first be a community before it can be a society, and it remains a community but also becomes something more than a community. When it is said that a society must be a community before it can be a society, the relation between the two is logical and not necessarily temporal. Where the relation is temporal 'a particular society may have been a community during a time when it had not yet become a society. During that time it was what I shall call a *non-social community*.'[29] The distinction between a community and a society is, then, a distinction within the notion of a community, a society being a particular type of community. The distinction between the two can thus be restated in terms of community by calling the former a non-social community and the latter a social community: the important thing to remember is that both are communities and that when Collingwood writes of 'community' he may be referring to either or both of these things. Generally speaking this occurs when the relations between the two or the transition from one to the other is being outlined; the context makes clear the sense being employed.

All communities depend for their existence on the establishment and maintenance of their *suum cuique*: 'The establishment and maintenance of the *suum cuique* is called *ruling*.'[30] The difference between a society and a community in respect of ruling is that a society (qua social community) is a self-ruling community whereas a non-social community is not. The existence of a non-social community depends on its being ruled by something other than itself.

Where that which rules, rules itself, ruling is immanent; where that which rules rules something other than itself, ruling is

---

[27] N.L., 20.12.
[28] N.L., 20.2–20.23.
[29] N.L., 20.32.
[30] N.L., 20.35.

transeunt.[31] A society, in ruling itself, is self-originating and self-maintaining: it comes into existence by an act of joint will, and is kept in existence by the exercise of the same joint will. This joint will which maintains a society can also originate and maintain a non-social community, in which case the latter depends on the former, and its members are dependents.[32]

Within a society the relation between parts may be one in which one part has authority over another; we must be careful, however, to distinguish carefully between authority and force. What then is authority?

> Something capable of ruling itself sometimes appears to be (but is not in fact) ruled by something else. I refer to the case in which one thing is said to have *authority* over another. Authority is the name of a relation between B who 'has authority' to do something and A who 'authorizes' him or 'gives him authority' to do it. Where 'it' is a transeunt action there is a third party C to whom A authorizes B to do it. In that case B's relation to C may involve the use of force.[33]

Authority is an internal relation between the parts of a society, not a relation between a society and anything outside it, such as a non-social community: in the latter case the relationship is one of force. By force in politics Collingwood means not physical force but mental force: and force is a relative term. Force signifies not mental strength as such but one man's superiority in mental strength to another.[34] A relation of force is one in which the person with the higher degree of mental development acts so as to stimulate the emotions of the weaker in such a way that he renders the victim incapable of his normal emotional control. In other words, force presupposes a relative, degree of mental weakness and lack of control on the part of the person who is being forced. What the operation of force does is to deprive the victim of that degree of control and mastery over his passions that he has attained; when a man suffers force the origin of the force is always something within himself, some irresistible emotion[35] which makes him do something he does not intend to do; force is thus employed in order to make the victim do what the stronger partner wants.

There seems to be a difference between force as used between members of a society and force as used by a society against a non-social community. Collingwood does not make the difference

---

[31] N.L., 20.37–9.
[32] N.L., 20.43–5.
[33] N.L., 20.45–6.
[34] N.L., 20.5–51.
[35] N.L., 20.59.

quite clear, but it seems to be this: within a society force is a relation between members of that society; the members of a society are free agents and hence force is employed with the consent of the agent and patient; the agent and patient together constitute a society and it is this society as a whole which authorizes the use of force: between a society and a non-social community, force is a transeunt relation and there is no consent on the part of the forced party. The difference between these types of relation is brought out in the following paragraphs:

> *Authority is a relation between a society and a part of that society to which the agent assigns the execution of a part of its joint enterprise.* This may involve the use of force by one part upon another part of the society. As thus exercising force upon C, B is not ruling the society; the society, as always, is ruling itself; B is a part of itself which it is using in the course of its rule over itself to exercise force on another part of itself. This force is exercised by authority of the society; and therefore according to the free will of every member of the society, including C.[36]

Where, on the other hand, force is employed against a member of a non-social community the position is this: 'if B is a member of a non-social community he has no will of his own. His orderly life as a member of a community cannot be based on his own will, for he has none; it must be based on what from his point of view is force.'[37] The relation of force between a society and a member of a non-social community is the foundation of the institution of punishment, and this will be dealt with in section 6.

No existing society is wholly social, and therefore no actual society can be a universal society. A universal society would be a society pure and simple with no aim other than that of being a society.[38] The idea of a universal society is implied in the idea of a particular society, and is always to some extent realized in that every actually existing society exists only because its members partly achieve social consciousness. A society is constituted by social consciousness: a universal society would be one in which social consciousness were fully achieved — it would be a society *tout court*. By the law of primitive survivals,[39] which states that 'when A is modified into B there survives in any example of B, side by side with the function B which is the modified form of A, an element of A in its primitive or unmodified state', every society contains traces of that out of which it has grown, that is, traces of the non-social community. And this,

---
[36] N.L., 20.48.
[37] N.L., 20.56.
[38] N.L., 21.42.
[39] N.L., 9.51.

Collingwood explains, is the reason that a universal society is never realized:

> The reason why no actual society can be the universal society is that no actual society can ever lose all traces of the non-social community out of which it has emerged. To be a universal society is the same as to be a society: to exist only because its members, by freely embarking on a joint enterprise, constitute it a society. But every society that actually exists comes into existence because its members do partly achieve this social consciousness. Every society that actually exists is a partly non-social community whose members, awaking to consciousness of their own and each other's freedom, have begun to convert it into a society and have carried the process of conversion up to a certain point, but have left it unfinished. If the process had been brought to completion everything that distinguishes the particular society from any other particular society would have vanished; the society would have become completely social; it would have become the universal society, which it never does.[40]

At this point Collingwood returns to further discussion of authority, command, obedience, and freedom; these will be left until sections 5 and 6 which contain a full account of ruling and punishment drawn largely from the unpublished manuscripts.

To conclude this section I shall briefly mention Collingwood's distinction between a permanent society and a temporary society. The distinction is not between societies that last for a short time and those that last for ever; it is a matter of intention:

> It is a distinction between two kinds of enterprise, one intended to terminate within a length of time, planned to reach a conclusion at some definite period in the future; this I call a *temporary* enterprise; the other intended, in Stevenson's words, to 'travel hopefully' but not 'to arrive': no time of termination being either stated or implied; this I call a *permanent enterprise*.[41]

Corresponding to these two types of enterprise are two types of society:

> Every society is formed for the joint prosecution of some enterprise. Where it is a temporary enterprise, I call the society a temporary society; where permanent, a permanent society. Examples of the former would be two people going for a walk or a one off football team; examples of the latter would be an antiquarian society or a college.

The state, as the political function in human life, is of course permanent because necessary; any particular state is permanent in intention, although of course, empirically speaking it may turn out to be temporary.

---

[40] N.L., 21.5–51.
[41] N.L., 21.92.

4: The Body Politic

Political theory is specifically a theory of the body politic. But what sort of community is the body politic? For modern thinkers, the body politic comprises two elements, a positive and a negative, both of which are present: it is, in Collingwood's terms, a non-social community in process of turning into a society.[42] The relation between the non-social community and a society in a body politic is a dialectical one:

> According to Hobbes . . . *a body politic is a dialectical thing*, a Heraklitean world in which at any given time there is a negative element, an element of non-sociality which is going to disappear, or at least is threatened with abolition by the growth of the positive element; and a positive element, an element of sociality. . . . The world of politics is a dialectical world in which non-social communities (communities of men in what Hobbes called the *state of nature*) turn into societies.[43]

Chapters XXII and XXIII of *The New Leviathan* deal at length with the family, treating it first as a mixed community and secondly as a society. By a mixed community he means a community of which one part is a society and the other part a non-social community; and he thinks that most communities, if not all, are mixed communities.[44] It might be of value here to insert a terminological reminder: a society is the same as a social community; and this is the opposite of a non-social community (which is a community incapable of ruling itself). Both social and non-social communities are communities and by this is meant that they both have a *suum cuique*, (which is something shared in common between its members). Any actual community is a mixed community, as defined above, and a body politic is a mixed community. A society, then, is a social community, and is always found in conjunction with a non-social community, the two together constituting a mixed community. However, a society not only lives in conjunction with a non-social community; it also contains traces of the non-social community out of which it has emerged, and it is this element of its origin which prevents any particular becoming a universal society, or what is the same thing, becoming a society, no more and no less. It is important to bear in mind that the distinction between a society and a non-social community is not the same as the distinction within a society between its character as social and its character as containing within it traces of non-social community. The distinctions are, in a certain way, paral-

---

[42] N.L., 24.13.
[43] N.L., 24.68; 24.71.
[44] N.L., 22.1–11.

lel, but should be carefully differentiated; although, as we shall see later, it is the element of non-sociality that always remains within even the most well developed society which makes it possible for a society to break down into a non-social community.[45]

In a family we find a society (the parents) and a non-social community (the nursery). The nursery is not self-ruling, but is ruled by the parents; the parents constitute a society which is self-ruling, and because capable of being self-ruling, capable also of ruling others.

> The parents are able to exercise *transeunt* rule over their children because they are capable of *immanent* rule over themselves. And so there is a self-ruling community, or society, upon which the children are dependent; and into this society the children are drawn as they grow up: not inexorably, again, because something may go wrong with them, we will not ask what; but that incorporation of the now adult child into the family-society is what generally happens. By a dialectic of the same kind the *subjects* in a body politic grow up into sharing the work of rule.[46]

This makes it clear that the relations within a body politic are analogous to the relationships inhering in a family. The claim that parents rule over the children because they are capable of rule over themselves introduces the important and recurring principle that in the world of politics men and women rule others only because they can rule themselves. Likewise, a society can rule a non-social community only because it can rule itself. The relation between self-rule and rule of others thus reproduces itself in an individual person, in a family, and in a body politic.

From this outline of the general nature of the body politic we pass to consideration of the relations between the parts of a body politic. Collingwood argues, in the chapter 'The Three Laws of Politics' in *The New Leviathan* that:

> Political life is the life characteristic of a body politic. A body politic is a non-social community which by a dialectical process also present in the family, changes into a society. At a relatively early stage in this process (there is no stage at which it has not yet begun to operate) the body politic is a mixed community consisting of a social nucleus and a non-social circumnuclear body. The first are called the rulers; the second the ruled. The first class is a society and rules itself. Its members are 'persons' or agents possessed of free will. It also rules the second class, which is a community only because it is ruled. Members of the second class are devoid of free will. Let us call the first class the 'council' of the body politic; the second its 'nursery'. The body politic, as consisting of council and nursery, has to provide for the recruitment of each. It recruits the council

---

[45] See N.L., 21.87.
[46] N.L., 24.73–5.

by promotion from the nursery; it recruits the nursery by breeding babies and taking the consequences.[47]

The body politic differs from the family at one key point: each has a social and a non-social part, 'but whereas the family society is a temporary society the political society is a permanent society. The council or 'state' or 'sovereign' is a permanent society because its work is never done.'[48] The work of the 'state' is never done because the composition of the body politic is always changing, and therefore the constitutional problems arising can never be solved once and for all. There must always be a 'state', and it must always be addressing the constitutional problem — the state is for this reason a permanent society.

What follows from this is that any body politic is divided into rulers and ruled. Rulers are people who having reached a certain stage in mental development are possessed of free will; that is, they have achieved consciousness of freedom and are capable of free action. The ruled are those who have not reached mental maturity and who therefore have no will and are not conscious of being free. Freedom is a matter of degree.[49] This fact complicates the analysis as it means that there is no clear dividing line between those who have free will and those who do not. In some situations and on some questions a man may be free and able to make a rational decision; on others he might not. With increasing difficulty of circumstance a man in this position becomes increasingly unable to decide and increasingly incapable of free and rational action. The criterion for inclusion into the ruling class, for Collingwood, seems to be this: a man is eligible for inclusion into the ruling class if he can to any degree rule himself (control his passions and desires) and so be in that degree capable of ruling others (or taking part in the political activities of those who rule others). Freedom, possession of will, and mental maturity being a matter of degree, Collingwood allows that whoever has these things in any degree whatever should be included within the ruling class: the ruling class includes all those who are, in same degree, possessed of free will.

This has the corollary that the ruling class itself is stratified by its inclusion of people who are able to rule in differing degrees; ruling is a matter of degree, and the ruling class can therefore be seen as making up a scale of those in varying degrees capable of ruling. Some of these points are perhaps best put in Collingwood's own words.

---

[47] N.L., 25.1–25.18.
[48] N.L., 25.21–3.
[49] N.L., 25.41–25.59.

The minimum qualification for fitness to be a member of the ruling class is a very low one. People having that qualification and no more are capable of free action only when the problem to be solved is the easiest possible kind of problem and the circumstances in which they have to solve it are the easiest possible kind of circumstances. Where the strains are greater, greater strength of will is needed to resist them and make a free decision. The ruling class may, therefore, be subdivided into a multiplicity of graded subclasses demanding as their qualification for membership strength of will in different degrees. The highest subclass will consist of those members who are able to resist the severest emotional strains and make a free decision about the hardest political problems in the hardest circumstances. Lower subclasses will find places for persons who can only solve easier problems or solve them in easier circumstances. Thus the ruling class as a whole becomes a hierarchy of ruling subclasses, differently endowed with strength of will.[50]

All the above Collingwood summarises as 'The Three Laws of Politics'. These laws are meant to hold good of every body politic without exception, irrespective of differences between them.[51] They are therefore not empirical laws derived from induction, but fundamental rules of political activity which hold good of all political action: they are fundamental conceptions presupposed in our attitude towards political facts; we might call than absolute presuppositions of political action.[52]

The First Law is that a body politic is divided into a ruling class and a ruled class. Human beings are born babies, babies can survive only in nurseries which they cannot rule; nor can they authorize the rule of others for they have no free will. But they are still a part of the body politic and therefore 'every body politic, whatever else it contains, contains at least a *nursery*, that is, a ruled class or the nucleus of one; and a ruling class.'[53]

The Second Law is that 'the barrier between the two *classes is permeable in an upward sense*. That is, members of the ruled class must be

---

[50] N.L., 25.43–9. This pattern is repeated in the ruled class: members of this class are not capable of will (or are capable only in a low degree); but through proximity to someone capable of will a man in this condition may be inspired to behave as though he were capable of will (or capable in a higher degree). This Collingwood calls *induction*, and he considers that through wise and vigorous leadership from above such men may be rendered fit for participation in the ruling class: 'Subdivisions thus appear in the ruled class, based on the varying wisdom and vigour with which *induction* is administered from above, and the varying capacity to welcome it below. The better the rulers, and the better the ruled, the more this process will elevate sections of the ruled class to temporary and induced membership of the rulers.' (N.L., 25.58).
[51] N.L., 25.61.
[52] See E.P.S., p. 162 where Collingwood discusses the fundamental presupposed conceptions of economics.
[53] N.L.,25.73.

susceptible of promotion into the ruling class.'[54] Membership of the ruling class depends on a judgement being made as to who is fit to rule. Collingwood does not seek to give an answer to the question of the criteria to be employed in such judgement but claims that he is merely implying 'that *there is some quality which is held to make a man fit to be a ruler* and that by some kind of test the presence of this quality can be recognized. Let us call this quality *rule-worthiness*.'[55]

The Third Law is that there is a correspondence between the ruler and the ruled in which the ruler becomes adapted to ruling the particular ruled, and the latter to being ruled by this particular ruler. 'Working *directly*, or from the ruling class downwards, the ruler sets the fashion, and the ruled fall in with his lead. But the Third Law also works *inversely*, from the ruled class upwards, and determines that whoever is to rule a certain people must rule them in the way in which they will let themselves be ruled.'[56]

Through the operation of this third law the ruled class receive a training for political action which enables them to succeed their rulers. If the rulers are vigorous, freedom percolates downwards simply through the process of ruling; if the rulers are slavish then slavishness percolates. In this case, rather than elevating the highest sections of the ruled class into the ruling class, the ruled class throws up leaders which are as devoid of free will as itself and which can be trusted to do what is dictated by the desires of the mob. A leader so thrown up is 'a piece of flotsam floating on the political waves he pretends to control.'[57]

Collingwood's conception of the body politic is not free from ambiguity; I hope that his guiding ideas are now fairly clear, but still there is one ambiguity that I think needs to be examined further. The question is this: is the ruling class coextensive with society, and the ruled class coextensive with the non-social community? I will try to clear this up with the aid of Collingwood's lecture on 'The Three Laws of Politics'.

It would seem that the relation between a society and a non-social community is one of force: 'so far as the ruled are not yet capable of ruling and therefore not yet able to rule themselves they must be ruled without their consent by those who are capable of it.'[58] Thus, 'if it is the rulers' duty to pursue the good of the body politic as a whole, it is part of their duty to rule those members of it who cannot rule

---

[54] N.L., 25.8–81.
[55] N.L., 25.84–5.
[56] N.L., 25.9–92.
[57] N.L., 25.48
[58] N.L., 27.13.

themselves. They must be ruled by force, for they cannot be ruled otherwise.'[59] But rulers do not rule simply through force, they also rule by, and this is 'a relation between a society and a part of that society to which the society assigns the execution of part of its joint enterprise.'[60] Authority is not exercised over those who cannot rule themselves (those who cannot rule themselves can be ruled only by force, as we have seen above, or brought into the ruling class through induction), but only aver those who can rule themselves. So we have a state of affairs where 'something capable of ruling itself sometimes appears to be (but is not in fact) ruled by something else. I refer to the case in which one thing is said to have *authority* over another.'[61]

Bearing these distinctions in mind I will now try to make sense of the relation between rulers and ruled. What seems to be the case for Collingwood is this: 1) All members of the non-social community are members of the ruled class and are ruled by force except in so far as they are 'temporary and induced members of the rulers.'[62] 2) All members of a society are capable of ruling because they are capable of ruling themselves. 3) That the members of a society, in relation to any particular problem, divide into rulers and ruled where the relation between the two is not one of force but one of authority. 4) That there is a certain ambiguity about Collingwood's conception of the 'ruling class': sometimes it appears to mean those who happen to be rulers in relation to a particular political problem; at other times it appears to mean those who by virtue of being capable of self-rule are eligible as members of the ruling class whether or not they are engaged in ruling in relation to any particular problem.

This ambiguity can perhaps be resolved. The ruling class is composed of those who in relation to a particular political problem are ruling. The relation of this class to those in the non-social community is one of force. The relation of this class to those in society who, on this occasion, are not ruling and so find themselves members of the ruled class, is not force but authority. The essence of authority is that there is an appearance of rule by another, whereas the person who appears to be so ruled is actually ruling himself. Those who are ruled by authority and not by force are in one sense members of the ruled class as, in relation to that particular issue, they did not initiate the

---

[59] N.L., 27.18–21.
[60] N.L., 20.48.
[61] N.L., 20.45.
[62] N.L., 25.58.

ruling.[63] But in another sense they are members of the ruling class as, although they did not take the initiative in this instance, they are ruled only by consent, only by authority: in other words they rule themselves. This is precisely Collingwood's original criterion. Only those can rule who can rule themselves; and a society is a self-ruling and self-maintaining body, capable of rule over others only because able to rule itself. In this sense of the term, the ruling class is coextensive with society; in the other sense it is not.

It is probably best to restrict the term 'ruling class' to those who, on a particular occasion, are in the position of ruling; and to use the term 'society' to refer to all those who are free agents capable of self-rule who, if not on this occasion ruling, are at least ruled only through their consent: the rulers ruling through authority granted them by the ruled. This interpretation does most justice to Collingwood's explicit statements, especially those in 'The Three Laws of Politics' itself; it also enables us to understand the conception of the positive function of the ruled in ruling, a conception which makes no sense when the relation between ruled and ruler is understood as being one based on the use of force. It is this conception which Collingwood is characterising when he writes that 'the ruler rules as helping the ruled to rule themselves.'Consent' here passes over into active cooperation: the ruled's being ruled is itself an activity, i.e. their side of the bipolar act which constitutes the 'state'.'[64] These and related considerations will be dealt with in §5; I shall conclude this section by quoting some passages from 'The Three Laws of Politics' which bear out my interpretation, and make clear the relation between the ruling class and the ruled class:

> At any point in the development of a body politic's experience, and therefore in any body politic, there will be in it a distinction between two classes of its members; the class which decides how to deal with a political problem, and the class which, with regard to a political problem now being dealt with, does what the first class tells it. These two classes are called the rulers and the ruled. Such classes form themselves almost automatically in every body politic in relation to any political problem; and having formed themselves disappear as soon as their work is done; though there are psychological reasons for expecting a man or group of men whose advice has once proved acceptable to offer acceptable advice in the future.[65]

But what is the status of these political laws? Are they generalisations? Do they hold fast in all instances? Do they require conscious

---

[63] On initiative see N. L., 21.64 ff.
[64] 'Outlines of a Concept of the State'.
[65] T.L.P., p. 5.

effort to maintain them? Collingwood goes some way towards answering these questions when he remarks that:

> No political law enforces itself automatically. It might seem at first sight as if the first law did so; but it does not; granted a body politic confronted by a problem that calls for a solution, it does not follow automatically that those members who are capable of solving it should solve it, and that the rest should follow their lead. In order that this should happen the body politic throughout its fabric must be sensitive to political realities, quick to recognize political leadership, and resolute to draw the consequences of that recognition.[66]

A corollary of this is that the ruled have a positive function in the life of the body politic. Collingwood draws this point out by contrast with what it would mean to be a passive subject: 'to be a mere recipient of a ruler's behest, an obedient subject, is to have a merely negative function; to have a positive function is to have a will of your own which your ruler must take into account.'[67] The ruling class, is then (in one aspect) the social element within a body politic; in its other aspect it is that part of the social community which on a given occasion takes the initiative in ruling and whose subjects actively participate in being ruled. From this we can now turn to consider the problem of ruling and being ruled in a little more detail; and for this purpose I will draw on some unpublished manuscripts on politics.

5: Ruling and Being Ruled

We have seen that there is a twofold relation between ruler and ruled which varies according to the status of the ruled in the body politic. In the next section I shall discuss the relation between ruler and ruled where the ruled are members of the non-social community. (Which includes those whose actions place them, in respect of those actions, in the non-social community). In this section I shall discuss the relation between ruler and ruled where both are members of the social community.

The essential concepts in ruling are command and obedience, the relation between the two differing according to the relative status of those issuing the commands and those obeying them. In this section we shall deal only with those cases where, in principle, it can be said that the relation between the commander and the obeyer is a relation of authority and not one of force.

Political action at its simplest is action according to rule — regularian action. In its elementary form this consists in an agent

---
[66] T.L.P., p. 9.
[67] T.L.P., p. 14.

issuing commands to himself, in the form of rules, and obeying these commands. In such a case the agent is self-governing: he is neither ruler nor ruled, for he is both; and his ability to rule himself is a sign of mental maturity and freedom or autonomy. It is also a prerequisite for his ruling others.

However, the transition from ruling oneself to ruling another raises complications: some of these complications we have agreed to postpone (viz. where the ruler rules by force, although as we shall see in the sequel even rule by force presupposes a certain degree of agreement on the part of the ruled); but the other complications must now be dealt with. There are, obviously, certain empirical problems such as 'who shall rule and why should we let him?' But the problems we are concerned with are philosophical problems such as 'How is it possible for a society to be ruled and yet for each member to rule himself?'[68]

In 'Notes Towards a Theory of Politics as a Theoretical Science', Collingwood states that 'command is the keynote of politics as exchange is the keynote of economics.'[69] He goes on to state that command has sanctions, such as reward and punishment. As my view is that the sanctions of command only come into play where the command is given by a member of the social community to a member of the non-social community, and that within a society punishment and reward are redundant, I shall leave this aspect of command until later.

The concept of command requires for its completion the conception of obedience. In the case of a single agent issuing commands to himself both commander and obeyer are the same. In the case of political relations they are different, although political relations presuppose that the commander as ruling himself, also obeys himself.

> Command requires a commander and an obeyer. In exchange, the giver and the taker are perfectly reciprocal, but it is not prima facie clear that the commander also obeys and the obeyer also commands. The commander seems merely to command and the obeyer to obey. But it takes two to command, just as it takes two to exchange. There is cooperation between the commander and the obeyer. Command is not pure force and obedience is not pure passivity to force. The obeyer is passive, but actively, consentingly, passive. His obedience consists in doing of his

---

[68] This is, of course, the fundamental problem of political philosophy; it is perhaps most clearly stated by Rousseau who writes of it as the problem of how 'to find a form of association which defends and protects the person and property of each member with the whole force of the community, and where each, while joining with all the others, still obeys no one but himself, and remains as free as before.' J.J. Rousseau, *The Social Contract*, pp. 14–15.

[69] 'Notes Towards a Theory of Politics as a Philosophical Science', (N.P.P.S), p. 1.

own volition what he is told to do. The type of 'force' in command could not exist but for the cooperation of a will which, *without ceasing to be a will*, permits itself to be enforced.[70]

The crucial and interesting phrases above are that 'it takes two to command' and that in command, 'force' can operate only with the cooperation of a will which 'without ceasing to be a will, permits itself to be enforced'. Collingwood thinks that, in a sense, all government is self-government in that, strictly speaking, no one can ever make any one else do anything which in same way they do not agree to do. Where the relation is one of force the person thus forced acts through the pressure of 'some irresistible emotion';[71] where the relation is one of force in the everyday sense of the term, the person forced may have free will but may be incapable of becoming free because of the actions of (for example if he is a slave) his master. Even a slave, insists Collingwood, does not *have* to obey his master: the master is only a master because the slave obeys him.[72] This may be so, but little consolation for the slave if his master has him put to death: in this event the master loses his status as a master, but the slave loses his life: whether the sacrifice is worthwhile is a matter for the slave to decide, but at the very least, it can hardly be said that the slave's freedom in refusing to do his master's bidding amounted to much. What we are looking for is a third type of case, in which the obeyer does not merely acquiesce in the command for fear of sanctions or whatever, but obeys the command because he understands it as a rational command, a command worthy of being obeyed. In this case we could say not only that it takes two to command, but that both parties to the transaction are commander and obeyer at once and hence that the obeyer permits himself to be enforced without ceasing to be a will.

In ruling the ruler promulgates laws: 'law is the political form of right; it is regularian action in its political form';[73] law is the objectified form of rule, where the rule is made by one person for another; the problem is that of how the objective form of law can be subjectively appropriated and enacted by the obeyer, and understood by him as issuing from his own will. The bare bones of an answer to this are provided by Collingwood in his very short 'Outlines of a Concept of the State':

> State = government. This is a pure act. The state is not a substance but an activity. False antithesis of the 'state and the individual' becomes com-

---

[70] N.P.P.S., p. 3.
[71] N.L., 20.59.
[72] 'Stray Notes on Ethical Questions', Section 2, p. 10.
[73] N.L., 28.6

prehensible when it is reduced to the true antithesis between the political and non-political activities of one and the same person. The act of government is . . . an act with two sides, an active and a passive side. There must, that is, be a ruler and there must be a ruled. I) In the dialectically primitive case the ruler is a pure ruler and the ruled a pure ruled, i.e. government is despotic . . . This, however, generates *coincidentia oppositorum*, and the tyrant becomes a slave (so Plato) while his subjects become themselves tyrants. This is the ground of the *instability* of despotic rule. II) The ruler now becomes mutually ruled, and the ruled mutually rulers: i.e. the rulers become a mere magistrate. This is *democracy*, which is faulty because there is no absolute centre of power — hence degeneration into anarchy. III) The ruler and the ruled are conceived as *koinonoi*, i.e. the ruler rules as helping the ruled to rule themselves. Consent here passes over into active cooperation: the ruled's being ruled is itself an activity; i.e. their side of the bipolar act which constitutes the state. This is *autonomy* or freedom.[74]

The relation between ruler and ruled in a society is thus not a relation of dominant activity to passivity: the ruled play a positive part in the act of ruling, they have a positive function which means that they have a will of their own which their ruler must take into account.[75] Self government of a society becomes possible because the members of that society are all fit for rule as they can rule themselves. And they can recognize the validity of commands issuing from others who on this occasion form the ruling class, because as themselves capable of ruling (although not on this occasion initiating law) they are also capable of recognizing the rationality of law made by others. 'We speak of a society, but the society is not anything except the people in it. Its actions are their actions.'[76] The agent is always a human being, and the society always acts through individual human beings acting on behalf of that society. An agent so acting is said to have authority, and he is obeyed by others who, recognizing that authority, at the same time recognize it as being an expression of their own will: in obeying an agent acting on behalf of a society they are, therefore, obeying themselves as the originators of that authority. The presupposition of all political action in that society is thus the existence of that society itself; and the existence of that society depends on the maintenance of the *suum cuique* of that society: the sum total of that society's arrangements with respect to the common life its members share. The maintenance of the social consciousness of the members of a society is the same thing as the maintenance of that society itself, as the society is nothing more than those

---

[74] 'Outlines of a Concept of the State' (O.C.S.).
[75] T.L.P., p. 14.
[76] Pol. A., p. 169.

of whom it is composed: hence what is important in all political action is that that consciousness is nourished and allowed to thrive.

For Collingwood, the political system is a *liberal* political system and 'the essence of this conception is, or was, the idea of a community as governing itself by fostering the free expression of all political opinions that take shape within it, and finding some means of reducing this multiplicity of opinions to a unity.' There is no necessary connection between liberal principles and particular forms of representation because 'the one essential of liberalism is the dialectical solution of all political problems: that is; their solution through the statement of opposing views and their free discussion until, beneath this opposition, their supporters have discovered some common ground on which to act.'[77]

The other essential, and that which underlies the dialectical solution of political problems, is the conception of the common good itself; the conception that political differences are differences in opinion as to the best action to be taken for the common good, or as to the best interpretation of the general will, and that therefore differences in political opinion presuppose the common good and presuppose the existence of the society in which the common good has its life. Without such a presupposition political argument hardens into eristic: 'An eristic discussion is one in which each party tries to prove that he was right and the other wrong.'[78] A dialectical discussion, on the other hand, is a discussion motivated not by antagonism, but by a common desire to get to the bottom of things:

> In a dialectical discussion you aim at showing that your own view is one with which your opponent really agrees, even if at one time he denied it; or conversely that it was yourself and not your opponent who began by denying a view with which you really agree. The essence of dialectical discussion is to discuss in the hope of finding that both parties to the discussion are right, and that this discovery puts an end to the debate.[79]

A discussion about private ends, or class interests, or any other partial interest will tend to generate eristical discussion. There is nothing in common between those arguing in favour of their interests and those, who holding different interest, argue against them. If, however, it can be recognized that both sides do have something in common, that what they have in common is more important than their private interests, and that it alone is what makes their pursuit of

---

[77] 'Man Goes Mad', (M.G.M.), 1936, p. 16. and see A., pp. 253–4 and also Collingwood's translator's preface to G. De Ruggiero, *The History of European Liberalism*, vii–viii.
[78] N.L., 24.58.
[79] N.L., 25.59–6.

private interests possible; then the conditions for a dialectical discussion begin to be created. If a discussion changes from one about purely private interests to one about the common good and the correct balance of private interests within that common good, then the possibility of agreement is opened up as both sides now have something in common which transcends their merely personal ends. It is this which Collingwood comments on in a brief manuscript, 'The Breakdown of Liberalism'.[80]

> The ethical-political theory known as liberalism is a criticism and refutation of the theory that ethical and political divergences can be resolved only either by warfare (in some shape) or by compromise. The situation is that in a society A + B, A desires to do a and B desires to do b, where a and b can be done only if they are done by the whole society. It is thus impossible for both A and B to get what they want. This is what I call a divergence. The solution by warfare is that A and B shall engage in a trial of strength: the winner then does what he wants and prevents the loser from opposing him or getting in his way — if indeed the loser has not been destroyed in the process. The solution by compromise is that each shall modify demands until the two come to an agreement, each getting something which is not what he really wants. The objections to these methods are obvious. In the first a trial of strength is substituted for a judgement of right: and the method is plausible only if the substitution can somehow be justified or explained away. In the second, nobody is satisfied; and consequently a reason needs to be shown why either party should accept the solution.

The liberal idea is that in addition to a, which is the particular good of A, and b the particular good of B, there is also a general or common good, the welfare (i.e. the existence) of the society A + B. This (and this is the key to liberal theory) is to A more important than a, and to B more important than b, because it is the presupposition of both: whatever A or B is to get, he must get as a member of the society A + B, and hence his first and foremost desire is the desire that this society may continue to exist.[81]

A liberal community is a self-governing community, that is, it is a society. In order to be self-governing a society must be conscious of itself as a society: its members must have a social consciousness; as we have seen above, this translates into practical terms as the acceptance of the common good. Each member of a society understands that whatever he pursues he pursues as a member of the society of

---

[80] 'The Breakdown of Liberalism', (B.L.). *Pace* Maurice Cowling, the title signifies the *analysis* of liberalism and not its collapse, see M. Cowling, *Religion and Public Doctrine in Modern England*, pp. 160–89.
[81] B.L., and the translator's preface to De Ruggiero, *The History of European Liberalism*, op. cit.

which he is a part, and his social consciousness consists in precisely this understanding.

There is yet more to be said about the concept of a self-governing society. We know that, for Collingwood, the state is not a thing but is (philosophically understood) 'the collective name for a certain complex of political actions'[82] and that 'the state' at any one moment is equivalent to the 'ruling class' at that moment, and that 'the state' in this sense is not a permanent; we also know that within a society the rulers rule over the ruled by authority and not by force: the question that now arises is that of the legitimacy of law not generally, but in particular. Generally, law is the medium of political action, and therefore law as such can be denied or rejected only if political action as such is also rejected. This is of course impossible. But what of particular laws? It might be plausibly maintained that law as such cannot be wrong, but this is not at all the same as maintaining that therefore each individual law must always be right. Collingwood is, as we have seen, a long way from holding the view that either rulers or ruled are omniscient or omnicompetent; how then can we deal with the question of the rightness or wrongness of individual laws while at the same time maintaining that laws as such have to be obeyed and that therefore disobedience to law is prima facie unjustifiable?

These questions were addressed in a manuscript entitled 'Stray Notes on Ethical Questions'; in the section 'A Political Antinomy'. In this essay Collingwood begins by asking the question 'can it be right (i.e. politically right) to disobey the law?' He begins his answer by examining two opposite responses. First, that 'it *Cannot*. For the state has a right to command the subject in a particular way.' The rights of subjects are rights only because they are assigned to him through the state by legislation. Unless the state has the right to legislate, that is, to demand obedience, there are no rights. There can therefore be no right to disobey the state as rights depend for their very existence on the state. Again, it might be said that the state has the right to command only what is right, and that if it commands anything else its command carried no obligatory force. The question is: who judges what is right? If the subject judges then the state's right to command is null and void: if the subject were to obey only what he personally believed to be right then the notion of command collapses into persuasion or request, and this is to deny the state by denying its right to command. If the state issues commands in the form, not, do this, but 'do this if you think it is right (in the general interest, etc.).' then the

---

[82] Pol. A., p. 157.

state is not only ceasing to command, but is also throwing on the individual subject the task of deciding what is right or in the general interest: but the *purpose* of the state is to answer precisely that question. There would be no need for the state or rulers if each individual subject were capable of deciding what was politically right and of implementing their decisions in the form of legislation in concert with other subjects. This is, of course, not so; and as it is not so, the state must therefore take the responsibility of deciding what is right and issue its commands in the following form: *'Whereas in virtue of the right vested in me I have decided that this is the way for you to act, I now command you to do so and so.'*

The alternative answer is that:

> *It Can.* For the legislature and executive powers of the state are made for the community, not the community for them; and the ultimate question as to the validity of a command rests with the person who obeys it — or does not obey it. . . . A government bombinating in a vacuum is not government. By failing to govern *de facto* it proves itself devoid of power *de jure*. Hence the individual subject to whom the state issues commands has it on his responsibility to obey or not to obey, according as he thinks the commands wise or unwise. (Just or unjust, expedient or inexpedient — whatever it is exactly that the command of a state ought or ought not to be).

Collingwood then seeks to mediate the opposing positions, first by making a series of observations:

> The dilemma is between despotism and anarchy. Each has a perfectly logical case. Despotism simply means that the ruler must rule; that no one can carry out any business unless he is allowed to carry it out properly, and that, since the business of ruling is issuing commands and getting than obeyed, no one can rule unless he has security that he will be obeyed and therefore can issue what commands he thinks fit, in the confident expectation of their being properly carried out. Anarchy simply means that the business of ruling is a cooperative business in which the power of the ruler *consists in* (rather than *depends on*) his being obeyed by his subjects. If the subject is coerced he is not a subject but a chattel and the ruler is not a ruler but a master of slaves (Rousseau). With further analysis it becomes clear that even the slave obeys freely. He obeys because he decides to obey. If he decided not to, the master's commands would be an ineffectual flow of mere words.
>
> Neither side can be omitted from the antinomy without radically falsifying political life. Anyone who does not see that law qua law must be obeyed is just obtuse to the first fundamental axiom of political life; he is failing to recognize the sanctity of law, the necessity of carrying on the work of government, the *a priori* character of political principles. In politics he is what the radically unconscientious man is in morals. On the other hand, any one who does not see that the power of rulers rests on

their subjects consent is accusing himself of political inexperience. He has not discovered a truth which any mature political life must have forced to his attention; he is still in the superstitious and foolishly innocent state of one who believes that the mere word issuing from the lips of a magically-consecrated ruler has power to compel obedience in the hypnotised mind of the subject.

Collingwood then moves towards stating a solution to the dilemma:

> The solution seems to be contained in the criticism of the original dualism between the state and the individual subject. The individual does not stand to the state merely in the relation of an obeyer to a commander. For what is the state apart from the individual subjects composing it? Clearly, all commands are given by someone: and this person is always an individual subject. Commands, then, are given not by the state but by a subject (e.g. judge, police constable, etc.) whose function it is to represent the state by giving this command. But who commands him thus to represent the state? Clearly, other subjects. And in the last resort it appears that the individual subject, by being a subject or professing himself a subject, is deliberately making the demand that someone else (some other subject) shall issue orders to him. Each of these two parties is thus mutually sovereign and subject to the other; each is at once obeying the other and commanding the other. There is no such thing as the state outside this mutual activity of commanding and obeying as between individuals. The so-called state is merely a relatively self-contained system (not absolutely self-contained because of international politics) within which the relation of mutual command and obedience are stabilised and generalised into a code of law.
>
> How does this solve the problem? 'The state' has a right to my obedience because it consists of those political obligations which I take (N. B. not *have taken* but *am taking*) upon myself. It is merely my own political activity as objectified to me in a political system which I will to exist.[83]

The state, therefore, has the right to command because it is the society commanding itself: the state is the society as organising itself politically, and its power resides in the authority invested in it by the members of that society. Each member of a society is capable of ruling themselves, and each act of obedience is a recognition that their will is mediated by the activity of those who, on this occasion, are taking the political initiative. The act of ruling is thus the act of mutual ruling and being ruled: the relation is one of authority in which 'something capable of ruling itself appears to be (but is not in fact) ruled by something else.'[84]

The relation between ruler and ruled in a society is one of authority, and 'authority is a relation between a society and a part of that

---

[83] Extended quotations from 'Stray Notes on Ethical Questions', (S.N.E.Q.), pp. 7-13.
[84] N.L., 20.45.

society to which the society assigns the execution of a part of its joint enterprise.'[85] Is the state coextensive with the society as a whole, or only with that part of it doing the ruling at any one particular time? In one sense the state is that part of the society which is actually ruling at any given moment through authority invested in it by the rest of society; in another sense, the state is the whole society ruling itself and is therefore coextensive with society as a whole. In the end, these two senses coincide, as the essence of a state conceived as ruling by authority is self-rule by a society: the state in relation to the society it governs appears not as an alien expression of an external will, but as the collective expression of the will of the individuals of which the society is composed; and it is therefore false to continue to oppose the state to the individual subject. It was this opposition, this original dualism, which generated the original antinomy; and the overcoming of that antinomy depended on the overcoming of this dualism.

The distinction between the state and the individual subject can be restated as a distinction between the political activities and the non-political activities of the subject or the society; or as a distinction between the subject as relatively active or relatively passive with respect to a particular piece of ruling: both these distinctions are made within the same whole and so do not constitute a separation between one thing (the subject) and another (the state) and so do not harden into an opposition between these two 'things'.

However, in all of the above we have been treating politics and 'the state' philosophically and not empirically. We have seen that the state is not a thing, but a name for a certain complex of political activities; and that the state so conceived is not identical with the state as empirically existing. Of the state as empirically existing we can give only an historical, not a philosophical account; but what is the relation between the two? This, is a point which Collingwood addresses in a section of his 1929 lectures on moral philosophy: here his remarks arise out of a consideration of the idea of all government being self-government; but they apply equally well to the relation between the state and an individual subject. The point is that the subject's willing the state to exist cannot and should not be used as justification for any possible state, no matter how it operates. When the subject wills the existence of a state he does not will it as the best possible state, but as the state that it is in the absence of any alternative which he can provide: his willing the existence of the state is therefore compatible with a critical attitude towards the state and with a desire to amend or improve it. To use the fact of the subject's willing

---

[85] N.L., 20.48.

the state as implying support and approval for the particular nature and actions of any one state is therefore inadmissible: what the subject wills is the state as such, not his particular state in its detail; he wills this particular state in so far as it is a state and this is not incompatible with willing its replacement by something better.

Collingwood emphasises the difficulty of political improvement: he does not suggest that it is in any way impossible, but he denies that it is easy:

> Political thinking is no easier than any other kind. To invent anything that is a real improvement on existing ideas is always very difficult; and a political system is the fruit of so much hard and skilful thinking (a fact that tends to be ignored except by lawyers and those whose business it is to follow that thinking in detail), that however much we may dislike the system we find in existence we go on willing its existence (much as a man wills to go on attending the office he dislikes and accepting the salary he thinks inadequate) because we cannot improve on it . . . the sense of being tyrannised over in the political world is really nothing but the sense of our own inability to think out a better political system. If we could do so we shall find no difficulty in bringing this better system into existence. This is a hard saying, because we all like to think that we have invented a beautiful perpetual motion machine whose one fault — that it won't go — is a trivial fault.[86]

This passage appears to be suggesting that improvements are never possible: but it is clear that this is not Collingwood's view. What he is opposing is the view which sees all political institutions ahistorically in isolation from their context; which is incapable of seeing what is good about an institution but all too able to see what is bad; and which seeks to change institutions completely as it were by the flick of a switch, in line with a blueprint generated not by political experience, but by its exact opposite. In other words he rejects political rationalism of a sort which seeks to create political institutions *ab initio* in the light of 'pure' reason.[87] The passage above was written in March 1928; a month earlier Collingwood had delivered his paper 'Political Action', in which his views on political change are set out quite clearly:

> On what principle do people adopt a new political system as better than one already in existence? The false answers to this question are many and easy. A political reform comes about, one might be tempted to say, for economic reasons, for moral reasons, for religious reasons, and so forth. But in fact it can only come about for political reasons. When the political spirit of a society is no longer satisfied with its existing structure, no longer finds that structure to express its own political aspira-

---

[86] S.N.E.Q., §2, p. 13.
[87] Cf. M. Oakeshott, *Rationalism in Politics*, pp. 3–5.

tions, it alters it. And this process is really going on at all times. To speak of a stable political system as 'existing' and then as suddenly altered with a jerk by a so-called reformation or revolution, is to be deceived by appearances. Every fresh political action is in reality a modification of the whole political poise and attitude ('constitution') of the agent.[88]

What the inventors of political perpetual motion machines fail to notice, according to Collingwood, is that the political system is in perpetual motion already; and that to see it as a static object which can only be altered by altering it all, and altering it all at once, is simply to see it wrongly. Collingwood's views of the nature of political change are directly related to his understanding of the idea of progress. If progress means that the sum of human happiness has increased and is increasing then there can be no progress, for human happiness cannot be summed;[89] if progress means moral progress, then there can be none for goodness is not a product of civilization but a product of individual human actions: 'A man's moral worth depends not on his circumstances, but on the way in which he confronts them.'[90] How then, and in what can there be progress?

For Collingwood political progress is possible because political progress means progress in political institutions, customs and laws; that is, it is concerned with external circumstances, not personal motivation or moral worth. He wrote in 'A Philosophy of Progress' that 'the development of political life down to the present day has undeniably been a progress in the sense that it has led to the creation of political systems more supple, more adaptable, more responsive to individual initiative from within, and to alterations of conditions without, than the systems of the past.'[91]

There can, then, be progress in politics in the sense that political institutions can change, and change for the better; but how do we judge such progress? Collingwood suggests an answer to this question in the final essay of the Epilegomena to *The Idea of History* — 'Progress as Created by Historical Thinking'. Here, in the context of a discussion of a hypothetical community he distilled the following response to the question 'What is progress?' First, the question could only be answered on the condition that the person who uses the word should use it in comparing two historical periods or ways of life, both of which he can understand historically . . . with enough

---

[88] Pol. A., p. 168.
[89] P.P., pp. 71–2.
[90] P.P., p. 73.
[91] P.P., p. 76.

sympathy and insight to reconstruct their experience for himself.'[92] And the answer to the question is, secondly, that:

> If thought in its first phase, after solving the initial problems of that phase, is then, through solving these, brought up against others which defeat it, and if the second solves these further problems without losing its hold on the solution of the first, so that there is gain without any corresponding loss, then there is progress. And there can be progress on no other terms.[93]

If this principle is applied to politics the answer to the question of political progress becomes clear, and it also becomes clear that, for Collingwood, talk of 'revolution'[94] was more a reflection of the historian's inadequacy than a true historical description of events. As we have seen he writes in 'Political Action' of political systems as in constant motion. All change is therefore from one specific state of affairs to another, and progress is a matter of the adequacy or inadequacy of the new state of affairs in expressing the political spirit of a society, and in solving those problems which arise in the course of its history, while retaining its hold on the solutions to its earlier problems.

Collingwood does, then, accept the possibility of political progress, and he accepts it because it is a consequence of looking at politics historically; but he insists that it must be carefully understood in these same historical terms; and that if this is done then false and ahistorical notions of automatic progress, 'revolutions' or historical cycles will not stand up to the light of historical scrutiny.

If we now return to the relation between the state as understood philosophically and the state as existing empirically, we can dismiss another political sophistry: that of using a philosophical conception of the state in support of a political programme. What happens in cases of this sort is that in attempting to justify same action or deed, the perpetrator seizes upon some aspect of a philosophical theory which (being philosophical) applies equally to all states whatever their relative adequacy or inadequacy, and seeks to appropriate this general principle in order to justify some particular act.

The example I have in mind is this: Collingwood maintains that all government is self-government; this is, of course, not an empirical thesis but a philosophical one, and it is no answer to it to point to examples of coercion. But there are certain obvious dangers in maintaining that all government is self-government. First, as we have

---

[92] I.H., p. 329.
[93] Loc. cit.
[94] See N.L., 26.7–26.96 for a discussion of the concept of 'revolution' as a pseudo-scientific term which has no place where the historian understands his business.

seen, this is true only of those who have a will and who are conscious of being free, those who do not have free will are not capable of self government in any way. Those who have free will can accept and obey the commands of others without ceasing to have free will; and they obey others because they are both members of a society (social community) which as a whole is self-governing and self-maintaining, and in which each member is a free agent cooperating in the joint enterprise of maintaining that society. In such cases we can justifiably assert that in obeying the commands of others each member is obeying a command of their own; and that even if such a command runs counter to their private preferences or inclinations, the desire to maintain the society itself in which their well being is alone possible transcends their desire for private gain at the expense of that society, or outside that society. In a situation of this type the rulers have authority over the ruled, the ruled having given (authorised) that authority freely in order to facilitate the ruling of the community.

Secondly, there is a sense in which the phrase might be thought to lead to or imply a diminution of the liberty of the subjects within a society: if the subject is always self governing, how can it matter if the state chooses to restrict the empirical liberties of its subjects?

Collingwood replies to this carefully by employing the distinction between empirical and philosophical concepts.

> All government is self-government, in this sense at least, that the ruler, the person who makes the scheme, must be a member of the community for which it is made, and conversely the ruled, the people whose activities are determined by the scheme, must acquiesce in it to the extent of obeying it, which they cannot be compelled to do, and will not do except of their own free will . . . Liberty in the political sense, like several other conceptions which we have already examined, is on the one hand a philosophical or transcendental conception, and, on the other, an empirical. Much confusion may be caused by failing to distinguish these two aspects of the term. For example, when people say that they have not, but wish to have, political liberty, they do not mean that they are being forced to obey laws against their will, for no one can possibly force anyone to obey a law which he chooses not to obey — an elementary truth to anyone who has grasped the idea of the freedom of the will; they mean that they lack certain empirical facilities for making their wishes known to the people who legislate, or for replacing these by other people if they think that this would lead to greater attention to their desires. Politics as an empirical science is concerned with the various ways in which this may be brought about. Empirically speaking, there are some governments which are self-governments and others which are not; philosophically speaking, all government is self-government, for the simple reason that no one can be governed except by his own will. It would be a mistake to use this philosophical conception as an argument either for a

so-called free or democratic constitution, on the ground that this alone corresponds with the idea of self-government, or against the proposal to introduce such a constitution, on the ground that the people who demand it already have all they can want. It would be equally mistaken to say that because, empirically, some people enjoy self-government and others do not, therefore the philosophical doctrine that all government is self-government is untrue to fact.[95]

This, I think, makes the point clear and it is also substantially the same point which Collingwood made against Green in 'The Three Laws of Politics' twelve years later:

> A famous lecturer on politics, T.H. Green, refused to give Russia the name of a 'State' because it had too strong an inclination towards despotism for a name to suit it, part of whose connotation was freedom ... Green, if I understand him, was allowing the issue to become confused in his own mind. Unless I am mistaken, he was not clear as to the nature of the act which he was expressing, or was about to express, or had expressed, by uttering the words: 'Russia is something less than a body politic' or, in his words, 'a State'.
>
> Such a formula, as uttered by a speaker in Green's position, is likely to be ambiguous.
>
> (I) The ostensible or obvious meaning of the phrase is *scientific* and in particular classificatory. It means: 'Here we have something whose superficial characteristics would lead you to classify it as an 'x'. Do not be deceived; look again; and you will see that it is really a 'y''
>
> (II) Very closely connected with this is a *practical* meaning of the same phrase. It runs: 'Here we have a thing towards which we might act in either of two ways. Now is the time to make up our minds between them. Do not be seduced into treating the thing as an 'x', treat it as a 'y' and damn the consequences.'
>
> I hope I need not pause to argue, either that these two ideas are different, or that they are easily confused owing to the identity of the phrases that commonly serve us to express them; ... What Green was doing was to utter a statement about the contemporary character of Russia, which was in fact a practical statement, as if it had been a scientific statement. In effect what he said was that the Russia of his time had no business in the civilised world and that decent people would not recognize Russians as equals. This is as if someone had asked a second party what sort of meat had been offered him, and the reply had been given, 'It is a perfectly beastly sort of meat'; telling you not what the meat is, but what his practical reaction to it is ... Should not a cobbler stick to his last? Was it not Green's business as a political scientist to analyse facts without indulging in condemnation?[96]

If we substitute 'philosophical' for 'scientific', and 'empirical' for 'practical', we can see that Collingwood is objecting to the same mis-

---

[95] L.M.P., 1929, p. 110.
[96] T.L.P., pp. 11–12.

take in both cases: that of confusing a philosophical conception which applies to all possible cases with an empirical conception which applies to only some. For example, all action is political action in that all action can be understood as action according to rule; but this no more makes everybody a 'politician' than the existence of 'politicians' implies that political action is reserved only for themselves or that politics is confined to the activities of the state alone. Politics as an empirical concept is generally restricted in use to the description of the activities of government; as a philosophical concept it can be used to characterise any rational human activity.

From examining Collingwood's view on the relation between the rulers and the ruled within a society, we turn to the relation between the rulers and the ruled where the rulers belong to a society (social community) and the ruled belong to the non-social community. In the former rule operates by authority, in the latter through force. I shall not attempt to present a complete account of Collingwood's view, but will restrict myself to his views on punishment.

6: Punishment

Collingwood's published writings contain no extended discussion of punishment, although there are interesting passages in *The New Leviathan* and *Speculum Mentis*, and a longer discussion in *Religion and Philosophy*. However, this lack of extended treatment of punishment in the published writings is amply compensated by several passages from lectures and an essay on punishment to be found in Collingwood's unpublished manuscripts. Of these manuscript sources I shall concentrate on two: the section on punishment from the 1929 lectures on moral philosophy; and a discussion from 'Stray Notes on Ethical Questions'.

Punishment in General

Before examining the role of punishment within the theory of the social and non-social community I shall consider Collingwood's account of the general features of punishment.

Punishment is a political act; it is a direct consequence of regularian action: 'Punishment is a political act, and therefore deals with political values and no others.'[97] Punishment does not deal with moral but only political values:

---

[97] S.N.E.Q., §III, p. 33.

This is the basis of the philosophical theory of punishment. Men are punished, so far as they are rightly punished, not for neglecting their duties and acting otherwise than as conscience bids them, but for disobeying the laws of their country; and not for disobeying those laws in particular, but for disobeying law as law; that is, they are not punished for making private laws of their own — we all do that — but for making self-contradictory laws of their own. So far as punishment fails to conform to this criterion, it is exercised not by right but only by might. But so far as it does conform to this criterion, it is an essential element in all right action; it is the affirmation of the ideal of acting according to rule, operating negatively in the repression of whatever action is not according to rule; for a self-contradictory rule is no rule.[98]

Punishment, then, is the consequence of a person acting according to a self-contradictory rule, which is the same as acting according to two conflicting rules at once. Collingwood uses the example of someone presenting a forged cheque to a bank for gain.

A man forging a cheque may think that he has a right to do so, because he desperately needs the money, and the man whose name he is forging will never know and will not be harmed by the loss of so small a sum. This reason gives the rule by which he regards this individual act, or any act resembling it in essentials, as justifies. He may have no objection to applying this rule universally and saying that anybody else would have a right to do the same in his place. But he knows that in presenting the cheque over the counter of the bank he had better keep those views to himself, because it is impossible that they should be shared by the cashier. He knows, that is to say, that the rules on which he is acting are not only different from, but actually in conflict with, the rules of the institution within which and by whose means he is trying to procure his ends, namely the institution of banking. He is therefore willing the existence of two conflicting systems of law at once, not one for himself and one for other people, or one for this act and one for other acts, but both coinciding in one and the same act: a system of rules forbidding forgery and a system of rules permitting forgery. This constitutes the objective wrongness of his action. And this is the only thing that can constitute objective wrongness in any action: namely its having a reason which on analysis will be found to consist of two conflicting rules.[99]

Punishment is a political act and is not therefore concerned with the specifically moral side of the criminal's actions. 'The purpose of criminal justice is not the punishment of moral guilt as such.'[100] Typically, of course, acts that are punishable by law are immoral acts, but what is being punished is not their immorality as such but their character as contrary to law. Thus Collingwood argues that 'a criminal act is as a rule immoral; and therefore the acts for which people

---
[98] L.M.P., 1933, p. 163.
[99] L.M.P., 1933, pp. 162-3.
[100] L.M.P., 1929, p. 116.

are punished are as a rule morally wrong. But they are never punished *because* they are morally wrong. They are punished as politically bad, not as morally bad; and many other acts that are just as immoral are allowed to go unpunished.'[101] And of those immoral acts which the state does choose to punish, it is never the immorality of the act, but its objective wrongness as self-contradictory that is being punished. This is because 'moral guilt as such slips between the fingers of the law courts. What they can do is to insist that the law shall be obeyed; not law in general, not even the laws by which a particular country lives, but those of these laws which are selected for this particular kind of treatment.'[102]

Punishment, then, deals with immoral acts, but only with that aspect of an immoral act — its submission to conflicting rules, its running counter to the law — which is a relevant consideration in judging an act as wrong in regularian action. But not all immoral acts, as we have seen, are the business of the law, and the law courts are not the only means of inflicting punishment; social means of punishment — ostracisation of offenders and other social pressures — operate as effective methods of punishment.

> Punishment, being a determination of action as such, is a transcendental, and not limited in its occurrence to the activity of any particular agent or body ... any penalty for the breach of any rule is punishment ... We cannot argue that punishment turns on issues other than moral ones because there are cases of immoral action which meet with no punishment. The answer is that they are punished elsewhere than in the courts.[103]

The question of the relation between the state and morality will be dealt with in a little more detail in section 7; for the moment I shall concentrate on the justification of punishment. The question is: What theory of punishment provides the best justification of punishment in general? It is to Collingwood's answer to these questions that I shall now turn.

Collingwood is quite emphatic as to which theory of punishment is the correct one: he states that if the retributive, reformative and deterrent theories are viewed as rivals then the retributive theory is the only justifiable one. The deterrence theory is open to the objection that unless a malefactor deserves to suffer, it is immoral to inflict suffering upon him in order to frighten other people. Again, the reformatory theory is immoral for similar reasons: if punishment is an attempt to reform somebody, that is, to make him change his hab-

---
[101] S.N.E.Q., p. 33.
[102] L.M.P., 1924, p. 116.
[103] L.M.P., 1929, p. 115.

its, it is an immoral method of education unless his habits are such that he deserves to be hurt. The retributive theory implies neither anger nor cruelty. The victim is hurt because he or she is judged to deserve it, and this demands careful consideration, not passion. The other theories, as we have seen, lead to cruelty in order to deter or reform. The retributive theory, on the other hand rests on desert, and so asks first, before any other question arises, whether the punishment is deserved. From the standpoint of the retributive theory, then, we can, for example, reject any increase in the severity of a sentence on grounds of supposed deterrence value and insist that unless the increased sentence is actually deserved by the criminal it is immoral.

Collingwood concludes by stating that 'punishment is certainly retributive, whatever else it may be.'[104] However, this leaves open the possibility that it may also be something else; if we cease to view the three theories of punishment as rivals we may be able to account for the undoubted attraction that each theory has for us. As Collingwood has made quite clear, taken as rivals the retributive theory is the only justifiable theory: any other theory fails to account for the initial act of punishment: if punishment were always and only reformative, would it then apply to everyone (for could it truthfully be said of anyone that in certain respects he or she did not need to be reformed?) or only to those who stand in need of reform as a consequence of some action on their part which merited such treatment? If the latter, then the process of reform follows upon a judgement that *this* person and not *that* person, on account of *this* criminal action, must undergo reformative treatment; and this is to judge the person as deserving such treatment in a penal institution. Hence we arrive back at the notion of desert; and we realize that without such a notion there could never be any justification for the initial separation of the criminal from society which must be prior to the process of reformation.

Again, if punishment were always and only deterrent, how should we choose which persons to incarcerate as a deterrent to others? If we choose people at random, that would not only be immoral, but it would also fail to deter: if victims are chosen at random there can be no possible deterrent effect on a criminal who in this case is no more likely to be incarcerated than anyone else; if anything, the reverse would be true, as it would be rational for the criminal to suppose that if detention were random his chances of being detained were no higher than anyone else's, and that therefore he had nothing

---

[104] L.M.P., 1929, p. 114.

to lose by his criminal activities. On the other hand, if we say that we should incarcerate only those found guilty of criminal action, and that the notion of deterrence comes into play only at this point in deterring those who might otherwise seek to follow the example of the incarcerated criminal, then we have admitted the point at issue. We have admitted that punishment in the first place can be justified only on grounds of desert that deterrence only works by deterring those who if they performed the criminal action would deserve to be punished for it; and that punishment could only in fact deter at all if it were understood that only those people were imprisoned who deserved to be imprisoned.[105]

Understood as rivals, then, the theory of punishment as retributive wins outright: but if we take punishment as retributive and then look for what else it might be in addition, we find that it may also be both deterrent and reformatory:

> Those who say that punishment ought to be deterrent or reformatory really mean it ought to be these things *as well* as being punishment. Deterrence and reform may, therefore, be *properties* of punishment even if not its essence. A good punishment would produce good effects from both the other points of view.[106]

We have arrived at a position in which we can say that 'punishment consists in the infliction of deserved suffering on an offender',[107] while also recognizing that the character or properties of punishment may also include deterrence and reformation. As we shall see later, punishment, in relation to the social community, is meted out to those who, in behaving criminally, thereby cease to be members of that social community. Because 'crime is an action by one member of a society prejudicial not to the rights of another member but to the pursuit of its self appropriated task by the society as a whole',[108] punishment is thus inflicted by a society upon those who threaten the pursuit of the society's common good. In breaking the law, the criminal threatens not merely the individual against whom his criminal act is directed, but the whole system of law. The system of law is the expression of a society's attempt to pursue a common good; hence in attacking the system of law the criminal is also attack-

---

[105] A.M. Hoff made the point forcefully: 'What could be more immoral than to inflict punishment on a criminal for the sake of deterring others if he does not *deserve* it? or would it be justified to subject him to a compulsory attempt at reform which includes a denial of his liberty unless, again, he *deserves* it? In P. Devlin, *The Judge*, viii.
[106] L.M.P., 1929, p. 114.
[107] *Religion and Philosophy*, p. 176.
[108] N.L., 21.86.

ing the pursuit of the common good and therefore the society itself, the society itself being nothing but the joint will of its members in their pursuit of a joint enterprise. Thus, in threatening the common good the criminal ceases to be a member of the society. In punishing a criminal the society is punishing him not merely as an individual but as a threat to the society's way of life:

> Punishment, then, is injury inflicted by a person, acting consciously as the representative of a community, upon a person, also a member of that community, who has ignored the community by impeding the pursuit of its common ends. The same act, if reference to the community were absent, would be mere vengeance; but punishment is still vengeance, though communal and not private vengeance.[109]

Punishment is retribution; this as Collingwood points out contains an element of vengeance; but retribution as such is not vengeance as such. Vengeance is the infliction of injury upon someone because he has injured me or (either directly or indirectly through injuring someone or something I care for); but vengeance must be distinguished from retribution because it is not based on the idea of desert. I do not injure someone, in revenge, because I think he deserves it, but because I feel angry towards him. Anger at the action of the criminal is always a part of punishment, and therefore vengeance is always an element also, but it is never merely vengeance: as Collingwood points out in *Religion and Philosophy*, 'revenge is a second crime which does nothing to mitigate the first; punishment is not a crime but something which we feel to be a duty.'[110] The element of vengeance in punishment does not reduce punishment to vengeance as the element of desert or retribution is present also.

A society chooses to punish, then, because the criminal deserves to be punished; but the matter does not end there. Presumably a society wishes to ensure other ends as well: first, that further crimes of a similar kind do not take place; secondly, that the criminal, who in acting criminally ceased to be a member of society, can at some future time be re-admitted as a member of that society. The former desire implies that the society will wish to deter others from breaking its laws; the latter implies that it will wish to reform criminals so that on completion of their sentences they are fit to be re-admitted as members of society. We have therefore arrived at the conclusion that a society, while justifying punishment only on the grounds of criminal desert (and therefore adhering to the retributive theory), will at the same time wish to deter other criminals and also to reform its

---
[109] S.N.E.Q., p. 24.
[110] R.P., p. 172.

already existing criminals. Neither reform nor deterrent are here operating as the justifications for punishment; that is provided by retribution on the grounds of criminal desert; but both are operating as elements in the execution of a legally ordered punishment (though never as its ground).

Punishment in Particular

In his 1929 Lectures on Moral Philosophy Collingwood roundly declared that 'the essence of punishment is the frustration of the criminal's will. He is not allowed to do what he wants to do, because his choice runs counter to the choice of the society in which he lives.'[111] This is the general ground of punishment, and we know that punishment is inflicted by a person acting as the representative of a community upon the criminal: but Collingwood's account of punishment is complicated by his theory of the non-social community. A person acting as the representative of a community has authority vested in him by the other members of that community, and it is by this authority that he is enabled to punish criminals. Authority is essentially a relation holding between members of a social community or society; and those members of a society who obey the commands of those in authority do so because they recognize those commands as issuing from their own will, from their granting the ruler the authority to act on their behalf. But punishment is seen, typically, by the criminal, as arising not from authority but from force, as not an expression of his will, but as something alien and hostile to his will. The reason seems, for Collingwood, to be this: that the criminal, by being a criminal, is *ipso facto* not a member of a society. To say that a criminal is a member of society is self-contradictory: to be a member of society is to act in a certain way and to recognize authority and obey its commands; to be a criminal is to fail to do this and hence to fail to be a member of society.

> Punishment is inevitable and necessary in the sense that no one can violate any kind of good without bringing upon himself the corresponding kind of harm. The good that consists in my own pleasurable sensations — the only good recognized by hedonists — can only be violated by hurting myself; the moral good, by making myself immoral; the political good by making myself to that extent unpolitical, or detaching myself in certain ways from the common life of my society. In some form or other, acts of this kind are automatically followed by punishment; for if I detach myself from the common life of my society, I am detached from that common life. Some kind of punishment cannot but be inflicted on

---

[111] L.P.M., 1929, p. 121.

me, for essentially punishment is just that detachment or forfeiture of the common life of society which I have myself deliberately brought about.[112]

To be criminal is thus to detach oneself from the common life which one previously enjoyed: it is to act unpolitically. By the criminal act itself the criminal ceases to be a member of a society: if and when the members of a society 'lapse into criminality, they have already (before joining the body of criminals) ceased to function as members of society.'[113] The relation between those in authority and the criminal is not therefore a relation between equals, but between a member of a society and a member of a non-social community; and hence the theory of punishment belongs not to the theory of society but to the theory of the non-social community.

I shall illustrate Collingwood's understanding of the relation between command, obedience, authority and punishment by reference to appropriate passages from *The New Leviathan*. Command and obedience, he argues, are related to the performance of a common task:

> Command and obedience are found, not in all societies, but in all where the nature of the common task is such as to require them. Watch two men moving a piano; at a certain moment one says 'lift', and the other lifts. The authority whereby one is empowered to give this order is not based on one man's superior skill in furniture removing, nor on his superior rank in feudal hierarchy, nor on his superior literacy or greater age or ability to hold more beer; cases might be found in which any one of these or a hundred other conditions were taken into account, but none is relevant: 'the *decision who shall give advice is part of the structure of the society* and exists, like every other part, by an act of joint free will. Each partner agrees to the formation of the society, and hence agrees to give such orders as it is his business to give and obey those which it is his business to obey. And reciprocally, each authorizes the other to do the share that falls to him. This is the theory of command and obedience (or, in one word, authority) as a feature of social life. As a feature of non-social life it is an utterly different thing. In a society a command is given because the partners have agreed that in certain circumstances it shall be given. It is obeyed because they have agreed that it shall be obeyed. Giving the order and obeying it are social functions, allotted by common agreement to certain members of the society. In commanding and obeying each is doing what he has decided to do with the authorization of his fellow members, and doing it because, being a man of free will, he is a man whose decisions stand firm. What is called authority in a non-social community is an entirely different thing. It is not authority, it is force.

---

[112] S.N.E.Q. p. 38.
[113] N.L., 21.88.

The so-called command of A over B is A's exercise of force upon B. The so-called obedience of B to A is B's enforcement by A.[114]

Punishment, it follows, is essentially a relation between a society and a non-social community, and it arises when, for whatever reason, a member of the non-social community disobeys a command issued by a representative of a society acting with that society's authority. It is the correlative of force: this Collingwood makes clear as he continues:

> A man may force B to do something by promise of *reward* or threat of *punishment*. By the first A excites in B an irresistible desire; by the second an irresistible fear. These are irresistible only if B is slavish enough for the promised reward or the threatened penalty to overwhelm any will he may happen to possess. If his will is strong enough he will laugh at them. Reward and punishment have no weight with free men, and the theory of them has no place in the theory of society. It belongs to the theory of the non-social community. It is by such methods that non-social communities are established and maintained.[115]

This account of the place of punishment is the bare minimum: at this level it is merely a relationship between a society and the non-social community over which it rules. Punishment here is characterised by its deterrent value: criminals are punished because they deserve punishment, but the point of punishing someone who belongs to the non-social community is essentially deterrent and threatening. However, as Collingwood almost immediately goes on to make plain, there are other occasions for punishment: the first is that in which a member of a society falls away from membership through his conduct; in this case the criminal is not throughout a man incapable of free will, but starts as a man with free will and at some point or in respect of some action enjoined on him, regresses below the level of free agency. The second is when the 'criminal' remains throughout a member of society in that he has free will, and when his 'crime' consists not in violation of the common ends of the society, but from a different conception of the common good. In this case the 'criminal' at all times remains a free agent, and his actions spring not from his willing contradictory laws or his inability to rule himself, but from precisely their opposite: he is a critic of the social order, criticising it not for what it is but for not being what it ought to be, for not living up to its own professions.

Punishment, then, in respect of a member of the non-social community will be primarily deterrent in respect of a lapsed member of society, primarily reformative; in respect of a social critic its purpose

---

[114] N.L., 21.68–21.72.
[115] N.L., 21.73–4.

is ambiguous: the breach of law must be punished, but the criticism must also be heard: the 'criminal' can be neither reformed not deterred; their crime springs from their free will, not from its absence; he is a member of a society criticising that society from within, not a member of society who ceases to be a member through his inability to live up to its standards.

The case of the criminal inhabiting the non-social community has already been addressed; Collingwood's views on the other two cases will now be considered. The immediate issue is why punishment becomes necessary; that is, why do people fall away from the condition of freedom into a relative unfreedom which no longer fits them for membership of society? Collingwood's answer is that:

> *Freedom is a matter of degree.* On certain questions and in certain circumstances an agent may be capable of decision, or free; on other questions or in other circumstances the same agent may be utterly unable to prevent a certain passion or a certain desire from taking charge. It is always possible that a given society may break down into the non-social community out of which it has arisen, and cease to exist as a society, because it is confronted by a certain kind of question or practical problem. This happens when the agents of whom that society is composed degenerate from a condition in which they are capable of free decision into one in which their will may be said to *crack* and for any man, I suppose, there are conditions under which a crack of the will would happen. Persons who constitute themselves as a society may foresee the possibility of its breaking down into a non-social community, and provide against this in two ways: first by so organizing the society that the duty of giving orders is assigned to those of themselves whom they judge best able to resist the strains to which the society is likely to be exposed. The second method, in case the first should prove insufficient, is a kind of machinery whereby anyone of themselves whose will may happen to crack may be forcibly prevented from impeding the rest in their work of living politically. This machinery is called *criminal law*. It is not for everyday use; it is meant to come into operation only if and when the society to whom is serves as a life saver shows signs, in spite of all other precautions, of breaking down into a non-social community.[116]

As Collingwood elsewhere reminds us, society is nothing over and above the activities of its members in their mutual arrangements and activities; so to talk of a society breaking down into a non-social community is the same thing as to talk of individual members of that society breaking down and ceasing to be members of that society. Crime as such is incompatible with society as such, which is why crime must be punished: the criminal is punished for failing to be what he ought to be and, as failing, acting as a negative element in

---

[116] N.L., 21.8–84.

the body politic, a hindrance to the common life pursued by a society. Ruling requires obedience on the part of the subject and therefore a refusal to obey is a refusal by the subject to undertake his share in the common political task: the task of ruling falls on both ruler and subject and a refusal by either to that extent weakens or signals the breakdown of society. Where the idea of providing against crime occurs:

> it rests on the assumption that crime will be committed only when the society has to some extent broken down into a non-social community by the cracking of some member's will and the member's ceasing in consequence to function as a member of that society; thought he may perfectly well continue to be a member of the non-social community from which it was derived. Crime and society are incompatible. Not that, when once a society has been formed, its members are protected by some magic against lapsing into criminality; but that, if and when they do lapse into criminality, they have already (before joining the body of criminals) ceased to function as members of society.[117]

As to the state's right to punish, there can be no question: 'the state is the community (society) as organised for certain political purposes',[118] and to ask whether a society has a right to punish is to ask whether it has a right to be a society, which is absurd. A society is a group of people sharing a common end, and therefore an integral part of what it means to be a society is the punishment of those who violate the pursuit of that common end. Without the common end, the society could not be a society and the criminal could not be a criminal: 'a criminal, be it noted, is not an anarchist. He does not deny or repudiate society as such. He lives in it and on it like everyone else. And this he could not do unless it really were a society — unless it did actively pursue its common ends and punish those who ostracised them.'[119] Criminals, through their criminal action, oppose not merely the ruler or sovereign, but their fellow subjects:

> The criminal, then, is a person who sets his own will in opposition not merely to the will of a ruler or sovereign, in which case he would be not a criminal but a rebel, and even perhaps a hero, but in opposition to the will of his fellow subjects in so far as they are in the habit of obeying this particular law and are therefore making it something more than a dead letter ... The corporate will of the society is against the criminal ... and his inability to overcome this mass of opposition is the essence of his punishment. It must always be painful, simply because it is a failure, a passivity, the breakdown of an attempted action ... and this is of the very nature of pain ... It is not open to the society to refrain from punish-

---

[117] N.L,. 21.87–8.
[118] 'Notes on R.M. MacIver, *The Modern State*', note to p. 279
[119] S.N.E.Q. p. 39.

ing such a person. A society will no doubt consider whether a better law cannot be found, but pending this discovery it cannot acquiesce in the breach of the existing law. To do so would be to surrender the plan of action which at present is controlling its movements, without adopting any alternative plan; and this is impossible, because, as we know, all action must organise itself according to same plan or other . . . For the present there is no option but to override the will of the objector and carry on with the plan to which he objects. This is called punishing him and enforcing the law . . . The essence of punishment is this frustration of the criminal's will. He is not allowed to do what he wants to do, because his choice runs counter to the choice of the society in which he lives.[120]

It follows that there is no real question about whether the state has the right to punish, because

If the state has a right to do anything, it has a right to punish . . . just as it has a right to tax, to defend life and property and so on . . . In a word, to legislate and to execute its own laws; hence the question what right the state has to govern itself is open to Locke's old objection against the question whether the will is free; the will, he pointed out, was nothing but our name for man's freedom, so that, though we can ask whether man is free, i.e. whether man has a will, we cannot ask whether his will is free, i.e. whether he is free freely. Similarly, it may be held that society has no right to govern itself, i.e. that society is not a state; but it cannot be asked whether the state has a right to govern, for to be a state is the same thing as having a right to govern.[121]

The right of society, acting politically through the state, to punish is therefore unquestionable: and we have seen how punishment applies to members of the non-social community, and to members of a society who lapse, through a 'cracking' of their will, into being members of the non-social community. But what of the critic of a society or the rebel against society? Both are members of society and remain so despite their punishment; and their punishment is essentially a formal response to their critical activity rather than the exercise of force; indeed, as Collingwood insists, free men *cannot* be subjected to force and 'reward and punishment have no weight with free men.'[122] What then is the distinguishing feature of punishment in this case?

So long as a social and political system is only one possible system, one historical manifestation of the ideal of social life, a single finite thing, so long crime will arise: that is, acts will be done which show that their agents are out of harmony with the system under which they live. Such lack of harmony follows inevitably from the finite character of the social organisation. It is notorious that every act of legislation creates a new

---

[120] L.M.P., 1929, pp. 120–1.
[121] S.N.E.Q., pp. 45–6.
[122] N.L., 21.74.

crime, by declaring criminal a class of acts which previously were not so. This is a confession that there is a class of agents which will not be in harmony with the new law; and the lack of harmony may very well be due not to self-interest but to a different conception of the social good.

A crime that springs from a conception of the social good is no less a crime than one that springs from self-interest, and it must be punished. But a crime of this kind, characteristic as it is of a person with a high degree of political intelligence, has redeeming features. In especial, its punishment may be endured wholly without resentment. The criminal knows enough of politics to recognise that any social ideal must promote and defend itself by political action. He is fighting against an existing ideal for the sake of an ideal of his own, and he knows that weapons are used in that war. He probably knows also that the ideal against which he is fighting is as strong as it is only because of its merit as an ideal. In that case, he respects not only the abstract idea of punishment but also the particular punishment that is being imposed upon him. If this seems a somewhat shadowy and remote contingency, it is enough to remember the death of Sir Thomas More.[123]

7: The Law and Morality

The question now facing us is that of the relation between law and individual conduct. This can be divided into two. First, what is the relation between the law and morals? and secondly, when and under what circumstances is state interference permissible and what can it achieve?

These questions can be resolved into the general questions of the relation between politics and ethics, and the character of the overlap between them. In 1933 Collingwood summarised this relation and outlined the role of the state thus:

> As a philosophical science, politics is the science of rightness or conformity to rule. Its first task is to distinguish its own field from that of economics and that of ethics in the special sense, by distinguishing rightness from utility and duty. Rightness means the same as law and order, civil peace, and the various other phrases which the political consciousness has used as names for its own proper end. Its relation to utility is expressed by various phrases which define what the state does, as opposed to what the state is. The state is the rule of law; what it does is to provide for the security of person and property, the safeguarding of the subject's legitimate interests, and the like: that is to say, law and order or civil peace affords a framework within which interests or utilities may be pursued, and without which they could not be pursued without entering into a mutually destructive conflict. Its relation to duty is, roughly, expressed by such phrases as respecting the liberty of con-

---

[123] S.N.E.Q., pp. 45–6.

science: that is, laws do not usurp the function of conscience but provide a basis upon which the moral life of the individual may freely develop.[124]

The task of the state is to maintain the conditions necessary for the common life of society: to make laws in furtherance of the common ends of the society and to enforce them. But, as we have seen, those who break these laws are punished not for moral badness but for political badness, that is, not for their immorality but for their acting in such a way as to threaten political order and thereby imperil the common life of the society. The badness of the criminal lies not in his moral badness, although this is undoubtedly present, but in his political badness. Political goodness, for Collingwood, is order, hence political badness is the threat to order; and it is the criminal's action as a threat to order, rather than its motive, that is punished. Likewise, although the state aims at the common good, it does not aim at making its citizens good. The moral goodness of the subject slips through the fingers of the law, just as does the moral badness of the criminal.

> Political action, as such, is not moral action . . . The moral good, I believe . . . is not different from the moral action that realizes it. Nothing has moral value, I submit, except the will of a moral agent. If that is so, the moral good and moral activity, are not related as end to means: they are identical. To do good and to be good are the same.[125]

In politics, as Collingwood elsewhere notes, there is a separation between means and ends and what is of value is the end alone:

> Political action aims at bringing into existence a state of things which is an end conceived as good for somebody, this end being regarded as good in itself and in abstraction from the means adopted to bring it about. Hence, in Political action, one conceives the end first in logical order and then thinks out the means to fit it. From self-interest, politics are distinguished because the end is not the good of the individual agent but of a whole of which he regards himself as the part. Hence the concept of the general will = will which wills the general good. Political force consists in the abstractness of the end. In willing the end I take no account of the means: therefore the means have in themselves no value; e.g. if somebody's will is recalcitrant to the end as I conceive it, that will must be bent or broken in the endeavour to reach the end.[126]

What matters in politics, then, is that the law is obeyed: it is possible to obey the law as a duty, in a spirit of willing and free cooperation, and this will be, typically, how the members of a society will obey it; but from the law's point of view it does not matter whether it

---
[124] L.M.P., 1933, p. 100.
[125] Pol. A., p. 154.
[126] Rough Notes on Politics, (R.N.P.), p. 1.

is obeyed in this way or not, and if people obey the law only through fear of the consequences of failure to do so, that is a matter of indifference so far as the political goodness attendant on obedience and order is concerned.

Collingwood deals with this question of political and moral goodness in 'Stray Notes on Ethical Questions':

> The state certainly does aim at the promotion of a common good; and this certainly is the common good of its members; but it does not follow that the state aims at making its subjects good. The word good is here ambiguous. The good life, which the state promotes is good in the sense in which a life promoted by political means can be good, and in no other way. You certainly can make people good by acts of parliament, but only good in certain well-defined senses and not in others. What is sometimes called moral goodness — the peculiar type of goodness which is exemplified in the good will of a man who does his duty because it is his duty — cannot be promoted or impeded, cannot be created or destroyed, cannot even be fostered or discouraged to however small an extent, by political means. But this is not the only kind of goodness. There is another kind which may be called political goodness, the goodness of a society whose members live together under good laws well administered and loyally obeyed. This is a goodness which can be promoted by political means, and no other.[127]

This leaves us with three related questions: first, to ask when it might be a duty to act politically; and secondly, given that political action cannot impede moral goodness, what is the relation between the two and, thirdly, how and when is state interference justified and how does such interference affect moral actions.

> It is a politician's moral duty, so far as he is a politician at all, to be a good politician: that is to say it is the moral duty of a legislator to promulgate good laws, the moral duty of a magistrate to enforce them, and the moral duty of a subject to obey them . . . doing our duty (creating moral goodness) and doing the work of the state (creating political goodness) are different things, but it may be a man's duty to do the work of the state.[128]

'Doing the work of the state' may be our duty, but equally, it may not: both the legislator and the subject may have other duties. The legislator, if caught between two conflicting claimants for the title of his duty might justifiably choose not to legislate, but to be at his wife's bedside and so not pass a law which would have been, if passed, a good law.[129] Again, the subject, generally speaking, should obey the law: but as we have seen it does not matter whether he

---

[127] S.N.E.Q., p. 30.
[128] S.N.E.Q., p. 31.
[129] Pol. A., p. 160.

obeys it dutifully or not, and it may be (in addition) that there are circumstances in which his duty might lie in breaking the law.

When might it be a duty to do the work of the state?

> First, when if the man in question is responsible for the active work of the state: if, that is, he is in some sense a ruler. And in a democratic country where the franchise is practically universal, practically everyone comes under this category. Secondly, if the man in question has a passive part in the work of the state; that is, if he is a subject. For no ruling can be done without obedience on the part of the subject, and therefore a refusal to obey is a refusal to undertake the subject's share in the common political task, a task which falls not merely on the ruler but on the subject as well. A ruler who rules badly or a subject who obeys badly is therefore doing two things: he is being politically bad, and (in so far as it is his duty to be politically good) he is also being morally bad.[130]

There is, therefore, an overlap between politics and morals in so far as the same action may be both right and our duty, both politically good and morally good; and on this occasion there will be 'a distinction in the concepts without a difference in the instance.'[131] The concepts nonetheless must be carefully distinguished: political action may be a duty, but its characteristics as duty are not therefore its characteristics as political.

The second question to be dealt with is that of the intrusion of political considerations into moral actions and the justification of state interference. Collingwood discusses these issues in his 'Notes Towards a Theory of Politics as a Philosophical Science' and in his notes on R.M. MacIver's *The Modern State*.[132]

We have seen that it may be a duty to obey the law, but that what matters politically is not *why* we obey the law, but *that* we obey the law. The imperative of the law is not the imperative of duty or moral obligation:

> It is in the form 'I will' not 'I ought'. This is the explanation of the difficulties about relations between the 'state' and morality ... Morally, there is no value in my paying my taxes if I only do it for fear of punishment; and the 'state' can only make me do this or anything else for motives of this kind; therefore the state cannot promote morality; but surely the state exists to promote the good of its members, and is not morality the best of goods?[133]

---

[130] S.N.E.Q., p. 32.
[131] E.P.M., p. 50.
[132] Published 1926.
[133] N.P.P.S., p. 5. As Collingwood points out elsewhere, the attempt to command a moral act by law is bound to fail because if we make it penal to do right from fear of punishment, 'you are trying to prevent people from doing right for fear of punishment by threatening to punish them if they do.' S.N.E.Q., p. 34.

We can agree that this is so, but, Collingwood insists, it is not this good which the state exists to promote: the state promotes the political, not the moral good. For example; it is politically good that I should pay my taxes, whatever my motives; it is politically good that travellers are not robbed on the roads, whatever the reason for the robber refraining from robbing; it is politically good that children do not work down the pit and so on, even if mine owners release them from employment only through the fear of punishment. 'There is in short a kind of goods which are independent of the moral character of the agent's motives; to this class belongs political good.'[134] Nevertheless, there is a connection between moral and political action arising out of the fact that it may be a duty to pursue a good of this kind. For example:

> The state might not be able to make the highway man do his duty, it may not be able to make him stop robbing for the *right* reasons; but it is my (the state's) duty to stop you by hook or by crook, and whether or not you intend to do your duty, I mean to do mine. Correlatively, it may be thought a duty to obey the commands of a political power. For example; I may regard it as my *duty* to pay taxes and not just in order to avoid punishment. That is, I might think it obligatory on me to do what I am legally bidden. But neither of these is indispensable to political action . . . The ruler need not regard it as his duty, but only as his function, to rule . . . Similarly, the subject may obey not as a duty but simply because obedience is demanded.[135]

From this Collingwood develops a criticism of Green's and Bosanquet's political theories which maintain that 'the state is in its right when it forcibly hinders a hindrance to the best life or common good.'[136] He is not objecting to this as such, nor the assertion that 'the state . . . as such, can only secure the performance of external actions,'[137] nor, as Green says, that only such acts should be enforced by the state as it is better should take place from any motive whatever than not take place at all. Collingwood objects to none of this. What he does object to, however, is any suggestion that by commanding a certain action the state is depriving those who are thus commanded of the opportunity for doing the action for a moral reason. This, he says, is simply not so; and there is nothing whatever stopping those who wish from performing the action from a moral motive; all that matters to the state is that those who would not oth-

---

[134] N.P.P.S., p. 5.
[135] N.P.P.S., P6.
[136] B. Bosanquet, *The Philosophical Theory of the State*, p. 178. For Collingwood the crucial point is '*what*, exactly, can be hindered?'
[137] op. cit., p. 176.

erwise perform the action at all are made to perform it, irrespective of their reason for doing so.

> A further point to the relation between politics and duty is that when people are commanded to do things which it is their duty to do, they may be said to be deprived of the opportunity of doing than for the right reasons, and thus the state is morally degrading them — making them immoral by wrongly trying to make them moral . . . This is a commonplace of arguments against state interference in moral questions. It involves a sophism . . . from the premiss that moral questions are wholly decided *in foro interno* it draws the conclusion that they are decided, but always wrongly, by the action of the state. There is an obvious contradiction: if motives alone make acts moral, and if the state bids me (e.g.) to maintain my children decently, I cannot blame the state for my own immorality if, not recognizing that I ought to maintain than, I do so only through fear of punishment. I am immoral, but the state is doing its duty in treating me with the only argument to which I will listen. The state does not dictate my motive — it still leaves me free to maintain my children through a sense of duty. If it is suggested that a selfish motive . . . e.g. punishment . . . in itself destroys the morality of the act, the answer is that duty is now being regarded as purely subjective, dependent on the agent's recognition of it: therefore what he does not recognize as a duty is not a duty, and he has no right to complain to the state for depriving him of opportunities for moral action, since such opportunities are entirely of his own making and can be made with equal ease in all circumstances.[138]

That is, the government's threat of punishment does not mean that one is obliged to take that as one's motive for action; there is no reason why one cannot act through duty alone. Punishment, on this view, only becomes a selfish motive if it is made so, e.g. if the duty is not subjectively recognized. From these considerations Collingwood draws the conclusion that:

> This removes not only the theory of the state as the source and propagator of morality, (Greek), and the theory that it is the enemy of morality and a creature of evil (abstract moralism), but equally the view that it exists to promote the moral life indirectly by 'removing hindrances' to it. If you cannot promote morality in another, for the same reason you cannot hinder it in another, and therefore the conception of hindrances to morality, which can be removed by political action, is baseless and self-contradictory.[139]

Collingwood suggests that Green tried to compromise between the Greek and the Mill view of the state. The advantage of the Greek view was that it saw the state as necessary and beneficent; the advantage of the Mill view was that it limited the sphere of the state's

---

[138] N.P.P.S., p. 7.
[139] N.P.P.S., p. 8.

action, and denied any suggestion that the state could claim authority over the whole of human action. 'Green, in trying to combine these advantages, forfeited both'. The objection here seems to be the same as that expressed in 'A Philosophy of Progress' denying the possibility of moral progress:

> Goodness, like beauty and happiness is not a product of civilization. A man's moral worth depends not on his circumstances, but on the way in which he confronts them. It was a good act to abolish slavery, but the men who are born into a slaveless world are not automatically made good men by that fact. All it can do for than is to confront than with moral problems of a new kind. This the nineteenth century believers in progress failed to see. They thought that external circumstances, by being better, made man better. You might as well say that we are better soldiers than Napoleon because our guns have a longer range, or better musicians than Bach because our orchestras are larger.[140]

Collingwood's point is that moral worth depends not on circumstances but on how we deal with them; and that the value of our actions, as moral actions, depends on the intrinsic motivation of the action itself, not on its outward conformity to rule. He is further maintaining that (*pace* Green and Bosanquet)[141] the intervention of the law can in no way deprive people of the opportunity of acting morally: and that if morality can be neither furthered nor hindered by political action, hindrances to morality cannot be hindered. The state can do no more than secure the performance of external acts,[142] and a hindrance to morality, in Collingwood's view, cannot be an external thing: just as external circumstances cannot promote morality, so external circumstances cannot hinder it; in consequence it is absurd to suppose that the state can 'hinder hindrances' when, as both Green and Bosanquet admit, it can penetrate no further than external acts and circumstances. I shall not pause here to ask whether this is a correct reading of Green and Bosanquet; it is enough for our purposes that it is Collingwood's understanding.[143]

If we refer back to the passage from the 1933 lectures on moral philosophy quoted above, we find Collingwood stating that the state's 'relation to duty is, roughly, expressed by such phrases as respecting the liberty of conscience: that is, laws do not usurp the function of conscience but provide a basis upon which the moral life of the indi-

---

[140] 'A Philosophy of Progress', p. 115.
[141] T.H. Green, *Lectures on the Principles of Political Obligation*, pp. 38–9. B. Bosanquet, *The Philosophical Theory of the State*, p. 180.
[142] T.H. Green, op. cit.; B. Bosanquet, op. cit., pp. 175–6.
[143] For an alternative view, see W. Sweet, *Idealism and Rights: the social ontology of human rights in the political thought of Bernard Bosanquet*.

vidual may freely develop.'[144] Now, in this passage Collingwood quite clearly affirms his view that laws as such do not inhibit or usurp the function of conscience or duty, while at the same time suggesting that a society well governed and well administered provides (in same way) the conditions in which the moral life of the individual may flourish. What precisely can Collingwood mean by this? He rejects the idea that Political action can promote morality either directly or indirectly by the removal of hindrances to it; how, then, can it be said to 'provide a basis upon which the moral life of the individual may freely develop'?

The answer, on Collingwood's terms, can only be that somehow the state can overcome its inability to deal only with the external aspects of action and penetrate to its internal side. If this is possible, it will not be possible for it in its dealings with those who have free will and are members of a society. To have free will is to have self-control, to be capable of self-government and of rational action. 'The freedom of the will is, positively, *freedom to choose* freedom to exercise a will; and, negatively, freedom from *desire* not the condition of having no desires, but the condition of not being at their mercy.'[145] The activities of the state can do nothing to a person who has achieved that degree of mental maturity we call freedom. Such a person will obey laws because he sees why they were made and why they have to be obeyed; and, it seems to me, when Collingwood denies that law can have any effect on motive, he has in mind only those who are free agents.

However, as we know, freedom is a matter of degree: on certain questions and in certain circumstances we may be free and able to decide a course of action rationally and freely; on other questions and in other circumstances we may not be able to do so. This, I think, is the key. People are not born free, nor do they necessarily remain free once having achieved freedom. The state (or any other external circumstance) can neither promote nor hinder morality in a free man: but in an unfree man or in a man only relatively free both possibilities are open.

For example: in considering punishment above it was argued that in the case of a person who lapses from society, punishment which is inflicted retributively and for reasons of desert also carries with it the property of being reformatory. What this clearly implies is that, by same process of education or other, a man who has lost (or lost relatively with respect to the required capacity for free choice

---

[144] L.M.P., 1933, p. 100.
[145] N.L., 13.25.

demanded by a society) his free will, can come to regain it. In punishment, force is always present; and by force is meant a certain sort of mental superiority by which the stronger can induce the weaker to obey him by exciting his emotions. Punishment is inflicted on those who are already in, or have reverted to, the non-social community: with respect to those already in the non-social community (who will typically be children) the aim is to raise them out of the non-social community; with respect to those who have lapsed into membership of the non-social community the aim is to enable them to regain sufficient mental maturity to take their places once again in a society. In the former case punishment will be primarily deterrent as those punished have not ever had free will; in the latter case it will be reformatory as its intention is to restore a free will that has been lost. But in all cases, the ultimate aim of the society with respect to the non-social community, is to raise its members to the condition of free will in which they will be able to become members of that society.

Now, force of itself, although acting directly on the emotions, is not sufficient to bring those on whom it operates up to the level of free will; but Collingwood mentions two other principles which can and do fulfill this function. If freedom is a matter of degree it would seem to follow that we can make a person more free and rational by appealing to the level of freedom and rationality he has already attained. The two principles Collingwood develops both have this effect. Further, although to a free man the fact of something's being enjoined by law is no hindrance to the performance of his duty, it might very well be to a man who is relatively unfree; and therefore in the latter case laws might be made which 'check the development of the moral disposition'. The interesting point here is that, if I am right, Green is talking not of those already free and mature, but of those in the process of becoming so and that on this point Collingwood agrees with him: in other words the state cannot remove hindrances to the moral life of the free and mature man, but it can remove hindrances to the moral life of someone whose self-control is as yet precarious, who has not yet attained that degree of free will that enables him to be a strong and dependable member of society. The more the scale is ascended, the less external acts and circumstances can hinder or promote it.[146]

The first principle is this: where faced with someone who has achieved the state of mental maturity, but who for one reason or another is not aware of having done so, 'arouse his self-respect'.

---

[146] For a development and discussion of the points raised here see J. Connelly and W. Sweet in S. Panagakou (ed.), Symposium on *Idealism and Rights*.

What this means is to make him conscious of the freedom he was unaware he possessed. In the terms of our present discussion, what will such an injunction imply? It will imply, I suggest, that we treat the person concerned as mentally adult, as no longer a member of the nursery or non-social community; and that therefore we will treat him as capable of making his own decisions. In which case we will free him from the rules and regulations necessary for the well-ordering of the non-social community; and the grounds on which we will do this will be that it is insulting to a mature and free person to be constantly told what and what not to do; and further, what our action will thus imply is that these rules and regulations, the enjoining of actions which a person is capable of doing freely, will actually be debilitating to his free will, will hinder his moral progress by depriving him of responsibility for his own conduct. A person who, having a degree of freedom, is never allowed to make a decision, will find that his freedom atrophies and that he becomes incapable of making a decision at all. This is a common occurrence; it is often called 'being institutionalised'.

We free the person from the rules and regulations appropriate only to a member of a non-social community, and thereby introduce them to the life of the social community. An essential part of this life is sharing in the maintenance of its *suum cuique* and such sharing not only contributes towards the maintenance of the society, but also towards the maintenance of the man's social consciousness, towards the strength of his will. Thus, Collingwood says in *The New Leviathan*:

> *Law and order mean strength.* Men who respect the rule of law are by daily exercise building up the strength of their own wills; becoming more and more capable of mastering themselves and other men and the world of nature. They are becoming daily more and more able to control their own desires and passions and to crush all opposition to the carrying out of their intentions. They are becoming day by day less liable to be bullied or threatened or cajoled or frightened into courses they would not adopt of their own free will by men who would drive them into doing things in the only way in which men can drive others into doing things: by arousing in them passions or desires or appetites they cannot control.[147]

And the key to progress here is appealing to the agent's self-respect:

> This arousing of self respect is extremely important in the practice of government and education. Persons thus engaged constantly find themselves meeting men who are incapable of decision. The rule for overcoming this state is: 'Arouse his self respect'. There is also the converse rule

---

[147] N.L., 39.92.

for depriving a man of his ability to make a decision: 'Undermine his self respect'.[148]

One possible way of arousing a person's self respect is to treat her as an autonomous agent responsible for her own actions; one possible way of undermining her self respect is to treat her as incapable of acting freely and autonomously through weighing her down with rules and regulations which deprive her of the need to choose and of her self respect as a free agent. The danger is most acute at that stage where the person's hold on her freedom is not quite firm, because 'there is a stage of mental growth at which self respect is precarious. The consequent desire is achieved, but there is, or is fancied to be, a danger that some desire more powerful than the rest may break loose and take charge.'[149] On an occasion of this sort, if it were to occur, the will of the person would crack and she would cease to be a member of a society and revert to being a member of the non-social community as no longer capable of free decision.

The second principle has already been touched on, and I shall not develop it further: it is the principle of 'induction'.

> The 'induction' of which I speak is something whereby a human being incapable of will (or capable in only a low degree) behaves as if he were capable (or capable in a higher degree) owing to the proximity of a being thus capable... This inspiration of a weak will by a stronger is what I call 'induction'. It happens not only where a man of weaker will is in contact with a man of stronger but where a man almost but not quite capable of voluntary action is in contact with a man who is so capable. It thus enables men not quite fit for membership of a ruling class in right of their own mental powers to become fit for it when they are well led by their mental superiors. It does not enable them to do everything their superiors can do; it only narrows the gap between them without abolishing it; but it does at least bring into existence a class, recruited from those members of the ruled who, being by mental development most near to being fit for the life of ruling, are rendered fit for that life when they are inspired by wise and vigorous leadership from above.[150]

This process of induction is similar to education; indeed it is a part of all education: 'response to good leadership is part of becoming a good leader. And conversely a good leader is always teaching his followers to become leaders in their turn.'[151] Induction is part of the third law of politics:

> An example of this law occurs when vigorous rulers teach the ruled to cooperate with them and to develop, under their tuition, a vigorous

---

[148] N.L., 13.64–5.
[149] N.L., 13.67.
[150] N.L., 25.52; 25.56–7.
[151] N.L., 25.59.

political life, a similarity in political enterprise and resource, like their own. In this way that portion of the ruled class which is more closely in contact with the ruling class receive a training for Political action which enables them to succeed, in time, their rulers. Here the *freedom* whereby the rulers rule percolates, owing simply to the process of ruling, without any intention that it shall do so, downwards through the strata of the body politic. But this only happens when the rulers are vigorous. Let the rulers be of a slavish sort, and what will percolate will be slavishness.[152]

The solution to the riddle, it appears, is political education: Collingwood's remarks about the relation between law and motive are concerned with those who are already free agents; it does not apply to those who are becoming free agents, or who are regaining their free agency. The life of the body politic is a life of political education: the major task of politics is political education which involves initiation into political life, the gaining of free will, the gaining of the ability to rule oneself and thereby the ability to rule others. *The New Leviathan* provides an account of political education, an account in which Collingwood corrected the one-sided picture he presented in discussing Green and Bosanquet, and accepted some of their arguments, but suitably amended and placed within the framework of a dynamic theory of politics which repairs the deficiency of the classical theory by providing an account of political education. Political education is central to political life, which 'involves the conversion of human beings fit as yet only for membership of the nursery into human beings fit for membership of the council chamber . . . the work done in the council chamber is to recruit itself, with all that this implies. The life of politics is the life of political education.[153]

8: Conclusion

This chapter has ranged widely over Collingwood's political thought on society, the body politic, ruling, punishment, the relation between law and morality, and certain aspects of the question of state interference. In the next chapter these matters are placed within the wider context of the concept of civilization. The common element in all political action is the attempt to live a civilized life, that is, to behave with civility and to organise one's society in such a way as to render this possible. Civilization is an historical process, and within its bounds spring up a world of laws and institutions and customs, which together with its other features, define its character at any given time. But what is meant by calling something 'civilized' or

---

[152] N.L., 25.94–5.
[153] N.L., 32.34.

by the term 'civilization'? What is meant by 'barbarism' and what by 'savagery'? Is 'civilization' a matter of degree or of kind? These topics are addressed in Chapter Six.

Chapter Six
Civilization and Barbarism

1: Introduction

The first part of this chapter consists of an exposition of the concepts of civilization and barbarism as developed in *The New Leviathan*; the second consists of an exposition of the same and related topics as they are treated in some of the unpublished manuscripts. These are illuminating both in that they provide valuable supplements to the published account and also in that they shed additional light on some of the vexed questions raised by Collingwood's later published work. These manuscripts contain discussion of ideals, philosophical method and historical relativism which bear directly on the issue of Collingwood's conception of philosophical method and his alleged conversion to radical historicism.

2: Civilization and Barbarism

For Collingwood, civilization is primarily a process, rather than an end-point. It is a process of approximation to an ideal state, that is, a process of transition from the ideal of 'barbarity' to the ideal of civility. There is no such thing as a perfectly civilized or uncivilized society, and any existing society will be a mixture of civility and barbarity. Collingwood suggests that, as in mixing paint, just as the addition of white paint to black never results in pure white, so the process of civilization never succeeds in producing the condition of pure and complete civility. That is to say, traces of the original condition must always remain, and although prevailed over will never completely vanish. Further, the activity of civilization itself produces its own occasions for barbarity: the greater civilization's achievements the more power it puts in the hands of men for evil as well as good: 'for those who wish to behave in a civilized manner it gives new opportunities for civilized behaviour; for those who wish to behave barbarously it gives opportunities to create new forms of barbarism.'[1] As a consequence of these two factors the most that can be hoped for is an 'asymptotic approximation to the ideal condition of civilization.'[2]

Civilization is a thing of the mind:[3] it is Collingwood's view that all mental activities possess this asymptotic character, and therefore that civilization must possess it as well. The method employed by Collingwood in dealing with the science of mind is of course the method of scale of forms analysis as developed in *An Essay on Philosophical Method*. This method pervades *The New Leviathan*: the structure of the book is a scale of forms. In particular, the idea of civilization as a continuous process with both complete barbarity and complete civility conceived as abstractions — ideal limiting cases — is a direct application of the concept of a scale of forms which has no beginning (the first term being not zero, but unity) and no end (there being no highest term, the scale is open ended).

Collingwood distinguished 'civility' as an ideal from 'civilization' as the process directed towards realizing that ideal state. At this point he examines the etymology of the word 'civilization'. Three clear, but related, senses of the word emerge: 1) Civilization as the process itself (Dr. Johnson's usage); 2) Civilization as the result of the process (i.e. as the condition to which in any given case it leads or has led; 3) Civilization as the equivalent of 'civility' (Boswell's usage). There are three corresponding senses of 'barbarism'.

From this point on Collingwood's discussion focuses on the specific meaning of 'civilization', and he concentrates his attention on the first sense of the word as given above; although he does allow that the other two meanings are in accordance with common usage as usefully describing the results of processes of civilization.

Civilization is the process whereby a community becomes more 'x'.[4] The character of 'x' is indeterminate as it depends on the specific character of the particular process of civilization in question. Here 'x' is divided into two elements, a and b. A community is a 'we' that is always correlative to a 'non-we'. *a* represents the relations of a community with itself and *b* represents the relations of a community with what stands outside itself. Relations with what is outside the

---

[1] 'What Civilization Means', (W.C.M.), p. 24.
[2] N.L., 34.56
[3] N.L., 34.14
[4] N.L., 35.22

community may be relations with an absolute 'non-we' (b_1) or with a relative 'non-we' (b_2), in which b_1 is the world of nature and b_2 is another community as a whole or a member of another community.

'In relation to members of the same community, civilization means *coming to obey rules of civil intercourse*. In relation to the natural world civilization means *exploitation*, or, to be more exact, *scientific or intelligent exploitation*.'[5] In relation to members of other communities civilization means behaving civilly towards them.

I will now elaborate on the first two constituents (a and b_1) of civilization.

a) Behaving civilly involves respecting men's freedom and self respect, and abstaining from the use of force against them. Force is here understood to mean a manner of acting towards a man which, by arousing his passions at the expense of his intellect, causes him to lose self control thereby causing a breakdown of his will.

> Behaving 'civilly' to a man means respecting his feelings: abstaining from shocking him, annoying him, frightening him, or (briefly) arousing in him any passion or desire which might diminish his self-respect; that is, threaten his consciousness of freedom by making him feel that his power of choice is in danger of breaking down and the passions of desire likely to take charge.[6]

b_1) In relation to the natural world, civilization is scientific or intelligent exploitation. This exploitation represents man's scientific understanding of the natural world, and his consequent ability to convert it into a source of supply for his demands. The common factors linking man's treatment of men and his treatment of nature is to be found in the chapter on 'The Essence of Civilization'. We have seen that, generically, civilization is a mental process which goes on in a community, and that specifically it has been characterised as a combination of three such processes. These are 1) Members of a community becoming less addicted to the use of force in human relations; 2) Intelligent exploitation of the natural world; 3) The recognition of those outside the community as agents entitled to be treated civilly rather than as objects of exploitation.

The common fact in all three processes is civility. Natural science is only possible as an organised enterprise (which is to say, only possible at all) where and when conditions of civility obtain. Without civil relations there could no accumulation and passing on of acquired knowledge of the natural world (both practical and theoretical). Without cooperation between men in exploitation the rela-

---

[5] N.L., 35.35–6
[6] N.L., 35.4

tion of man with the natural world could never rise above the level occupied by animals in their relation with the natural world. 'Civilization in part consists in civility and in part depends on civility: consists in it in so far as it consists of relations of man to man; depends on it so far as it consists in relation of man to nature'.[7] 'The mainspring of the whole process is the spirit of agreement.'[8] Collingwood sees the heart of civilization as 'living dialectically'[9]; he draws a distinction between relations between men which are conducted eristically and relations which are conducted dialectically. Eristic is a process of disagreement, dialectic a process of agreement. In dialectic we begin by supposing that there is a real, though hidden, agreement between our view and that of our opponent; in eristic we begin by supposing that we are right and our opponent is wrong. Both processes start with non-agreement: dialectic seeks to convert this into agreement; eristic hardens non-agreement into disagreement.

Being civilized, whatever else it may be, means at the very least the pursuit of agreement and harmony; in particular, it means '*living, so far as possible, dialectically*, that is, in constant endeavour to convert every occasion of non-agreement into an occasion of agreement. A degree of force is inevitable in human life; but being civilized means cutting it down, and becoming more civilized means cutting it down still further.'[10] Thus civilization rests upon the possibility of cooperation and agreement; this in turn rests upon the free will by which men can choose whether they wish to live dialectically or eristically. The development of free will, if dialectical living is chosen, leads to a process of civilization in which each man, through training his intellect, learns to control his desires; and to a process of civilization in which the various members of the community assert themselves as will: both individual and collective will — for Collingwood the two are inseparable; 'the idea of oneself as having a will is correlative with the recognition of something other than oneself having a will.'[11]

So far we have said only that civilization is a process which happens in a community: the question now arising is what kind of community? 'Civilization is the process in a community by which the various members assert themselves as will: severally as individual will, corporately as social will (the two being inseparable).'[12] Specifi-

---

[7] N.L., 36.7
[8] N.L., 36.46
[9] N.L., 39.15
[10] N.L., 39.15
[11] N.L., 21.14
[12] N.L., 36.89

cally, 'civilization is the process of converting a non-social community into a society. For 'to convert into a society' let us say 'to socialize'; then *to civilize is to socialize.*'[13] Civility is the same as sociality: 'It is the condition in which every member of the community, as a free man in a community of free men, respects himself and all his fellow members, and expects them to treat him likewise.'[14]

In the section 'Social Civilization' of 'What Civilization Means',[15] Collingwood phrases it in these terms:

> In this sense being 'civilized' means treating others 'civilly'; treating them without the use of force. This is a negative definition, but the idea defined is not a negative idea, it is the idea of joint action; that is, action involving two or more parties where each party is an agent and therefore a free agent. Joint action is the same thing as society. A society and a civilized society are thus the same.[16]

This clarifies the relation between civilization and the theory of the body politic. Collingwood's dynamic theory of the conversion of the non-social into the social community is a theory of civilization: and one of the most important elements in such a conversion, as already intimated, is education. *The New Leviathan* contains a provocative and lively chapter on 'Civilization as Education': for our present purposes all we need to know is that he saw education as a process of initiation into a civilization.[17]

Much of the substance of Collingwood's understanding of barbarism is contained implicitly in his account of civilization: it is essentially the negative aspect of civilization. Originally the word 'barbarian' meant simply 'foreigner' or 'not Greek' — people whose language was unintelligible to the Greeks. Those who did not speak Greek were called *'barbaroi'* because that is how their language sounded. This did not imply contempt — indeed, the Greeks respected the cultures of the Persians and the Egyptians: but nonetheless, the difference was not simply one of language. Not speaking Greek began to imply something more: it implied that foreigners did not live or think Greek either; and gradually a sharp distinction began to be made between a Greek and a *Barbaros*, the latter being not only not-Greek, but also by implication unfree, slavish, uncivi-

---

[13] N.L., 37.22
[14] N.L., 37.25
[15] 1939–40.
[16] *Ibid.*, p. 36.
[17] For an account of Collingwood's views on education, see D. Boucher, 'The Place of Education in Civilization'; for further discussion of his conception of civilization, see also A.J.M. Milne, 'Civilization and the Open Society: Collingwood and Popper'.

lized and uncultured. From this root grew the modern sense of the word 'barbarian'.

Collingwood distinguished two ways of being uncivilized: savagery and barbarism. Savagery is simply an absence: it is the condition of not being civilized, that is, of being only minimally civilized and relatively uncivilized. Barbarism, on the other hand, refers to a condition of active hostility towards civilization: it is the effort to become less civilized than you already are. This distinction between savagery and barbarism may be clarified by reference to a passage in an unpublished manuscript 'Untitled Fragments on Barbarism':

> The word 'Barbarian' as here used means not being a savage, but behaving like a savage; that is, imitation of savagery (or of what savagery is thought, perhaps wrongly, to be) by persons who are not savages. It involves not the absence of civilization but a revolt against civilization. There is a warrant for this use of the word: words ending in -ism (x-ism let us say) are Greek words: and in Greek they signify, not being an x but behaving like an x; often, though not necessarily, without being one. 'Hellenism' means, not being a Hellene but behaving like a Hellene; adopting Greek mannerisms and customs, in particular the Greek language. You would never ascribe Hellenism to a Greek.'[18]

Barbarism, then, is not being a savage, but behaving like a savage; not being uncivilized, but revolting against civilization: it is the conscious effort to become less civilized than you are. Barbarism, therefore, unlike civilization, is necessarily conscious and aware and cannot be promoted unawares.

For the civilized person, the existence of the sentiment of approval towards civilization (which is partly emotional and partly rational) means that he can promote civilization without necessarily being aware that he is doing so. The sentiment is practical, beginning with an emotional impulse towards some end, and concluding in a rationalisation of this impulse, whereby the intellect judges the action and presents the reasoned case for the action. Rationalisation as a word is not (necessarily) pejorative: it is a legitimate and rational way of behaving. Sentiment, as it approaches the intellectual end of the scale, becomes more conscious; but the emotional element is still present in the agent who is now more aware of the workings of sentiment. The outcome of the working of sentiment is that a civilized man can work unconsciously at promoting civilization; for the barbarist this unconscious promotion of his aims is impossible. He must possess a clear idea of the character of that which he is fighting: in order to aim at the destruction of civilization he must first identify his target.

---

[18] 'Untitled Fragments of Barbarism', 1939–40, pp. 1–2.

The barbarist, the active opponent of civilization, is unable to defeat civilization in the long term, however successful he may be in destroying particular manifestations of the civil spirit. Collingwood presents six reasons in support of this view. 1) The position of the barbarist is self contradictory; he is engaged in willing the suppression of his free will, he is denying his own freedom. The will to barbarism is a will to do nothing, a will to acquiesce in the chaotic rule of pure emotion. It asserts itself as will and proceeds to deny itself as will.[19] 2) As a consequence of 1), barbarism cannot organize itself and make alliances in its effort to destroy civilization. In other words, there cannot be a society for the suppression of sociality. Thus, barbarists are condemning themselves to war not only with civilization, but also with other barbarists. 3) There is no such thing as 'civilization'. If there were it could be destroyed irrecoverably. What exists are only approximations to the ideal condition of civilization; particular manifestations, in what has been built, both physically and mentally, by the civil spirit. Barbarism, as negativity, is parasitic upon civilization: the converse is not true: wherever there are human beings, civilization will spring up, and barbarism can spring up only in opposition to that civilization. 4) As a consequence of 3), civilizations react to attacks not by submission but by expansion. Each attempt at destruction results only in more activity of the civil spirit manifesting itself in an infinite number of ways and with an infinite variety of possible expressions. Civilization is not a particular culture or set of buildings: these are only the external forms of the civil spirit, and their destruction results only in the destruction of those external forms, not in the destruction of the spirit itself. 5) There will always be partisans of civilization ready to defend its achievements. Unlike the barbarist, the partisans of civilization will be able to act in concert; to make alliances and to present a unified and harmonious front against the attack of the barbarist. The barbarist is capable, at most, of achieving a shifting series of unstable alliances. His very existence precludes the possibility of harmonious and joint civil action. 6) Only the barbarist is interested in waging war. The civilized society has peace as its fundamental objective. As a result of his persecution mania, the barbarist pursues a hopeless war. He will never want, or be able to, end the war, but will continue fighting until he is himself destroyed.[20]

Throughout *The New Leviathan* (published before the defeat of Nazi Germany), Collingwood appears to have been confident that

---

[19] N.L., 39.64
[20] N.L., 41.88

civilization will win in the end. A different, more pessimistic tone prevails in the article published in 1940, 'Fascism and Nazism'. In this article he is deeply pessimistic about the possibility of beating the forces of barbarism. He stresses the fanaticism of the barbarist, and declares that those who 'think with their blood' will always be able to beat those who think with their brains. By the time of writing the final version of *The New Leviathan*, he was much more confident that barbarism could not achieve its ends and would be beaten. The above sketch of his understanding of civilization and barbarism indicates the reasons why he believed this.[21]

3: Civilization as an Ideal

The manuscripts 'What Civilization Means' and the untitled fragments on 'Barbarism' are undated, but as both include references to books published in 1939 and as both were written before the final draft of *The New Leviathan*, they can be dated to around 1939–40. The value of these manuscripts, especially the former, lies not only in the light they throw on Collingwood's conceptions of civilization and barbarism, but also in what they say or imply about other topics such as, for instance, the notion of an ideal, historical relativism and philosophical method.

Collingwood begins his account with the simple statement that 'the act of civilizing ... involves two opposite conceptions: the conception of a state of society towards which it is orientated, called civilization, and the conception of a state of society away from which it is orientated, called barbarism.'[22] What is the relation between these two conceptions? Collingwood considers three possible ways of answering this question. The first is that employed in the seventeenth and early eighteenth centuries, which was perhaps the

[21] That Collingwood's views cannot be categorised simply as either optimistic or pessimistic is demonstrated in a letter he wrote to Knox on the day of the outbreak of war on September 1939: in this letter he confidently expressed the view that the Nazis would be beaten and that 'Nazi Germany is doomed in any case'. But he is less sanguine about what might happen to Britain and the immediate prospects for European civilization: 'if this country went Nazi for the sake of beating the German Nazis, victory in the field would be the worst fate. I am not confident about the immediate future of the thing we have called European civilization any more than yourself. But I am quite sure that in the long run the spirit in which you and I believe will create a better civilization ...' Later, in a letter on 6th January 1940, he echoes some of the themes of 'Fascism and Nazism' and wrote that 'we are engaged in a war of ideas, and ... Nazi ideas have the explosive force of novelty: what we call 'democratic' ideas are old and stale, and ... likely to become absolutely decrepit in war conditions, whose effect might easily be the intellectual bankruptcy of our own side.'

[22] W.C.M., p. 9.

simplest way: it conceived the relation between civilization and barbarism by drawing a line between them, and placing any given society on one side of the line or the other. They are then called 'contradictories', and the relation between them a 'dichotomy'. The essence of this dichotomy was that the act or process of civilizing should be telescoped into a vanishing point, with the result that there is no class of societies which is at any given moment undergoing the process of performing that act upon themselves: there is only the one class of those who have finished undergoing it, and another of those who have not yet begun to do so.

Collingwood regards this way of viewing the relation between civilization and barbarism as characteristic of the unhistorical outlook of the time, and he considers that the historians of the late 18th century rendered obsolete the view of history as a succession of 'epochs' or 'periods' each with its own proper and fixed character. There are, Collingwood admits, people who still accept this point of view and who continue to accept the dichotomy between civilized and barbarous societies; 'but to accept it in the middle of the 20th century is a sure sign of retarded development: of being a century and a half behind the times in your habits of thought.'[23]

The conception of history as a series of epochs with the processes leading from epoch to epoch telescoped into vanishing points, rendered the historian's task impossible. The processes leading from period to period eluded the grasp of the historian: he could never say what they were or why they happened, but only that they did happen. By the late eighteenth century change had come to be regarded as intelligible, and accordingly historians focused their attention on the dynamics of history — the dynamic events leading from one period to another. The idea of history as describing static conditions existing in the past at this or that period was obsolete:

> History had become the history of processes ... it had become a commonplace that every period was a period of transition, and that processes of transition were all the historian had to describe...for a mind that has assimilated the results of this late 18th century development in historical thought there can be no sharp line between civilization and barbarism; it becomes clear that any such line is only the effect of telescoping into nothing a process which has no absolute beginning and no absolute ending.[24]

This leads us on to the second way of answering our initial question, and this answer is more complex than the first. The terms civilization and barbarism or civilized and barbarous now have not one but two

[23] W.C.M., p. 9.
[24] W.C.M., p. 11.

pairs of meanings. First, they may be used absolutely. In this sense they are contraries: they are names for the two ends of a scale, between which there are many intermediate terms. But these two ends are not really existing conditions of society: no society is or ever has been either civilized or barbarous in this absolute sense. Secondly, they have a relative meaning. Any given society at any given time stands somewhere on the scale between absolute civilization and absolute barbarism: although in an absolute sense it is neither civilized nor barbarous, in a relative sense it is civilized as compared with one lower down the scale, and barbarous as compared with one higher up.

This relativity of terms does not mean that the absolute meanings drop out of use: but their function is now not one of describing existing or possible states of affairs, but one of describing ideals, or 'points in a frame of reference'.[25]

> Civilization in the absolute sense is the point towards which the civilizing process is directed: barbarism the point away from which it is directed. Civilization as a fact, the actual civilization of any given society at any given time, is always intermediate between these two points. The question about any given society at any time is no longer whether it is civilized or not, but how civilized it is.[26]

Collingwood grants the merit of this way of looking at the matter as relatively more adequate than the first way; but he insists that it is both false and out of date. This conception of civilization as a matter of degree is, Collingwood points out, a typical 19th century one: to us it seems almost as archaic as the previous conception.

> This is because it rests on a presupposition which is no longer made, namely that the civilizing process, wherever it goes and whenever it has gone on, is always and everywhere one and the same process, directed toward one and the same goal; so that the only difference between one civilization and another are differences in the degree to which that process has been operative and that goal approached.[27]

According to Collingwood we no longer think of the civilizing process in this way: such a view is, for us, a mark of the 'historical monism' which we now regard as the chief defect of 19th century historical thought. We no longer suppose that there is only one possible scale of civilization upon which we can place individual civilizations according to their degree of civilization: on the contrary, we suppose that there are many such scales, and therefore different ideals of civilization at different times and among different people. The

[25] W.C.M., p. 12.
[26] W.C.M., p. 12.
[27] W.C.M., p. 12.

'historical pluralism', which twentieth century historians take for granted, regards civilization as differing in kind and not merely in degree, and this leads us to the present day conception of the relation between civilization and barbarism. For us any given society at any given time has its own standard of civilized life, and thinks of itself as civilized in so far as it recognizes that standard, and of other societies as barbarous in so far as they do not.

This leads to a third way of answering the question:

> The question with regard to any given society, then, is not how high it stands in the scale of civilization, for there is no one scale; still less whether it is just civilized or just barbarous, for every society is civilized or it would not be a society: but in what way is it civilized. And from the point of view of any one civilization any other is merely one of the innumerable forms of barbarism.[28]

Such a view would seem, on the surface, to indicate Collingwood's acceptance of a complete historical and cultural relativism of precisely the kind which his critics accuse him of espousing in his later writings. What is particularly interesting is that Collingwood is fully aware of this danger, raises the problem, and shows how it can be solved, without on the one hand giving up the diversity of culture and civilization, or on the other giving up their essential unity; and furthermore, the way Collingwood does this is by applying the principles of method which he laid down in *An Essay on Philosophical Method*.[29] As we shall see, the solution is basically the assertion that civilizations differ in both degree and in kind, and therefore cannot be placed on a scale as differing in degree alone: if civilizations are to be placed on a scale, that scale can only be a scale of forms in which differences in degree are fused with differences in kind, and in which relations of opposition are fused with relations of distinction. The passage on historical relativism is important and interesting enough to be quoted in full:

> The question with regard to any given society, then, is not how high it stands in the scale of civilization, for there is no one scale; still less whether it is just civilized or just barbarous, for every society is civilized or it would not be a society: but in what way is it civilized. And from the point of view of any one civilization any other is merely one of the innumerable forms of barbarism. This may seem a dangerous option. It may

---

[28] W.C.M., p. 14.
[29] Collingwood regards an up to date approach as essentially identical with his approach in E.P.M. Whether this merely shows the degree to which his theory of method follows its own precepts by developing a systematic and considered account of his own experience as a philosopher and historian; or whether it shows that Collingwood uses it as a touchstone against which to test the claims of any rival and 'out of date' view I shall not here enquire.

seem to imply that for any given society the proposition 'we are civilized' has a sense peculiar to that society, for 'civilized' has no constant meaning in such propositions; the definition of civilized conduct varies from society to society, and in any given society from time to time, in such a way that every society thinks its own present way of behaving civilized and the others barbarous.

This is called 'historical relativism', and is rightly regarded with suspicion, because it really amounts to denying what it professes to explain. It amounts to denying that there is any such thing as an ideal of civilized conduct: not merely that there is one single ideal valid for all societies and all times, but that there are many ideals each valid for one society at one time. For if 'civilized conduct' as a phrase in the mouth of certain persons at a certain time merely means 'the way in which we behave', the ideal element in the meaning of the word 'civilized' has vanished, and only a factual element is left. In that case the verb 'to civilize' has lost all meaning; for it cannot refer to a process or act unless it implies that the process has direction and the act purpose, and these imply a distinction between fact and ideal.

The conception here defined as number (3) does not, therefore, imply 'historical relativism'. It does not imply the negation of all ideals and the substitution for social ideals of social facts. All it asserts is that the social facts which are called civilization are orientated towards different ideals. To say that Chinamen and Europeans have different ideals of civilized conduct is not to say that neither has any ideal of civilized conduct. On the contrary, it is to say that each of them has an ideal.[30]

Collingwood suggests that there is a further implication: which is that different ideals of civilized conduct, though in one way divergent, are in another way convergent. They are both called ideals of civilized conduct, and unless this phrase means that in some way they are the same ideal it means nothing. Thus, he concludes, 'the historical pluralism of the present day does not exclude a sense in which all civilization is one.'[31]

---

[30] Cf. 'Untitled Fragments on Barbarism', pp. 3–4: 'Savages have a civilization of sorts; a different kind of civilization according to what kind of savage they are, but always a civilization. They have manners and customs which to you and me may possibly seem uncivil, at any rate in the first shock of novelty, but do not seem so to them. They consider it well-bred to behave in ways which we consider ill-bred. You or I, visiting a strange house, look or ask for the chief person there and report to him. A Bantu sits down and waits until he is noticed. ... He shows politeness in a way different from ours, for politeness is a part of civilization; but he has a civilization.'
[31] W.C.M., pp. 14–16.

Collingwood is attempting here to give an account of a concept such as civilization which is neither simply descriptive, nor simply prescriptive. An account which was simply descriptive would be, in effect, a type of sociology, leaving aside all questions of validity or universality — it would be an admission of historical relativism. A simply normative account, on the other hand, would ignore how people actually behave, and address itself solely to the question of how they ought to behave. Neither approach can be a philosophical approach: for philosophy is a criteriological science which treats its subject matter as operating according to principles and self-governing criteria: the former approach ignores the self-critical aspect of moral or political conduct, the latter ignores its actual existence. Philosophy, as a criteriological science, must embrace the question of both what is actually done and also what ought to be done. A philosophical approach to the question of civilization is therefore both normative and descriptive, treating its subject matter both as something really existing, and also as something which operates according to criteria whereby it can judge the success of its own performance in being the thing it is trying to be. In considering moral philosophy in *An Essay on Philosophical Method*, Collingwood summarises the point thus:

> It would be better, combining a normative with a descriptive conception, to define moral philosophy as giving an account of how people think they ought to behave. Here the facts and ideals of conduct are alike included in the subject matter... but the ideals might seem to be reduced to a mere new kind or order of facts. To correct this, it must be borne in mind that the question how people think is not in any philosophical science separate from the question whether they think rightly or wrongly; and thus moral philosophy has to face the responsibility either of holding that people are always right when they think they ought to do some act, or of instituting some kind of comparison and criticism of moral judgement. In the first alternative, the view is taken that the moral ideal already exists as an ideal in the minds of all moral agents; in the second, that it partially so exists, and more completely as... they try to think out more clearly what they believe their duties to be. In either case, the science is both normative and descriptive; it describes, not action as opposed to ideas about action, but the moral consciousness; and this it is forced to describe as already being in some sense what it ought to be. This in turn will affect the account which it gives of action; for no theory of moral ideals is conceivable which does not admit that to some extent moral ideas affect action.[32]

This passage is concerned, of course, with moral philosophy, but it is nevertheless to the point: in one sense all who act according to some

---
[32] E.P.M., pp. 131–2.

particular ideal of how they ought to act, in particular, according to some ideal of civilized conduct; but, as Collingwood makes plain, in some way all particular ideals of civilized conduct converge — in some way all these ideals are the same ideal. If this is granted then what follows is this: that although it is not possible to arrange civilization on a scale structured according to differences of degree alone, it is nevertheless possible to judge the relative performance of each individual ideal, that is, to judge its performance as an ideal of civilized conduct. Unless this were possible we should fall back into an historical relativism of the kind already rejected: the question remaining is, of course, upon what principles can we adjudicate between various civilizations and ideals of civilized conduct?

As I have already indicated, the principles are those of a scale of forms, and the method that elaborated in *An Essay on Philosophical Method*. If the argument of that book is sound, and if it can be successfully applied, then this is precisely the sort of problem to apply it to. What needs to be done is to examine different civilizations and ideals and to arrange them on a scale which takes full notice of differences in kind as well as differences in degree. I shall not attempt to apply the doctrines of *Philosophical Method* here, but to let them speak through their application in what Collingwood goes on to say in the extremely interesting and important discussion of the concept of an ideal with which he follows and develops in detail the remarks on the convergence of ideals quoted above. Before proceeding, I shall first quote a passage from the 'Untitled Fragments on Barbarism' which deal with the possibility of comparing and evaluating different civilizations. As the passage from *Philosophical Method* quoted above makes clear, philosophy cannot treat the question of how people think separately from the question of whether they think rightly or wrongly; how then do we apply this in the case of comparing and evaluating civilizations and ideals of conduct?

> If people prefer their own civilization to other peoples', it certainly follows that there are different kinds of civilization and that each kind is good; and that it is a mark of ignorance to call one's own kind civilization and all other kinds savagery. But it doe not follow that any one kind is as good (that is, as civilized) as any other. It may still be possible to compare two civilizations by a standard applicable to both, and to decide that by this standard one is better than another. For example, if Europeans and Bantu express politeness towards the head of the household in different ways, there is no contradiction between admitting that what is done in each case is a genuine expression of genuine politeness, and holding that one belongs to a superior type of civilization and the other to an inferior type. They must in that case be judged by reference to the

same standard, and it must be a standard that each civilization regards as valid.[33]

So far this statement, like the one above rebutting the charge of historical relativism, is more an assertion of logical possibility than an attempt to work out the solution to the problem in detail. However, as I have already indicated, in the same manuscript ('What Civilization Means') Collingwood devotes a lengthy section to the notion of an ideal. This section is called 'Ideal and Fact', and does constitute a serious attempt to provide a solution in detail to the problem. I shall quote extensively from this section; it is, I judge, of very great importance in all considerations of Collingwood's supposed conversion to historicism, his supposed relativism, and his view of the relation between philosophy and history.

Collingwood's discussion here seems to take its cue from his remarks in *Philosophical Method* that moral philosophy (which I take to include political philosophy) — 'describes the moral consciousness and this it is forced to describe as already being in some sense what it ought to be.'[34] Such a notion lies behind the whole of the account of society and civilization in *The New Leviathan*, and it is equally central here:

> Any given civilization is in one sense an ideal and in another a fact. In any society that is a society at all (that is, in any group of agents which have risen at all, even though rarely and only on certain kinds of occasion, to the level of joint action) a certain kind and degree of civilization has been actually achieved and does actually exist. As actually existing, it is a fact. This fact is itself an ideal. It began to exist only because the agents in whom it began to exist conceived it as something desirable. It continues to exist only because they think it desirable that it should continue. The fact of civilization actually existing in a certain kind and a certain degree is thus both fact and ideal.
>
> But this realized ideal implies a further ideal conceived but not realized. The consciousness that one has achieved civilization of a certain kind, and to a certain degree, implies the consciousness that even in that kind there are degrees of civilization still unattained.
>
> With regard to degree: a given society at a given time has trained itself to refrain from force between man and man on occasions of a certain kind. For example, a man with money in his pocket goes into a shop to buy cigarettes. He finds no one serving. It would be easy for him to take the cigarettes from the counter and slip away; but in so far as he is civilized he dos not do it, not so much because he is afraid of the policeman as because he thinks it would be an 'uncivilized' or barbarous act, it would be an offence against his own ideal of civilized conduct. And even if he is influenced by fear of the policeman, the fact remains that the

---
[33] 'Untitled Fragments on Barbarism', pp. 21–2.
[34] E.P.M., p. 132.

policeman stands in his mind not as representing mere force, but as representing force directed to upholding the ideal of civilized conduct.

But the same man, if he were hungry and had left his children very hungry at home, and had no money in his pocket, and had entered a baker's shop where no one was serving, might have been tempted to take a loaf from the counter and slip out, knowing it to be an offence against his own ideal of civilized conduct, but being unable to resist the temptation. He has been trained to recognize an obligation to honesty; but trained to carry out that obligation only when the emotions which he must control in carrying it out have no more than a certain degree of strength. The question 'At what point will this strength become irresistible?' is a question concerning the degree of civilization achieved in that degree.[35]

There are also differences of kind in individual ideals of civilized conduct: a person may recognize honesty as part of his ideal of civilized conduct, and be strong in resisting temptation; yet he may completely fail to recognize other kinds of courtesy. For example, if he drives fast cars, he may drive them in such a way as to cause annoyance and inconvenience to others on the road, but it may simply never occur to him that he is behaving barbarously. He acts barbarously not because he cannot resist the temptation to do uncivil things, but because his ideal of civilized conduct quite simply contains no reference to occasions of that kind.

> Such defects, both in degree and in kind, exist in every civilization, where the word 'civilization' refers to the fact that a given society at a given time lives up to its ideal of civilized conduct and up to a certain degree. Every man who is civilized in a certain way and up to a certain degree recognizes other ways and other higher degrees in which he might be civilized, and is to that extent conscious of shortcomings in his own civilization. This implies that, in addition to the ideal of civilization which he both recognizes and realizes, he has another ideal of civilization which he recognizes but does not realize. Let us call this an ideal of the second order.[36]

Ideals of the first order, then, are ideals which are also social facts; they are both recognized and realized in the actual conduct of people and societies. What Collingwood seems to have in mind in talking of first order ideals are our normal everyday customs and manners: the way in which, for example, we normally express politeness. But if there are standards or criteria by which we judge our thought and actions, this necessarily implies the possibility that our thoughts and deeds may not realize the standard or ideal which it sets itself. In

---

[35] W.C.M., pp. 16–7.
[36] W.C.M., pp. 17–8.

other words, we may recognize an ideal of conduct which we do not realize in our actions: thus ideals of the second order are generated.

> How widely this second order of ideals differs from the first will, no doubt, vary enormously from man to man and from society to society; and in the same man or society from time to time. Some men and some societies are relatively self-satisfied, in this respect, others relatively self-critical. But it is very difficult to find out how self-satisfied or how self-critical a given man or a given society really is; partly because the question is an unreal one, since most of us are self-satisfied about some things and self-critical about others; partly because a parade of self-satisfaction is often a disguise for self-criticism and a show of self-criticism a cloak for self-satisfaction, This at any rate is certain: that every man who is conscious of realizing one ideal of civilized life is also conscious of entertaining a second ideal which he does not realize.
>
> Ideals of the first order, which are also social facts, differ among themselves, it would seem, indefinitely. Every Englishman knows that the civility which English people demand of themselves and one another differs from the civility which Frenchmen, or Italians, or Spaniards, demand of themselves and one another; and that even among Englishmen there are many different groups which are civilized to different degrees and in different ways. Only a very ignorant and very foolish person expects that everyone to whatever society he belongs, will agree with everyone else as to what kinds of actions are civilized and what barbarous.[37]

We saw in the previous section that there were three ways of thinking about differences in civilization: the first in which we divide civilized from uncivilized absolutely; the second in which we treat them as constituting a scale on which each differs from its neighbour merely by degree; and the third in which they constitute a scale in which each differs from its neighbours both in degree and in kind. Collingwood now goes on to suggest that we can fit these different ways of conceiving differences in civilization together, and can do so by using the distinctions he is now drawing between different orders of ideals.

The first implied a hard and fast line between civilization and its opposite. This makes perfect sense when being civilized means acting in accordance with an ideal both recognized and realized in a certain social group — but it cannot be applied outside this group.

> The second implied a difference of degree. One action is called civilized and another barbarous, by one and the same ideal of civilized conduct, in so far as they realize this ideal in a higher or a lower degree. We can now see that these two belong to the same social group, by persons agreeing as to what kinds of actions are civilized and what barbarous; but differing in ability to resist the temptation, arising from emotional

---
[37] W.C.M., p. 18.

pressure within them, to do what they regard as barbarous.

The third implied a difference of kind, as for example between European civilization or Chinese civilization; for we may still keep that example, although European civilization (we know, and Chinese civilization, we may suspect) is not homogeneous throughout, but includes many civilizations differing in kind; such differences in kind are not incompatible with resemblances which would justify the statement that all Europeans in some sense have a single civilization.

Ideals of the first order, we have seen, may vary indefinitely. Ideals of the second order may also vary indefinitely. But they may vary less than ideals of the first order. It is a fact that the line between civilized and barbarous conduct is drawn in different places by different groups of English people; but there is a tradition to the effect that many of these groups recognize, even if they do not all realize, a single ideal which is both recognized and realized by one group: the ideal of conduct as 'gentlemanly'. How far this tradition is based on fact I do not ask; I only point out that the people who think it is believe that the idea of a 'gentleman' is a first order ideal for one group of Englishmen and a second order ideals for other Englishmen or even for all Englishmen. Similarly, it used at one time to be thought, and is still perhaps thought by some, that the French ideal of civility is an ideal valid for all Europeans. This implies that French civility is a first order ideal for all Frenchmen, and a second order ideal for others.

And it makes little difference if the Englishmen who claim actually to be gentlemen are found to behave in an ungentlemanly way, or if Frenchmen are sometimes justly accused of not living up to the French standard of civility. It would follow that gentlemanly conduct is a second order ideal for all Englishmen, including those who falsely claim it as a first order ideal for their own caste, and that French politeness is a second order ideal even for the French nation. It would still be true that second order ideals are regarded as differing among themselves less than first order ideals admittedly do.[38]

But even second order ideals, Collingwood suggests, are only partial, and any particular ideal of conduct (realized or not) would appear peculiar if stated in detail. The issue at this point, however, is to consider what there is about first and second order ideals which justify us, logically, in calling them ideals of the same thing. In some way all ideals of civilized conduct are the same, they are all ideals of civilized conduct, and hence there is some sort of unity lying behind their very real diversity.

---

[38] W.C.M., pp. 18–20.

In the previous section we found Collingwood concluding his refutation of historical relativism with the statement that different ideals of civilized conduct, although divergent, must also be in some sense convergent, for they are both ideals of the same thing, and, he suggests, 'unless this phrase means that in some way they are the same ideal it means nothing. Thus the historical pluralism of the present day does not exclude a sense in which all civilization is one.'[39]

The distinction between different order of ideals is an attempt to put flesh on the bones of this skeletal statement. We have so far distinguished first and second order ideals of civilized conduct: Collingwood goes on to distinguish a third order ideal which is both a truly universal and universalizable ideal, and also the logical ground of both first and second order ideals: all the ideals governing our actual conduct and our hoped for conduct, presuppose and depend on this third order ideal which alone makes them intelligible.

> There is an ideal of civilized conduct in which these elements of particularity are left behind: an ideal of universal civility; civility on every kind of occasion, civility under any kind of provocation, civility to every kind of person. It has not left itself without a witness. Christian literature teams with references to it, from the Sermon on the Mount downwards.
>
> This, which may be called the third order ideal, is logically the source of all other ideals of civilized conduct. Not that it was reached before them; on the contrary, civility began, no doubt, at home; but on reflection it became evident that being civil to certain kinds of person, on certain kinds of occasion, and under certain kinds of provocation, is only a special case or (as Spinoza would say) a 'mode' of being civil: and that the particular ideals of civility which are realized, or recognized without being realized, by this or that particular logically presupposes the ideal of civility as such.
>
> This is the sense, and the only sense, in which all civilizations, or ways of living in a civilized manner, are one. They are one in the sense that they all converge upon this one ideal. It must be one ideal, there can be no other beyond it, because it is absolutely unqualified. There can be no fourth order ideal of civilized conduct between man and man. Every man must recognize it when he reflects on his own life as a member of a civilized society. He finds himself behaving civilly in certain limited ways. On reflection, he discovers that he is trying to behave civilly in other and more far-reaching, but still limited, ways. On further reflec-

---

[39] W.C.M., p. 14.

tion, he discovers that he is trying to behave civilly without any limit whatever.[40]

Although the manuscript continues after this point, for our present purpose there is nothing further to draw from this essay but this: at the beginning of the next section Collingwood asks the question: 'Why is the second order ideal not realized?'[41] The answer he gives to this question indicates, I think, the relation between these three order of ideals and the scale of forms; and they also show how scale of forms analysis can be used by Collingwood to allow, on the one hand, for the relativity of things (their difference in kind), while on the other hand insisting on their essential unity, and thus avoiding the pitfalls of relativism.

Why is the second order ideal not realized? 'To recognize an ideal is to try to realize it: recognizing it is not just an intellectual act but an act of will.' The attempt to realize the second order ideal does not entirely fail: 'The second order ideal, considered simply as an ideal, includes the first order ideal as part of itself; realization of the first order ideal, therefore, is a partial realization of the second order ideal. The failure to realize the second order ideal is failure only to realize that part of the second order ideal wherein it goes beyond the first order ideal.'[42]

As we have already seen, a second order ideal, once realized, would become a first order ideal: it would become a social fact. Again, a first order ideal, if it ceased to be fully realized would become a second order ideal: no longer a social fact, but an ideal recognized but not realized. What I am trying to establish is that, on Collingwood's own account of the matter, first and second order ideals are what they are only relatively and not absolutely. Furthermore, they overlap: the second order ideal, as an ideal, contains the first order ideal as a part of itself; realization of the first order ideal is, therefore, at the same time a partial realization of the second order ideal. When we say that we fail to realize a second order ideal what we mean is not that we do not realize it *at all*, but that we only realize it to a limited extent: where we fail is in not realizing that part of the second order ideal in which it goes beyond the first order ideal.

This account can now be further developed through consideration of the formulation for the overlap of classes as expressed in *An Essay on Philosophical Method*. This states that:

---

[40] W.C.M., pp. 20–1.
[41] W.C.M., p. 22.
[42] W.C.M., p. 22.

The higher of any two adjacent forms overlaps the lower because it includes the positive content of the lower as a constituent element within itself. It only fails to include the lower in its entirety because there is also a negative aspect of the lower, which is rejected by the higher: the lower, in addition to asserting its own content, denies that the generic essence contains anything more, and this denial constitutes its falsehood ... The lower overlaps the higher in a different sense: it does not include the higher as part of itself, it adopts part of the positive content of the higher, while rejecting another part.[43]

Comparison of this formulation with the relation between first and second order ideals presented above shows that the second order ideal overlaps the first order ideal in precisely the same way as the higher of two adjacent terms overlaps the lower; and vice versa. My contention is, of course, that the relation between first and second order ideals is exactly the same relation as that holding between adjacent members on a scale of forms. A possible objection to this — that first and second order ideals are absolute and not relative, whereas the terms on a scale of forms are relative and not absolute — has already been overcome by pointing out that first and second order ideals are not, in fact, conceived by Collingwood as absolute: the difference between them is a logical one resting on their relative degree of realization, not on any intrinsic feature.

If I am right in regarding first and second order ideals as adjacent members on a scale of forms, there still remains the question, 'what, then, is a third order ideal?' The answer to this question is, I suggest, this: the third order ideal is not a still higher term on a scale of forms, but rather the philosophical concept which is the logical ground of the scale itself: the genus of which each term in the scale is a specification.

If our concept is civilization understood as an ideal governing our conduct, this concept will articulate itself as a scale of forms in which first and second order ideals will be alternative names for any two adjacent members of the scale, and in which the third order ideal will be the concept which the specifications logically presuppose. First order ideals may be fully realized so far as they go; second order ideals are not fully realized; third order ideals are in one sense fully realized and in another not realized at all: they are realized in so far as any ideal of civilization is realized, and not realized in so far as no realization of the ideal of civilization is complete or perfect. In *Philosophical Method* Collingwood asserts that in a philosophical scale of forms 'the variable is identical with the generic essence itself'[44] and

---

[43] E.P.M., p. 90.
[44] W.C.M., p. 60.

that each term is, therefore, a specification of the generic essence but, as compared with its successor, a relatively inadequate one; and as compared with its predecessor a relatively adequate one. Each term in the scale sums up the scale to that point. Wherever we stand in the scale we stand at an end; but only at a relative end. This is because the specific form at which we stand is the generic concept itself, so far as we yet conceive it. As remarked above, we might say that the generic concept is intimated, anticipated and presupposed in each of its specifications. This is, it should be remembered, a logical point: it does not mean that the ideal of universal civility is somehow present in content; if we knew how to be absolutely and universally civil on each and every kind of occasion then we would already be doing it. What is meant by saying that such an ideal is presupposed by our first and second order ideals is not that we know the way in which such an ideal (universally realized) would empirically manifest itself, but simply that the notion of such an ideal lies behind our everyday conduct and our everyday description of different ideals of civilized conduct as ideals of one and the same thing — civility itself.

4: Conclusion

I have shown the importance and interest of Collingwood's understanding of civilization and barbarism and also indicated that he was aware of the difficulties inherent in attempting to account for the relativity of moral and political ideals without falling into relativism. He saw the danger and sought to avoid it, and in so doing he not so much employed as displayed the method first developed in his lectures on moral philosophy and propounded in *An Essay on Philosophical Method*.[45]

We have thus examined civilization conceptually. But to fully understand civilization as an historically existing condition we must also consider its roots in what it means to be human. Thus we next consider the 'dimensions of civilization'.

---

[45] In 'On the Notion of an Ideal' I address the character of ideals using ideas in part derived from Collingwood.

Chapter Seven

The Dimensions of Civilization

1: Introduction

The previous chapter examined the concept of civilization, showing how it relates to the concept of barbarism and coheres with Collingwood's conception of philosophical method. However, the abstract conceptual discussion needs to be complemented and fleshed out by a consideration of civilization in relation to human nature and human history. As is well known, Collingwood denied that there was such a thing as human nature outside history; however, this claim has to be understood carefully because at the same time he is clear that all human beings share a physiological and emotional nature. Indeed, the analyses of the role of the emotions in *The Principles of Art* and *The New Leviathan*, and the analyses of the role of magic and art in life in relation to the expression and use of emotion presuppose a commonality of human nature without which they would be unintelligible.[1]

This chapter, therefore, examines Collingwood's understanding of the dimensions of civilization as rooted in human nature and experience.

2: Man Goes Mad?

'Man Goes Mad' was written in 1936, and comprises three distinct but related essays: 'The Marks of Madness', 'Modern Politics' and 'The Destruction of the Countryside.' The first two essays are primarily concerned with topical political matters and were considered

---

[1] For an interesting comparison of Collingwood's and Husserl's understanding of civilization, its underpinnings, and threats to it, see, M. Eisenstein, *Phenomenology of Civilization: Reason as a Regulative Principle in Collingwood and Husserl.*

in Chapter Four, §3, 'Collingwood's Politics.' It is the outline of 'the dimensions of civilization' found in the third essay which is relevant here and which I take as the starting point for this chapter.

Collingwood begins by stating that European civilization is at bottom an agricultural civilization. Man, as a mere member of the human species, finds the roots of his emotional life to be found in his feelings concerning his own body and personality, and in his relation to all those beings with whom he has necessary contact. Injury to these fundamentally and generally human emotions, Collingwood argues, is the profoundest injury of which the human mind is susceptible. But man is more than a mere abstract of human nature; he possesses a civilization. A civilization is a traditional way of life, acquired through an historical process in which the later developments are specialized outgrowths from the earlier. Collingwood then goes on to maintain that in order to be real any civilization must have three dimensions: these are: *Complexity*: an elaborate system of responses to various situations; *Continuity*: identity with itself in its own past; *Vitality*: those to whom it belongs must possess it, treasure it and hang on to it. Corresponding to these dimensions of civilization are three dimensions of mental life: Complexity is a function of *intelligence*; Continuity is a function of *memory*; Vitality is a function of *emotion*.

After enumerating these dimensions, Collingwood declares that 'If any of these failed civilization would perish.' For example, if intelligence failed, adaptability would disappear, and the civilization would become rigid, 'like the social structure of bees';[2] if memory failed, the power of comparison of what man is with what he was would be lost — man would become the slave and not the master of his responses; if emotion failed, 'the whole fabric of civilization would crumble in his hands to dust and vanity, and he would sink back into the condition of a human brute.'[3] He continues by arguing that: 'changes in civilization seem to have been as a result of the dying away of certain emotions; (for example) where men care about one thing for centuries and then cease to care and care about something else.'[4]

I shall postpone consideration of the role of emotion in civilized life until later, and turn first to the other dimensions of complexity and continuity. I shall take Collingwood's remarks on the dimensions of civilization and mental life as a starting point, and sketch out

---

[2] Man Goes Mad, (M.G.M.), p. 30.
[3] M.G.M., p. 29.
[4] M.G.M., pp. 29–30.

their place in relation to his detailed discussions of these and similar matters as they are to be found elsewhere in his writings.

3: Complexity and Intelligence: The Role of Critical Thinking

In 'Man Goes Mad', Collingwood suggests that if intelligence failed, adaptability would disappear, and the civilization would become rigid, like the social structure of bees.[5] However, this is not the only way in which intelligence can fail. Elsewhere he draws a distinction between two kinds of unintelligence: *negative* unintelligence, which is simply stupidity, and *creative* unintelligence, which is craziness.[6] Negative unintelligence might very well lead to rigidity, but Collingwood's concern seems, more often than not, to be with the causes and effects of creative unintelligence: this he saw as presenting the greater practical danger.

Creative unintelligence is described as the condition in which 'your mind creates illusions or hallucinations about the things of which you are trying to think.'[7] This conception, which amounts to a form of self-deception, Collingwood examines at length in *The Principles of Art* where he terms it the 'corruption of consciousness'. What did he mean by the term? When the mind refuses to acknowledge and attempt to overcome its error, we have an indication of the presence of a corrupt consciousness. A corrupt consciousness is one that arrests itself and refuses to acknowledge its own true nature: it abdicates its critical function and wallows in the mud of anti-intellectual emotionalism. A full account of the notion of the corruption of consciousness is provided as part of the wider account of expression, consciousness and language in chapters X, XI, and XII of *The Principles of Art*. Without entering into all the complex and fascinating detail of Collingwood's inquiry into art and its place in life we can nonetheless extract the unadorned essentials and see how they fit into our account.

Corruption arises in the transition from the psychic level of experience to the conscious level of experience. This transition is the basis of language, the attempt to express our emotions, the conversion of the preconscious into the conscious. Corruption of consciousness is said to occur when this transition is not performed properly; that is, when the expression of emotion is distorted. This distortion takes place through consciousness disowning some part of its own experi-

[5] M.G.M., p. 30.
[6] 'Three Laws of Politics' (T.L.P.), p. 18.
[7] T.L.P., p. 19.

ence; repressing it; refusing to admit its existence. The feeling thus disowned does not disappear, but lives on in its unexpressed form. Thus the mind's account of itself and of its activities is distorted at the very root, at the lowest level of consciousness. This corruption affects everything subsequently erected upon it; it is a rotten foundation which distorts and renders false the superstructure. Collingwood expresses it this way:

> To know ourselves is the foundation of all life that develops beyond the merely psychical level of experience. Unless consciousness does its work successfully, the facts which it offers to the intellect, the only things upon which intellect can build its fabric of thought, are false from the beginning. A truthful consciousness gives intellect a firm foundation upon which to build; a corrupt consciousness forces intellect to build on a quicksand. The falsehoods which an untruthful consciousness imposes upon the intellect are falsehoods which intellect can never correct for itself. In so far as consciousness is corrupted, the very wells of truth are poisoned. Intellect can build nothing firm. moral ideas are castles in the air. Political and economic systems are mere cobwebs. Even common sanity and bodily health are no longer secure.[8]

Corruption of consciousness is obviously not to be taken lightly. If Collingwood is correct then where and when the consciousness of a civilized people is habitually corrupt, the entire fabric of their civilization is in danger of decay from within. Is there a cure for the corruption of consciousness. And if there is a cure, what is it, and how can it be applied? There are, it would seem, two types of medicine. The first medicine is art and the second philosophy and metaphysics.

It would be hard to overestimate the importance that Collingwood throughout his career attached to the role of art in human life. For example, in 'The Place of Art in Education' (1926) he declares that 'a right training in art is the absolute bedrock of all sane human life.'[9] And in the the manuscript 'Art and the Machine', after discussing the art education of children, he concludes that 'children so trained may or may not turn out to be great artists, they may or may not turn out learned scholars; but they will begin life sane.'[10] This view of art as a necessity for all sane human life rests on two presuppositions, first, that art or imagination is primordial in the life of the mind; secondly, that it is universal in the life of the mind. Collingwood sums up the first of these presuppositions in *Outlines of a Philosophy of Art*:

---

[8] P.A., pp. 284-5.
[9] 'The Place of Art in Education', p. 448.
[10] 'Art and the Machine', n.d., p. 14.

the relation between imagination and thought is that thought presupposes imagination, but imagination does not presuppose thought. This fact is of crucial importance for the attempt to determine the place of art in life as a whole. As thinking presupposes imagination, all those activities whose theoretical aspect take the form of thought presuppose art; and art is the basis of science, history, 'common sense' and so forth. Art is the primary and fundamental activity of the mind, the original soil cut of which all other activities grow. It is not a primitive form of religion or science or philosophy, it is something more primitive than these, something that underlies them and makes them possible.[11]

The second presupposition is stated perhaps most clearly in *The Philosophy of History* (1930), where art is characterised, along with history and religion, as 'a universal and necessary characteristic of things.' Further, Collingwood contends that:

> If the philosophy of art is the study of certain things called works of art, and of the minds of certain people called artists, then it studies only a selected part of the world, not the world as a whole; it is science not philosophy, and its methods ought to conform to the model of scientific (in this case psychological) research, not that of philosophical thinking. If it is to be a branch of philosophy, it must be able to show that, in the sense in which it uses the word art, every work is a work of art, locomotives and business letters no less than statues and sonnets; it must even show that natural objects are *objets d'art* and that everyone is an artist.[12]

Furthermore, in Collingwood's terms, to write a philosophy of art is at the same time to situate art in its relation to other activities of mind.[13] These points concerning Collingwood's understanding of the philosophy of art are essential to an understanding of his writings on the subject; and their being overlooked or ignored has led to much irrelevant criticism of his writings on aesthetics. But if art is universal and necessary, and if it is of vital importance to all other activities of the mind and hence also to the creation and sustaining of civilization, how is this practical effect achieved? Is art merely political propaganda?

On Collingwood's account, art is the expression of emotion; the self discovery by the artist of his or her real feelings through the act of imaginative expression. The artists express their own feelings through their aesthetic activity, but because they are members of a community, they do not express their own feelings alone, but also the feelings of the country of which they are members.[14] Through

---

[11] *Outlines of a Philosophy of Art*, 1925, (O.P.A.), p. 14.
[12] *The Philosophy of History*, 1930, p. 2.
[13] P.A., p. 2; O.P.A., p. 4.
[14] Collingwood does not use the term 'community' in P.A. in the technical sense employed in N.L.

being a member of a community (that is, being possessed of social consciousness) artists have insight into the real feelings of their community; by expressing their own emotions they enable the community as a whole to express its emotions: the artist expresses the emotions of the whole community and so enables it to become aware of the feelings of which it would be otherwise unaware.

For this to be possible, the artists' own feelings must be in tune with those of their community. If successful in their expression of these feelings, they will be conveying to their audience the truth of their feelings which they otherwise do not (or do not wish) to know. They will be exposing to their gaze the feelings which their consciousnesses wish to disown and repress. it is in this sense that the artist may be said to be a prophet: not that he or she predicts the future, but that they tell their community the secrets of its own heart. The artist makes explicit what is implicit; thereby enabling us to see or admit to what we did not see or admit to before.

However, it should be remembered that Collingwood did not reserve the terms 'art' and 'artists' for use only in description of officially designated persons called 'artists' and officially designated aesthetic products called 'art'. He does not seek to minimise the importance of these things: indeed, as we have just seen, he places the greatest value upon their work: but they are not alone in combatting the corruption of consciousness, although they are perhaps more important in so far as they are the spokespeople of an entire community, expressing not only their own private emotions, but those of their audiences also. But, nevertheless, there is a clear sense in which *every* person is an artist, and in which everyone therefore has a personal responsibility in the fight against the corruption of consciousness. Art is a universal and necessary category of mind, and therefore no person can evade their responsibility as an artist.

Collingwood contends that art and language are the same thing. Language is the expression of emotion: the act of expression is language. That is what language is, and as already indicated, that is what art is: the two are complementary aspects of the same activity. Thus each one of us is an artist, and each of our gestures and utterances is a work of art, the act of an artist:

> The effort towards expression of emotions, the effort to overcome corruption of consciousness, is an effort that has to be made not by specialists only but by everyone who uses language, whenever he uses it. Every utterance and every gesture that each one of us makes is a work of art. It is important to each one of us that in making them, however much he deceives others, he should not deceive himself. If he deceives himself in this matter, he has sown in himself a seed which, unless he roots it up

again, may grow into any kind of wickedness, any kind of mental disease, any kind of stupidity and insanity. Bad art, the corruption of consciousness, is the true *radix malorum*.[15]

As we have already seen, the artist is a prophet, and art must be prophetic. *The Principles of Art* concludes on this note:

> The artist must prophesy not in the sense that he foretells things to come, but in the sense that he tells his audience, at risk of their displeasure, the secrets of their own hearts. His business as an artist is to speak out, to make a clean breast. But what he has to utter is not, as the individualistic theory of art would have us think, his own secrets. As a spokesman of his community, the secrets he must utter are theirs. The reason why they need him is that no community altogether knows its own heart; and by failing in this knowledge a community deceives itself on the one subject concerning which ignorance means death. For the evils which come from that ignorance the poet as prophet suggests no remedy, because he has already given one. The remedy is the poem itself. Art is the community's medicine for the worst disease of mind, the corruption of consciousness.[16]

Art is the cure for the corruption of consciousness; the remedy for emotional self-deceit. Philosophy, by contrast, is the cure for intellectual self-deceit. All that Collingwood here says of art is applicable also to metaphysics; from the importance of knowledge 'on the one subject concerning which ignorance means death' down to the displeasure of the audience at being told the secrets of their own hearts: people, as Collingwood reminds us in *An Essay on Metaphysics*, 'are apt to be ticklish in their absolute presuppositions.'[17]

The other cure, then, the remedy for intellectual self-deception, is metaphysics, whose role in the intellectual life of a community is to theorise activity and thereby to give an account of the principles and presuppositions underlying first order activities. An inaccurate or incomplete account will result in a distortion of the activity itself. Philosophy has its function in civilization by virtue of its nature as the activity which engages in the examination, analysis, and criticism of the underlying conditions and assumptions of all other forms of activity: and its task once this is complete is to inform those activities of its conclusions.

The work of philosophy cannot be ignored: metaphysics is a necessary part and corollary of all and any activity. Without metaphysics (not necessarily carried out by professional metaphysicians) the other forms of activity would wither and die as a result of the torpor

---

[15] P.A., p. 285.
[16] P.A., p. 336.
[17] E.M., p. 31.

introduced into their workings by the lack of awareness of their conditions or error as to their presuppositions. Such knowledge is, according to Collingwood, the powerhouse which generates their internal momentum, and makes progress and development possible through the struggle to overcome perceived inadequacies and limitations.[18]

Philosophy is at bottom the same kind of activity as the first order activities — it is an activity of rational thought. A science or body of organized thought or knowledge which refused to recognize and accept its own true nature (that is, in particular, the nature of its foundational presuppositions) could be said to be exhibiting symptoms of corruption of consciousness. This corruption would impede all further progress.

> As regards its *modus operandi* . . . all analysis is metaphysical analysis; and since analysis is what gives its scientific character to science, science and metaphysics are inextricably united, and stand or fall together. The birth of science, in other words the establishment of orderly thinking, is also the birth of metaphysics. As long as either lives the other lives; if either dies the other must die with it.[19]

But, as Collingwood later points out, it is not only science and metaphysics which live or die together, but also metaphysics and civilization:

> Because metaphysical analysis is an integral part of scientific thought, an obstinate error in metaphysical analysis is fatal to the science with which it is concerned. And because science and civilization, organized thought in its theoretical and practical forms, stand or fall together, the metaphysical error which killed (e.g.) Greco–Roman science killed Greco–Roman civilization with it . . . The Greco–Roman world was failing to keep alive its own fundamental convictions . . . because, owing to faults in metaphysical analysis it had become confused as to what those convictions were. The remedy was a metaphysical remedy. It consisted in abandoning the faulty analysis and accepting a new and more accurate analysis.[20]

Metaphysics, like art, has the task of informing a civilization and its science, culture and other activities what its fundamental beliefs actually are, whether they want to hear it or not. If either art or philosophy fail to do their work properly then both science and civilization are, on this account, in danger: the danger being brought about through their dependence on, and attempt to live up to, a false account of their true nature. In 'Political Action', Collingwood sum-

---

[18] See, e.g., I.N., pp. 1–3.
[19] E.M., p. 41.
[20] E.M., pp. 224–5.

marises the task of theory thus: 'the business of sound theory, in relation to practice, is not to solve practical problems, but to clear them of misunderstandings which make their solution impossible.'[21]

Theory cannot do the work of practice for it, but it is nonetheless indispensable for the success of sound practice, and without this critical analysis and clarification, practical problems are rendered intractable. If Collingwood is right, philosophy is indispensable and necessary to the well being of any and every society: it is not irrelevant to practice, but inseparable from it as an aspect of its activity. But philosophy itself, as an activity of mind can be placed in danger by the corruption of consciousness: there may, for example, be emotional impediments to good critical thinking:

> People may have a motive for deceiving themselves and each other. Where certain things which may happen in people's minds are conventionally regarded with disapproval, the lengths to which people in whose minds they actually do happen will go, in order to persuade themselves and others that they do not happen, are most remarkable. In Modern Europe absolute presuppositions are unfashionable. The smart thing to do is to deny their existence.[22]

This is quite clearly an example of corruption of consciousness: where consciousness is corrupt, then all acitivities of the intellect which are normally built upon the foundation of a sound and healthy emotional life are threatened. I shall return to the question of the emotions in considering the third dimension of civilization: the reason for dealing with both them and the corruption of consciousness here is Collingwood's insistence that the intellect can build nothing without a sound foundation of emotional honesty, and that consequently, the work of the intellect is endangered by emotional dishonesty. Where the wells of truth are poisoned no drinkable water of the intellect can be drawn.

However, we have so far looked only at the emotional threats to intellectual life: we still have to examine other, and equally dangerous threats to that life. The intellect can be undermined from beneath by the corruption of consciousness; it can also be undermined from within itself: the intellect can be a danger to the intellect. How is such a thing possible? It is possible, Collingwood suggests, when the intellect develops a science which denies the work of the intellect, thereby undermining itself. Such a science, he avers is psychology considered as a science of the mind. He does not deny that psychol-

---

[21] Pol.A., p. 158.
[22] E.M., p. 42.

ogy is as science, nor that it has a place among the other sciences: what he denies is that it can be a science of thought.

During the 1920s Collingwood reviewed a number of books on psychology, and as a reading of these reviews shows, his attacks on the pretensions of psychology were no late development: he attacks them as vigorously in the 1920s as he was later to do in the 1930s.[23] The major difference is simply that in books published throughout the late 1930s he devotes considerable attention to demolishing the pretensions of psychology as a pseudo-science of thought: there are lengthy passages in *The Principles of Art*, *An Autobiography* and *An Essay on Metaphysics*.

The most succinct statement of Collingwood's views on the proper scope and limits of psychology can be found in *The Principles of Art*. Here he distinguishes thinking (traditionally spirit) from feeling (traditionally the psyche or soul) and goes on to state that 'the proper business of psychology is to investigate this level of experience and not the level which is characterised by thought.'[24] His view of the proper place of psychology is then developed further in an explanatory note:

> whereas, in order to study the nature of feeling, it is necessary to ascertain what persons who feel are actually doing, in order to study the nature of thinking it is necessary to ascertain both what persons who think are actually doing and also whether what they are doing is a success or a failure. Thus a science of feeling must be 'empirical' ... but a science of thought must be 'normative', or criteriological, i.e. concerned not only with the 'facts' of thought but also with the 'criteria' or standards which thought imposes upon itself, e.g. logic, ethics, have long been accepted as giving the correct approach to the study of thought. In the sixteenth century the name 'psychology' was invented to designate an 'empirical' science of feeling. In the nineteenth century the idea got about that psychology could not merely supplement the old 'criteriological' sciences by providing a valid approach to the study of feeling, but could replace them by providing an up to date and 'scientific' approach to the study of thought. Owing to this misconception there are now in existence two things called 'psychology': a valid and important 'empirical' science (both theoretical and applied) of feeling, and a pseudo-science of thought, falsely professing to deal 'empirically' with things which, as forms of thought, can be dealt with only criteriologically'.[25]

---

[23] See, for instance, his highly critical reviews of C.G. Jung, *Psychological Types*; C. Spearman, *The Nature of Intelligence and the Principles of Cognition*; E. Rignano, *The Psychology of Reasoning*.
[24] P.A., p. 164.
[25] P.A., p. 171.

What Collingwood seems to have in mind is that psychology can give a perfectly coherent account of all the levels of what he calls psyche or feeling (which, in the language of *The New Leviathan* are presumably all levels of consciousness below reason and will, which functions appear only at the level of choice); and that they are incapable of giving an account of any mental activity which contains within itself reference to a standard or criterion by which its success or failure is judged. It may be, as Donagan points out, that psychology is not trying to undermine the criteriological sciences, and that psychology and the sciences of mind can work hand in hand, the one (for example logic) showing that a given argument is valid or invalid, the other (psychology) explaining why one day we reason validly and the next day we do not.[26] This line of approach is suggested by Collingwood himself when, in his 1927 lecture on 'Aesthetic' he remarks that 'psycho-analysis can do infinite service to art-criticism by takings cases of bad art and showing why each is bad . . . Not how it is bad; that is the art-critic's business.'[27] Such an approach, in which psychology and the criteriological sciences work in a complementary rather than in an opposed fashion might, on Collingwood's own terms, be possible. It is possible that Donagan is right in suggesting that Collingwood was mistaken in trying to show that no activity of which there is a criteriological science is properly also a possible object of psychological investigation: on balance I think that Donagan is probably wrong on this point, and that Collingwood did allow that psychological investigation might have some part to play in examining processes of thought; but I shall leave this aside. The main point is this: Collingwood, whether rightly or wrongly, believed that psychologists were trying to substitute psychology for the traditional philosophical sciences, and that such an attempted substitution could only be disastrous because logically impossible. This point is discussed in *Speculum Mentis*:

> If psychology is a correct account of thinking, it is a correct account of the thinking of psychologists; that is to say, psychology itself is only a kind of event which goes on in the minds of people called psychologists, a complex of mental idiosyncracies innocent of any distinction between truth and falsehood. But no psychologist believes that his own psychological theories and inquiries can be described in this way. He tacitly excepts his own activity of scientific thinking from the analysis which he is giving of mind in general: that is to say, the mind which he is describ-

---

[26] Donagan, *The Later Philosophy of R.G. Collingwood.*, p. 167.
[27] 'Aesthetic', p. 240.

ing is not the mind which is doing the description, but something not merely different but absolutely heterogeneous.[28]

What the psychologist is studying is not mind at all, not mind in the sense in which the psychologist's own thinking itself is mind:

> In ignoring the distinction between truth and falsity, the psychologist has not ignored something alien to thought, namely its accidental relation to an object other than itself, he has simply ignored thought; for thought is nothing but the drawing of this distinction. And yet, in ignoring the distinction, he has asserted it implicitly in his own person, and is thus the living refutation of his own principles. Psychology is refuted by the psychology of psychology.[29]

If the attempt is made to substitute psychology for a criteriological science of thought, then, a simple destructive dilemma ensues: either the psychologist provides an account which tacitly exempts his own thinking from consideration, or he provides an account which attempts to cover his own thinking as a psychologist. By attempting the former he is admitting failure by being unable to provide an account which holds universally; by attempting the latter he presents an account of thought which refutes itself by the very fact of its being presented.

What are the consequences of the encroachment of psychology — the science of feeling — upon the territory of the sciences of mind? This question is answered in *An Autobiography* and *An Essay on Metaphysics*. In the former Collingwood argues that psychology was created in order to study not mind in its traditional sense (reason, will, consciousness), nor body, but *psyche*, (that is, such functions as appetite and sensation) and that it existed quite happily in close proximity to the sciences of mind and body until early in the 19th century. Psychology:

> marched on the one hand with physiology, and on the other with the sciences of mind proper, logic and ethics, the sciences of reason and will. And it showed no desire to encroach on its neighbour's territories until, early in the nineteenth century, the dogma got about that reason and will were only concretions of sense and appetite. If that was so, it followed that logic and ethics could disappear, and that their functions could be taken over by psychology. For there was no such thing as 'mind'; what had been so called was only psyche . This is what underlies the modern pretence that psychology can deal with what were once called the problems of logic and ethics, and the modern claim of psychology to be a science of mind. People who make or admit that claim ought to know what it implies. It implies the systematic abolition of all those distinctions which, being valid for reason and will but not for sensation and appetite,

---
[28] S.M., pp. 275-6.
[29] S.M., p. 276.

constitute the special subject matter of logic and ethics: distinctions like that between truth and error, knowledge and ignorance, science and sophistry, right and wrong, good and bad, expedient and inexpedient. Distinctions of this kind form the armature of every science; no one can abolish them and remain a scientist; psychology, therefore, regarded as the science of mind, is not a science . . . it is the fashionable scientific fraud of the age.[30]

Psychology so conceived becomes what Collingwood referred to in *An Essay on Metaphysics*, as 'the propaganda of irrationalism'. Psychology as a pseudo-science of thought, he there contends in chapter XI, 'is actually teaching that there is no difference between the pursuit of truth . . . and the pursuit of falsehood',[31] and this follows from its ignoring the distinction between truth and falsehood, which distinction belongs to the very essence of thinking. But, in Collingwood's view, the matter does not end here. What the psychologists are in fact doing is not erecting a science of thought, but something else. What they are doing is acting as the propagandists of irrationalism by denying the importance of truth, science, and thought and erecting in their place a contempt for systematic and orderly thinking in science and politics and religion; substituting the appeal to emotion for the appeal to reason. In relation to politics (which is here our special concern) the results will be disastrous. Since all argument is, from a psychological point of view, nothing more than the expression of feeling or emotion, the identification of psychological with philosophical method destroys the possibility of rational political argument, and public discussion of principles and politics; public statements of facts. Public debate on all political matters — in particular the relation between principles and policies, between means and ends and the rest, will all be replaced by a style of politics in which the tendency is to choose leaders:

> not for their intellectual powers but for their ability to excite mass-emotions; to induce in followers not an ability to think about political problems, but certain emotions which in persons untrained to think will explode into action with no questions asked as to where such actions will lead; and to suppress discussion and information in favour of what

---

[30] A., pp. 94–5. This passage also perhaps contains the answer to Donagan. Collingwood's point is that psychology *denies* the existence of mind by reducing mind to psyche; but he says nothing of the possibility of a non-reductive science of mind, which, while admitting the primacy of criteriological sciences of mind, conceived its own task as inquiry into the 'how' of mental processes while leaving aside the 'why' for the true sciences of mind. There is really nothing in Collingwood's writings which would preclude this possibility. For a discussion of Collingwood's attitude to psychology see J. Connelly and A. Costall, 'R.G. Collingwood and the Idea of a Historical Psychology'.

[31] E.M., p. 120.

is called propaganda, that is, statements made not because they are fact but because they generate these emotions or spark them into action.[32]

Further, there will be a tendency to promote men to positions of authority who have not reached the level of rationality required for the highest forms of political and moral life. And the consequences for political life, for societies and for their civilization will be equally disastrous:

> Civilizations sometimes perish because they are forcibly broken up by the armed attack of enemies without or revolutionaries within; but never from this cause alone. Such attacks never succeed unless the thing that is attacked is weakened by doubt as to whether the end which it sets before itself, the form of life which it tries to realize, is worth achieving. On the other hand, this doubt is quite capable of destroying a civilization without any help whatever. If the people who share a civilization are no longer on the whole convinced that the form of life which it tries to realize is worth realizing, nothing can save it. If European civilization is a civilization based on the belief that truth is the most precious thing in the world and that pursuing it is the whole duty of men, an irrational epidemic if it ran through Europe unchecked would in a relatively short time destroy everything that goes by the name of European civilization.[33]

We are now able to answer the original question we set ourselves, that is, how is it possible for the intellect to deny and destroy the work of the intellect? The answer is that it is possible if a pseudo-science of thought is erected in place of a criteriological science of thought. By denying the distinction between truth and falsity, such a pseudo-science of thought undermines thought itself: it is thought denying the power of thought: it is logically self-refuting, but this in no way affects its ability to corrupt; and if it does corrupt then the consequences can be nothing less than serious.

The success of the propaganda of irrationalism makes the way clear for the success of the forms of unintelligence distinguished earlier. If systematic and orderly thinking is belittled and denied then what will take its place will be creative unintelligence, which is craziness supplemented by the chaotic rule of the passions and emotions. If we return to our starting point we might conclude this section by recalling that philosophy is an indispensable aspect of organized knowledge, and thus a vital part of the intelligent adaptability to circumstances — one of the dimensions of civilization. If philosophical thought dried up (from whatever cause, whether it be

---

[32] E.M., p. 139. I am here following closely N.K. O'Sullivan 'Irrationalism in Politics', pp. 143–4.
[33] E.M., pp. 139–40.

the corruption of consciousness or the success of irrationalism — perhaps the two together) creative intelligence would dry up with it, and creative un-intelligence would take its place. It was this danger Collingwood was passionately committed to warding off; and it was the perception that something of precisely this sort was actually happening in Europe that spurred him into writing his later books and to conclude *An Essay on Metaphysics* with these words:

> The fate of European science and European civilization is at stake. The gravity of the peril lies especially in the fact that so few recognize any peril to exist. When Rome was in danger, it was the cackling of the sacred geese that saved the Capitol. I am only a professional goose, consecrated with a cap and gown and fed at a college table; but cackling is my job and cackle I will.[34]

4: Continuity: The Place of Order and Tradition

A healthy society needs identity with itself in its past: this is one of its dimensions. 'A civilization is a traditional way of life acquired through an historical process in which the later developments are specialised outgrowths from the earlier.'[35] It is only through immersion in a tradition, through the practical knowledge of an established manner of living, that the individual political agent can go about his business. Freedom is only possible within a society working with an ordered set of arrangements and an authoritative way of doing things. All action has to take place in a context of some sort; and political action is possibly only where the agent understands his situation, is fairly confident of the likely consequences of his actions, and shares a set of implicitly understood social and political presuppositions with his fellow citizens which, being commonly understood, render his and their actions rational and intelligible. Thus one of the central conditions of a civilization is a shared tradition, and a shared sense of the value of political order. A society must be rooted in its past, and its citizens must be rooted in its traditions as exemplified and made concrete through the institutions, activities, and practices of that society.

A tradition is a shared and inherited world; but it is not transmitted automatically. Its inheritance has to be earned: the tradition has

---

[34] E.M., p. 343.
[35] M.G.M., p. 30.

to be understood and learned if its inheritors are to own and possess it. Goethe wrote: 'what from your fathers you received as heir, acquire if you would possess it'.[36] Hegel, following the spirit of Goethe's remark, developed the point in this fashion:

> Since the substance of the individual, the World-Spirit itself, has had the patience to pass through these shapes over the long passage of time, and to take upon itself the enormous labour of world-history, in which it embodied in each shape as much of its entire content as that shape was capable of holding, and since it could not have attained consciousness of itself by any lesser effort, the individual certainly cannot by the nature of the case comprehend his own substance more easily. Yet, at the same time, he does have less trouble, since all this has already been implicitly accomplished.[37]

Michael Oakeshott once remarked that 'a tradition of behaviour is a tricky thing to get to know',[38] and certainly the task facing the individual is great. The tradition has to be learned and re-created by those who learn it; but its existence, while not sparing its practitioners the task of learning it, takes away the task of creating it out of nothing.

The only way to know, possess, and maintain a tradition is to act within it. The only form of political education is political action.[39] Political education occurs only in the school of political experience, not in the school staffed and run by political 'projectors'. Learning how to act within a tradition is like learning how to use a language. It is not possible to first acquire a language, and then to put it to use. To possess a language and to use a language are one and the same thing: we can only come to possess it by repeated and progressive attempts to use it.[40]

Similarly, a tradition exists only in use. A tradition that is not in use is an extinct tradition, which is to say no tradition at all. It is false to speak of a tradition as existing apart from or independently of its being put into practice. It is likewise false to suggest that a tradition somehow resides in objects. The so called 'British Heritage' does not reside in the artefacts produced by artisans within a society, but only in the continuing traditional activity which demands that those objects be made and which governs the skill and craft of those who make them. All this is, of course, equally true of civilization: Collingwood, in the definition quoted above, defines a civilization

---

[36] J. Goethe, *Faust*, lines 682ff.
[37] G.W.F. Hegel, *Phenomenology of Spirit*, Preface, p. 17.
[38] M. J. Oakeshott, *Rationalism in Politics*, p. 128.
[39] N.L., 32.34
[40] 'Observations on Language', n.d.

as a 'traditional way of life'. This definition serves to draw the connection between the notion of tradition and the concept of civilization. Whatever civilization is, it most certainly is not country houses, antique chairs, chamber pots or any suchlike object: Collingwood raises this point in *The New Leviathan*:

> For example, under the destructive energy of barbarism's first onslaught it may seem dreadful that the monuments of civilization in bricks and mortar, in paint and canvas, in human customs and institutions, should be destroyed. But these things are not civilization itself, they are only example of what it can do. What made them once can make them again; their destruction is a challenge to such remaking; it can be an effective challenge only if the creative power is already dead.[41]

Implicit in Collingwood's remarks on the nature of tradition is his doctrine of incapsulation: this is the process which accounts for historical continuity as such. In any process of historical change, what was present in the earlier stages is still present in the later stages: it is incapsulated in the present. The process p_1 leaves traces of itself in the process p_2 which succeeds it. There is no dividing line where it can be said that one stops and the other starts: p_1 never stops, but continues in the changed form p_2 and p_2 never begins, but was previously going on in the earlier form of p_1. The elements making up the historical process p are those of the living past as incapsulated in the present. It is this incapsulation which makes historical knowledge possible as the re-thinking of the past. The past is always implicit in the present, perhaps as a 'minority report' making up part of the fabric of the present, or as physical evidence surviving as artefacts waiting to be interpreted and understood by the historian. We are thus able to re-think the past because, in a sense, it has never gone away.[42]

Of what value is historical knowledge in action? What knowledge of the past provides for those who wish to act in the present is knowledge of their situation: that is, knowledge of how their situation came to be what it is: 'what history can bring to moral and political life is a trained eye for the situation in which one has to act.'[43] By grasping the past — as living in the present — the political agent is able to grasp the implications and antecedents of the situation. She knows how and in what way to act because she is aware of the possibilities available: she has her thumb in the pie of tradition; she is able and ready to discern intimations and to act upon them. Thus the tra-

---

[41] N.L., 41.71
[42] See A., chapters IX–XI where Collingwood propounds his theory of 'incapsulation' in the context of a discussion of the revival of Celtic Art after the Roman occupation.
[43] A., p. 100.

dition provides both the context and the opportunity for political action; and this action is itself the continuation, the self enactment, the concrete embodiment, of the tradition — a tradition that does not exist save in 'use'.

Yet this action within the tradition; this exemplification and continuation of its substance is at the same time a modification of it. It is created anew with each action. A tradition is a dynamic thing whose essence is constant movement and alteration: a tradition which ceased to flow would be a tradition which ceased. No tradition is the mere static repetition of what has already gone before; no tradition is the eternal reiteration of one fixed, idealised and glorious moment in history. A fossilized tradition is a dead tradition: if still called a tradition this is so only because it is given the name as a courtesy title. In 'Political Action', as we saw earlier, Collingwood expressed this general conception of 'tradition' thus:

> When the political spirit of a society is no longer satisfied with its existing structure, no longer finds that structure to express its own political aspirations, it alters it. And this process is really going on at all times. To speak of a stable political system as 'existing', and then as suddenly altered with a jerk by a so-called reformation or revolution, is to be deceived by appearances. Every fresh political action is in reality a modification of the whole political poise and attitude (constitution) of the agent.[44]

Allied with the idea of tradition (central to Collingwood's conception of civilization) is the idea of political order, which we have already examined, but a few additional remarks are apposite here. All political action takes place within a civilization; within a way of life rooted in its past; that is, within a tradition. But if this is so, the direct aim of political action itself cannot be the maintenance of the tradition which makes it possible. The tradition is a presupposition of political activity, not its end: of course, all sound political activity will remake the tradition and thereby enhance and continue it, but this is an indirect consequence of political action, not its direct and immediate objective. A tradition is the naturally occurring outcome of shared activity: it is the name we give to a form of shared activity as it exists through time; but it is impossible to have a shared activity whose object is the founding of a tradition as such. A tradition is exemplified in and by shared activities and enterprises; its presence can be shown, but it cannot be detached from its historical existence and defined in the abstract. It follows that there can be no such thing as a piece of legislation providing for the continuation of a tradition.

---

[44] Pol. A., p. 168.

Traditions cannot be made by laying down the law. What is more, the very attempt to legislate in this way would be tantamount to an admission (or recognition) that the tradition was already dying; and if it were dying, the political activity predicated upon its existence would also be dying.

In summary, a tradition is a shared sense of political order over time; it cannot be legislated into existence; and that the search for political order and the attempt to live a civilized life, while on the one hand presupposing a tradition, on the other carries that tradition forward by acting within its spirit. We now come to the third dimension of civilization.

5: The Vitality of a Civilization: Emotion and the Place of Religion

Those who belong to a civilization must possess and treasure it. We have already looked at some of the ways in which this is done, but there is a third: the health and strength of the basic human emotions. In 'Man Goes Mad', Collingwood insists that: 'the sanity of man as man depends on the health of his fundamentally human emotions ... the sanity of a man as civilized depends on the health in him of the emotions fundamental to his type of civilization.'[45]

Before proceeding further, it is worth recalling some of Collingwood's general remarks about the place of emotion in life. At no point in his career did he seek to separate emotion from intellect: just as he insisted on the inseparability of will and intellect,[46] so he insisted on the inseparability of emotion from all rational living. In *Faith and Reason*, published in 1928, Collingwood avers that faith is present not only as theoretical practical faith, but also in the form of feeling:

> We have feelings toward this or that finite object, but we also have feelings toward the universe as a whole. Nor can these two kinds of feeling be completely separated; our feeling toward a particular thing is very often, perhaps always, more or less conditioned by a sense that the thing is somehow typical or symptomatic of things in general. Few people, except through failure to observe their own experiences, will deny that they sometimes have feelings about the world at large: we feel the world sometimes as a familiar place, as our home, sometimes as alien and strange, and formidable or menacing in its aloofness, sometimes as cold and rigid, sometimes as palpitating with life, sometimes as a single concentrated focus of meaning, a thing that could be completely expressed in a single word if we knew the word, sometimes as a riot of differences

---
[45] M.G.M., p. 32.
[46] See R.P., pp. 30–1 and the lectures on moral philosophy.

inexhaustible to the most patient enumeration. Poetry (that is to say, the work of people who make it their business to express feelings accurately) is full of the record of such cosmic emotions, which are the emotional aspects of faith.[47]

Again, in reason (which is the attitude we take towards things as parts of a whole as distinct from an attitude towards the whole itself which is the province of faith), we find the same distinctions. We find a theoretical aspect, a practical aspect, and an emotional aspect 'in which everything excites in us a feeling proper and peculiar to itself.' It should be noted that the three aspects; theoretical, practical and emotional, of both faith and reason, are aspects of the same thing: they may be distinguished but not separated. Thus, for example, practical faith (which is the certainty that life is worth living) cannot exist apart from theoretical faith (i.e. that the universe as a whole is rational); the belief that life is worth living is nothing apart from the belief that it can be lived, that is, from the belief that our actions will have the effects we intend or hope for. If we believed the world to be irrational and random, action would be impossible. On the other hand, the certainty that life is worth living would be nothing if we did not feel that it were worth living: a merely intellectual faith could have no grip, could excite no enthusiasm.

If we turn now to the 1933 lectures on moral philosophy we find, in the section 'Rational Emotion', a similar emphasis on the role of emotions: 'the forms of rational action have their own emotional colourings. In a sense, each is a peculiar emotion or complex of emotions; but only in the sense that they are emotions of a special kind, proper to rational beings as rational, and constituting the emotional aspect of their rationality.'[48] There is thus an emotional attitude towards, for example, any activity which we regard as means to any of our ends; and 'similarly, there is an emotional attitude towards any rule which we recognize and obey; our common name for this is respect or reverence, and this is akin to love, but is an intelligent or rational love, not love as an appetite.'[49] To these intellectual emotions correspond intellectual passions, such as a rational fear of frustration in the pursuit of our ends, and a rational anger at breaches of recognized rules.

At this point Collingwood's inquiry into rational emotion takes a turn which anticipates the argument of 'Fascism and Nazism' seven years later. This is the view that ethical and political principles are predicated on the religious love of a God. In the later article he

[47] F.R., pp. 141-2 in Rubinoff (ed.) *Faith and Reason*.
[48] L.M.P., 1933, p. 125.
[49] L.M.P., 1933, p. 125.

writes: 'The real ground for the 'liberal' or 'democratic' devotion to freedom was religious love of a God who set an absolute value on every individual human being.'[50] The lectures of 1933 continue in this vein:

> But although there is an element of hunger in our emotional attitude towards the useful, there is also an element of love in it. This must be so, for it is a rational hunger, and reason always apprehends the universal, and our emotional attitude towards the universal is love. Regarded as love, our emotional attitude towards the useful is self-love in the sense of devotion to our own interests; not self-love as a mere appetite, the blind force that drives us on to new acts, but cool or rational self-love, the enlightened emotion that pursues what we think will be to our advantage, the emotional characteristic of the economic life. From this point of view, our respect for law may be described as love of our neighbour, that is, the desire to put others on an equality with ourselves before a law that applies without discrimination to all. This again is not a mere appetitive impulse to interfere in the lives of others, but a rational desire, a desire to create an intelligible or reasonable order in the world of finite wills. The rational love of our neighbour is the emotional spring or expression of political activity.
>
> The third kind of love is the love of God, and this is the emotional aspect of duty. In doing our duty we are aiming at realizing in ourselves an absolutely good will, and this is the will of God; our devotion to this ideal is therefore the love of God. Our will is here wholly active, and therefore no passion corresponds to duty; the love of God, it is is an intelligent love, has no place for fear or for anger with those to fail to do his will. Passions only exist so far as our will is impeded in its activity by its own weakness and defective intelligence; we fear God so far as we do not yet truly love him, and are angry with those who defy his will only so far as we do not understand his ways. The disappearance of these passions is a sign that we are beginning to love him truly.
>
> The love of God is the sea into which all our passions and appetites flow. At first we think that we have two appetites, hunger and love; but hunger, when we understand it, turns into self-love. We think that we love ourselves and our neighbours, but when we come to know our own minds better we recognize that in these various loves we have from the first been loving God, from whom all love comes and to whom it all returns.[51]

To complete this brief survey of Collingwood's views on the place of emotion I will turn to *The Principles of Art* and pinpoint the relevant passages; there is no space here either to develop or defend his theory of art.

---

[50] 'Fascism and Nazism', p. 190.
[51] L.M.P., 1933, pp. 126–7. At this point Collingwood proceeds to the concluding passage quoted on pp. 176–7.

Collingwood maintains that 'every sensation has its own emotional charge',[52] and that there are also emotions of consciousness' which, 'unlike the purely psychical emotions, admit of expression in language: in a phrase, a controlled gesture, or the like.'[53] Later, in dealing with language and the expression of emotion, Collingwood has this to say:

> I have been speaking hitherto as if discourse had two functions, one to express thought, the other to express emotion; and as if the misconception I want to remove were the doctrine that scientific discourse or intellectualized language has the first function without the second. I do want to remove that misconception; but I want to go a good deal farther. An emotion is always the emotional charge upon some activity. For every kind of activity there is a different kind of emotion. For every different kind of emotion there is a different kind of expression. Taking first the broad distinction between sensation and thought, the emotional charges upon sense experience, felt as they are at a purely psychical level, are psychically expressed by automatic reactions. The emotional charges upon thought experiences are expressed by the controlled activity of language. Taking next the distinction within thought of consciousness and intellect, the emotions of consciousness are expressed by language in its primitive and original form; but intellect has its emotions too, and these must have an appropriate expression, which must be language in its intellectualized form. Intellect has its own emotions . . . If it is once granted that intellectualized language does express emotion, and that this emotion is not a vague or generalized emotion, but the perfectly definite emotion proper to a perfectly definite act of thought, the consequence follows that in expressing the emotion the act of thought is expressed too. There is no need for two separate expressions, one of the thought and the other of the emotion accompanying it. There is only one expression.[54]

A little later Collingwood develops the point that intellect has its own emotions, and that therefore intellectualization is not the same thing as the expulsion of emotions:

> The progressive intellectualization of language, its progressive conversion by the work of grammar and logic into a scientific symbolism, thus represents not a progressive drying up of emotion, but its progressive articulation and specialization. We are not getting away from an emotional atmosphere into a dry, rational atmosphere; we are acquiring new emotions and new means of expressing them.[55]

---

[52] P.A., p. 162. Collingwood goes on to refer to the habit among modern Europeans of 'sterilizing sensa' by ignoring their emotional charge. This, as we shall see, has its parallel in the demand for a religion purged of its emotional and magical elements.
[53] P.A., p. 232.
[54] P.A., pp. 266–7.
[55] P.A., p. 269.

For Collingwood, then, emotion and rational life are inseparable: I shall illustrate the place of emotion in life, first by looking at religion, and secondly by looking at our emotional attitudes towards the land and agriculture. As a preliminary we need to take a look at Collingwood's account of magic. The reason for this is that, for Collingwood, magic is not a matter of pseudo-science or control over natural events by supernatural means, but a matter of the expression and orientation of emotion. Religion, along with other activities, has both an intellectual and an emotional side. In dealing with the place of religion and the emotions in civilized life we are, therefore, to a large extent dealing with one and the same thing. The spirit of a civilization is sustained by the strength of its religious conviction, and the strength of this conviction is an emotional truth as much as an intellectual matter.

Collingwood inquires into the nature of magic in a lengthy unpublished manuscript devoted to the subject; this manuscript became the source of the discussion of the topic in *The Principles of Art*. I shall accordingly draw the account from the latter source only, as (although not so detailed and wide ranging as the former) it provides a good summary of Collingwood's basic position.[56]

In Collingwood's view magic, properly understood, should not be seen as an attempt to control natural events through supernatural means. It was precisely the error of taking magic as this sort of activity that led anthropologists such as Taylor and Frazer to characterize magic as pseudo-science. This was, in Collingwood's estimation, a failure to grasp the essential nature of magic, and it resulted in such distortions as the belief that 'savages' had a 'primitive mentality' which prevented then understanding the relation between cause and effect in nature.

In opposition to this account, Collingwood insists on the rationality of magic. Magic, he suggests, is a means to a preconceived end. It is utilitarian in purpose, and the end it seeks is not the control of nature by 'supernatural' means, but the arousal of particular sorts of emotion on particular occasions. Unlike amusement-art, in which the emotions aroused are discharged by the act of being amused itself (catharsis), magic has the purpose of arousing emotions and keeping them aroused. It is, that is to say, the direct opposite of catharsis: its intention is to focus and crystallise the emotions aroused, and to direct them upon the conduct of practical life. Thus

---

[56] For discussion see H. Saari, 'R.G. Collingwood's Emotivist Theory of Magic'. For a consideration of Collingwood's account of magic in relation to anthropology, see W. James, 'Tales of Enchantment: Collingwood, Anthropology, and the "Fairy Tale" Manuscripts'.

the function of a war dance is to arouse war-like emotions which will spur warriors on to fight more fiercely; the purpose of a rain dance is to arouse the emotion necessary in dealing with the problems arising from the rain and flooding, and so on.

The particular form that the emotional representation and its accompanying ritual takes is not important in itself, so long as it is successful in fulfilling its function. The basic condition for success is that those taking part in the ritual are aware of the type of ritual being performed and of the objective: they must know whether it is a rain dance or a war dance; and, of course, the ritual must have sufficient magical potency to arouse the required emotions. A quiet and restrained war dance would probably fail. For a magical ceremony to be successful in arousing emotions, the participants must know what emotions are desired, the use to which they are to be put, and the ceremony must be somehow consonant with the desired end result. Collingwood is fully prepared to admit that magic may, on occasion, be mistaken by those who practice it for something that really does produce rain or prevent earthquakes, but this, he assures us, is an error and not the essence of magic. Further, it is an error which can be recognized by 'savages' themselves: 'I am quite prepared to think that they do entertain such beliefs; savages are no more exempt from human folly than civilized men'.[57] While magic does not entail belief in supernatural intervention, this mistake may nevertheless by made, and it will probably aid rather than hinder the potency of the magic. However, the mistake, if it is made, is nonetheless refuted by the content, context, and timing of magical rituals: as Wittgenstein once remarked, the important thing to notice about a native rain dance is that it is conducted at the onset of the rainy season.[58]

Magic is no less a part of 'civilized' society which contains innumerable performances, rituals and activities whose partial or sole function is the stimulation of emotion for the purpose of its discharge in the conduct of practical life. Collingwood lists National anthems, military bands, the Eiffel Tower, fox hunting, funeral and marriage services, debutante dances, dinner parties, religious rites and services in general; and we could add the Royal Jubilee and World Cup football. These are all excellent examples of activities which any respectable savage would immediately recognize as magical.

---

[57] P.A., p. 67.
[58] L. Wittgenstein, 'Remarks on Frazer's Golden Bough', pp. 71–2.

In the modern civilized world there are some who would deny the existence of magic among themselves, while attributing a belief in it to others: this they can do only by misunderstanding magic as a pseudo-science, and then patting themselves on the back for having freed themselves from such superstitious nonsense. Collingwood's riposte to those people is:

> Magic is a representation where the emotion evoked is an emotion valued on account of its function in practical life, evoked in order that it may discharge that function, and fed by the generative or focusing activity into the practical life that needs it. Magical activity is a kind of dynamo supplying the mechanism of practical life 'with the emotional current that drives it. Hence magic is a necessity for every sort and condition of man, and is actually found in every healthy society. A society which thinks, as our own thinks, that it has outlived the need of magic, is either mistaken in that opinion, or else it is a dying society, perishing for lack of interest in its own maintenance.[59]

I shall first discuss religious emotion. Collingwood began his 1940 article on 'Fascism and Nazism' dramatically:

> When travellers are overcome by cold, it is said, they lie down quite happily and die. They put up no fight for life. If they struggled, they would keep warm; but they no longer want to struggle. The cold in themselves takes away the will to fight against the cold around them. This happens now and then to a civilization. The vital warmth of the heart of a civilization is what we call a religion. Religion is the passion which inspires a society to persevere in a certain way of life and to obey the rules which define it.[60] Without a conviction that this way of life is a thing of absolute value, and that its rules must be obeyed at all costs, the rules become dead letters and the way of life a thing of the past. The civilization dies because the people to whom it belonged have lost faith in it. They have lost heart to keep it going. They to longer feel it as a thing of absolute value. They no longer have the sense of its rules as things which at all costs must be obeyed. Obedience degenerates into habit and by degree the habit withers away.[61]

Collingwood's conviction was that the whole of western civilization was built upon a religious foundation. The ideas of freedom, free thought, free discussion, free assembly which constitute the body of liberal or democratic principles, had been distilled from Christian practice by a long line of thinkers: 'The real ground for the 'liberal' or 'democratic' devotion to freedom was religious love of a God who set an absolute value on every individual human being.'[62]

---

[59] P.A., pp. 68–9.
[60] That is, to uphold what Collingwood refers to elsewhere as its *suum cuique*.
[61] F.N., p. 168.
[62] F.N., pp. 170–1.

So far so good: if the religious life of a society is healthy, its emotional life (in that aspect) will be healthy, and so the society as a whole will be healthy. But what if this religious foundation crumbles? What will be the consequences? In Collingwood's opinion, as we have seen, liberal principles are derived from Christian practice, but their health and strength depend on the continuation of a sound and vigorous religious life. Liberal principles cannot be distilled, bottled, labelled, and applied to matters of conduct while at the same time their religious underpinning is jettisoned. If the superstructure of civilized life is to remain stable, its religious foundation must stand firm.

The emotional impetus — the dynamo — driving a civilization forward cannot provide sufficient power if it is disowned and repressed. If a society habitually sterilizes not only sense-data but also all emotional charges on practical and theoretical activities, if it denies itself the emotional impetus needed to sustain itself, then it will slowly but surely die. This was the ground for Collingwood's pessimism in 'Fascism and Nazism': he there believed that 'Liberalism or democracy may be wise, but the people who care for it do not care for it passionately enough to make it survive.'[63]

By the time he came to write *The New Leviathan*, this pessimism has vanished and we find Collingwood declaring that 'barbarists have always in the end been beaten.'[64] Whatever the reason for this change of heart, there is no doubt that there was no change in the belief in the importance of emotion in civilized life; the change arose out of an altered evaluation of the tenacity of the emotions sustaining liberal democracy. In 1940 Collingwood believed that Fascism and Nazism would be victorious:

> Fascism and Nazism, then, are successful because they have the power of arousing emotion in their support. They can annihilate even the most widespread liberal-democratic opposition in their own countries because those who believe in them 'think with their blood', as the Nazis say: care intensely about their beliefs, and can therefore overwhelm the liberalism or democracy which, because its votaries have for two hundred years progressively purged it of emotional elements, has become as purely as possible what the French call *cerebral*, an affair of unemotional thinking. A man who thinks with his blood, even if what he thinks is silly, will always get the better of a man who thinks merely with his brains, even if what he thinks is wise.[65]

---

[63] F.N., p. 172.
[64] N.L., 45.95
[65] F.N., pp. 172–3.

The Dimensions of Civilization 311

The Nazis and Fascists care intensely about their beliefs; the protagonists of liberal democracy no longer do: why is this? It is because liberal and democratic principles:

> are derived from Christianity; and the emotional force, the 'drive or 'punch' that once made them victorious was due to Christianity itself as a system of religious faith rich in the superstitious or magical elements... which generate the emotion that gives men the power to obey a set of rules and thus bring into existence a specific form of life . . . Illuminism and other anti-religious movements have long ago exhausted liberalism or democracy of this emotional force and reduced it to a mere matter of habit. A mere habit has no 'punch'. It holds together with a success directly proportional to its own tenacity, which depends chiefly on the completeness with which it has been established, and inversely proportional to the strength of the destructive forces operating upon it.[66]

If all this is true, and the practice of a religion rich in emotional elements is an indispensable foundation of a civilization, then the threat is twofold: first, the rise of a devitalised *cerebral* religion; secondly, the rise of widespread atheism, (or of a religion so devoid of distinctly religious elements as to be indistinguishable from atheism). In one sense neither of these is possible: religion is, says Collingwood, 'a universal and necessary characteristic of things... it is a universal and necessary human interest, the interest in a universal and necessary aspect of the world.'[67] We must, however, be careful to be sure exactly what is meant by such a statement. Just as the universal and necessary human interest called history does not make everyone a professional historian, so the universal and necessary human interest called religion does not make everyone a practicing Christian. In other words, what we are dealing with here is the relationship between a category of mind and its empirical application: to say that the category is universal is to say nothing of the health, vigour or intellectual merits of its empirically existing manifestations. 'Religion' in general may be universal, but no one is 'religious in general', they can only be religious in particular, i.e. as a Christian, Moslem, Hindu and so on; and what matters in appraising each religion are its virtues and vices as the particular religion it is, not the general characteristics it shares with all religions whatever, or with a universal religious 'habit of mind'.

I make these points to forestall misunderstandings. For example, it might be said that if religion is universal and necessary, then it cannot alter for either better or worse, nor even less die out altogether.

---

[66] F.N., p. 174.
[67] *Philosophy of History*, pp. 2–3.

Again, it might be said that the emotional punch, by Collingwood's own admission, does not necessarily have to derive from religion at all, and if this is so, why bother overmuch if religion as we have hitherto known it dies out?

Collingwood's answer to both points of view is that religion is both necessary and contingent: it is necessary as a universal aspect or characteristic of things; it is contingent in that its practical and theoretical existence depends entirely upon the character of an historically existing religion in all its empirical detail. The adequacy of any religion is not, then, a given datum; each religion or religious practice can be judged on both its theoretical and practical merits, and there is no reason at all to suppose that any religion is immune from decay or debilitation. A final point might be the significance of ritual: if religion, as a universal, already gave the emotional punch we are looking for then ritual would be unnecessary: the fact that it is necessary is an indication that any emotion, and particularly religious emotion, needs focusing and strengthening by what Collingwood would call the appropriate magical ceremonies.

At the time of writing 'Fascism and Nazism' Collingwood was not alone in perceiving an upsurge of atheism, which went hand in hand with the general resurgence of positivism. As far as religious belief was concerned, this followed (in Collingwood's view), a long line of 'Illuminists' who sought to purge all trace of superstition and emotion from the lives of modern men. Accordingly, when dealing with Christianity, their attitude was that the rational principles, if any, should be filtered off leaving a residue of superstitious and magical elements which could then be safely discarded to the advantage of all. This, of course, was for Collingwood simply a way of killing off Christianity completely.

However, as suggested above, there was another (and a more insidious) danger. If it is the case that only a religion rich in magical and superstitious elements can provide the 'punch', the emotional power behind a civilization, then it follows that if a religion continues in existence but divested of this vital side of its nature, the threat to the fundamental values and spirit of the civilization will be just as great as the threat posed by out and out atheism.

To conclude this section on the importance of religion and the emotions it generates and focuses in practical life, consider the concluding passage of 'Fascism and Nazism':

> The time has long gone by when anyone who claimed the title of philosopher can think of religion as a superfluity for the educated man and an 'opiate for the masses'. It is the only known explosive in the economy of

that delicate internal-combustion engine, the human mind. Peoples rich in religious energy can overcome all obstacles and attain any height in the scale of civilization. Peoples that have reached the top of a hill by the wise use of religious energy may then decide to do without it; they can still move, but they can only move downhill, and when they come to the bottom of the hill they stop.[68]

The second form of emotion to be remarked on is our emotional attitude towards the land and agriculture. Collingwood's question is this, 'European civilization is at bottom an agricultural civilization. Are our emotions about the land in good health or not?'[69] This question was for Collingwood no idle query, but a matter of the utmost pressing concern:

> If man outrages his body by refusing to eat, he dies. If he outrages his mind by injuring the foundations of his emotional life, he goes mad. So far as man is merely a member of the human species, the roots of his emotional life are to be found in his feelings concerning his own body and personality and his relation to his mother, his possible and actual mates, and the other beings with whom, no matter to what type of society he belongs, he comes into necessary contact. Injury to these fundamentally and generally human emotions is the profoundest injury of which the human mind is susceptible. If grave enough, it can make the sufferer cease, in any true sense, to be a man at all.[70]

Our emotions towards the land are equally fundamental, and injury to them would, in Collingwood's view, have the gravest consequences. Our civilization is at bottom an agricultural one; it is commercial and scientific as well, and, we must feel strongly about these things also, but that from which they originally sprang is not dead and past, but present and so cannot be ignored. The love of our country is not aesthetic or patriotic, but something 'far deeper and more primitive than that . . . it is an experience neither aesthetic nor political, but in the deepest sense religious . . . and upon the vitality of this religious feeling depends the vitality of our civilization as a whole.'[71] Until the nineteenth century this feeling for the land was strong and general, and this was shown by the way that the land was actually treated. But with the rise of industrialisation came the ruin of the countryside. For Collingwood, this was not because mills and mines were necessarily fatal to it; in fact they are as intimately related to the earth as barns, dovecotes or oast-houses. The reason the countryside was ruined was simply that it lost its vitality. With the rise of the motor car, and the growing desire of town dwellers to escape from

---

[68] F.N., p. 176.
[69] M.G.M., p. 29
[70] M.G.M, pp. 29–30.
[71] M.G.M., p. 33.

the horrors that modern towns had become, the countryside was further damaged. Again, this was not inevitable, it happened because there was no longer any traditional country life intact. If there had been a flourishing tradition of agricultural village life, then the invasion from the towns could have been met by a flood of buildings in the living tradition of country architecture, and they would have become part of the countryside. But the tradition was dead, and so it was the town that provided the buildings thereby spoiling the very thing which they sought to enhance and enjoy.[72] There were, wrote Collingwood, two common responses to this process: one is the response of the exploitative builder, the other the response of those who wish to preserve the beauties and amenities of the countryside. The conservers protest against the erection of new buildings. They are right to do so, because it is rightly assumed that new buildings will be blots on the landscape, a defacement of the beauty of the countryside. Our fore-fathers made no such assumption, they could build what they liked, confident that it would only be a further adornment of the land. Why have we lost this confidence?

> It is because we no longer feel toward the country as towards a garden in which God has put us to dress and keep it: we no longer have that sense of a loving union with its soil ... Those who wish to preserve its amenities are as far from having this sense as those who recklessly destroy them ... The speculative builder looks upon it as something to exploit for his own advantage; his enemy, its would be preserver, looks upon it as an object of aesthetic enjoyment, a museum exhibit.[73]

We have killed the agricultural life of our fathers and the least we can do is to preserve the choicer relics as museum exhibits: 'That whole villages should become part of a vast national museum is neither impossible nor unreasonable.'[74] But there is a difficulty, because 'the thing which it is proposed to divide into a town-dwellers' playground and a museum exhibit is the dead body of our agricultural life. If it is true that agriculture is the root of our entire civilization, we cannot do that, not because our bodies will starve, but because the emotional foundations of our civilized life will perish.'[75] Our industry lacks the vitality at its roots, and we therefore turn to the countryside for a renewal of emotional power: 'industry, if it consciously nourishes itself from roots in agriculture, is well. Cut off from these roots it is a kind of madness, which may endure for a time

---

[72] Paraphrase of M.G.M., pp. 34–5.
[73] M.G.M., p. 36.
[74] M.G.M., p. 37.
[75] M.G.M., p. 37.

in a feverish restless consciousness, but can have no lasting vitality.'[76] We are, Collingwood thinks, beginning to be aware of this; because we 'know that our civilization has in it a sickness of the mind, a morbid craving for excitement, a hyperaesthesia of emotion for which it offers no cure. There is a cure, if only we could get it: the deep, primitive, almost unconscious emotion of the man who, wrestling with the earth, sees the labour of his hands and is satisfied.'[77]

7: Conclusion

All this is taken from the third part of 'Man Goes Mad' — 'The Destruction of the Countryside'. It is in many ways highly speculative, but at the very least it shows the extent to which Collingwood took human emotion seriously, and this was the point which this chapter was designed to convey. In many ways his words seem prophetic and much of his concerns are at the centre of current discussion in environmental ethics and philosophy.[78] From that point of view his analysis may be judged profoundly right, in which case our present attitude to the countryside leaves much to be desired; but there is a counterview brutally expressed by Maurice Cowling who referred to Collingwood's 'idiotic commitment to the countryside.'[79] Collingwood's account of the 'Dimensions of Civilization' is a unity and it fits, as I attempted to show, his pronouncements on these and related topics elsewhere in his writings. It unites intellectual and emotional needs with the concept of tradition, and with the concept of political order. This passion for unity, this refusal on Collingwood's part to accept anything less than the whole person in all aspects (practical, theoretical and emotional, together with his repeated attempts to characterise the relationship properly), is a major unifying themes (or, 'big worry')[80] of his entire philosophy.

---

[76] M.G.M., p. 37.
[77] M.G.M., p. 42.
[78] For discussion and references, see J. Connelly and G. Smith, *Politics and the Environment: from theory to practice.*
[79] M. Cowling, *Religion and Public Doctrine in Contemporary England*, p. 189.
[80] P. Johnson, *R.G. Collingwood: An Introduction*, chapter ten.

Chapter Eight

Conclusion

In considering 'Ruskin's Philosophy', Collingwood singled out for attention Ruskin's belief in the indivisibility of the spirit; but why did he focus on this theme? Was it because of its intrinsic importance as a theme in Ruskin or because of its importance as a central theme in Collingwood's own thinking? Without adjudicating on the former, I would suggest that Collingwood found in Ruskin reflections of his own views that he was happy to elaborate and attribute to Ruskin. The belief in the unity and indivisibility of the spirit is central to Collingwood's philosophical vision, his assessment and criticisms of other philosophers, and his understanding of the importance of philosophy to practice; hence his words on Ruskin can be re-deployed in self-description:

> this kind of assumption betrays the presence of a definite theory of the human mind: the belief, namely, that each form of human activity springs not from a special faculty — an organ of the mind, so to speak — but from the whole nature of the person concerned: so that art is not the product of a special part of the mind called the 'aesthetic faculty', nor morality the product of a special 'moral faculty', but each alike is an expression of the whole self. Thus, if the ancient Greek was a man of definite type and character, his art exhibited this character in one way, while his political systems and his religious beliefs exhibited the same character in another way, translated, as it were, into another language, but otherwise identical. This principle — the unity and indivisibility of the spirit — Ruskin never questioned and never attempted to prove.[1]

By contrast with Ruskin, Collingwood *did* attempt to question and prove this assumption. But he never ceased to presuppose it. He refused to accept an abstract separation of the forms of experience and he denied the existence of separate faculties of reason or emotion. He insisted that whatever activities a person pursues in one mood, idiom, capacity or mode has both logical and existential

---

[1] R's. P., pp. 6–7.

implications for all the others. These implications can only be ignored, he maintained, at the risk of shattering the unity of the mind, and so producing fragmented and deracinated human beings.

Collingwood's life work was the conceptual overcoming of this fragmentation: conceptual, but this work was, for Collingwood, necessarily also practical. As he remarked in a letter of Knox in 1937, 'is there a philosophical science of action as distinct from one of thought? I am pursued by the notion that these are not distinct or different at all, but that there is only one thing . . . action, for which thought would be an appropriate name . . . I don't know how far you would go in your repudiation . . . of the dualism between "theory" and "practice". I would go a terrible long way myself.'[2] The unity of the spirit and the closeness of the relationship between thought and action and theory and practice was central to Collingwood's concerns. But how far did he demonstrate it in his own life and writings? How far do his philosophical writings unite into a broadly coherent whole? These are the questions I have sought to answer

The New Leviathan, Collingwood's first book devoted entirely to political theory, was also his last. That book did not aim at completeness and therefore did not include treatment of all those subjects typically falling under the general head of 'political theory'. Even allowing for material contained in a number of earlier published articles, much was left undiscussed. Some of these omissions I have rectified through the use of unpublished manuscripts: in particular the sections on theory and practice, punishment, law and morality and state interference, are largely derived from this source. The vital point, however, is that to label Collingwood's work in this field 'political theory' or 'political philosophy' is in some degree misleading. *The New Leviathan* is as much a philosophy of civilization as a philosophy of politics in any narrower sense. Collingwood's inquiry is far more engaged with the theory and practice of civility and civilization than with (for example) the issue of political obligation.

In presenting Collingwood's treatment of civilization as an ideal I was also able to bring into the account his own extremely interesting and important remarks concerning the dangers of historical relativism. In the final chapter I explicitly returned to the theme of the book as a whole, which is not only to argue for the unity and coherence of Collingwood's philosophy, but also to suggest that his account of the conditions of civilization is a direct and unifying outcome of all his inquiries and writings on philosophical method, metaphysics, history, anthropology, political theory, art and religion. It is a recog-

---

[2]   Letter to Knox, 2/11/37.

nition of this thorough intertwining of all the major themes and focal points of Collingwood's philosophy which justifies and underpins the basic approach of this book. That approach rests on two key points. First, that it is necessary to deal with issues in political philosophy not in isolation from, but in direct relation to, debates in metaphysics and philosophical method. Secondly, that it was necessary to include critical consideration of the claim that Collingwood's views underwent a 'radical conversion' and the extent to which they are mutually compatible or contradictory. Whatever may be the case with other political philosophers, it is certainly the case that with Collingwood it is mistaken to separate the narrower questions of political theory from the broader questions of method and metaphysics.

The discussion of Collingwood's political philosophy, then, comes full circle back to our starting point: the unity and coherence of Collingwood's philosophy. The unity of a philosophy is no two-dimensional jigsaw in which every part fits statically with every other part; but a developing structure of thought in which each part co-exists dynamically with other parts. Strains and tensions are therefore inevitable, but they should not obscure the underlying unity of purpose and direction. Inconsistency and contradiction are alike to be expected, as are both progress and regress. The issue is not the mere existence of these things (on that there is no dispute) but whether or not they go down to fundamentals. The conclusion for which I have argued is that the fundamental characteristics of Collingwood's philosophical outlook remained constant throughout his academic life.

Bibliography

Writings by Collingwood

Books and Pamphlets

Religion and Philosophy. London: Macmillan, 1916.
Ruskin's Philosophy. Kendal: Titus Wilson, 1922. (Reprinted in Donagan, 1964).
Speculum Mentis. Oxford: Clarendon Press, 1924.
Outlines of a Philosophy of Art. London: Oxford University Press, 1925. (Reprinted in Donagan, 1964).
Faith and Reason. London: Benn, 1928. (Reprinted in Rubinoff, 1968).
An Essay on Philosophical Method. Oxford: Clarendon Press, 1933.
The Principles of Art. Oxford: Clarendon Press, 1938.
An Autobiography. London: Oxford University Press, 1939.
An Essay on Metaphysics. Oxford: Clarendon Press, 1940. Revised edition with an Introduction and additional material edited by Rex Martin, 1998.
The First Mate's Log. London: Oxford University Press, 1940.
The Three Laws of Politics. L.T. Hobhouse Memorial Trust Lecture, No. 11, London: Oxford University Press, 1940. (Reprinted in Boucher, 1989).
The New Leviathan. Oxford: Clarendon Press, 1942. Revised edition with an Introduction and additional material edited by David Boucher, 1992.
The Idea of Nature. Oxford: Clarendon Press, 1945.
The Idea of History. Oxford: Clarendon Press, 1946. Revised edition with an Introduction and additional material edited by W.J. van der Dussen, 1993.
The Principles of History and other writings in philosophy of history. Edited and with an Introduction by W.H. Dray and W.J. van der Dussen. Oxford University Press 1999.

Articles

'The Devil' in *Concerning Prayer*, ed. B.H. Streeter, London: Macmillan, 1916. (Reprinted in Rubinoff, 1967).
'Croce's Philosophy of History', *Hibbert Journal*, vol 19, 1921, pp. 263–78. (Reprinted in Debbins, 1965).

'Can the New Idealism Dispense with Mysticism', (*Proceedings of the Aristotelian Society*, supp. Vol. 3, 1923, pp. 161-75. (Reprinted in Rubinoff, 1967).

'The Nature and Aims of a Philosophy of History', *Proceedings of the Aristotelian Society*, vol. 25, 1924-5, pp. 151-74. (Reprinted in Debbins, 1965).

'Plato's Philosophy of Art', *Mind*, vol 34, 1925, pp. 154-72. (Reprinted in Donagan, 1964).

'Economics as a Philosophical Science', *International Journal of Ethics*, vol. 36, 1925, pp. 162-85. (Reprinted in Boucher, 1989).

'The Place of Art in Education', *Hibbert Journal*, vol. 24, 1926, pp. 434-48. (Reprinted in Donagan, 1964).

'Oswald Spengler and the Theory of Historical Cycles', *Antiquity*, vol. 3, 1927, pp. 311-25; 435-46. (Reprinted in Debbins, 1965).

'Aesthetic', in J.S. McDowall (ed.) *The Mind*, London: Longmans, 1927. (Reprinted in *Collingwood Studies*, vol. 3, 1996, pp. 195-215).

'Reason is Faith Cultivating Itself', *Hibbert Journal*, vol. 26, 1927, pp. 3-14. (Reprinted in Rubinoff, 1966).

'Political Action', *Proceedings of the Aristotelian Society*, vol. 29, 1928-29, pp. 155-76. (Reprinted in Boucher, 1989).

Notice of 'Political Action', *Transactions of the Cumberland and Westmorland Antiquarian and Archaeological Society*, Vol. 29, 1929, p. 355.

'A Philosophy of Progress', *The Realist*, vol.1, 1929, pp. 64-77. (Reprinted in Debbins, 1965).

'The Present Need of a Philosophy', *Philosophy*, vol. 4, 1934, pp. 262-5. (Reprinted in Boucher, 1989).

'Human Nature and Human History', *Proceedings of the British Academy*, vol. 22, 1936. (Reprinted in *The Idea of History*).

Notice of *The Principles of Art*, *Transactions of the Cumberland and Westmorland Antiquarian and Archaeological Society*, vol. 38, 1938, p. 314. (Reprinted in Collingwood Studies, vol. 4, 1998, pp. 192-3).

'Fascism and Nazism', *Philosophy*, vol. 15, 1940, pp. 168-76. (Reprinted in Boucher, 1989).

Collections of Articles

Boucher, D., (ed.) *Essays in Political Philosophy*. Oxford: Clarendon Press, 1989.

Debbins, W. (ed.), *Essays in the Philosophy of History*. Austin: University of Texas Press, 1965.

Donagan, A., (ed.) *Essays in the Philosophy of Art*. Bloomington: Indiana University Press, 1964.

Rubinoff, L., (ed.) *Faith and Reason: Essays in the Philosophy of Religion*. Chicago: Quadrangle, 1967.

Reviews

Psychological Types, or the Psychology of Individuation by C.G.Jung, *Oxford Magazine* 7/6/23. (Reprinted in *Collingwood Studies*, vol. 1, 1994, pp. 188–90).

The Nature of 'Intelligence' and the Principles of Cognition by C. Spearman, *Oxford Magazine*, 15/11/23. (Reprinted in *Collingwood Studies*, vol. 1, 1994, pp. 190–2).

The Psychology of Reasoning by Eugenio Rignano. *Oxford Magazine*, 6/12/23. (Reprinted in *Collingwood Studies*, vol. 1, 1994, p. 192).

The Philosophy of the Good Life by C. Gore. *The Criterion*, vol. 10, No. 40, 1931, pp. 561–2. (Reprinted in *Collingwood Studies*, vol. 5, 1998, pp. 139–42).

Philosophy and History: Essays presented to Ernst Cassirer, ed. R.K. Klibansky and H.J. Paton, Oxford: Clarendon Press, 1936, in the *English Historical Review*, vol. 52, 1937, pp. 14–16. (Reprinted in *Collingwood Studies*, vol. 5, 1998, pp. 145–51).

Translations

Croce, B. *The Philosophy of Giambattista Vico*. London: Howard Latimer, 1913.

Ruggiero, G. de *The History of European Liberalism*. Oxford: Clarendon Press, 1927.

Unpublished Manuscripts

Truth and Contradiction, Chapter II, (1917). Bodleian Library, Dep. 16/1.

'The Spiritual Basis of Reconstruction', (1919). Bodleian Library, Dep. 24/3.(Extract published in Boucher, 1989).

'The Philosophy of the Christian Religion', (1920). Bodleian Library, Dep. 1/5.

'Notes on Hegel's Logic', (1920). Bodleian Library, Dep. 16/2.

'Utility, Right and Duty', (n.d. c1920). Bodleian Library, Dep. 6/3.

Lectures on Moral Philosophy, (1921). Bodleian Library, Dep. 4.

'Action': Lectures on Moral Philosophy. (1923) Bodleian Library, Dep. 3/1.

'Notes Towards a Theory of Politics as a Philosophical Science.' (n.d., c.1925–27) Bodleian Library, Dep. 24/6.

'Art and the Machine', (n.d. c.1926) Bodleian Library, Dep. 25/8.

Notes on R.M. MacIver, *The Modern State*, (1927). Bodleian Library, Dep. 6/7.

'The Idea of a Philosophy of Something, and, in particular, a Philosophy of History', (1927). Bodleian Library, Dep. 14/2. (Published in revised edition of *The Idea of History*).

'Outlines of a Concept of the State.' (n.d., c.1928). Bodleian Library, Dep. 24/9.

'The Breakdown of Liberalism', (n.d. c.1928). Bodleian Library, Dep. 24/7.

'Rough Notes on Politics', (n.d., c.1928) Bodleian Library, Dep. 24/8.

'Stray Notes on Ethical Questions.' (1928) Bodleian Library, Dep. 6/1.

Commentary on the Preface to Kant's *Critique of Pure Reason*, (n.d. c.1928). Bodleian Library, Dep. 22/4.
'Outlines of a Philosophy of History', (1928). (Published in the revised edition of *The Idea of History*).
Lectures on the Philosophy of History, (1929). Bodleian Library, Dep. 12/6.
Lectures on Moral Philosophy, (1929). Bodleian Library, Dep. 10. (Extracts published in Boucher, 1989).
'War in its Relation to Christian Ethics', (1930). Bodleian Library, Dep. 1/8.
Lectures on Moral Philosophy, (1932). Bodleian Library, Dep. 7.
Lectures on Moral Philosophy, (1933). Bodleian Library, Dep. 8. (Extracts published in Boucher, 1989).
'List of Work Done', (1933). Bodleian Library, Dep. 22/2.
'Notes towards a Metaphysic', (1933). Bodleian Library, Dep. 18/3-7.
'Outline of a Theory of Primitive Mind', (1933). Bodleian Library, Dep. 16/8.
'The Metaphysics of F.H. Bradley: An Essay on *Appearance and Reality*', (1933). Bodleian Library, Dep. 29.
'The Nature of Metaphysical Study', (1934). Bodleian Library, Dep. 18/2. (The second lecture is published in the revised edition of *An Essay on Metaphysics*).
'Method and Metaphysics', (1935). Bodleian Library, Dep. 19/3.
'Man Goes Mad', (1936). Bodleian Library, Dep. 24/4. (Extract published in Boucher, 1989).
'Magic', (1936-7). Bodleian Library, Dep. 21. (Extract published in Boucher, 1989).
'Folklore: Three Methods of Approach', (1936-7). Bodleian Library, Dep. 21/5
'The Historical Method', (1936-7). Bodleian Library, Dep. 21/6.
'Function of Metaphysics in Civilization', (1938). Bodleian Library, Dep. 19/7.
'Notes on Historiography', (1938-9). Bodleian Library, Dep. 13/3. (Reprinted in *The Principles of History*).
'Untitled Fragments on Barbarism', (1939-40). Bodleian Library, Dep. 24.
'What Civilization Means', (1939-40). Bodleian Library, Dep. 24. (Published in revised edition of *The New Leviathan*).
'Goodness, Rightness, Utility.' (1940) Bodleian Library, Dep. 9. (Published in revised edition of *The New Leviathan*; extracts reprinted in Boucher, 1989).
Draft Preface to *The New Leviathan*, (1941). Bodleian Library, Dep. 24/12. (Published in Boucher, 1989).
'Observations On Language', (N.D.) Bodleian Library, Dep. 16/3.

Correspondence

Letters to the Clarendon Press are held in the Clarendon Press Archives, Oxford. (See Johnson, pp. 6-34.)
Letter to O.G.S. Crawford, 14 April 1941. Bodleian Library, MSS. Crawford 4, fol. 118. (See Johnson, pp. 42-3.)

Letters to B. Croce. (Biblioteca Benedetto Croce, Naples. See Johnson, pp. 43–50.) Five letters are reprinted in whole or in part in Donagan, 1962, pp. 314–7.
Letters to G. de Ruggiero. Bodleian Library, Dep. 27. (See Johnson, pp. 51–9.)
Letters to Tom Hopkinson. (In private possession, Johnson, pp. 61–3.)
Letters to T.M. Knox held in the library of St Andrews University. The letters of 2/11/37, 3/9/39 and 6/1/40 are reprinted in Boucher, 1989, pp. 232–3. (See Johnson, pp. 67–74.)
Letter to A.D. Lindsay, 20 October 1938. Reprinted in D.Scott, *A.D. Lindsay: a Biography*, Oxford University Press, 1971. (See Johnson, pp. 76–7.)
Letters to Gilbert Ryle, 9 May & 6 June 1935. Bodleian Library, MS. Eng. Lett. d.194. (See Johnson, pp. 100–1.)
Letters to F.G. Simpson. (In private possession, see Johnson pp. 101–7.)
Letter to W. von Leyden, 31 May 1941. (In private possession, see Johnson pp. 111. Extract in W. von Leyden, 'Philosophy of Mind: An Appraisal of Collingwood's Theories of Consciousness, Language, and Imagination'.
Letter from Joseph Needham to *The New Statesman*, 1940, Vol. 19, pp. 174–5.
Letter from Joseph Needham, 14 January 1940. (In the possession of Teresa Smith).

Writings on Collingwood

Bibliographies

Burchnall, R.A., *Catalogue of the Papers of Robin George Collingwood (1889–1943)*. Bodleian Library, Oxford.
Dreisbach, C., *R.G. Collingwood: a Bibliographic Checklist*. Bowling Green, Ohio: The Philosophy Documentation Centre, 1993.
Johnson, P., *The Correspondence of R.G. Collingwood an Illustrated Guide*. R.G. Collingwood Society, 1998.
Taylor, D., *R.G. Collingwood: a Bibliography*. New York: Garland, 1988.

Collections of Essays

Boucher, D., Connelly, J. and Modood, T., (eds) *Philosophy, History and Civilization: Interdisciplinary Perspectives on R.G.Collingwood* Cardiff: University of Wales Press, 1995.
Krausz, M., (ed.) *Critical Essays on the Philosophy of R.G.Collingwood*. Oxford, Clarendon Press, 1972.
Collingwood Studies, 1994–9 and *Collingwood and British Idealism Studies* 2000–, (D. Boucher, B. Haddock and A. Vincent, eds.) publishes both primary and secondary articles and reviews.

Reviews

Knox, T. M. Review of *An Essay on Philosophical Method*, *Oxford Magazine*, 23 November 1933, pp. 257–9.

Oakeshott, M. Review of *The Principles of Art*, *The Cambridge Review*, 9 June, 1938, p. 487. (Reprinted in *Collingwood Studies*, 4, 1998, pp. 189-92).
Laski, H.J., Review of *The New Leviathan*, *New Statesman*, Vol. 24, 1942, pp. 97-8.
Webb, C. C. J., Review of *The Idea of Nature*, *Journal of Theological Studies*, vol. 46, 1945, p. 251.

Books and Monographs

Boucher, D., *The Social and Political Thought of R.G. Collingwood*, Cambridge University Press, 1989.
Donagan, A., *The Later Philosophy of R.G. Collingwood*. Oxford: Clarendon Press, 1962. Second edition, University of Chicago Press, 1985.
Eisenstein, M., *Phenomenology of Civilization: Reason as a Regulative Principle in Collingwood and Husserl*. New York: University Press of America, 1999.
Ficarra, F. T., *Collingwood's New Leviathan*, unpublished Ph.D. Thesis, University of Illinois, 1961.
Hinz, M., *Self-Creation: Collingwood and Nietzsche on Conceptual Change*. New York: University Press of America, 1994.
Johnson, P., *R.G. Collingwood: An Introduction*. Bristol: Thoemmes, 1998.
Mink, L., *Mind, History and Dialectic*. Bloomington: Indiana University Press, 1969.
Rubinoff, L., *Collingwood and the Reform of Metaphysics*. Toronto: University of Toronto Press, 1970.
Tomlin, E.W.F., *R.G. Collingwood, Writers and Their Work*, No. 42, Longmans, Green & Co., 1953.
Van der Dussen, W.J., *History as a Science: The Philosophy of R.G. Collingwood*. The Hague: Martinus Nijhoff, 1981.

Articles

Boucher, D., 'The *Principles of History* and the Cosmology Conclusion to the *Idea of Nature*, *Collingwood Studies*, vol. 2, 1995, pp. 140-174.
Boucher, 'The Significance of of R.G. Collingwood's Principles of History', *Journal of the History of Ideas*, vol. 58, no.2, 1997, pp. 309-30.
Boucher, D.'The Place of Education in Civilization', in D. Boucher, J. Connelly and T. Modood (eds) *Philosophy, History and Civilization*, 1995.
Connelly, J., 'Metaphysics and Method: A Necessary Unity in the Philosophy of R.G. Collingwood', *Storia, antropologia e scienze del linguaggio*, Anno 5, fasc. 1-2, 1990, pp. 33-156.
Connelly, J., 'Art thou the Man: Croce, Gentile or de Ruggiero', in D. Boucher, J. Connelly and T. Modood (eds) *Philosophy, History and Civilization*, 1995.
Connelly, J., 'Natural Science, History and Christianity: the Origins of Collingwood's Later Metaphysics' in *Collingwood Studies*, vol. 4, 1997, pp. 101-32.
Connelly, J., 'Bradley, Collingwood and the 'Other Metaphysics'', *Bradley Studies*, vol. 3, no. 2, 1997, pp. 89-112.

Connelly, J. and Costall, A., 'R.G. Collingwood and the Idea of a Historical Psychology', in *Theory and Psychology*, vol. 10, no. 2, 2000, pp. 147–70.

Connelly, J., 'A Mistake in the Interpretation of Collingwood', *Collingwood and British Idealism Studies*, Vol. 9, 2002, pp. 112–122.

Connelly, J. 'Sweet, Bosanquet and the hindrance of hindrances', in S. Panagaku (ed.) Symposium on William Sweet's 'Idealism and Rights', *Collingwood and British Idealism Studies*, vol.9, 2002.

Croce, B., 'In Commemoration of an English Friend, a Comparison in Thought and Faith' in *Thought, Action and Intuition as a Symposium on the Philosophy of Benedetto Croce*, L.M. Palmer and H.S. Harris (eds), Hildesheim, 1975. (Reprinted in *Collingwood Studies*, vol. 3, 1996, pp. 174–187).

Crossman, R.H.S. 'When Lightning Struck the Ivory Tower', *New Statesman*, 1939, xvii, pp. 222–3.

D'Oro, G., 'How Kantian is Collingwood's Metaphysics of Experience?', *Collingwood Studies*, 6, 1999, pp. 29–52.

D'Oro, G., *Collingwood and the Metaphysics of Experience*, London: Routledge, 2002.

Emblom, W.J., Review of A. Donagan, *The Later Philosophy of R.G. Collingwood* in *Journal of Aesthetics and Art Criticism*, vol. 23, 1963, pp. 84–5.

Hopkinson, H.T., 'Robin Collingwood', *Pembroke Review*, 1982.

James, W. 'Tales of Enchantment: Collingwood, Anthropology, and the "Fairy Tale" Manuscripts', *Collingwood Studies*, vol. 4, 1998, pp. 133–56.

Knox, T.M., Preface to *The Idea of History*, Oxford: Clarendon Press, 1946, v–xxiv.

Knox, T.M., 'R.G. Collingwood', *Dictionary of National Biography*, 1941–1950. Oxford University Press, 1959, pp. 168–70.

Knox, T.M., Review of W.M. Johnston, *The Formative Years of R.G. Collingwood*, *Philosophical Quarterly*, April 1969, pp. 165–6.

Knox, T.M., Review of L. Mink, *Mind, History and Dialectic*, *Mind*, vol. 70, 1971, pp. 150–2.

Krausz, M., 'The Logic of Absolute Presuppositions', in M. Krausz (ed) *Critical Essays on the Philosophy of R.G. Collingwood*.

Mackay, D.S., 'On Supposing and Presupposing', *Review of Metaphysics*, vol. 2, 1948, pp. 1–20.

McCallum, R.B., 'Robin George Collingwood: 1889–1943', *Proceedings of the British Academy*, vol. 29, 1943, pp. 463–68.

Martin, R., 'Collingwood's Doctrine of Absolute Presuppositions and the possibility of Historical Knowledge' in L. Pompa and W.H. Dray (eds) *Substance and Form in History: A Collection of Essays in Philosophy of History*. Edinburgh: University of Edinburgh Press, 1981.

Martin, R., 'Collingwood's *Essay on Philosophical Method*', *Idealistic Studies*, Vol. 4, 1974, pp. 224–50.

Milne, A.J.M., 'Collingwood's Ethics and Political Theory', in M. Krausz (ed.) *Critical Essays on the Philosophy of R.G. Collingwood*.

Milne, A.J.M., 'Civilization and the Open Society: Collingwood and Popper', in D. Boucher, J. Connelly and T. Modood (eds.) *Philosophy, History and Civilization*, 1995.

O'Sullivan, N.K., 'Irrationalism in Politics', *Political Studies*, Vol. 20, 1972, pp. 141–151.
Passmore, J., Review of L. Rubinoff, *Collingwood and the Reform of Metaphysics*, *Australasian Journal of Philosophy*, vol. 51, 1973, pp. 175–6.
Peters, R., 'Collingwood's Logic of Question and Answer, its Relation to Absolute Presuppositions: another Brief History', *Collingwood Studies*, Vol. 6, 1999, pp. 1–28.
Rotenstreich, N., 'Metaphysics and Historicism', in M. Krausz (ed.) *Critical Essays on the Philosophy of R.G. Collingwood*,
Ryle, G., 'Mr. Collingwood and the Ontological Argument', *Mind*, vol. 44, 1935, pp. 137–151.
Ryle, G., 'Back to the Ontological Argument', *Mind*, vol. 46, 1937, pp. 53–57.
Rynin, D., 'Donagan on Collingwood: Absolute Presuppositions, Truth and Metaphysics', *Review of Metaphysics*, vol. 18, 1964, 301–33.
Saari, H. 'R.G. Collingwood's Emotivist Theory of Magic', *Collingwood Studies*, vol. 5, 1998, pp. 90–108.
Stock, G., 'Collingwood's Essay on *Appearance and Reality*: some Contemporary Reflections', *Collingwood Studies*, vol. 4, 1998, pp. 34–50.
Panagaku, S. (ed.), Symposium on *Idealism and Rights: The Social Ontology of Human Rights in the Political Thought of Bernard Bosanquet, Collingwood and British Idealism Studies*, vol. 9, 2002.
Toulmin, S., 'Conceptual Change and the Problem of Relativism', in M. Krausz (ed.) *Critical Essays on the Philosophy of R.G. Collingwood*.
Van der Dussen, J., 'Collingwood on Process, Progress and Civilization', in D. Boucher, J. Connelly and T. Modood (eds.) *Philosophy, History and Civilization*, 1995.
Von Leyden, W., 'Philosophy of Mind: An Appraisal of Collingwood's Theories of Consciousness, Language, and Imagination'. In Krausz (ed.) *Critical Essays on the Philosophy of R.G.Collingwood*.
Walsh, W.H., 'Collingwood and Metaphysical Neutralism', in M. Krausz (ed.) *Critical Essays on the Philosophy of R.G. Collingwood*.

Other Books and Articles

Ayer, A. J., *Language, Truth and Logic*, London: Gollancz, 1936.
Ayer, A.J., *A History of Modern Philosophy* London: Allen & Unwin, 1984.
Ayer, A.J., *Part of my Life,* London: Collins, 1977.
Bosanquet, B., *The Philosophical Theory of the State*. London: Macmillan, Fourth Edition, 1923.
Boucher, D. and Vincent, A., *A Radical Hegelian*, Cardiff: University of Wales Press, 1993).
Bradley, F.H., *The Presuppositions of Critical History* [1876] (reprinted in *Collected Essays*, Oxford: Clarendon Press, 1935).
Bradley, F.H., *Ethical Studies*. Oxford: Clarendon Press, Second Edition, 1927.
Connelly, J., 'On the Notion of an Ideal', *The Gadfly*, vol. 7, no. 1, 1984, pp. 35–53.

Connelly, J. and Smith, G., *Politics and the Environment: from theory to practice*, (second edition) London: Routledge, 2003.
Cowling, M., *Religion and Public Doctrine in Modern England*. Cambridge: Cambridge University Press, 1980.
Devlin, P., *The Judge*. London: Oxford University Press, 1979.
Emmet, D.M., *The Nature of Metaphysical Thinking*. London: Macmillan, 1945.
Grant Duff, S., *The Parting of Ways*. London: Peter Allen, 1982.
Green, T. H., *Prolegomena to Ethics*, Oxford: Clarendon Press, Third Edition, 1890.
Harré, R. and Krausz, M., *Varieties of Relativism*, Oxford: Blackwell, 1996
Harris, E. E., *Nature, Mind and Modern Science*. London: Allen & Unwin, 1954.
Harris, H.S., Introduction to G. Gentile, *Genesis and Structure of Society*. Urbana: University of Illinois Press, 1960.
Harris, H.S., 'Gentile's "The Reform of Hegelian Dialectic": An Introductory Note', *Idealistic Studies*, vol. 11, 1981, pp. 187-8.
Hegel, G.W.F., *Phenomenology of Spirit*, translated A.V. Miller, Oxford: Clarendon Press, 1977.
Hegel, G.W.F., Preface to *The Phenomenology of Spirit*, translated by W. Kaufmann in *Hegel: Reinterpretation, Texts and Commentaries*, London: Weidenfeld and Nicolson, 1966.
Hegel, G.W.F., *The Logic of Hegel*, Translated W. Wallace, Oxford: Clarendon Press 1959.
Hopkinson, H.T., *Of This Our Time: A Journalist's Story 1905-50*, London: Hutchinson, 1982.
Jones, H., *A Faith That Inquires*, London: Macmillan, 1922.
Kant, I., *Critique of Pure Reason*, London: Macmillan, 1929, trans. N.K. Smith.
Knox, T.M., *Action*. London: Allen & Unwin 1969.
Krausz, M., *Limits of Rightness*, Rowman & Littlefield, 2001.
Lamont, W. D., *Introduction to Green's Moral Philosophy*, London: Allen and Unwin, 1934.
Mackinnon, D.M.,'Teilhard's Achievement' in *Teilhard de Chardin: Pilgrim of the Future*, ed. N. Braybrooke, London: Libra Books.
Minogue, K. R., Introduction to *Hobbes's Leviathan*, London: Dent, 1973,
Mure, G.R.G., 'Change: Part II', *Philosophy*, vol. 9, no. 36, 1934, pp. 450-64.
Oakeshott, M.J., *Rationalism in Politics*, London: Methuen, 1962.
Quinton A., *Thoughts and Thinkers*, London: Duckworth, 1982,
Rousseau, J.J., *Political Writings*. trans. F.M. Watkins, London: Nelson, 1953.
Sweet, W., *Idealism and Rights: the social ontology of human rights in the political thought of Bernard Bosanquet*, Maryland: University Press of America, 1997.
Watt, A.J., 'Transcendental Arguments and Moral Principles', *Philosophical Quarterly*, 1975, pp. 40-57.
Wittgenstein, L., *On Certainty*. Oxford: Blackwell, 1969.
Wittgenstein, L. 'Remarks on Frazer's Golden Bough', in *Wittgenstein: Sources and Perspectives*,C.G. Luckhardt (ed.), Hassocks: Harvester Press, 1979.

Index

Action 184-204; moral action or duty 190, 199-204; political 190, 195-9, 206-10, 251; regularian 190, 195-9, 100-1, 223-4; utilitarian or economic 190, 191-6
Anselm, St. 123
Aristotle 77, 81, 95, 141, 153
Art 61-2, 288-91; and expression of emotion 289-90
Ayer, A.J. 15n, 27, 51n, 97-9, 134n

Barbarism 267-70; barbarity 263-4
Body politic 216-223
Bosanquet, B. 33n, 67n, 254-6, 261
Boucher, D. viii, 43n, 79n, 115n, 188, 206, 267n
Bradley, F.H.. 115n, 127-34, 165n

Christianity; and natural science 153-4; and civilization, 311
Civilization 262-7, 268-9, 270-84, 285-315, 318-19; and art 288-91; and civility 264-6, 284; and Christianity 311; and emotion 268, 284, 286, 303-15; and magic 307-9; and metaphysics 292; and the natural world 265-6, 313-15; and religion 303-15; as an ideal 270-84; as a scale of forms 52n, 273-84; dimensions of 285-315
Collingwood, R.G. illness 11-12, 17, 20, 23-5, 26, 75, 205-6; planned series of books 12-14, 16-17, 20, 52n, 76n, 75, 76; 'central thread' 34-46, 53; political views of 177-89; style and terminology 30, 46-53; radical conversion hypothesis 1, 7-11, 19-36, 55-6, 155, 319; unity of thought and philosophy 8-54

Community 289, 211-12; social 212-18, 220-2, 223, 245-8, 267; non social 212-18, 220-2, 223, 245-8, 267
Concepts: philosophical 15, 52, 77, 141-52, 236-8, 189-91, 206, 236-9; and absolute presuppositions 97, 141-56; and definition 16, 41-2, 51, 66, 80-1, 95n; and differences in degree and kind 11, 15, 77; and opposition and distinction 77-8, and scale of forms 14-16, 32-3, 37-8, 41-3, 50-1, 77-85, 116, 136, 138, 150, 189-90; non-philosophical or empirical 141-52, 236-9; overlap of 15, 21-2, 67, 77-9, 142, 189-90, 253, 282-4; transcendental 141-52, 189-91, 206
Consciousness, corruption of 287-8, 289-91, 293
Convention and habit, value of 172-4
Costall, A.P. 297n
Cowling, M. 228n, 315
Croce, B. 47-8, 115
Crossman, R.H.S. 188n

Descartes, R. 126, 128
Dialectic, dialectical process 32, 50-2, 63n, 73-4, 94-5, 104, 105, 149, 183-4,185, 187, 227, 266
D'Oro, G. 61n, 71n
De Ruggiero, G. 114-15
Donagan, A. 8n, 26-9, 72-3, 105, 138, 295, 297
Duty 199-204

Eisenstein, M. 285n
Emblom, W.J. 75
Emmet, D. 137

Emotion 122, 303-15; expression of 289-90, 306-10; and the natural world 313-15
Faith 121-2, 123, 303-4; and natural science 9
Fascism 48, 185-6, 309-11
Ficarra, F.T. 43, 76n
Frazer, J.G. 307
Freedom and free will 122, 212, 218, 236, 245-7, 249, 257-61, 266-7
Freud, S. 129

Galileo 126, 132
Gentile, G. 47n, 48, 113-14n
Goethe, J. W. 300
Gore, C. 9, 123
Grant Duff, S. 164n
Green, T.H. 162-7, 237, 254-6, 261

Harris, E.E. 92-4, 112-13, 139-40
Harris, H.S. 48-9, 113-14n
Hegel, G.W.F. 51, 61, 63n, 67n, 73-4, 87n, 107, 131, 141, 187, 300
Hinz, M. 105n
Historicism, see relativism, historical
History and philosophy 18, 19, 21-2, 23n, 25, 26-7, 28, 43, 67, 72-3, 114-15, 155, 273-5, 281-2
History, philosophy of 120, 146-9
Hobbes, T. 43, 206, 216
Hoff, A.M. 242
Hopkinson, H.T. 172-4
Human nature 114-15, 284, 286, 313
Husserl, E. 284n

Idealism 50-1, 128n
Identified coincidents, fallacy of 22

James, Wendy. 307n
James, W. 10
Johnson, P. vii, 81n, 161n, 315n
Jones, H. 115n

Kant, I. 61n, 81, 102, 108, 202, 203
Knox, T.M. 7n, 13, 14, 17-26, 35, 105, 110n, 112, 144, 170, 179, 182
Krausz, M. 89n

Lamont, W.D. 165
Laski, H.J. 188n, 205
Liberalism 183-7
Lindsay, A.D. 182
Locke, J. 126, 249

McCallum, R.B. 179
Mackay, D.S. 15n
Mackinnon, D.M. 15n
Magic 307-9
Martin, R. 102-3, 115n
Marx, K. 178, 181-2, 188-9
Metaphysics 44-5, 65, 71-2, 75, 86-95, 98-100, 110-11, 113, 115, 116, 122, 123-31; and civilization 291-2; and natural science 126-32; and system 90-95, 104; as the science of absolute presuppositions 65, 71-2, 86-94, 100-2, 115, 129-41; as the science of being 86-7, 113, 124-5, 144
Mill, J.S. 255
Milne, A.J.M. 191n, 267n
Mind, as activity 113-14; and history 113-15
Mink, L. 8n, 19, 33-4, 57n
Minogue, K. 43
Morality and law 250-61
Moral philosophy, lectures on 37-8, 40-2, 45-6, 53; and practice 175-77
Mure G.R.G. 151

Nazism 185, 270, 309-11
Needham, J. 188

O'Sullivan, N.K. 298n
Oakeshott, M. 16n, 233n, 300
Ontological argument 65

Passmore, J. 32n
Peters, R. 115n
Philosophy 57-69; and experience 65, 82-3; and method 14-16, 38-9, 50-1, 62-3, 69-76, 77-85, 273-7, 282-4; and system 57-8, 90-5; as activity 67-68; as categorical thinking 63-7; as criteriological 58n, 59, 68-9, 81, 275; as self knowledge 167-8,

169-70; as self-referential 58; as thinking about thinking 59-62, 81; conceives its object as activity 68-9; elucidates what in some sense we already know 44, 62-3, 71n, 79-82, 94

Plato 81, 140n

Politics and political action 190, 195-9, 206-10, 251; and morality 250-61; political education 260-1, 267, 300; political good as order 197-8, 250-2, 254, 259, 299-303;

Precarious margins, fallacy of 21-2

Presuppositions, absolute 8-9, 19, 52, 65, 70, 71, 74, 86-95, 97-157, 191, 219; (un)awareness of 88-9, 104, 105-7; and Christianity 153-4; and criticism 112-13; and philosophical concepts 97, 141-56; and scale of forms 109-11,138; as *a priori* 100-2, 135; change in 103-7, 109-12, 136-40; consupponibility of 90-1, 92-3; relative 71, 88, 138-9; (non)verifiability of 86, 98-9, 117-19, 132-7, 138n

Prichard, H.A. 168

Primitive survivals, law of 42-3n, 79, 214-15

Progress 233-5

Psychology 10, 58n, 68-69, 113, 129-30, 293-7; studies mind as object, not activity 10, 58n, 68-9, 113, 293-7

Punishment 238-50, 255, 257-8

Question and answer, logic of 24, 65-6, 86, 87-8, 116, 141

Quinton, A. 188n

Radical conversion hypothesis 1, 7-11, 19-36, 37, 55-6, 75, 115, 155, 319

Realism/realists 128n, 162-4, 167-9

Relativism, historical; historicism 18, 19, 21-2, 23n, 25, 26-7, 28, 43, 56, 67, 114-15, 155, 273-5, 281-2, 318

Religion 303-15; and civilization 303-13;

Rotenstreich, N. 155n

Rousseau, J.J. 224n

Rubinoff, L. 8n, 29-33, 113, 120n

Rule and ruling 212-31; and authority 213-4, 221, 244; and force 213-5, 220-1, 224-5, 246, 257-8, 266-7; ruling class 218-23; self-rule 217-19, 222, 226; and being ruled 223-38; and command 223-6, 231, 236, 245

Rule, action according to 195-9, 199-201, 223-4

Ruskin, J. 118, 317

Ryle, G. 99-101

Rynin, D. 72-3, 136

Saari, H. 307n

Savagery 268

Scale of forms 14-16, 32-3, 37-8, 41-3, 50-1, 77-85, 116, 136, 138, 150, 189-90; and civilization 52n, 264, 273-84

Smith, G. 315n

Smith, J.A. 115n

Socialism 180, 185-7

Society 42, 210-18, 222, 247, 249; *suum cuique* of 210-12, 216, 226, 259, 309n

Spengler, O. 122-3

Spinoza, B 95, 129

State, the 207-10, 215, 218, 229-33, 248-9, 251-4

Stock, G. 127n

Sweet, W. 256n, 258n

Theory and practice 161-77, 318; and self knowledge of mind 167-8, 169-70

Tomlin, E.W.F. 36

Toulmin, S. 189

Tradition 299-303

Tylor, E.B.

Utility 191-95; utilitarian or economic action 190, 191-5, 196; utilitarianism 190, 193-5, 196

Vico, G. 166

Vincent, A 115n

Walsh, W.H. 154n
Watt, A.J.. 152
Webb, C.C.J. 20n
Whitehead, A.N. 128n, 143
Wittgenstein, L. 308

REFERENCES TO WRITINGS BY R.G. COLLINGWOOD

Books

An Autobiography 9-12, 17, 18, 19, 24, 25, 27; 28, 33, 44, 46, 47, 48-9, 51n, 75, 86, 116, 122, 123, 132n, 141, 151, 162-3, 168-9, 177-9, 180, 181, 183, 185, 189, 190, 199-200, 209, 296-7, 301n; reliability of 19-20, 47-9

An Essay on Metaphysics 8-12, 15, 17, 18, 21, 24, 25, 27, 28, 36, 40, 43, 44, 45, 49, 51, 56, 65, 70, 71, 74-5, 86-90, 94, 95, 97, 100, 103-5, 106, 107, 109-11, 117, 119, 120, 122, 123, 130, 132-5, 134n, 138-41, 150, 153-4, 155, 169, 179, 291-3, 297-9

An Essay on Philosophical Method 8-11, 12, 14, 15, 17, 18-19, 21, 24, 26, 27, 28, 29, 30, 33, 37-39, 40, 41, 43, 44n, 45, 46, 47, 48, 49, 50, 51, 52, 56, 62, 64, 65, 68, 69-70, 73-4, 76, 77-83, 85, 91-2, 94, 95, 101, 106, 109, 110, 116, 123, 135, 142, 156, 253, 264, 273, 275, 276, 277, 283-4

Faith and Reason 9, 121-22, 303-4

Outlines of a Philosophy of Art 11n, 61-2, 150n, 288-9

Human Nature and Human History 18, 108-9

Religion and Philosophy. 10, 18, 39, 64, 76, 115, 238, 242, 243

Ruskin's Philosophy. 34-5, 116, 117-18, 119, 317

Speculum Mentis. 10, 11n, 18, 20, 26, 28, 30-1, 32, 33, 34, 37-8, 39, 45, 46, 48, 50, 51n, 61, 62, 70, 76, 84, 85, 86, 106, 114, 116, 135n, 143, 162, 169-70, 180, 182, 238, 295-6

The First Mate's Log 194-5

The Historical Imagination 18

The History of European Liberalism by G. de Ruggiero, Preface. 183, 227

The Idea of History 9, 12-13, 18,19, 20, 21, 27, 35, 39, 49, 76, 84, 85, 114, 139, 155, 234-5

The Idea of Nature 9, 12-13, 14, 15, 18, 19, 20, 27, 39, 46, 49, 76, 84, 85, 105, 106, 107, 109-10, 114, 131, 139, 154-5

The New Leviathan 19, 24-5, 27, 28, 34, 36, 40-3, 45, 46, 49, 50, 52, 75, 76, 84, 85, 114, 122n,162, 174, 179, 181, 182, 183-5, 189, 191-4, 196, 203-4, 205-6, 210-222, 238, 245-8, 249, 257, 259-61, 264-7, 269, 270, 285, 301, 310, 318

The Philosophy of History 64, 70, 142-3, 289, 311

The Principles of Art 11,12, 13, 14, 15, 16, 19, 20, 22, 26, 28, 43, 47, 49, 50, 65n, 68, 76, 85, 114, 122n, 285, 287, 290-1, 294, 305-6, 307-9

The Three Laws of Politics 179, 211, 222-3, 237, 287

Articles

'A Philosophy of Progress' 234, 256
'Aesthetic', 295
'Can the New Idealism Dispense with Mysticism' 51n
'Croce's Philosophy of History' 51n
'Economics as a Philosophical Science' 8, 45, 69, 94, 120
'Fascism and Nazism' 52, 122n, 174-5, 179, 270, 304-5, 309, 310-13
'Human Nature and Human History' 11
'Oswald Spengler and the Theory of Historical Cycles' 8, 122
'Plato's Philosophy of Art' 11n
'Political Action' 45, 69, 167, 181, 196-8, 202, 207, 208, 211n, 229, 233-4, 235, 251, 252, 302

'Reason is Faith Cultivating Itself' 9, 121
'Sensation and Thought' 50
'The Nature and Aims of a Philosophy of History' 120
'The Place of Art in Education', 288
'The Present Need of a Philosophy' 166
'The Devil' 122n

Reviews

Review of C. Gore, *The Philosophy of the Good Life* 9, 123
Review of C.G.Jung, *Psychological Types, or the Psychology of Individuation*, 294
Review of H.J. Paton and R. Klibansky (eds) *Philosophy and History*, 48
Review of E. Rignano, *The Psychology of Reasoning*, 294n
Review of C. Spearman, *The Nature of 'Intelligence' and the Principles of Cognition*, 294n

Unpublished Manuscripts

'Art and the Machine', 288
'Function of Metaphysics in Civilization' 40, 44-5, 63n, 73, 95, 134, 141, 175
'Goodness, Rightness, Utility' 37n
Kant's *Critique of Pure Reason*, Commentary on the Preface 102
List of Work Done 37n
'Man Goes Mad' 3, 182, 184, 186-7, 188, 227, 285-7, 299, 303, 313-15
'Method and Metaphysics' 38, 76
Moral Philosophy, Lectures (1921) 157
Moral Philosophy, Lectures 'Action', (1923) 37-8, 173, 192, 202
Moral Philosophy, Lectures (1929) 63, 142, 149, 232, 238, 239-42, 244, 249
Moral Philosophy, Lectures (1932) 204

Moral Philosophy, Lectures (1933) 167, 175-7, 201, 202, 207, 208-9, 239, 250-1, 257, 304-5
Notes on Hegel's Logic 94
'Notes on Historiography' 16
Notes on R.M.MacIver, *The Modern State* 248, 253
'Notes Towards a Metaphysic' 110-11
'Notes Towards a Theory of Politics as a Philosophical Science.' 224-5, 253-4
Notice of *The Principles of Art* 22
Notice of 'Political Action' 196
'Outlines of a Concept of the State.' 222, 225-6
Philosophy of History, Lectures (1929). 181-2
Realism and Idealism, Lectures 128n
'Rough Notes on Politics' 207
'Stray Notes on Ethical Questions.' 42, 229-31, 233, 238, 239, 243, 248, 249-50, 252-3
'The Breakdown of Liberalism' 228
'The Idea of a Philosophy of Something, and, in particular, a Philosophy of History', 145-9, 156
'The Metaphysics of F.H. Bradley: An Essay on *Appearance and Reality*' 127n
'The Nature of Metaphysical Study' 123-30
The New Leviathan, Draft Preface 45, 174
'The Philosophy of the Christian Religion' 66-7
The Principles of History 12-13, 14, 16, 20, 21, 85
'The Spiritual Basis of Reconstruction' 180
Truth and Contradiction 10, 86, 116-17, 119-20, 123
Untitled Fragments on Barbarism 268, 270, 274n, 276-7
'Utility, Right and Duty' 201
'War in its Relation to Christian Ethics' 180

'What Civilization Means' 264, 267, 270-74, 277-283

Correspondence

Letter to the Clarendon Press, 9/3/33. 70
Letter to the Clarendon Press, 14/11/38. 28n, 76n
Letter to the Clarendon Press, 3/6/39. 12, 76n
Letter to the Clarendon Press, 6/8/41. 25
Letter to O.G.S. Crawford on 14th April 1941 174
Letter to B. Croce. 20/4/38. 47
Letter to G. de Ruggiero, 12/6/37, 114-15
Letter to H.T. Hopkinson, 7/5/41. 44
Letter to T.M. Knox, 3/9/39, 270n
Letter to T.M. Knox, 2/11/37, 318
Letter to W. von Leyden, 31/5/41. 206
Letter to A.D. Lindsay, 20th October 1938. 182
Letter to Gilbert Ryle, 9/5/35. 51n, 53n, 100
Letter to F.G. Simpson, 17/6/25 181